Marriage in America

Rights and Responsibilities: Communitarian Perspectives

Series Editor: Amitai Etzioni

Marriage in America

A Communitarian Perspective

Martin King Whyte

Editor

ROWMAN & LITTLEFIELD PUBLISHERS, INC.
Lanham • Boulder • New York • Oxford

ROWMAN & LITTLEFIELD PUBLISHERS, INC.

Published in the United States of America
by Rowman & Littlefield Publishers, Inc.
4720 Boston Way, Lanham, Maryland 20706
http://www.rowmanlittlefield.com

12 Hid's Copse Road
Cumnor Hill, Oxford OX2 9JJ, England

British Library Cataloguing in Publication Information Available

Library of Congress Cataloging-in-Publication Data

Marriage in America : a communitarian perspective / edited by Martin King Whyte.
    p. cm. — (Rights and responsibilities)
    Includes bibliographical references and index.
    ISBN 0-7425-0770-X (alk. paper)–ISBN 0-7425-0771-8 (pbk. : alk. paper)
    1. Marriage–United States. 2. Family–United States. 3. Divorce–United States. I.
Whyte, Martin King. II. Rights and responsibilities (Lanham, Md.)

    HQ734.M3887 2000
    306.81'0973–dc21

                                  00-024862
Printed in the United States of America

∞™ The paper used in this publication meets the minimum requirements of American
National Standard for Information Sciences—Permanence of Paper for Printed Library
Materials, ANSI/NISO Z39.48-1992.

*To Alice Clare Hogan
and
to our daughter,
Julia Hogan Whyte*

Contents

Boxes, Figures, and Tables

Preface

The chapters assembled in this volume represent an effort to consider a variety of innovative practices and policies intended to help strengthen American marriage as an institution and to enhance the chances for couples to have enduring and satisfying marriages. Some of this material was first presented at a conference convened in Washington, D.C., in November 1996, entitled "A Conference on Communitarian Pro-Family Policies." Both the impetus and funding for the conference came from the Communitarian Network, a nonpartisan organization founded by Amitai Etzioni devoted to seeking changes in policies and practices that will strengthen the moral, political, and social foundations of American society. This is not the place to elaborate at length on what communitarianism means. However, at the core of this political philosophy is a view that for society and the individuals within it to flourish, there needs to be a better balancing of community with individual interests and of responsibilities with rights.[1] From its inception, the Communitarian Network has targeted the family as one of four priority areas[2] (along with communities, character education, and societal diversity), and Dr. Etzioni, a colleague at George Washington University, asked me to organize the 1996 conference and then this expanded volume of the papers presented.

Along the way the project grew in scope and intersected with an independent effort launched by Don Browning, a professor in the Divinity School at the University of Chicago, and William Doherty, a family studies scholar at the University of Minnesota, to produce a set of papers dealing with communitarian approaches to the family. It eventually became apparent that the most sensible way to proceed was to merge the two sets of papers.

The chapters in this volume are divided into three main sections. These are concerned, broadly speaking, with (1) new approaches designed to enhance the chances for successful marriages, (2) whether or how to use the law in an effort to make divorces less common, and (3) reducing the economic harm to children if divorce should occur. The authors of the various chapters represent a mix of backgrounds and include academic researchers, practitioners, family advocates, and officials who develop and implement family policies. Given this diversity in backgrounds and approaches, the chapters contain more than the usual variation in tone of contributions to an edited volume. Some are heavily footnoted academic treatises; some are fervent pleas by advocates of a particular approach to America's marital problems; still others contain thoughtful personal reflections on the difficulties confronting couples and marriages today. Some authors explicitly frame their discussions in terms of communitarian principles, while others do not. Our authors do not agree in their specific recommendations; in some instances, they disagree quite vehemently. What unites these diverse pieces is a common concern for finding new ways that may help provide a more supportive environment for marriages in America. Taken together, the chapters in this volume are intended to present a broad array of ideas that have been stimulated by national debates about how to reduce the social costs of America's high divorce rate.

Chapter 1, by Martin Whyte, a sociologist at George Washington University, reviews debates about trends in marriage and divorce in America. While the divorce rate is no longer climbing year by year as it did during the 1960s and 1970s, concern about the impact of divorce on children has been growing. Whyte argues that part of the reason for the disparity between actual divorce trends and public concern over the impact of divorce can be attributed to changing political and religious moods. However, a more important explanation can be found in recent social science research that concludes that for children, a parental divorce is less benign than most experts previously thought. This overview essay sets the context for the discussion in subsequent chapters of a variety of ways to support marriages and reduce the harm that children may suffer when marriages end.

Chapter 2, by Linda Waite, a sociologist and demographer at the University of Chicago, is concerned with assessing why one increasingly popular practice—premarital cohabitation—does *not* contribute to the effort to promote satisfying and enduring marriages.[3] Many had hoped, and young people in particular have often told their parents, that living together prior to marriage would be a beneficial way to learn whether someone was a suitable marriage partner. However, Waite summarizes a growing body of research that disproves such claims. She contends that the tentative, impermanent, and weakly institutionalized nature of cohabitation impedes the ability of this type of partnership to provide many of the benefits of marriage. Cohabitation relationships are significantly less stable than marriages, even in cases where the couple has children. Cohabiting couples have more difficulties relating to their extended families, they often do not consolidate their financial resources, they distance themselves from important social institutions, and they bring a shorter time perspective into their relationship. Finally, even in cases where cohabiting couples get married, the resulting marriages are on average less satisfying and enduring than those of couples who did not live together prior to getting married. In view of these limitations of cohabitation, Waite recommends that strong social and legal distinctions be maintained between married and cohabiting couples. In short, she suggests that the marriage relationship should remain privileged.

Chapter 3 on responsible fathering, by William Doherty and Martha Erickson, family studies and child development specialists, respectively, at the University of Minnesota, reviews extensive research on the impact fathers have on their children's development.[4] They note a variety of ways in which the relationship fathers have with their children is more variable and more threatened by recent social trends than mother–child relations. They stress that a caring, committed, and collaborative marriage is the best context for responsible fathering. Past research indicates a variety of influences that can strengthen or weaken the involvement of fathers in their children's lives, both within and outside existing marriages. Based on their review of this evidence, the authors conclude with specific policy recommendations that can enhance responsible fathering, thus contributing to the welfare of children.

Chapter 4, by Pepper Schwartz, a sociologist at the University of Washington as well as a magazine columnist and television commentator on family issues, addresses a slightly different issue.[5] She is concerned with the contention of some analysts that marital stability requires a traditional division of roles between husband and wife, so that each feels they need and depend on the other. To the extent that this claim is true, couples who structure their marriages in an egalitarian way, so that each is simultaneously a breadwinner and a performer of domestic duties, are asking for trouble. In highly personal and reflective material drawn from her recent book on the same subject,[6] Schwartz points out a number of ways in which "peer marriages" build distinctive bonds and strengths that may be more durable and rewarding than bonds based on mutual dependency. Since the traditional division of marital roles was based on an uneven dependency, with the wife much less able to function without the husband than vice versa, she points out that particularly for wives, peer marriages have special meaning and potential.

The question of what we know about what husbands and wives could do to make their relationship more satisfying and enduring is the subject of chapter 5, by Kimberly Ryan, Sybil Carrère, and John Gottman, psychologists also at the University of Washington who have been pioneers in research on the patterns of successful versus unsuccessful marriages. Their chapter presents a wide-ranging overview of recent research of their own and by others on the patterns that make it possible to predict whether a given marriage will survive or break up. This research, which has been the focus of several recent television documentaries on how to improve and preserve marriages, shows that it is not so much the frequency or even the intensity of conflicts between couples that is predictive of divorce. Rather, conflict is inevitable, but the particular ways in which such conflicts are expressed and resolved may be either healthy or damaging to the marital relationship. If couples can learn how to minimize or avoid falling into damaging ways of engaging in conflicts with their partner while emphasizing modes that reaffirm their bond, their chances for preserving a mutually satisfying relationship will be enhanced.

When married couples encounter difficulties in their relationship, they may turn to marriage counselors or psychotherapists for assistance. However, William Doherty, in chapter 6, contends that the dominant orientations among marital therapists are at best neutral toward, and at worst work against, the preservation and improvement of marriages.[7] By focusing primarily on the individual happiness of each spouse, rather than on the benefits of preserving the marriage or the welfare of children involved, therapists may be, as the saying goes, "part of the problem rather than part of the solution." Doherty advocates a fundamental change in the orientations of practitioners of marital therapy, with the preservation of marriages, where possible, given a higher priority. They should do this, however, without giving up good therapeutic practices. This effort might involve making use of the sorts of accumulated wisdom summarized in the chapter by Ryan, Carrère, and Gottman to help couples learn how to resolve their marital conflicts before confronting the question of divorce. Doherty believes that good therapeutic practice and a gentle, pro-marriage stance can be combined to make marriage counselors and therapists more effective.

Chapter 7, by Don Browning, a professor of religious ethics and social sciences at the University of Chicago, takes an approach that parallels Doherty's and applies it to America's religious institutions.[8] Browning notes that there is often a disjunction between the role of the church in initiating marriages and in sustaining them. Over 70 percent of all weddings in America occur in churches and synagogues, and in weddings it is not uncommon to ask the congregation to pledge to support the newly married couple. Later, however, most couples struggle on their own to deal with their marital problems, without much involvement or support from either church leaders or congregations. Browning advocates a more activist approach in which churches attempt to develop ways to help support marriages of members of their congregations while also becoming advocates of public policies designed to have the same effect. He considers a variety of innovative practices that churches could develop (and in some cases are developing) for their parishioners, including extensive premarital and marital education as well as the mentoring of young spouses by older married couples. Community marriage policies as advocated by Michael McManus,[9] in which the various churches and synagogues in a community form a compact designed to share and promote such marriage-friendly practices, also are worthy of consideration. The other front for church efforts to support the marriage institution involves their advocacy of public policies. Here Browning gives special emphasis to a proposal to develop public policies that enable employed parents to limit their joint work burden to a total of sixty hours a week, thus enabling such parents to devote more time to their homes and children.

Chapter 8, by Enola Aird, an activist mother and director of the Motherhood Project at the Institute for American Values, is a very personal consideration of the stresses of contemporary family life and of innovative initiatives arising within mainline American churches that can help couples deal with those stresses more effectively. While Aird covers some of the same ground as Browning, her canvas is broader than simply husband–wife relations. She correctly observes that a whole range of tensions and problems, including those associated with bringing up children, contribute to marital difficulties. Despite a general pattern of "benign neglect" of parishioners' marriages and families, in recent years a number of churches and denominations have developed family ministries, children's charters, and other innovations. Although more illustrative than exhaustive of the new forms of church activism in support of families and marriages, this chapter provides a range of useful examples of new ways a vital segment of society (religious communities) is becoming involved in the effort to create more support for successful marriages. The examples provided also show that the effort to take active steps to reinforce "family values" is not confined to America's conservative and evangelical religious communities.

The final chapter in part 1, by C. Eugene Steuerle, an economist at the Urban Institute, points out that marriage is the only living arrangement achieving economies of scale that is taxed disproportionately by the federal government.[10] Hence, married couples are discriminated against in U.S. tax laws, which likely discourages some from marrying. Furthermore, tax penalties against married couples affect the poor just as much as they do the middle and upper classes, and the federal income tax is only one form in which Americans suffer from a marriage penalty. Steuerle advocates comprehensive reform proposals aimed at these inequities, all in an effort not only to remove marriage penalties but also to positively support marriage as an institution.

Taken together, the chapters in part 1 reflect several common beliefs, as indicated at the outset: that marriage is an institution deserving of support; that social science research can help us choose better ways to provide such support; that both married couples and the networks, communities, and institutions in which they live can absorb new lessons and change the way they operate in the quest for more satisfying marriages; and that public policy interventions can help facilitate such changes. However, should we also contemplate changing the ways in which the U.S. legal system regulates entry into, and exit from, marriage?

The chapters in part 2 are all concerned with whether in the effort to reduce the prevalence of divorce in America, changes should be made in the laws that regulate marriage and divorce. Chapter 10, by Elizabeth Scott, represents a further elaboration of her earlier pioneering work on "marital precommitments,"[11] a proposal that Amitai Etzioni championed in an opinion piece in *Time* magazine some years ago as "marriage supervows."[12] Throughout the United States, couples can marry with quite minimal qualifications and without making any particular commitments about steps they will take to try to make sure the marriage will last. Scott, a member of the law faculty at the University of Virginia, points out that couples could voluntarily take upon themselves a variety of more demanding commitments as they marry—for example, to seek marital counseling if problems arise or to agree to an extended waiting period before seeking to divorce or re-marry. Such marital "precommitments" should increase the barriers to divorce. State laws could be changed to encourage couples to assume such extra commit-ments. In 1997, the state of Louisiana enacted into law a very similar set of ideas, by providing two different options for couples approaching marriage: conven-tional marriage commitments and "covenant marriages," with the latter involving a set of additional obligations. Similar legislation was subsequently passed in Ari-zona and is being considered in other states. All of those concerned with the ef-fort to promote more enduring marriages are watching the Louisiana and Arizona cases to see how many couples opt for the more demanding, covenant marriages and how much difference it makes for the fate of those marriages.

The remaining chapters in part 2 are concerned primarily with laws regulating divorce rather than marriage. The context in which these essays fit is the recent emergence of legislative proposals in a number of states to modify or repeal the no-fault divorce legislation that spread throughout America in the 1970s.[13] These proposals are motivated by concern that no-fault divorce procedures make the barriers to exit from marriage too low and deprive women and children, in par-ticular, of the sorts of protection against abandonment and impoverishment that was contained in the previous, fault-based divorce laws.[14] William Galston, a pro-fessor of philosophy and director of the Institute for Philosophy and Public Pol-icy at the University of Maryland and former White House adviser on domestic policy in the Clinton administration, has been a persistent advocate of a reexam-ination of no-fault divorce laws, and chapter 11 is a cogent summary of his views on the subject.

Chapter 12, by Ira Ellman, a professor of law at Arizona State University, pres-ents the contrary view, forcefully arguing against a return to mandatory fault-based divorce procedures. He maintains that the original reasons for the repudia-tion of fault-based divorce are still valid,[15] that the no-fault divorce option did not contribute to the rise in the divorce rate that occurred after 1960, and that revival of mandatory fault-based divorce would have a number of undesirable conse-quences for society. Ellman also argues against the extended waiting period prior to divorce that Scott advocates, on the grounds that this would encourage the same sorts of deceptions that undermined respect for the law under the fault-based divorce regime, while also undesirably obstructing individuals from getting on with their lives.

Chapter 13, by Milton Regan, a professor of law at the Georgetown Law Cen-ter, specifically addresses the issues raised in the Scott, Galston, and Ellman chapters. In effect Regan puts forth a compromise position. He agrees with Galston and others that the current no-fault divorce procedures convey an unde-sirable moral message about marriage—that it represents a private agreement be-tween spouses that can be dissolved whenever the parties to that agreement (or even one party alone) wish to do so, and that society has no business interfering in such private decisions. However, he contends that a return to mandatory fault-based divorce would not be a desirable way to convey the message that marriage represents a serious commitment that society has an interest in preserving, and it would not help lessen the damage that results if the marriage dissolves. Regan presents arguments in favor of both the sort of extended waiting periods prior to divorce that Scott advocates in chapter 10, as well as for provisions that require income sharing after divorce in the case of marriages of some duration. He contends that these kinds of legal innovations would convey a stronger message about how society values the marital commitment and might help make divorces somewhat less common, while at the same time avoiding the undesirable consequences that Ellman and others describe as flowing from a mandatory fault-based divorce regime.

Part 3 consists of three closely related essays. All are concerned with one of the most serious problems America faces as a result of its high divorce rate: the fact that many custodial parents receive little or none of the child support payments awarded them during the divorce procedure, so that they and their children face severe economic difficulties.[16] There may be debates about a wide range of issues regarding marriage and divorce, but there is little debate about the fact that children raised in poverty face multiple difficulties in life. Despite widespread recognition of the need to see that custodial parents (most often mothers) and their children regularly receive the child support payments due them and are thus protected from the economic damage a divorce may precipitate, a combination of factors (varying state laws, the changing job and residential situations of noncustodial parents, the protracted nature of legal enforcement procedures, etc.) have made it difficult to raise the rate of child support collections.

Chapter 14, by Katherine Shaw Spaht, a professor in the Louisiana State University Law Center and a primary drafter of the Louisiana covenant marriage law, addresses a different area in which the laws affecting marital relations might be modified.[17] Spaht presents and then provides a detailed elaboration and justification for an innovative approach to family property, "the family as community act." Inspired by the work of Mary Ann Glendon of the Harvard Law School on the "children first" approach to property settlement, this model legislation is an attempt to better protect children's interests in the event of divorce. Spaht contends that the wealth accumulated in a family should not be seen as belonging only to the mother and father but to the whole family. If this contention is accepted, then having the property divided between husband and wife at the time of divorce is unfair. Instead, children should have a share of the family wealth set aside for their support until their maturity, and only then should the shares of the husband and wife be negotiated. Spaht concludes that this approach to the division of family property not only is fairer than current practice but also might inject greater financial realism into the negotiations that surround divorce.

The remaining two chapters in part 3 deal with efforts to improve the rate of payment of child support under current practice, given the fact that a "children first" system of property division has yet to be legally established. Judge David Ross has served since 1993 as commissioner of the Federal Office of Child Support Enforcement of the Department of Health and Human Services in Washington, D.C. His chapter presents a broad overview of both changing federal legislation affecting child support payments and of efforts coordinated by the federal government to help states increase their degree of success in collecting child support payments. A substantial part of that federal program has involved efforts to construct a national system for keeping track of mobile, noncustodial parents and to enable the responsible agencies in various states to cooperate so that cases do not fall between the cracks of different jurisdictions.

Chapter 16, by Marilyn Ray Smith, a lawyer in the Child Support Enforcement Division of the Department of Revenue, Commonwealth of Massachusetts, describes the innovative and complex system developed in Massachusetts, one of the pioneers in this effort, designed to make enforcement of child support collections speedy and effective.

The topic of child support payment enforcement might seem far removed from the emphasis on finding ways to create a more supportive environment for successful marriages in America, the orientation for earlier chapters in this volume. However, if we take into account the arguments Regan makes in his chapter, we can see the link. If parents contemplating divorce know that they have inescapable, long-term financial commitments to their ex-spouse and their children, this recognition may make divorce seem a less attractive option than at present.

Our volume concludes with another chapter by Don Browning, who reviews attempts to apply communitarian theory to the family, as exemplified particularly in the writings of Amitai Etzioni, the founder of the Communitarian Network.[18] Etzioni, Browning contends, exemplifies a new trend in the social sciences—a trend toward combining the descriptive and explanatory tasks of social science disciplines with critical moral and social theory. Etzioni believes that humans have intuitive moral insights that frame their pursuit of satisfactions. These insights inform Etzioni's views on the family—his support, for example, for two-parent families, his gender egalitarianism, his advocacy of marriage "supervows," and his strong emphasis on the welfare of children.

Obviously this volume does not deal with all the sorts of steps that might be taken to try to create a more supportive environment for enduring and satisfying marriages. There are obvious gaps in our coverage; for example, we have not dealt here with things that corporations and employers might be doing to be more supportive of the marriages and the children of their personnel. (However, the policy advocacy portion of chapter 7 by Don Browning includes a range of specific family-friendly policies that he feels religious organizations should be pressing employers and governments to enact.) As noted earlier, the material presented here is not intended to be the last word on the subject. Instead, we hope this volume makes a contribution to a growing debate that will help us find ways to provide better support for American marriages and protect children from the harm that may be precipitated by divorce.

NOTES

1. This approach implies a conviction that in late twentieth-century America individualism and individual rights have been allowed to overshadow community interests and individual responsibilities, and that citizen action and public policy changes should be attempted to right the balance. See the Communitarian Network, "The Responsive Community Platform: Rights and Responsibilities" (Washington, D.C.: Communitarian Network, 1997), and Amitai Etzioni, *The Spirit of Community* (New York: Simon & Schuster, 1993).

2. See Jean Bethke Elshtain, Enola Aird, Amitai Etzioni, William Galston, Mary Ann Glendon, Martha Minow, and Alice Rossi, "A Communitarian Position Paper on the Family" (Washington, D.C.: Communitarian Network, 1993).

3. An earlier version of this chapter appeared as a position paper of the Communitarian Network in 1999.

4. An earlier version of this chapter appeared as a position paper of the Communitarian Network in 1999.

5. A version of this chapter appeared earlier in the journal of the Communitarian Network, *The Responsive Community* 8 (1998): 48-60.

6. Pepper Schwartz, *Peer Marriages* (New York: Free Press, 1994).

7. A version of this chapter appeared earlier in *The Responsive Community* 7 (1997): 31-42.

8. A version of this chapter, which incorporates work of the Communitarian Task Force on the Family, appeared as a position paper of the Communitarian Network in 1999.

9. See Michael McManus, *Marriage Savers* (Grand Rapids, MI: Zondervan, 1995); also, by the same author, "What Churches Can Do to Reduce the Divorce Rate," unpublished paper presented at the 1996 Conference on Communitarian Pro-Family Policies.

10. A version of this chapter appeared as a position paper of the Communitarian Network in 1999.

11. Elizabeth Scott, "Rational Decisionmaking about Marriage and Divorce," *Virginia Law Review* 76 (1990): 9-94.

12. Amitai Etzioni, "How to Make Marriage Matter," *Time*, September 6, 1993, 50-54.

13. One of the discussants at the 1996 panel at which these essays were presented was Jesse Dalman, a state legislator in Michigan who has introduced legislation in that state to return to a fault-based system of divorce. (As of early 2000, none of these efforts to repeal no-fault divorce had been enacted.)

14. An influential although controversial critique of no-fault laws as they were implemented in California, and particularly of their impact on women and children, is Lenore Weitzman, *The Divorce Revolution: The Unexpected Social and Economic Consequences for Women and Children in America* (New York: Free Press, 1985).

15. Those original reasons included the claim that fault-based divorce proceedings aggravated the conflicts between couples to the possible detriment of their children and led

those eager to get a divorce to manufacture false accounts of abuse or other "faults," thus reducing public respect for the laws involved.

16. Obviously the problem of child support payments applies not only to divorced, noncustodial parents but also to absent parents who never married—most often unwed fathers. The chapters that follow by Ross and Smith deal with the issue of child support payments generally, and not solely following a divorce. However, as noted in chapter 1 the primary focus of this volume as a whole is on marriage and divorce rather than on nonmarital births and parenthood.

17. A version of this chapter appeared as a working paper of the Communitarian Network in 1999.

18. A version of this chapter appeared in *The Responsive Community* 9 (1999): 52-61.

1

The State of Marriage in America

Martin King Whyte

In recent years a wide-ranging debate has erupted about the state of the American family, particularly about the present health and future prospects of the central building block of family life in society, the institution of marriage. Whereas in earlier eras those who saw signs of family decline were countered by other observers who interpreted family trends in neutral, evolutionary terms or even as indicating progress,[1] in the 1980s and 1990s the pessimists have far outnumbered the optimists. High levels of divorce, the rise of premarital cohabitation, declining marriage rates, increased births out of wedlock, and other trends have given rise to increasing fears that marriage might be on its way to becoming simply one of a number of "lifestyle options" in America.[2] Debate has raged about the accuracy of this diagnosis, the causes of the trends involved, and the long-term consequences for America of a weakened institution of marriage. Once again, few analysts can be found who argue that America would be a better place if marriage as an institution becomes still weaker and more brittle.[3] Yet even with a growing consensus that the decline of American marriage constitutes a serious problem, there has been precious little agreement on whether anything can be done to reverse these worrisome trends, and if so what.[4] The chapters that follow represent an attempt to grapple with these troubling questions.

The contributions to this volume share a number of concerns and assumptions. From a reading of the available evidence, some of which will be briefly reviewed here, we assume that marriage is an institution worth supporting and that American society would be better off if marriages were more common, long-lasting, and satisfying. In particular, we accept the basic view that the declining popularity and increasing brittleness of American marriages impose social costs, particularly by endangering the prospects that children will be raised so that they become competent, happy, and productive adults. Thus, it is particularly in terms of the ability to provide a supportive environment in which to raise our children that we think proposals to provide better support for the institution of marriage in America must be evaluated.

We also do not assume that the forces buffeting American marriages are so powerful that nothing can be done. In other words, we assume that if problems with American marriages exist, there must be things that can be done to help address those problems and create more supportive conditions for satisfying and long-lasting marriages. However, we did not start this initiative with any pet list of new family policies and practices. Rather, the purpose of the 1996 conference mentioned in the preface, and of subsequent efforts to supplement the papers from that conference with other contributions, was to examine in some depth a variety of potential approaches to see whether some seemed more feasible and desirable than others.

One final basic assumption guided this effort. We do not assume that it is either desirable or possible to turn back the clock to recapture the family patterns of the 1950s or earlier, with male breadwinners and dependent housewives once again the norm. Although rising female employment and growing gender equality are arguably among the major causes of worrisome recent family trends, including the rise in the divorce rate,[5] we are seeking ways to strengthen marriages without undermining the recent gains that women have made in society. Thus, we are assuming that what Pepper Schwartz refers to as "peer marriages" do not have to be brittle and unsatisfying marriages. The trick is to find new policies and practices that will help provide a more supportive atmosphere for long-lasting marriages without undermining the chances for wife–husband equality. In pursuing this agenda, we consider a wide range of ideas, as the chapters in this volume will show, although we cannot claim to have exhausted all of the possibilities. Indeed, we see the goal of this volume not as ending the discussion but as stimulating further debate and the consideration of these and other innovative approaches to strengthening American marriage as an institution.

At first glance the timing of the recent debate about the state of American marriage, and about the high divorce rate in particular, may seem odd. Broadly speaking, the American divorce rate has been rising during most periods for roughly a century and a half.[6] However, for much of this time the rise was gradual and irregular, with occasional reversals and lowered rates. Then a much more rapid and dramatic rise in divorce frequency began, starting during the 1960s. For two decades rates of divorce in America climbed rapidly, so that in 1980 there were roughly three times as many divorces as two decades earlier, and the likelihood of newlyweds ending up in divorce court had risen from roughly 25 to 50 percent or even higher. However, since the early 1980s the divorce rate has stabilized and even declined slightly—from 5.2 divorces per thousand population in 1980 to 4.4 per thousand in 1995.[7] Why, if the rate of divorce in America peaked almost two decades ago, has the debate over what to do about the high divorce rate escalated much more recently?

At least three factors contribute to this lag between the peaks of divorce in America and debates about what to do about high divorce rates. The first factor involves the rising influence of conservative religious forces in American politics in the 1980s and 1990s and the social agendas and debates about "family values" that this shift has produced. Whether through Vice President Dan Quayle's attack on the unwed motherhood of TV character Murphy Brown or the calls for marital fidelity championed in revival meetings of the Promise Keepers, these voices have helped focus national attention as never before on trends in American family life.[8] These trends have thrust our high divorce rate to the center of national attention.

The second contributing factor is an increased recognition of the cumulative effect of a sustained high divorce rate, in combination with other trends, even if that rate is no longer climbing year by year. The effect of most relevance here is what this means for America's children. With more than one million divorces occurring in America every year for the past two decades, and with a sharp rise in births out of wedlock, the chances that a child will grow up in a "stable, two-parent family" have declined markedly (and have continued to decline in the 1980s and 1990s, despite the stabilization in the divorce rate). According to one set of estimates, white children born in 1950 had a 19 percent chance of spending some period of time in a single-parent family prior to age seventeen, and for blacks the probability was 48 percent. For a child born in 1980, these probabilities were projected to increase to 70 percent and 94 percent, respectively![9] Although the size of this shift is not due to brittle marriages alone but increasingly to births to unwed mothers as well, the sheer magnitude of the shift to which the high divorce rate has contributed evokes mounting concern. These sorts of statistics give rise to the conclusion that, even if the divorce rate is no longer climbing annually, divorce in America still qualifies as an "epidemic."[10]

The third and perhaps most significant factor in the recent rise in public concern about divorce in America is the accumulating evidence on the social costs of high divorce, particularly for America's children. Until relatively recently, much of the available scientific evidence discounted the potential costs of divorce in several ways. It is worth reviewing briefly this earlier consensus of research results before discussing how it has been challenged recently.

Critics of divorce generally argue that children whose parents divorce are likely to be harmed in several ways. First, the trauma of divorce itself is likely to cause psychological problems for the child and even lead some children to blame themselves for the breakup of their parents' marriage. Second, after the divorce, most children lack the daily role model and disciplinary influence of their non-custodial parent (most often the father), and their custodial parent will be hard-pressed to guide and supervise them adequately, making disciplinary and motivational problems more likely. Third, divorce often produces downward mobility economically, particularly for a divorced mother who has custody of young children, and children newly thrust into poverty are less well equipped to succeed in academic and other competitions than children in better-off, two-parent families.

In the earlier research consensus, several arguments were used to discount these dangers. Most studies showed that the immediate psychological pain of divorce was short-lived for the children, who tended to recover rapidly and showed few long-term emotional scars. Furthermore, if the alternative to divorce was parents who stayed married but constantly argued and fought, most analysts argued that divorce would be less harmful to the children.[11] In other words, the best of all worlds might be to grow up with happily married parents, but if that is not possible, then growing up in a single-parent home is better than in an intact but rancorous or even violent home. Furthermore, rates of remarriage tended to be high (family sociology textbooks often claimed that about three-fourths of husbands and two-thirds of wives remarried within five years), so that most children would not have to remain in a single-parent family into adulthood. Within a few years, a stepparent might appear on the scene to provide an acceptable substitute for the guidance and discipline (not to mention earnings) once provided by the divorced and now absent parent. Finally, in addressing the "economic harm" claim, many analysts pointed out that what harmed children's ability to make their way into successful adulthood was not divorce itself but poverty, and that if you controlled for the effect of income level, children who lived with one parent did just as well in school and in other realms as did children raised by two parents. If divorce led to impoverishment, then the solution was not to limit divorce but to find ways to prevent such impoverishment, such as through fairer child support policies and more effective payment enforcement systems (a major concern in part 3 of this book).

In other words, many analysts until recently argued that the impact of divorce on children was either neutral, harmful but temporary, or even beneficial. With the potential harm of divorce to children thus discounted, the interests and desires of the spouses themselves could be the determining consideration. Given this perspective, rising divorce could be seen benignly as indicating that more and more spouses were getting out of unhappy marriages and trying again, without creating long-term social costs and damage to their children. Indeed, if they succeeded in finding a more satisfactory mate, the result of a higher divorce rate could be interpreted as promoting greater marital happiness, with individuals no longer "stuck" in unsatisfying or even violent marriages. Children would presumably benefit as well by being raised by a parent and stepparent who are happily (re)married.

This "conventional wisdom" regarding the benign nature of divorce has been upset by more recent research that challenges its basic assumptions, and this new research has led to a revival of support for the view that divorce often harms children. Some of this research emphasizes shifts in popular behavior that weaken the claim that divorce causes only temporary problems. For example, the remarriage rate has fallen in recent years, so that one can no longer so readily assume that most children of divorce will end up living with two parents again after an interlude.

However, the most sweeping challenge to the "divorce as benign" view comes from careful research that shows that children who are living with only one parent (whether through divorce or through the parent not marrying in the first place) do more poorly in a wide range of outcomes (e.g., high school grades, graduation rates, college enrollment, employment, teenage pregnancy) than children who live with both parents, even when income, race, and other influences are taken into account. Furthermore, this new research indicates that a stepparent is not an acceptable substitute for an absent parent. Children who live with a parent and stepparent do not fare much better than children who live with a single parent.[12] Children in single-parent homes with moderate and even high incomes do not fare as well as children at the same economic levels who live with both parents. Exactly what social and psychological mechanisms translate single parenthood into multiple deficits for children are not entirely clear in this new research, but it has led to new alarm about the social costs of high divorce rates (as well as high rates of birth out of wedlock).[13]

Taken together, these recent trends have produced a situation in which the apparent leveling off of America's high divorce rate has produced not complacency but heightened concern. If large proportions of children are spending a significant part of their formative years in what used to be called "broken homes," and if the best evidence available now indicates that this experience is not benign but is often harmful to them and their future lives, shouldn't we try to do something about it? And if so, what sorts of things should we do? The chapters in this volume are dedicated to exploring a variety of things that might help produce a more supportive environment for American marriages and reduce the harm to children if the parents do divorce.[14]

NOTES

1. See the informative reviews in Stephanie Coontz, *The Way We Never Were: American Families and the Nostalgia Trap* (New York: Basic Books, 1992); Mary Jo Bane, *Here to Stay: American Families in the Twentieth Century* (New York: Basic Books, 1976).

2. See the discussion in David Popenoe, *Disturbing the Nest: Family Change and Decline in Modern Societies* (New York: Aldine, 1989). See also David Popenoe, "American Family Decline, 1960–1990: A Review and Appraisal," *Journal of Marriage and the Family* 55 (1993):527-42; Council on Families in America, *Marriage in America* (New York: Institute for American Values, 1995); David Popenoe, Jean Bethke Elshtain, and David Blankenhorn, eds., *Promises to Keep: Decline and Renewal of Marriage in America* (Lanham, Md.: Rowman & Littlefield, 1996).

3. For an iconoclastic exception to this generalization, see Barrington Moore Jr., "Thoughts on the Future of the Family," from his book, *Political Power and Social Theory* (Cambridge, Mass.: Harvard University Press, 1958), pp. 160-78.

4. See, for example, the skeptical views presented in Frank F. Furstenberg Jr., "Family Change and the Welfare of Children: What Do We Know and What Can We Do about

It?" in *Gender and Family Change in Industrialized Countries,* ed. Karen Mason and An-Magritt Jensen (New York: Oxford University Press, 1995).

5. See the discussion in Popenoe, *Disturbing the Nest;* Andrew Cherlin, *Marriage, Divorce, Remarriage,* rev. ed. (Cambridge, Mass.: Harvard University Press, 1992); and Steven Ruggles, "The Rise of Divorce and Separation in the United States, 1880–1990," *Demography* 34 (1997): 455-66.

6. See figure 1-5 in Cherlin, *Marriage, Divorce, Remarriage,* p. 21.

7. Furthermore, the leveling off of the divorce rate is not a consequence of the fact that the average age at marriage has increased since the 1960s (given the fact that those who marry young are most likely to divorce). See the evidence presented in Joshua Goldstein, "The Leveling of Divorce in the United States," *Demography* 36 (1999): 409-14.

8. See, for example, Barbara Dafoe Whitehead, "Dan Quayle Was Right," *Atlantic Monthly,* April 1993, 47-84.

9. Sandra Hofferth, "Updating Children's Life Course," *Journal of Marriage and the Family* 47 (1985): 93-115. To look at the same trend from the other side, the total time spent by white children born in 1950 living with both parents between ages zero and seventeen was 92 percent; for black children born in the same year, 78 percent. For children born in 1980, these figures were projected to be reduced to 69 percent and 41 percent, respectively. Hofferth more recently commented (personal communication to the author, October 22, 1999) that she thought that her 1985 projections might have been overstated by perhaps 5 to 10 percent for whites but were rather accurate for blacks. It should be noted, however, that children being raised by a single parent in a significant minority of cases have at least one other adult present in the household and presumably helping with the childrearing—most often a cohabiting partner of the parent or a grandparent. One recent study indicates that close to one-third of all children being raised by a single parent in the early 1980s in fact had other adults in the home. See Larry L. Bumpass and R. Kelly Raley, "Redefining Single-Parent Families: Cohabitation and Changing Family Reality," *Demography* 32 (1995): 97-109.

10. In comparative context, the United States has for some time had the highest divorce ' rate of any modern nation, although Popenoe contends that if we take into account the dissolution of Swedish unions that do not involve formal marriage, Sweden might be number one. See Popenoe, *Disturbing the Nest.*

11. See the review in Cherlin, *Marriage, Divorce, Remarriage.* However, for an alternative view, suggesting that children whose parents divorce suffer longer-term psychological problems, see Judith Wallerstein and Sandra Blakeslee, *Second Chances: Men, Women, and Children a Decade after Divorce* (New York: Ticknor & Fields, 1989).

12. See, in particular, Sara McLanahan and Gary Sandefur, *Growing Up with a Single Parent* (Cambridge, Mass.: Harvard University Press, 1994); Paul R. Amato and Alan Booth, *A Generation at Risk: Growing Up in an Era of Family Upheaval* (Cambridge, Mass.: Harvard University Press, 1997); and the review of evidence presented in David Popenoe, *Life without Father: Compelling New Evidence That Fatherhood and Marriage Are Indispensable for the Good of Children and Society* (New York: Free Press, 1996).

13. The work reported by McLanahan and Sandefur, and several similar recent studies, are mostly the product of demographic analysis, and the data used do not contain clinical observations and other evidence that would enrich our understanding of the underlying mechanisms involved. We also do not yet have good evidence about how adequately grandparents and others who not infrequently assist or even reside with the single parent

can compensate for the absent parent, but given the negative evidence presented about the role of a stepparent, the comfortable assumption that any other adult to help out will do seems unwarranted. Indeed, McLanahan and Sandefur found in their research (*Growing Up*, pp. 74-75) that children growing up in a home with a single mother and a grandmother were just as likely to have a teen birth, and even more likely to drop out of high school, than children living only with a single mother.

14. Arguably the rising proportion of Americans who never marry and the rise in non-marital fertility are as much or more a source of concern than marriages that end in divorce. However, the focus of the present volume is on how to create more supportive conditions for existing marriages and how to minimize the personal and social costs when the marriage breaks up, rather than on initiatives that might make the unmarried more eager to head toward the altar.

Part One

Supporting Marriage as an Institution
and Making Marriages Work

2

Cohabitation: A Communitarian Perspective

Linda J. Waite

Americans often talk as if marriage were a private, personal relationship. But when two people live together for their own strictly private reasons and carve out their own, strictly private bargain about the relationship, without any legal or social pressures, we call that relationship not marriage but "cohabitation."

In America, cohabitation is now more popular than ever. More men and women are moving in together, sharing an apartment and a bed, without getting married first. U.S. Census Bureau (1998) figures show four million couples living together outside marriage (not counting gay couples), eight times as many as in 1970. In 1970 there was one cohabiting couple for every one hundred married couple households. Now there are eight couples living together for every one hundred married couples.

Not only are more couples living together, but also they are doing so more openly. Thirty years ago men and women who lived together generally presented themselves as married; often the woman would use the husband's surname and the title "Mrs." In many states, their relationship became a legal, common-law marriage after a certain number of years had passed. But as the moral prohibition against premarital sex weakened and more unmarried men and women began to conduct active sex lives openly, the stigma of living together also weakened, although it has not disappeared.

IS COHABITATION "TRIAL MARRIAGE"?

People used to believe that living together in a "trial marriage" told potential partners something about what marriage would be like. The information gained could help couples make good choices and avoid bad ones—cohabiting before marriage could lead to better marriages later. Survey evidence shows how widespread this belief is. Table 2.1 shows views on reasons for and against cohabitation among cohabitors under age thirty-five.

Most cohabitors say that making sure that they are compatible before marriage is an important reason that they want to live together. On the other hand, few cohabitors say that avoiding commitment, preserving each person's independence, sexual freedom, sexual activity, or saving on the rent were important considera-

Table 2.1. Views on Reasons for and against Cohabitation: Cohabitors under Age Thirty-Five

Reasons why a person might WANT to live with someone of the opposite sex without being married. How important is each reason to YOU?

	Important		Not Important	
Response	*Male*	*Female*	*Male*	*Female*
a. It requires less personal commitment than marriage.	14%	18%	46%	48%
b. It is more sexually satisfying than marriage.	17%	18%	49%	59%
c. It makes it possible to share living expenses.	28%	26%	32%	29%
d. It requires less sexual faithfulness than marriage.	12%	10%	64%	69%
e. Couples can be sure they are compatible before marriage.	51%	56%	18%	16%
f. It allows each partner to be more independent than marriage.	17%	19%	36%	41%

Reasons why a person might NOT want to live with someone of the opposite sex without being married. How important is each reason to YOU?

	Important		Not Important	
Response	*Male*	*Female*	*Male*	*Female*
a. It is emotionally risky.	13%	18%	47%	44%
b. My friends disapprove.	4%	4%	84%	82%
c. My parents disapprove.	8%	11%	71%	61%
d. It is morally wrong.	6%	9%	75%	60%
e. It is financially risky.	7%	7%	64%	55%
f. It requires more personal commitment than dating.	19%	25%	43%	40%
g. It requires more sexual faithfulness than dating.	24%	28%	42%	43%

Sources: National Survey of Families and Households, 1987–88; Bumpass, Sweet, and Cherlin (1991), table 7.

tions to them. This makes cohabitation sound like a trial marriage. Does it work that way?

What Is Cohabitation?

Because the social arrangement of cohabitation is becoming defined as people do it, we have to map the outlines like Aesop's blind men describing an elephant by each feeling a single part. We have to define cohabitation by looking at how cohabitors behave and how they describe their arrangement.

Couples who are cohabiting rarely refer to their arrangement with this term; they say that they are living with someone or refer to their "partner." The phrase "living with someone" implies a sexual relationship. Otherwise two people living together are just roommates. Shared quarters and a shared sex life are the minimum requirements of this social arrangement—no ceremony, no license, no long-term plans, no other sharing or accommodation necessary.

How Common Is Cohabitation?

The answer to this question depends on what, exactly, one means by "common." The proportion of people currently cohabiting is quite small compared to the proportion of people who are currently married. In 1995, cohabitors comprised 6.3 percent of all couples surveyed in the General Social Survey. Only 6 percent of all adults were cohabiting, and cohabitors comprised only 3.7 percent of all households (Smith 1997).

But a different picture emerges if one asks whether *experience* with cohabitation is common. Among those who have ever been in a "coresidential" union— meaning either cohabitation or marriage—experience with cohabitation has become the norm. Almost two-thirds of young adult men and women surveyed in the National Health and Social Life Survey—those born between 1963 and 1974—began their partnered adult lives through cohabitation rather than marriage. This compares to only 16 percent of men and 7 percent of women born between the mid-1930s and early 1940s (table B.5 in Laumann et al. 1994).

Cohabitation is even *more* prevalent among people who are divorced or separated; 60 percent of persons who remarried between 1980 and 1987 lived with someone before marriage—usually but not always the person they married. Just having been married before substantially increases the chances that a person chooses cohabitation instead of marriage for a new union (Lillard, Brien, and Waite 1995).

Most cohabitations are quite short-lived; they typically last for about a year or a little more and then are transformed into marriages or dissolve. Although many observers expected the United States to follow the path blazed by the Nordic countries toward a future of informal but stable relationships, this has not happened. We see no sign that cohabitation is becoming a long-term alternative to

**Table 2.2. Cumulative Proportion of Cohabiting Couples Married
or Separated by Duration of Cohabitation**

Months	Proportion Married (%)	Proportion Separated (%)
6	15.4	6.6
12	22.4	11.5
18	29.3	17.7
24	32.2	20.3

Source: National Survey of Families and Households; Smock and Manning (1997), table 1.

marriage in the United States. It has remained a stage in the courtship process or a temporary expediency, but not typically a stable social arrangement.

Cohabiting couples are somewhat more likely to marry than to split up. Table 2.2 shows the experience of couples living together in the late 1980s. By two years later, a third had married and one out of five had separated. Forty-seven percent remained cohabiting.

Cohabitation developed to meet the needs of the adult partners but now plays an important role in the lives of many children. Currently, nearly one-third of all births occur to women who are not married. About four in ten of these children were born into two-parent families, but with parents who were cohabiting rather than married. Additionally, as cohabitation has replaced marriage and especially remarriage, many children gain a "stepfather" through their mother's cohabitation instead of through her marriage. Two-thirds of children entering stepfamilies do so through cohabitation, although many of these couples marry at some point. Half of currently married stepfamilies with children began with cohabitation (Bumpass, Raley, and Sweet 1995).

Who Cohabits?

When social observers first noticed that people were living together, cohabitation was seen as something that college students invented as part of the sexual revolution of the 1970s. There was some truth to this belief. Among young women who came of age in the 1970s, cohabitation was more often chosen as a first union by the college-educated than by high school graduates. By the mid- to late 1980s, the situation had reversed so that many more high school graduate than college graduate women were cohabiting as their first union. So cohabitation shifted from a social arrangement with substantial appeal to college students and the well educated to a social arrangement more often chosen by those with no education past high school.[1]

Cohabitors seem to be different from those who marry in important ways besides education. Cohabitors more often report that one or the other member of the couple had personality problems, problems with money, or problems with drugs or alcohol that caused problems in the relationship (Johnson and Booth 1998). Cohabitors are more likely than those who marry to use illicit drugs (Bachman et al. 1997).

Cohabitors have different goals, values, and beliefs than people who marry or people who remain outside any union. They place a lower value on marriage for themselves. They hold more liberal views of sex roles than people who marry or remain outside a union. Cohabiting men are less committed to career success for themselves and cohabiting women are *more* committed to their own career success than those who marry. Cohabitors express less attachment to their parents and other kin than do people who marry. And men who value having leisure time to enjoy their own interests are drawn to cohabitation (Clarkberg, Stolzenberg, and Waite 1995). Living together may allow couples to ease into marriage, rather than assuming the commitments it brings directly.

Cohabitors see themselves as less religious than people who marry and entering a cohabitation distances people from organized religion. Young adults who choose cohabitation as their first union come disproportionately from families that are less religious than families of those who marry (Stolzenberg, Blair-Loy, Waite 1995; Thornton, Axinn, and Hill 1992).

THE (INCOMPLETELY INSTITUTIONALIZED) INSTITUTION OF COHABITATION

Cohabitation resembles marriage in some ways and differs from it in others. As a result, cohabitation brings some but not all of the costs and benefits of marriage. Cohabitation is a tentative, nonlegal coresidential union. It does not require or imply a lifetime commitment to stay together. Even if one partner expects the relationship to be permanent, the other partner often does not (Bumpass et al. 1991). Cohabiting unions break up at a much higher rate than marriages: in three-quarters of cohabiting relationships, at least one partner thought that the relationship was in trouble over the past year (Bumpass et al. 1991: 923). Cohabitors generally assume that each partner is responsible for supporting him- or herself financially. They have no responsibility for financial support of their partner, and most do not pool financial resources. Cohabitors are more likely than married couples to both value separate leisure activities and to keep their social lives independent (Blumstein and Schwartz 1983; Clark et al. 1995). Although most cohabitors expect their relationship to be sexually exclusive; in fact, they are much less likely than husbands and wives to be monogamous (Waite and Joyner 2000). Cohabitors may *choose* this arrangement because it carries no formal constraints or responsibilities.

The tentative, impermanent, and socially unsupported nature of cohabitation impedes the ability of this type of partnership to deliver many of the benefits of marriage, as do the relatively separate lives typically pursued by cohabiting partners. The uncertainty about the stability and longevity of the relationship makes both investment in the relationship and specialization with this partner much riskier than in marriage. Couples who expect to stay together for the very long run can develop some skills and let others atrophy because they can count on their spouse (or partner) to fill in where they are weak. This specialization means that couples working together in a long-term partnership will produce more than the same people would working alone. But cohabitation reduces the benefits and increases the costs of specializing—it is much safer to just do everything yourself for yourself since you don't know whether the partner you are living with now will be around next year. So cohabiting couples typically produce less than married couples.

The temporary and informal nature of cohabitation also makes it more difficult and riskier for the extended family to invest in and support the relationship. Parents, siblings, and friends of the partners are less likely to get to know a cohabiting partner than a spouse and, more important, less likely to incorporate a person who remains outside "the family" into its activities, ceremonies, and financial dealings. Parents of one member of a cohabiting couple are ill advised to invest in the partner emotionally or financially until they see whether the relationship will be long-term. They are also ill advised to become attached to children of their child's cohabiting partner because their "grandparent" relationship with that child will dissolve if the cohabitation splits up. Marriage and plans to marry make that long-term commitment explicit and reduce the risk to families of incorporating the son- or daughter-in-law and stepchildren.

The separateness of cohabitors' lives also reduces their usefulness as a source of support during difficult times. Cohabitors tend to expect each person to be responsible for supporting him- or herself, and failure to do so threatens the relationship. This risk-sharing feature of marriage is explicitly absent in cohabitation—each person must fend for him- or herself (Blumstein and Schwartz 1983). The lack of sharing typical of cohabitors disadvantages the women and their children in these families relative to the men, because women—especially mothers— typically earn less than men (Waldfogel 1998).

Cohabitation seems to distance people from some important social institutions, especially organized religion. Most formal religions disapprove of and discourage cohabitation, making membership in religious communities awkward for unmarried couples. Individuals who enter a cohabitation often reduce their involvement in religious activities, whereas people who get married and those who become parents become more active. Young men and women who define themselves as "religious" are less likely to cohabit, and those who cohabit subsequently become less religious (Stolzenberg et al. 1995; Thornton et al. 1992).

Cohabitors should get many of the economies of scale of married couples except that the short time horizon may limit the willingness of cohabiting couples to purchase durable goods "together," leading to more cohabiting households having two TVs or separately owning cars, furniture, dishes, or appliances. The clarity of the legal rights and responsibilities in marriage—of spouses to each other, between society and married couples, and between married parents and children—encourages high levels of productivity of the married. It also encourages high levels of savings and wealth accumulation (Lufton and Smith 1999).

Cohabiting partnerships are not legally bound together—that is the whole point of cohabitation. They are also not institutionally supported. This makes it difficult for others—family, society, social institutions—to offer support, since they are not sure what the cohabitors themselves expect from the relationship, how long it will last, or what form it will take. Cohabitors are less likely than married partners to have been introduced by family members, less likely to have met through church, less likely to know each other's family, and less likely to know each other's friends (Schumm and Laumann 1999).

The nature of cohabitation, the rules under which it operates, and the expectations that the partners have for each other and for the partnership are not clearly spelled out. This means that the partners have to negotiate many more issues than married couples do, creating potential for conflict and misunderstanding. This lack of clarity about expectations, rights, and responsibilities also means that cohabitors can avoid (or try to avoid) those aspects of marriage that they find burdensome or onerous (Clarkberg et al. 1995).

Cohabitation has become an increasingly important, but poorly delineated, context for childrearing. Recent estimates suggest that 30 percent of all children are likely to spend some time in a stepfamily. One quarter of current stepfamilies involve cohabiting couples, and a significant proportion of "single-parent" families are actually two-parent cohabiting families. The parenting role of a cohabiting partner toward the child(ren) of the other person is extremely vaguely defined. The nonparent partner—the man, in the substantial majority of cases—has no explicit legal, financial, supervisory, or custodial rights or responsibilities regarding the child of his partner. "Mom's boyfriend" carries less weight with school officials, friends, or family, or with the children themselves than "my dad" or "my stepfather." Cohabitation does not impose obligations on the partner of a single parent for help, either financial or instrumental, in raising the child. By the same token, it gives the partner no moral or legal stake in the child; if the couple splits up, the former "stepfather" can expect no visitation rights and no obligation to provide child support. This ambiguity and lack of enforceable claims by either cohabiting partner or child makes investment in the relationship dangerous for both parties and makes "Mom's boyfriend" a weak and shifting base from which to discipline and guide a child.

THE CONSEQUENCES OF THE COHABITING BARGAIN

People who choose to live with someone differ in important ways from people who marry and from people who remain single. So cohabitors differ from married and single people simply as a result of the characteristics of those who pick one type of arrangement over another.

But cohabitation also involves a different bargain between the individuals involved than marriage, and this bargain will change the way people behave and what they get out of the deal.

Marriage Alternative or Marriage Prelude?

All cohabiting relationships are not equal; those on their way to the altar look and act like already-married couples in most ways, and those with no plans to marry look and act very different. For engaged cohabiting couples, living together is a step on the path toward marriage, not a different road altogether. Three-quarters of cohabitors in some studies say that they plan to marry their partner (Brown and Booth 1996).

These engaged cohabitors seem to get all the emotional benefits of marriage (at least if this is the first marriage for both partners and neither one has children), express levels of commitment to their relationship as high as married couples, are as unlikely as married couples to be violent, and are not distinguishable from married couples in frequency of disagreements, happiness, conflict management, and levels of interaction (Brown and Booth 1996; Stanley and Markman 1997; Waite and Gallagher 2000). Where we can, it is important to distinguish between cohabitors who have the hall rented and the ring bought from those who see their relationship in different terms.

Marriage produces benefits for men, women, and children across a wide range of outcomes (Waite and Gallagher 2000). Does cohabitation produce the same benefits?

Cohabitation and Domestic Violence

We can't talk about what men and women get out of cohabitation versus marriage without addressing the issue of domestic violence, at least in part because there is substantial public concern with this problem. Since domestic violence is, by definition, restricted to couples (otherwise the same behavior is just assault), surveys generally only ask these questions of married and cohabiting couples, although some also include dating couples.

My own analysis of data from the 1987–88 wave of the National Survey of Families and Households shows that married people are about half as likely as cohabiting couples to say that arguments between them and their partner had become physical in the past year (8 percent of married women compared to 16 percent of cohabiting women). When it comes to hitting, shoving, and throwing things, cohabiting couples are more than three times more likely than the married to say things get that far out of hand.

One reason cohabitors are more violent is that they are, on average, younger and less well educated. But even after controlling for education, race, age, and gender, people who live together are 1.8 times more likely to report violent arguments than married people (Waite and Gallagher 2000).

It matters a great deal, however, whether cohabiting couples have definite plans to marry. Engaged cohabitors are no more likely to report violence than married couples, but cohabitors with no plans to marry are *twice* as likely to report couple violence as either married or engaged couples. Women in uncommitted cohabiting relationships seem to be especially at risk of violence directed toward them, as table 2.3 shows. Well-being of married and *engaged* cohabiting couples is substantially higher on this dimension than less committed cohabiting couples. Some researchers suggest that commitment to the relationship and to the partner reduces couple violence, and these differentials seem to support this view (Stets 1991).

Interestingly, when domestic violence does erupt, marriage makes it easier for the law to contain. When one scholar looked at the affects of mandatory arrest policies on future domestic violence, he found striking evidence that marriage matters: husbands who were arrested did become less violent as a result. But boyfriends actually became more violent toward their partners after being arrested for "minor" violent assaults. Marriage may decrease the level of couple violence; 54 percent of men and women in a community sample of engaged couples who reported physical aggression prior to marriage did not report any violence a year later (O'Leary, Malone, and Tyree 1994).

Marriage integrates men into the community. Men with a stake in conforming to the social rules are more likely to be deterred from violence when they are shown (by an arrest) how seriously society frowns on domestic violence. Cohabiting men, by contrast, appear to rebel against social control by inflicting more pain on their partners. Cohabiting men have less to lose from being publicly identified as an abuser than married men (Sherman 1992).

Table 2.3. Percentage of Married and Cohabiting Couples Who Say That Arguments between Them Became Violent in the Past Year

	Married	*Engaged Cohabiting*	*Not Engaged Cohabiting*
Male-to-female violence	3.6	4.7	9.9
Female-to-male violence	3.2	3.4	7.6

Source: National Survey of Families and Households, 1987–88; predicted probabilities net of age, race, and education.

Even when it comes to murder, killings are more likely to happen to unmarried cohabitors than spouses (Wilson and Daly 1992). As one scholar sums up the relevant research, "Regardless of methodology, the studies yielded similar results: cohabitors engage in more violence than spouses" (Jackson 1996: 200).

Cohabitation and Sexual Activity

Cohabiting couples are much less likely than married couples to pool their finances, to share leisure activities, to assume responsibility for support of their partner, and to own appliances or property together. What they do share is an active sex life.

Easy access to a sex partner is one benefit of marriage that is also enjoyed by cohabiting couples. For them, too, dinner and small talk with their lover is not a special date—time out that must be somehow subtracted from regular life—but part of their daily routine. Consequently, live-in lovers also have a lot of sex, at least as much, on average, as married couples do.

Sex appears to be a key part of the cohabiting deal. In fact, cohabiting relationships seem to be built around sex to an even greater extent than marriage. According to the 1992 National Health and Social Life Survey, cohabiting men and women make love on average between seven and seven and a half times a month, or about one extra sex act a month than married people (Laumann et al. 1994). The slight advantage in sexual quantity holds even after we take into account the length of the relationship (men and women report the most sex in the early years of a marriage or cohabitation, and most couples who live together either marry or break up within a few years).

While cohabiting couples have at least as much sex as the married, they don't seem to enjoy it quite as much. For men, having a wife beats living with someone by a wide margin on this dimension: 48 percent of husbands say sex with their partner is extremely satisfying emotionally, compared to just 37 percent of cohabiting men. Thirty-nine percent of cohabiting men find sex physically satisfying compared to 50 percent of married men. The comparable figures for women are 39 percent of cohabiting women and 42 percent of married women say they are extremely satisfied emotionally by sex with their partner. After controlling for age and other differences, married men and married women are substantially more satisfied with sex than cohabiting or single men and women (Waite and Joyner 2000).

Cohabitation and Sexual Exclusiveness

Norms about the relationship between sex and marriage have changed a great deal over recent years. For example, only a minority of Americans now view premarital sex as always wrong. But within this sea of sexual change, the norm of marital faithfulness has changed very little. Almost all people who are married or even living with someone say they expect the relationship to be sexually exclusive. In the 1992 National Health and Social Life Survey, 94.6 percent of cohabitors and 98.7 percent of married people expected their partner to be sexually faithful to them (Laumann et al. 1994, table 11.12).

Cohabiting men and women are less likely than those who are married to live up to this ideal. Data from the National Health and Social Life Survey, presented in Table 2.4, show the percentage of men and women who had another sexual partner in addition to their spouse or their cohabiting partner during their marriage or cohabitation.

Renata Forste and Koray Tanfer (1996) find strikingly similar figures in the National Survey of Women. Married women in their survey were least likely to have had a secondary sex partner—4 percent, compared to 20 percent of cohabiting women and 18 percent of dating women. Women's behavior changed dramatically when they married, with a huge decline in the chances of having a secondary sex partner. Forste and Tanfer conclude that marriage itself increases sexual exclusivity; cohabitation is no better than "dating" on this dimension.

Cohabitation and Commitment

Psychologists Scott Stanley and Howard Markman (1997) questioned a national sample of individuals in couples about their commitment to their relationship. They asked whether people agreed with each of four statements: "My relationship with my partner is more important to me than almost anything else in my life," "I may not want to be with my partner a few years from now," "I like to think of my partner and me more in terms of 'us' and 'we' than 'me' and 'him/her,'" and "I want this relationship to stay strong no matter what rough times we may encounter."

Markman and Stanley's questions, and the answers people give, are important social indicators—canaries in the coal mine—because they apply equally well to cohabitation and marriage. So we could, in theory, find that cohabiting partners are *more* committed to their union than married people. In fact, these questions show the opposite: cohabiting people with no plans to marry say that they are significantly less committed to their partner and to the partnership itself than husbands and wives say they are to each other and to their union. Men who were co-

Table 2.4. Percentage of Men and Women Born between 1963 and 1974 Who Had More Than One Sex Partner While Married or Cohabiting

	Men	*Women*
Married	9.9	6.2
Cohabiting	24.2	11.3

Sources: National Health and Social Life Survey, 1992; Laumann et al. (1992), tables 5.9A and 5.9B.

habiting scored lower on commitment than anyone else in the survey (Stanley and Markman 1997).

In fact, married men and women are more committed to their partners than cohabiting men and women or those in sexually active dating relationships. They are also more committed to the idea of sexual exclusivity, and they are much less likely to have been unfaithful (Waite and Gallagher 2000).

Cohabitation and Work

Married men earn substantially more than otherwise similar unmarried men. The wage premium married men receive is one of the most well-documented phenomena in social science, in this country and in many others. Married men earn at least 10 percent more than single men and perhaps as much as 40 percent more. Economists call this the "marriage premium." Women get no wage premium and pay no wage penalty for being married (Waldfogel 1997). Although high-earning men are more likely than others to get married, marriage itself seems to increase earnings (Daniel 1995).

The longer a man is married, the greater the wage premium he receives. One recent study of younger white men, for example, found that married men aged twenty-four to thirty-one earned $11.33 an hour, while single men earned $10.38, and divorced or separated men earned $9.61 (Gary 1997). For older men, the wage gap between husbands and bachelors is even larger. A study done from 1966 to 1976 of men aged fifty-five to sixty-four found that married men earned 20 to 32 percent more than their nonmarried counterparts (Bartlett and Callahan 1984; Grossbard-Shechtman and Neuman 1991).

Economists generally agree that the greater productivity of married men plays a role in their higher earnings. This productivity boost comes with the more settled, stable lifestyle of marriage, with its regular hours, adequate sleep, and decent meals. It also may come directly from the productivity-enhancing efforts of the wife herself, assisting her husband with his tasks for work, giving advice, or taking on other household duties that allow him to focus on his job (Daniel 1995).

Do cohabiting men get a "marriage premium"? Does cohabitation provide the same increase in productivity that comes with marriage? Only one study has compared the changes in men's earnings that come with entry into cohabitation with those that appear at marriage. According to Daniel (1995), cohabiting men receive just half the earnings premium of marriage. Daniel estimates that young black men get a marriage premium of 4.5 percent and a cohabitation premium of 3.6 percent. White men get a marriage premium of 6.3 percent and a cohabitation premium of 2.9 percent. These estimates take into account the selection of higher-earning men into marriage. When he does not take selection into account, Daniel finds a 12 to 15 percent premium for marriage. So selectivity accounts for about half the marriage wage premium for men; the other half of the premium is caused by marriage.

Cohabitation "causes" an increase in men's wages, according to Daniel's (1995) estimates. But the premium for cohabiting is about half the premium from marriage. The tentative, nonlegal nature of cohabitation, with its uncertain future, makes investing in their partner's productivity risky for cohabiting women. Under the most common agreement governing cohabitation, partners do not assume financial responsibility for support of each other so a woman will not gain from the higher current earnings of her partner. And the uncertain prognosis for the relationship over the long term means that the woman has little assurance that the man will be around for her to reap the benefits of any future gains in his earnings. But cohabitors clearly benefit from the more stable, ordered life led by couples, which increases the earnings of cohabiting men.

Cohabitation and Housework

Cohabiting men benefit from the housework done by the woman they live with. Couples who are living together generally do not share income. It is interesting that they don't share housework as much as one might expect, either. A recent study of housework done by cohabiting and married men and women shows that women who are cohabiting spend thirty-one hours a week on household tasks compared to nineteen hours per week spent by cohabiting men. Married women spend thirty-seven hours on housework a week compared to eighteen hours for married men. So, the "housework gap" is twelve hours for cohabiting couples and nineteen hours for married couples. Taking into account the presence of children and others and characteristics of the partners reduces the gap to about fourteen hours for married couples and about ten hours for cohabiting couples. On this dimension, cohabitation is a better deal for women than marriage (South and Spitze 1994). Some economists argue that husbands compensate their wives for their time in work for the family by sharing their income with them (Grossbard-Shechtman 1993). But cohabiting women generally don't share their partner's earnings, so they may be doing extra housework without extra pay.

Cohabiting couples organize their housework in a slightly more gender-neutral way than married couples. Cohabiting men spend over 2.5 more hours per week on "female" chores such as cooking and doing dishes than married men, but married men spend more time on tasks such as outdoor maintenance. But both cohabiting and married men spend less time on the "female" chores and more time on "male" chores than other men (South and Spitze 1994, tables 2 and 3).

Cohabitation and Parenting

Some cohabiting couples live with their own children, and some live with children that belong to only one of them. Cohabiting stepfamilies differ in important ways from cohabiting two-parent families but are often difficult to distinguish in most data used to study families.

Although cohabitation by the adults in their lives affects a sizable number of children, we know very little about how cohabiting families or stepfamilies function and how they compare to married two-parent families or married stepfamilies.

Among all families with children, cohabiting families have very low levels of net wealth, on average, comparable to the wealth of single-mother families. A recent study by Lingxin Hao (1996) compares the wealth net of debt for families with children. She finds that intact two-parent families and stepfamilies have mean levels of wealth six times as high as cohabiting couple families. They are also more likely to get substantial transfers of money from family. These financial transfers translate into greater wealth in the long run but only for intact families and stepfamilies, not for cohabiting or single-parent families. As a result, children in married couple families—both intact and stepfamilies—enjoy a much better economic environment than children in cohabiting couple families or single-parent families.

But the cohabitation deal generally does not include a parental role for the partner of the parent. As Hao (1996) points out, cohabitation does not impose obligations on the partner of a single parent for help—either financial or instrumental—in raising the child. So the low wealth of cohabiting couples with children may not be shared equally with the children in the family, especially if the nonparent partner has the higher income, as is usually the case. But even if "Mom's boyfriend" does share all his income with the woman he lives with and her children, Hao's study shows how economically disadvantaged children in this situation are.

Children in cohabiting couples families are disadvantaged in other ways as well. Hao (1997) compares children from different types of families on three measures of child development: emotional development, troublesome behaviors, and grades. She finds that children in cohabiting-couple families are disadvantaged on all these outcomes, showing poorer emotional development, lower grades, and more troublesome behaviors than children from married, two-parent families, closely resembling children in remarried and single-parent families. Family structure itself is strongly related to children's well-being, even when one takes into account parents' education, income, occupation, and parenting values and behaviors. Hao attributes the better outcomes of married two-parent families to positive role modeling in those families.

Cohabitation and Money

Cohabitation lacks the legal and institutional supports of marriage. Couples who live together lack clear guidelines, either legal or normative, on appropriate financial arrangements between them. The short time horizon and uncertain future of the relationship may discourage cohabiting couples from many of the behaviors that increase productivity and asset accumulation in married couples. Cohabitation also seems most attractive to people who lack the financial wherewithal for marriage. Both the bargain under which cohabitors operate and the selection of those with modest resources into the arrangement leave cohabiting couples worse off financially than married couples.

Married couples link their fates—including their finances. This is a more attractive proposition if one's intended has a decent income and few debts. But if not, living together is a way to avoid taking on the debts—current or future—of the partner. It also allows couples to avoid the "marriage penalty" in tax code—an issue for two-worker couples with fairly equal incomes (but couples with unequal earnings could see tax benefits if they marry and share income). Couples with the same income who live together are counted as separate in determining eligibility for many government programs such as food stamps and the earned income tax credit. Since the income of one's spouse (but not one's cohabiting partner) is counted in determining eligibility for benefits, the implicit tax on marriage in these programs can be very high (Steuerle et al. 1998; Steuerle, present volume).

Selection of those with few resources into cohabitation and/or the negative effects of the cohabitation bargain combine to leave couples who are living together with relatively little money. Hao (1996) shows that among all families with children, cohabiting couples have the lowest average level of wealth, comparable to families headed by a single mother. Intact two-parent families and stepfamilies have the highest level of wealth, followed at a distance by families headed by a single father (see table 2.5). Unlike single-parent families, cohabiting couples have two potential earners, so their very low levels of wealth are a cause for concern, especially for the children living in these families.

Cohabitation and Emotional Well-Being

Something about living together seems to lead to lower psychological well-being; cohabitors report being more depressed and less satisfied with life than do married people. The key seems to lie in being in a relationship that one thinks will last. Marriage is, by design and agreement, for the long run. So married people

Table 2.5. Wealth of Families with Children by Family Structure

	All	Intact	Step	Cohabit	Lone Mom	Lone Dad
Mean	67.83	79.69	77.61	12.18	12.74	47.41
Median	11.00	25.75	22.50	1.00	0	22.93

Net wealth is total assets less total liabilities in 1987, in thousands of dollars.

Source: National Survey of Families and Households, 1987–88; Hao (1996), table 1.

see their relationship as much more stable than cohabiting people do. And for any couple, thinking that the relationship is likely to break up has a dampening effect on the spirits. The result: cohabitors show less psychological well-being than similar married people. Worrying that one's relationship will break up is especially distressing for cohabiting women with children, who show quite high levels of depression as a result.

Cohabiting couples for whom living together seems to be an alternative to marriage—those who have lived together for a long time without marrying and those living with children—seem to suffer psychologically. Those in unions that seem to be a prelude to marriage—short unions without children—have levels of psychological well-being as high as the married (Brown 1998).

Perhaps cohabiting people are more depressed because depressed and dissatisfied people have trouble getting married. Susan Brown (1998) finds, to the contrary, that cohabitors' higher levels of depression are not explained by their scores before the start of the union. Perceptions of the chances that the relationship will break up seem to be the chief culprit in their poor emotional well-being.

DOES COHABITING INCREASE THE CHANCES OF HAVING A SUCCESSFUL MARRIAGE?

Couples who live together find out a good deal about each other in the process. One of the reasons that people often give for wanting to live together is to see whether they are compatible prior to marriage. But a large body of recent evidence now shows quite consistently that people who cohabited and then married are much more likely to divorce later than people who married without living together. This evidence indicates that couples who cohabit and then marry are more likely to divorce because they are less committed to the institution of marriage, or they have other characteristics, both which lead them to cohabit in the first place and make them poor marriage material. Selection of those most likely to divorce into cohabitation accounts for the relationship (Bennett, Blanc, and Bloom 1988; DeMaris and Rao 1992; Lillard et al. 1995).

CONCLUSION

The evidence suggests to me that compared to marriage, uncommitted cohabitation—cohabitation by couples who are not engaged—is an inferior social arrangement.

Couples who live together with no definite plans to marry are making a different bargain than couples who marry or than engaged cohabitors. The bargain is very much *not* marriage and is "marriage-like" only in that couples share an active sex life and a house or apartment. Cohabiting men tend to be quite uncommitted to the relationship; cohabiting women with children tend to be quite uncertain about its future. Levels of domestic violence are much higher in these couples than in either married or engaged cohabiting couples. Children in families headed by an unmarried couple do much worse than children in married parent families. Uncommitted cohabitation delivers relatively few benefits to men, women, or children. This social arrangement also probably benefits communities less than marriage.

Clearly, the men and women who choose uncommitted cohabitation do not have the same characteristics as those who marry without living together or who live together while planning their wedding. This selection into cohabitation of people least likely to build a successful marriage seems to account for their higher chances of divorce. But cohabitation itself seems to *cause* attitudes to change in ways inimical to long-term commitment, to damage emotional well-being, and to distance people from religious institutions and from their families. Some evidence indicates that cohabitation is less beneficial for children than marriage is. And some suggests that marriage—but not uncommitted cohabitation—reduces domestic violence.

If cohabitation is inferior to marriage, then we as a society should encourage marriage by privileging it over cohabitation. We should make a sharp distinction between the two social arrangements. This might involve allowing landlords to refuse to rent to cohabiting couples, removing penalties for marriage (but not cohabitation) in the tax code and in eligibility rules for government transfer programs, or giving benefits such as health insurance or housing preferences to married couples but not to domestic partners (except for gay couples who cannot legally marry). These are only examples; of course, any policy changes must be debated at length.

Alternatively, we could put in place something resembling the old common-law marriage provisions in the legal code, whereby people who lived together would assume the legal rights and responsibilities of marriage after some interval. Perhaps people who lived together at all and had children together would automatically assume the legal rights and responsibilities of married parenthood.

Society has a larger stake in the stability of a union when children are involved whether they are biological children of both partners or only one. Policies to encourage the delay of parenthood until a committed marriage has been formed, to encourage couples with children to marry, and to discourage cohabitation by single mothers should be considered and actively debated.

All cohabiting couples *could* marry if they wanted (unless one member is already legally married). If couples chose cohabitation rather than marriage because they don't want to get married, then making cohabitation legally just like marriage may cause those couples to avoid both marriage *and* cohabitation. We could see a move to visiting unions that did not involve coresidence, for example, if living together triggered a series of legal rights and responsibilities like those in marriage.

Encouraging marriage over cohabitation involves undoing a whole series of legal and social changes that have undercut the privileged status of marriage. To the extent that marriage delivers benefits that cohabitation does not, it is important to begin this process.

NOTE

1. Raley (1998) compares the experience with marriage and cohabitation by age twenty-five among young women born between 1950 and 1969. Among women born between 1950 and 1954, 18 percent of those who were college graduates cohabited as their first union, compared to 16 percent who had a high school degree. But fifteen years later, the nature of cohabitation had shifted so that women who were high school graduates were substantially more likely to cohabit in their first union than female college graduates (45 percent vs. 24 percent). In the earlier cohort, 70 percent of high school graduates married by age twenty-five without cohabiting first, compared to 43 percent of college graduates, who often had not entered any union by age twenty-five.

REFERENCES

Bachman, Jerald G., Katherine N. Wadsworth, Patrick M. O'Malley, Lloyd D. Johnson, and John E. Schulenberg. 1997. *Smoking, drinking, and drug use in young adulthood.* Mahwah, N.J.: Erlbaum.

Bartlett, Robin L., and Charles Callahan. 1984. Wage determination and marital status: Another look. *Industrial Relations* 23(1): 90-96.

Bennett, Neil, Ann Blanc, and David Bloom. 1988. Commitment and the modern union: Assessing the link between premarital cohabitation and marital stability. *American Sociological Review* 53: 127-38.

Blumstein, Philip, and Pepper Schwartz. 1983. *American couples.* New York: Morrow.

Brown, Susan L. 1998. Cohabitation as marriage prelude versus marriage alternative: The significance for psychological well-being. Paper presented at the meetings of the American Sociological Association, August, San Francisco.

Brown, Susan L., and Alan Booth. 1996. Cohabitation versus marriage: A comparison of relationship quality. *Journal of Marriage and the Family* 58: 668-78.

Bumpass, Larry L., R. Kelly Raley and James A. Sweet. 1995. The changing character of stepfamilies: Implications of cohabitation and nonmarital childbearing. *Demography* 32: 425-36.

Bumpass, Larry L., James A. Sweet, and Andrew Cherlin. 1991. The role of cohabitation in declining rates of marriage. *Journal of Marriage and the Family* 53(4): 913-27.

Clarkberg, Marin, Ross M. Stolzenberg, and Linda J. Waite. 1995. Attitudes, values and entrance into cohabitational versus marital unions. *Social Forces* 74(2): 609-34.

Daniel, Kermit. 1995. The marriage premium. In *The new economics of human behavior,* ed. Mariano Tommasi and Kathryn Ierulli. Cambridge: Cambridge University Press.

DeMaris, A., and K. V. Rao. 1992. Premarital cohabitation and subsequent marital stability in the United States: A reassessment. *Journal of Marriage and the Family* 54: 178-90.

Forste, Renata, and Koray Tanfer. 1996. Sexual exclusivity among dating, cohabiting, and married women. *Journal of Marriage and the Family* 58(1): 3-47.

Gray, Jeffrey S. 1997. The fall in men's return to marriage. *Journal of Human Resources* 32(3): 481-503.

Grossbard-Shechtman, Shoshana. 1993. *On the economics of marriage: A theory of marriage, labor and divorce.* Boulder, Colo.: Westview.

Grossbard-Shechtman, Shoshana A. and Shoshana Neuman. 1991. Cross-productivity effects of education and origin on earnings: Are they really reflecting productivity? In *Handbook of Behavioral Economics*, vol. 2A, ed. R. Frantz H. Singh and J. Gerber. Greenwich, Conn.: JAI.

Hao, Lingxin. 1996. Family structure, private transfers, and the economic well-being of families with children. *Social Forces* 75: 269-92.

———. 1997. Family structure, parental input, and child development. Paper presented at the meetings of the Population Association of America, Washington, D.C., March.

Jackson, Nicky Ali. 1996. Observational experiences of intrapersonal conflict and teenage victimization: A comparative study among spouses and cohabitors. *Journal of Family Violence* 11: 191-203.

Johnson, David, and Alan Booth. 1988. Premarital cohabitation and marital success. *Journal of Family Issues* 9: 255-72.

Laumann, Edward O., John H. Gagnon, Robert T. Michael, and Stuart Michaels. 1994. *The social organization of sexuality: Sexual practices in the United States.* Chicago: University of Chicago Press.

Lillard, Lee A., Michael J. Brien, and Linda J. Waite. 1995. Pre-marital cohabitation and subsequent marital dissolution: Is it self-selection? *Demography* 32: 437-58.

O'Leary, K. Daniel, Jean Malone, and Andrea Tyree. 1994. Physical aggression in early marriage: Prerelationship and relationship effects. *Journal of Consulting and Clinical Psychology* 62: 594-602.

Raley, R. Kelly. 1998. Recent trends in marriage and cohabitation. Paper presented at the NICHD conference "Ties That Bind: Perspectives on Marriage and Cohabitation," Bethesda, Md., June 29–30.

Schumm, L. Philip, and Edward O. Laumann. 1998. The roles of sex and social networks in the partnering process. Paper presented at the NICHD conference "Ties That Bind: Marriage, Cohabitation and Union Formation," Bethesda, Md., June 29–30.

Sherman, Lawrence. 1992. *Policing domestic violence: Experiments and dilemmas.* New York: Free Press.

Smith, Tom W. 1997. Changes in families and family values. Report prepared for the National American Foundation. NORC.

Smock, Pamela J., and Wendy D. Manning. 1997. Cohabiting partners' economic circumstances and marriage. *Demography* 34: 331-41.

South, Scott J., and Glenna D. Spitze. 1994. Housework in marital and nonmarital households. *American Sociological Review* 59: 327-47.

Stanley, Scott M., and Howard J. Markman. 1997. *Marriage in the 90s: A nationwide random phone survey.* Denver: PREP.

Stets, Jan E. 1991. Cohabiting and marital aggression: The role of social isolation. *Journal of Marriage and the Family* 53: 669-80.

Steuerle, C. Eugene, Edward M. Gramlich, Hugh Heclo, and Demetra Nightingale. 1998. *The government we deserve.* Washington, D.C.: Urban Institute Press.

Stolzenberg, Ross M., Mary Blair-Loy, and Linda J. Waite. 1995. Religious participation over the life course: Age and family life cycle effects on church membership. *American Sociological Review* 60: 84-103.

Thornton, Arland, William G. Axinn, and Daniel H. Hill. 1992. Reciprocal effects of religiosity, cohabitation and marriage. *American Journal of Sociology* 98: 628-51.

U.S. Bureau of the Census. 1998. *Marital status and living arrangements, March 1997.* Current Population Reports, Series P20, No. 506. Washington, D.C.: U.S. Government Printing Office.

Waite, Linda J., and Maggie Gallagher. 2000. *The case for marriage.* New York: Doubleday.

Waite, Linda J., and Kara Joyner. 2000. Emotional and physical satisfaction in married, cohabiting and dating sexual unions: Do men and women differ? In *Studies on sex*, ed. E. Laumann and R. Michael. Chicago: University of Chicago Press.

Waldfogel, Jane. 1997. The effect of children on women's wages. *American Sociological Review* 62: 209-17.

———. 1998. The family gap for young women in the United States and Britain: Can maternity leave make a difference? *Journal of Labor Economics* 16: 505-45.

Wilson, Margo, and Martin Daly. 1992. Who kills whom in spouse killings: On the exceptional sex ratio of spousal homicides in the United States. *Criminology* 30:189-215.

3

On Responsible Fathering: An Overview, Conceptual Framework, and Recommendations for Policies and Programs

William J. Doherty and Martha F. Erickson

For more than a century, American society has engaged in a sometimes contentious debate about what it means to be a responsible parent. Whereas most of the cultural debate about mothers has focused on what, if anything, mothers should do outside the family, the debate about fathers has focused on what fathers should do inside the family. What role should fathers play in the everyday lives of their children, beyond the traditional breadwinner role? How much should they emulate the traditional nurturing activities of mothers, and how much should they represent a masculine role model to their children? Is fatherhood in a unique crisis in late twentieth-century America (Blankenhorn 1995; Doherty 1997; Griswold 1993; LaRossa 1997; Popenoe 1996)?

The recent upsurge of interest in fathering has generated concern among supporters of women's and mothers' rights that the emphasis on the important role of fathers in families may feed long-standing biases against female-headed single-parent families, that services for fathers might be increased at the expense of services for single mothers, and that the profatherhood discourse might be used by the fathers' rights groups who are challenging custody, child support, and visitation arrangements after divorce. On the other hand, feminist psychologists have recently argued for more emphasis on fathering, suggesting that involved, nurturing fathers will benefit women as well as children (Phares 1996; Silverstein 1996). Only an ecologically sensitive approach to parenting, which views the welfare of fathers, mothers, and children as intertwined and interdependent, can avoid a zero-sum approach to parenting in which fathers' gains become mothers' losses.

These cultural debates serve as a backdrop to the social science research on fathering because researchers are inevitably influenced by the cultural context within which they work (Doherty et al. 1993). In their recent reanalysis of the historical trends of American ideals of fatherhood, Pleck and Pleck (1997) see the emerging ideal of fatherhood in the late twentieth century as father as equal coparent. (From 1900 to 1970, the dominant cultural ideal was the genial dad and sex role model; from 1830 to1900, the distant breadwinner.) Research on fathering, then, has attained prominence in the social sciences during an era of historically high expectations of men's involvement in the everyday lives of their children. Not surprisingly, a good deal of that research has compared levels of fathers' involvement with their children to mothers' involvement, because mothers have become the benchmark for norms for fathering (Day and Mackey 1989).

This post-1970s interest in fathering has been fueled by the reappraisal of family roles for women and by unprecedented demographic changes in the American family. In other words, scholarly, professional, and public policy interest in fathering has crystallized during the time that the foundation of traditional fathering—the physically present father who serves as the unique family breadwinner—has been eroding rapidly. With more than half of mothers in the workforce, with new marriages breaking up at a rate of 50 percent, and with nearly one-third of births to single women, the landscape of fathering was altered substantially in the late twentieth century (Bumpass 1990; U.S. Bureau of the Census 1994).

Sociological and historical work on fathering makes it clear that fathering (at least beyond insemination) is fundamentally a social construction. Each generation molds its cultural ideal of fathers according to its own time and conditions, and each deals with the inevitable gap between what LaRossa (1988) terms the "culture" of fatherhood and the "conduct" of fathers in families. Sociological and historical analyses also make it clear that fathering cannot be defined in isolation from mothering, mothers' expectations, and social expectations about child rearing in the society and that these social expectations were fairly fluid in the United States from decade to decade in the twentieth century. LaRossa (1997) has demonstrated how the culture of fatherhood and the conduct of fathers change from decade to decade as social and political conditions change.

In addition to this historical and social-constructionist perspective, fathering also lends itself to a systemic framework which views fathering not primarily as a characteristic or behavioral set of individual men or even as a dyadic characteristic of a father–child relationship but as a multilateral process involving fathers, mothers, children, extended family, and the broader community and its cultures and institutions. Fathering is a product of the meanings, beliefs, motivations, attitudes, and behaviors of all these stakeholders in the lives of children. Indeed, we will suggest here that fathering may be more sensitive than mothering to contextual forces, forces that currently create more obstacles than bridges for fathers but that potentially could be turned in a more supportive direction.

With these historical, social-constructionist, and systemic perspectives as a backdrop, this chapter examines the concept of "responsible fathering," offers a conceptual framework to organize past research on this topic, and makes communitarian-based recommendations for policy and program development.

RESPONSIBLE FATHERING

The use of the term *responsible fathering,* which was the original language by the Department of Health and Human Services in commissioning the work on which this chapter is based, reflects a recent shift among academics and professionals away from value-free language toward a more explicit value–advocacy approach *that is consistent with communitarian theory.* "Responsible" suggests an "ought," a set of desired norms for evaluating fathers' behavior. The term also conveys a moral meaning (right and wrong), since it suggests that some fathering could be judged "irresponsible." The willingness to use explicitly moral terms reflects a change in the social climate among academics, professionals, and policymakers, who until recently embraced the traditional notion that social science, social policy, and social programs could be value-free. The late twentieth century witnessed more appreciation of the inevitability of value and moral positions being part of social science and social interventions and a greater willingness to be explicit about value positions so that they can be debated openly and their influence on social science and policy can be made clear rather than being covert (Doherty 1995b; Doherty et al. 1993; Wolfe 1989). Indeed, fathering research has always had a strong but implicit undercurrent of value advocacy, much of it conducted by men and women interested in promoting more committed and nurturing involvement by men in their children's lives. Similarly, there has always been a moral undertone to the focus on fathers' deficits that has characterized much of the literature on absent, "deadbeat," and emotionally uninvolved fathers (Doherty 1990). The term *responsible fathering* as we use it applies to fathers across all social classes and racial groups, not narrowly to men in lower social classes or minority groups.

Now that value advocacy has become more explicit in the fathering area (Dollahite, Hawkins, and Brotherson 1997), responsible fathering needs to be clearly defined. Levine and Pitt (1995) have made an important start in their delineation of responsible fathering. They write:

A man who behaves responsibly towards his child does the following:

- He waits to make a baby until he is prepared emotionally and financially to support his child.
- He establishes his legal paternity if and when he does make a baby.
- He actively shares with the child's mother in the continuing emotional and physical care of their child, from pregnancy onwards.
- He shares with the child's mother in the continuing financial support of their child, from pregnancy onwards. (pp. 5–6)

Levine and Pitt's elements of responsible fathering have the advantage of referring to both resident and nonresident fathers, a reflection of the diversity of fathers' situations. The authors also assert that commitment to this ethic of responsible fatherhood extends beyond the father to the mother, to professionals who work with families, and to social institutions entrusted with the support of families. We employ Levine and Pitt's definition in this chapter but narrow our scope to men who are already fathers; we do not address the issue of postponing fatherhood.

The developmental backdrop for the discussion of fathering reflects children's needs for predictability, nurturance, and appropriate limit setting from fathers and mothers, as well as for economic security and a cooperative, preferably loving, relationship between their parents (Hetherington and Parke 1993). Furthermore, the specific needs of children vary by their developmental stage. Higher levels of physical caregiving by parents are required during infancy, and greater levels of parental conflict management skills are needed when children become adolescents. Although we do not review the literature on the effects of active fathering on children, a fundamental justification for promoting active, involved fathering is that children and adolescents benefit from this kind of relationship in many ways, including psychological, social, economic, and academic (Pleck 1997; Parke 1987). The prime justification for promoting responsible fathering is children's needs. A secondary but also important justification is that responsible fathering benefits men in their own adult development (Snarey 1993).

INFLUENCES ON FATHERING: A CONCEPTUAL MODEL

The fathering literature has been long on empirical studies and short on theory. Researchers mostly have adapted concepts from social sciences to fit their particular area, but work is beginning on overarching conceptual frameworks to guide research and program development. In his review of theory in fathering research, Marsiglio (1995) mentions life course theory (which emphasizes how men's experience of fatherhood changes with life transitions), social scripting theory (which emphasizes the cultural messages that fathers internalize about their role), and social identity theory (which focuses on how men take on the identity of a father in relation to their other social roles). Hawkins and colleagues (1995), Hawkins and Dollahite (1997), and Snarey (1993) have used Erik Erikson's developmental theory in their work on how fathering can promote generativity among adult men. Other scholars have explored the utility of economic theories to understand fathers' decisions to invest in, or withdraw from, their children (Becker 1991).

The most specific conceptual model frequently used in the fatherhood literature is Lamb's and Pleck's four-factor model of father involvement, which is not explicitly grounded in a broader theory such as Erikson's theory or social identity theory (see Lamb et al. 1985; Pleck 1997). Lamb and Pleck propose that father involvement is determined by motivation, skills and self-confidence, social support, and institutional practices. These factors may be viewed as additive, building on one another, and as interactive, with some factors being necessary prior to others. For example, motivation may be necessary for the development of skills. More recently, Parke (1996) has articulated a systems model of residential father involvement that includes individual, family, extrafamilial, and cultural influences.

Based on the research literature, prior theoretical work on fathering, and on the systemic ecological orientation mentioned earlier, we present a conceptual model of influences on responsible fathering (see Figure 3.1). Unlike prior work, the model is intended to include fathering inside or outside marriage and regardless of coresidence with the child. The focus is on the factors that help create and maintain a father–child bond. The model attempts to transcend the dyadic focus of much traditional child development theory by emphasizing first the child–father–mother triad and then larger systems influences.

The model highlights individual factors of the father, mother, and child; mother–father relationship factors; and larger contextual factors in the environment. Within each of these domains, the model outlines a number of specific factors that can be supported by the research literature. The center of the model is the interacting unit of child, father, and mother, each formulating meanings and enacting behaviors that influence the others. The three are embedded in a broader social context that affects them as individuals and the quality of their relationships.

We are particularly interested in highlighting factors that pertain to fathers, because one of the goals of this chapter is to guide father-specific research, program development, and public policy. All of the factors in the model affect the mother–child relationship as well, because they are generic to parenting (see Belsky 1984), but many of them have particular twists for fathers. Because the-

Figure 3.1. Influences on Responsible Fathering.

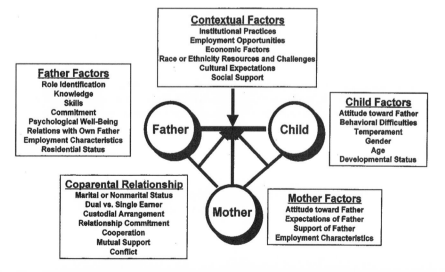

ory and research on parenting so often have been derived from work on mothers, it seems particularly important to illuminate the distinctive influences on fathering. The arrows point to the father–child relationship, in particular to the four domains of responsible fathering covered in this review: paternity, presence, economic support, and involvement. Although the model can depict fathers' indirect influence on their children through their support for the mother, the focus here is on direct father–child interaction. And although the influences depicted in the model also can be viewed as influencing the father directly, we prefer to focus on effects on father–child relations because enhancing those relations, and therefore children's well-being, is the ultimate goal of programs for fathers.

The research reviewed for this chapter supports the notion that father–child relations are more strongly influenced than mother–child relations by three of the dimensions of the model: the coparental relationship, factors in the other parent, and larger contextual factors.

Coparental Relationship

A number of studies have shown that the quality of father–child relations both inside and outside marriage is more highly correlated with the quality of the coparental relationship than is true for the mother–child relationship (Belsky and Volling 1987; Cox et al. 1989; Feldman, Nash, and Aschenbrenner 1983; Levy-Shiff and Israelashvili 1988). Fathers appear to withdraw from their child when they are not getting along with the mother, whereas mothers do not show a similar level of withdrawal. This is one way to understand the tendency of fathers to remove themselves from their children's lives after a breakup with the mother, especially if they have a negative relationship with the mother (Ahrons and Miller 1993). As Furstenberg and Cherlin (1991) have asserted, for many men, marriage and parenthood are a "package deal." Or one might say that in American culture, a woman is a mother all of her life, but a man is a father if he has a wife. Furthermore, if he has a wife but does not get along with her, he may be present as a father, but the quality of his relationship with his children is apt to suffer.

One reason that fathering is particularly sensitive to the marital or coparental relationship is that standards and expectations for fathering appear to be more variable than those for mothering. There is more negotiation in families over what fathers will do than what mothers will do and hence more dependence among fathers on the quality and outcome of those negotiations (Backett 1987). As Lewis and O'Brien (1987) state, men have a less clear "job description" as fathers than women do as mothers. Therefore, fathers' behavior is strongly influenced by the meanings and expectations of fathers themselves, as well as mothers, children, extended family, and broader cultures and institutions.

One of the most sensitive areas of research on fathering is the importance of fathers being married to the children's mothers. Because many fathers are not married to the mother, it can seem prejudicial to these men and their children—and perhaps to single-parent mothers—to emphasize the importance of marriage. On the other hand, an implication of our review of the research and our conceptual framework is that, for most American fathers, the family environment most supportive of fathering is a caring, committed, and collaborative marriage. This kind of marriage means that the father lives with his children and has a good partnership with their mother. These are the two principal intrafamilial determinants of responsible fathering.

Some of the controversy over the role of marriage in responsible fathering can be circumvented by specifying the quality of the marriage, as we have done. It is the quality of the marital process, rather than the legal or coresidential status, that most affects fathering. One might argue, then, that being married is not important, because cohabiting couples could have the same qualities of relationship. Although in principle this is true, the best national research on cohabitation indicates that cohabitation is a temporary arrangement for most heterosexual couples; they eventually either marry or break up (Bumpass et al. 1991). We conclude that in practice the kind of mother–father relationship most conducive to responsible fathering in contemporary U.S. society is a caring, committed, collaborative marriage. Outside this arrangement, substantial barriers stand in the way of active, involved fathering.

Mother Factors

Among external influences on fathering, the role of the mother has particular salience, because mothers serve as partners and sometimes as gatekeepers in the father–child relationship, both inside and outside marriage (De Luccie 1995). Mother factors in the conceptual model, of course, interact with the coparental relationship, because the mother's personal feelings about the father influence the coparental relationship. But evidence also indicates that, even within satisfactory marital relationships, a father's involvement with his children, especially young children, is often contingent on the mother's attitudes toward, expectations of, and support for the father, as well as by the extent of her involvement in the labor force (De Luccie 1995; Simons et al. 1990). Marsiglio (1991), using the National Survey of Families and Households data set, found that mothers' characteristics were more strongly correlated with fathers' involvement than fathers' own characteristics were. Indeed, studies have shown that many mothers, both inside and outside marriage, are ambivalent about the fathers' active involvement with their children (Baruch and Barnett 1986; Cowan and Cowan 1987). Given the powerful cultural forces that expect absorption by women in their mothering role, it is not surprising that active paternal involvement would threaten some women's identity and sense of control over this central domain of their lives. The evolution of a social consensus on responsible fathering, therefore, will necessarily involve a consensus that responsible mothering means supporting the father–child bond.

Contextual Factors

Research demonstrates the particular vulnerability of fathering to contextual and institutional practices—from the establishment of legal paternity to the greater impact of unemployment on fathering than on mothering. Lack of income and poor occupational opportunities appear to have a particularly negative effect on fathering (Thomson, Hanson, and McLanahan 1994). The prevalence of the abandonment of economic and psychological responsibilities among poor, unemployed men and among other men who undergo financial and employment crises is partly a function of the unique vulnerability of fathering to perceived success in the external environment (Jones 1991; McLoyd 1989). This analysis suggests that fathering is especially sensitive to changes in economic forces in the workforce and marketplace and to shifts in public policy. It also suggests that fathering suffers disproportionately from negative social forces, such as racism, that inhibit opportunities in the environment. McLoyd (1990), in a review and conceptual analysis of economic hardship in African American families, describes how poverty and racism combine to create psychological distress, which is, in turn, associated with more negative parenting styles and more difficulty in the coparental relationship.

Our conceptual model also depicts the positive contribution of ethnic and cultural factors to fathering. One aspect of responsible fathering, that of economic support, is nearly universally expected of fathers by their cultures (Lamb 1987a). LaRossa (1997), in his historical analysis, has demonstrated how changing cultural expectations in the first part of the twentieth century led to more nurturing father involvement in the United States. Allen and Connor (1997) have examined how role flexibility and concern for children in the African American community create opportunities for men to become involved in surrogate father relationships with children who lack day-to-day contact with their biological fathers. But, unfortunately, not much empirical research has been done that examines fathering in its cultural context, using representative samples of fathers to explore how cultural meanings and practices influence fathers' beliefs and behaviors.

The final contextual factor in the model is social support, which Belsky (1984) emphasizes in his theoretical model of parenting and which McLoyd (1990) documents as a crucial factor in diminishing the negative effects of poverty on parenting behavior. However, most of the research on social support specifically for fathers has focused on mothers as sources of social support. Pleck (1997) reviewed the limited research on extrafamilial social support for fathering and found the studies skimpy and inconsistent, except for the pattern that highly involved fathers tend to encounter negative attitudes from acquaintances, relatives, and fellow workers. Clearly, there is need for studies examining the sources and influences of social support on fathering, particularly the role of other fathers.

From the perspective of both the contextual factors and the mother factors discussed thus far, fathering can be conceptualized as a more contextually sensitive process than mothering is. Not that mothering is not also contextually sensitive, but the cultural norms are stricter on the centrality and endurance of the mother–child dyad, regardless of what is happening outside that relationship. Father–child relations, on the other hand, are culturally defined as less dyadic and more multilateral, requiring a threshold of support from inside the family and from the larger environment. Undermining from the mother or from a social institution or system may induce many fathers to retreat from responsible fathering unless their own individual level of commitment to fathering is quite strong.

This point about the ecological sensitivity of fathering is a principal conclusion of this report. It suggests that fathering programs and policy initiatives that focus only on fathers will benefit mainly fathers who already have a supportive social and economic environment. Fathers whose context is less supportive—for example, fathers who do not live with their children, who have strained relations with the mother, or who are experiencing economic stress—will need more extensive and multilateral efforts to support their fathering.

Child Factors

Individual child factors are included in the model for completeness, but the child factors studied in the research literature do not appear to be as important as the other dimensions in influencing fathering. Fathers do appear to find it easier to be more involved with their sons than their daughters, especially older sons, presumably because they identify with them and are more comfortable communicating with them (Marsiglio 1991). Most of the other child factors such as age appear to influence mothers as much as fathers, although Larson (1993) and Larson and Richards (1994) have documented how fathers withdraw more from parent–adolescent conflict than mothers do. More research is needed on the influence of the child's temperament and developmental status on relations with nonresidential fathers. Similarly, research is needed on how the child's beliefs about father involvement influence fathers' and mothers' expectations and behavior.

Mother–Child Relationship Factors

We include this domain for theoretical completeness, but we could find no research directly examining how the father–child relationship is affected by the mother–child relationship. Such effects may be tapped indirectly through other dimensions in the model, such as the mother's attitudes toward the father's involvement with the child. For example, a very close mother–child bond, combined with an ambivalent maternal attitude toward paternal involvement, might lead to less closeness of the father than a situation in which a mother had the same attitude but, herself, was less close to the child.

Father Factors

Fathers' role identification, skills, and commitment are important influences on fathering (Baruch and Barnett 1986; Ihinger-Tallman, Pasley, and Buehler 1995; Pleck 1997). These three appear to fluctuate from low to high levels along with a number of interpersonal and contextual factors such as the mother's expectations and the father's residential status with his children (Ihinger-Tallman et al. 1995; Marsiglio 1995). In American culture, fathers are given more latitude for commitment to, identification with, and competence in, their parental role. This latitude brings with it the price of confusion for many fathers about how to exercise their roles (Daly 1995).

The variability of the individual father factors suggests two important implications of our conceptual model: that the positive support from mothers and the larger context can move men in the direction of more responsible parenting even in the face of modest personal investment, and that strong father commitment, knowledge, and skills are likely to be necessary to overcome negative maternal, coparental, and contextual influences. This latter point is similar to Lamb's (1987b) hypothesis that high levels of father motivation can override institutional barriers and the lack of social support.

As for the father's experience in his own family of origin, some research suggests that the father's relations with his own father may be a factor—either through identifying with his father or through compensating for his father's lapses—in contributing to his own role identification, sense of commitment, and self-efficacy (Cowan and Cowan 1987; Daly 1995). Snarey (1993), in a longitudinal study, has documented the role of multigenerational connections between fathers.

The final father factors, psychological well-being and employment characteristics, have been studied extensively. Research examining psychological adjustment and parenting quality consistently shows a positive relationship between fathers' (and mothers') psychological well-being and their parenting attitudes and skills (Cox et al. 1989; Levy-Shiff and Israelashvili 1988; Pleck 1997). The research on job loss and economic distress generally has examined declines in psychological well-being as mediating factors leading to poorer fathering (Elder, Liker, and Cross 1984; Elder, Van Nguyen, and Caspi 1985; Jones 1991). In addition, fathers' work situations have been shown to have mixed relationships with involvement with children. Specific work schedules are not strongly related to involvement, but greater flextime and other profamily practices are associated with more father involvement (Pleck 1997). Indeed, consistent with other research on fathering, mothers' employment characteristics are more strongly associated with fathers' involvement than father employment characteristics. When mothers are employed, fathers' proportionate share of parenting is greater, although studies are inconsistent about the absolute level of father involvement (Pleck 1997).

The conceptual model outlines the multiple factors that influence fathering, from individual and relational to contextual. The factors can be viewed as additive. For example, low identification with the parental role, combined with low expectations from the mother, would be strongly associated with low involvement of the father in both residential and nonresidential contexts. Conversely, high identification with the parental role, combined with high expectations from the mother, would lead to greater father involvement in any residential context.

The factors in the model also can be viewed as interactive. For example, high role identification and good employment and income might be sufficient to offset low expectations from the mother. Similarly, not living with the child could be offset by the father's strong commitment to his children and the support of the mother. And strong institutional support through public policies could mitigate unmarried fathers' and mothers' reluctance to declare paternity.

Although the conceptual framework is intended to apply to the four domains of responsible fathering covered in this review (paternity, presence, economic support, and involvement), most of the research has focused on one or another of these areas. Indeed, the bulk of the empirical research has been on father involvement. Researchers have tended to assume that economic contextual factors uniquely influence economic support and that father factors uniquely influence father involvement. Putting a range of factors into one model challenges researchers to examine how all the factors might influence all the domains of responsible fathering. We acknowledge, however, that some components of the model are likely to influence some aspects of fathering more than others.

Finally, the model should be seen as depicting a dynamic set of processes, rather than a set of linear, deterministic influences. Systemic, ecological models run the risk of reducing the target behavior—in this case, responsible fathering—to a contextually determined phenomenon stripped of individual initiative and self-determination. Therefore, we want to emphasize the pivotal role of fathers themselves in appropriating or discarding cultural and contextual messages, in formulating a fathering identity and developing fathering skills with their own children, in working out their feelings about their own fathers, and in dealing collaboratively with their children's mother. The social construction of fatherhood is an evolving creation of all stakeholders in the lives of children, and contemporary fathers have a central role in this creation. The active construction of fathering by fathers themselves is not a prominent theme in the research literature, although it is crucial to programs that work with fathers. More qualitative research is needed to explore the kinds of identity development and social negotiation that constitute the experience of fathering in contemporary society.

DISCUSSION

This chapter delineates a conceptual model of influences on fathering that can serve as a stimulus for future research, programming, and policy development. The main premise, supported by a variety of studies, is that fathering is uniquely sensitive to contextual influences, both interpersonal and environmental. Fathering is a multilateral relationship, in addition to a one-to-one relationship. A range of influences, including mothers' expectations and behaviors, the quality of the coparental relationship, economic factors, institutional practices, and employment opportunities all have potentially powerful effects on fathering. These contextual factors shape the major domains of responsible fathering discussed in this report: acknowledgment of paternity, willingness to be present and provide economic support, and level of involvement with one's children. When these influences are not supportive of the father–child bond, a man may need a high level identification with the father role, strong commitment, and good parenting skills to remain a responsible father to his children, especially if he does not live with them.

This review and conceptual model deal with factors that promote active, involved fathering, not with the effects of that kind of fathering on children. (See the review by Pleck 1997.) Nor do we take a position on whether there are essential characteristics of fathering versus mothering or whether having parents of two genders is necessary for children's well-being. The growing literature on gay and lesbian parenting suggests that these kinds of questions are more complex than many scholars assumed in the past (Patterson 1992; Patterson and Chan 1997). However, it is not necessary to resolve these issues to address the factors that enhance and inhibit the parenting of men in the role of father.

A potentially controversial conclusion of this chapter is that a high-quality marriage is the optimal context for promoting responsible fatherhood. This position moves opposite the trend of contemporary family studies to disaggregate marriage and parenting. We do not suggest that men cannot parent adequately outside this context or that children must be raised in a married household to grow up well adjusted. However, we believe that the research strongly indicates that substantial barriers exist for most men's fathering outside a caring, committed, collaborative marriage and that the promotion of these kinds of enduring marital partnerships may be the most important contribution to responsible fathering in our society.

IMPLICATIONS

The model we propose is multifaceted, complex, and interactive and does not lend itself to simple prescriptive solutions. But it does suggest directions for action, including policy and program implications of varying degrees of specificity. Consistent with the communitarian emphasis on responsibilities, we begin with a broad call for responsible action by various stakeholders, including some suggestions for policy change. We then move to more specific recommendations for maximizing the effectiveness of father-serving programs.

Responsibilities of Men

Regardless of personal history or circumstances, a father needs to be accountable for his own behavior. As reviewed in this chapter, many factors can support or hinder a man's responsibility to his children; but acknowledging these factors does not imply that they should be viewed as excuses for irresponsible behavior.

The operational definition of father responsibility proposed by Levine and Pitt (1995) and adopted for purposes of this chapter is, in our opinion, only a starting point for considering what responsible fathers do. To fully and successfully share in the ongoing care of their children, men have a responsibility to learn and implement qualitative aspects of good parenting. This includes establishing a secure foundation through consistent, sensitive nurturance in infancy and early childhood; clear limits and firm, gentle guidance; moral teaching appropriate to a child's developmental level; and setting an example of respect for self and others (including maintaining a respectful relationship with the child's mother and encouraging the child to respect her as well). For fathers, as for mothers, good parenting requires a steady commitment of time and energy; this sometimes means setting aside self-interest (Communitarian Network 1997).

Responsibilities of Women

Women have a responsibility to support and honor a child's right to have a father in his or her life. This has several implications for women's choices and actions, some controversial and demanding a careful analysis of competing values. For example, while we support a woman's right to make her own childbearing decisions, we contend that, in making those decisions, a woman should consider the impact on the child if the father is nothing more than a sperm donor. Absent data on implications of new technologies for procreation, both men and women should at least consider the meaning children will make of the circumstances of their birth and life. Men and women should work together to study and understand the impact on children of alternative childbearing choices.

In making child-rearing decisions, women must recognize that they typically are the gatekeepers of children's lives. They must consider carefully the impact of their actions on their child's relationship with father. We understand that in too many situations women and children are at risk from abusive partners. But absent such harmful behavior, a mother has a responsibility to encourage a positive father–child relationship, just as a father has a responsibility to support a positive mother–child relationship.

Responsibilities of the Community

In the interest of children, families, and the larger society, communities have a responsibility to support fathers in maintaining positive relationships with their children and families. This responsibility can be carried out in several ways. Through schools, congregations, and other community organizations—and through informal relationships among members—communities should teach children from an early age about the importance of both mothers and fathers. Communities bear responsibility for instilling values that lead youth to careful consideration of childbearing and the importance of respectful, caring, committed relationships between mother and father.

In many specific ways (some delineated later), communities can and should support both men and women in their parenting roles and in their roles with each other as coparents. Communities should expect that all sectors (schools, hospitals, businesses) will clearly reflect in their policies and practices the notion that "parent" means both mother and father. This means, for example, that health care providers will engage fathers fully in prenatal care, childbirth classes, and pediatric visits. School personnel will engage fathers in school conferences, special activities, and ongoing support of student achievement and positive behavior. Finally, it means that workplaces will, at a minimum, support both mothers and fathers in taking full advantage of parental leave law and, even better, provide incentives for both mothers and fathers to be actively engaged in their child's school activities.

Community members also should advocate public policies that encourage father responsibility and that support (or at least remove barriers to) successful coparenting and strong marriages. Although we need careful research to study the impact of specific policies and programs, we recommend several promising approaches:

- School-based programs for the next generation of parents (see, e.g., "Dads Make a Difference," a peer education program for adolescents, developed by the University of Minnesota Extension Service [1994])
- Marriage education, a rapidly developing set of programs that support couples and teach the communication skills necessary for successful marriage and coparenting
- Mandated coparenting education for divorcing parents (e.g., "Parents Forever," developed by the University of Minnesota Extension Service [1997])
- Concerted multiagency efforts to establish paternity as early as possible
- Redesign of welfare policies that create disincentives to paternity establishment and/or marriage
- Child support enforcement policies that build on the multiple factors delineated in the research (e.g., economic factors; reaching fathers early to establish paternity and engage them emotionally in their child's life; understanding the link between support payment and father's access to child through visitation or shared custody)
- Workplace policies that encourage father involvement at each step in a child's life and educational programs in the workplace that bring about the culture change needed to allow full utilization of father-friendly policies

Finally, the research review and conceptual model we have presented here suggest a number of implications for the development and evaluation of programs that work directly with fathers.

Implications for Fathering Programs

The overarching implication is that fathering programs should involve a wide range of interventions, reflecting the multifaceted influences on responsible fathering. In fact, many of the best programs already use a systemic, ecological approach. This section delineates a number of specific implications and recommendations. Unfortunately, there is a paucity of research evaluating the effectiveness of these programs. Evaluation research on fathering programs has largely been confined to one-time father education groups, which have been found effective in increasing fathers' involvement and sense of competence with their young children (McBride 1990, 1991), and to limited interventions to enhance specific fathering behaviors such as infant care (Pfannenstiel and Honig 1991). Absent a solid body of research on multifaceted fathering programs, the following recommendations are based on the research literature, our conceptual model, conversations with practitioner/experts in the field, and a review of descriptions of leading fathering programs and consensus strategies for promoting responsible fathering (Levine and Pitt 1995; Ooms, Cohen, and Hutchins 1995).

1. *Fathering programs should target all the domains of responsible fathering that need remediation or enhancement: paternity, presence, economic support, and involvement.* Given the potential fragility of father–child bonds outside marriage or cohabitation with the mother, declaring legal paternity and paying regular child support are likely to be preconditions for a father's ongoing presence and active involvement in his child's life. Absent legal paternity, he is not likely to have institutional support for responsible fathering, and absent economic support, he is not likely to have either institutional or maternal support.

2. *Fathering programs should involve mothers.* In most contemporary families, mothers are the "senior partner" in parenting. For a residential father, the support, encouragement, and partnership of the mother are likely to be important enhancements to his learning fathering skills and to his ongoing connection with his children. Furthermore, involving a mother actively in a fathering program may offset the potential threat she may perceive to her centrality in parenting. For a nonresidential father, winning the mother's cooperation can be the key to his access to his child.

3. *Fathering programs should promote the well-being of mothers and of the mother-father partnership.* Whether inside or outside marriage, the father–child relationship is bound up with the mother and the mother–father relationship. In addition to involving mothers in promoting responsible fathering, programs should help fathers actively support mothers. They should provide vehicles for fathers and mothers to learn the skills of parental partnership both inside and outside marriage and coresidency. Absent such a pro-mother and pro-partnership orientation, fathering programs can create further splintering of male–female bonds in caring for children.

4. *Fathering programs should involve families of origin.* Some studies and much applied experience with fathers suggest that the father's family and the

mother's family may be key influences on fathering. For a residential father, his parents and other relatives may undermine his nontraditional efforts at parenting, particularly with infants. For a nonresidential father, especially an unmarried father, the acceptance by the mothers' parents of his fathering role can be crucial. The support of his own parents and other relatives can be equally crucial for a father, especially an adolescent one, in developing a father identity and learning the skills of fathering.

5. *Fathering programs should emphasize critical transition points for fathers and children.* Pregnancy and childbirth clearly are crucial times in the development of a father's role identity and for the mobilization of social support for responsible fathering. Similarly, becoming a father as an adolescent is a critical life transition for the new father. The transition from marital/residential fathering to divorce/nonresidential fathering is another key point for intervention. In this situation, the father must contend with developing more autonomous parenting skills, with less frequent contact with his children, with potential strains in the coparenting relationship, and with institutional practices that marginalize him as a father. Marital separation should be viewed as a high-risk transition for fathers and children that merits immediate and intensive programmatic help. Some counties in the United States are now experimenting with mandated parenting classes for divorcing parents to provide this kind of assistance.

6. *Fathering programs should involve an employment dimension.* Unemployment and underemployment are risk factors for underresponsible fathering for both residential and nonresidential fathers. The former are apt to withdraw emotionally from their children and become more punitive. The latter are at risk of becoming irregular in their contact with their children, falling behind in child support payments, losing parenting support from the mother, and losing contact completely. Comprehensive fathering programs already involve assistance for unemployed fathers in finding paid work and, if necessary, developing the skills that successful employment requires. Some fathering programs have found that sometimes when a nonresidential father becomes more involved with his child, he is more motivated to find employment. For residential fathers, fathering programs should also emphasize the work–family connection and the transition from work to home, both of which are frequent sources of stress for fathers, mothers, and children.

7. *Fathering programs should deal with the father's relationships with community systems.* Many nonresidential fathers must deal successfully with a variety of systems—courts, child support enforcement agencies, hospitals or clinics, social service agencies, and schools—to remain responsibly involved with their children. Comprehensive fathering programs coach fathers on how to deal with these systems and sometimes actively broker and advocate for fathers when they face opportunities or encounter problems with systems such as prenatal clinics, hospitals, schools, and youth programs.

8. *Fathering programs should train all staff who work with children and families to promote responsible fathering.* The matricentric culture of parenting affects most professionals and paraprofessionals who work with children and families. Until recently, "parent involvement" has meant "mother involvement." Absent specific training on working with fathers, staff are apt to either ignore fathers or have inconsistent expectations of them. This is especially the case for nonresidential fathers. Successful child and family programs that involve fathers as active participants have developed staff with high expectations of fathers and good skills in working with them. New training models are needed to enhance staff knowledge and skills to work intensively with fathers (and mothers) without crossing the line into doing therapy; one such model has been developed and implemented with parent educators in Minnesota (Doherty 1995a).

9. *Fathering programs should involve fathers working with fathers.* Although empirical research is lacking on the subject of fathers supporting other fathers, the consistent experience of fathering programs has been that father-to-father support groups are centrally important aspects of their programs. This kind of connection can be grounded conceptually in two aspects of a systemic, contextual model of responsible fathering: the importance of father role identification and relations with their own fathers, and the importance of social support. There may be a kind of support for fathering that only other fathers can provide, just as one can imagine certain support for mothering that only other mothers can provide. This support might be particularly essential in the face of coparental or contextual barriers to responsible fathering.

10. *Programs should be created to promote the viability of caring, committed, and collaborative marriage.* We expand more on this implication because of its potentially controversial nature and the lack of focus on it in most current fathering programs. All of the previous nine implications were intended for married and unmarried fathers alike and for residential and nonresidential fathers alike. Responsible fathering is possible inside or outside marriage, and not being married does not remove men's responsibilities to their children. But an inescapable implication of our review of the research, and of our conceptual model of responsible fathering, is that for most contemporary American fathers, the family environment most supportive of responsible fathering is a caring, committed, and collaborative marriage. This kind of marriage means the father lives with his children and has a good partnership for parenting with their mother; these are the two principal intrafamilial determinants of responsible fathering.

As described earlier, we include the three adjectives with *marriage* to suggest that it is not the legal status of marriage alone that conveys the advantage for fathering but the quality of the relationship. One might argue, then, that marital status is not important, because cohabiting couples could have the same relationship qualities. While in principle this is true, the research on cohabitation clearly indicates that cohabitation is a temporary phenomenon for the overwhelming majority of heterosexual couples—they eventually either marry or break up (Bumpass, Sweet, and Cherlin, 1991; DeMaris and Rao 1992). Thus, de facto the kind of mother–father relationship most conducive to responsible fathering in contemporary U.S. society is a caring, committed, collaborative marriage. Most scholars believe that this is also the optimal context for children's development.

This implication suggests two programmatic initiatives. First, programs for married fathers should involve a component of marriage enrichment, which can be done along with parent education. This could mean, for example, stressing the importance of maintaining couple connections in the face of the demands of parenting and of having couple enjoyment rituals that do not involve the child. Second, programs should take a long view of promoting responsible fathering by teaching males and females who are not yet parents the attitudes and skills necessary to create a caring, committed, and collaborative marriage.

These latter programs would have a broader reach than fathering or parenting programs and would involve a number of private and public institutions such as schools and religious communities. They would see the 31 percent nonmarital birthrate and the 50 percent divorce rate for newly married couples as indicators that men and women need help in learning to create viable marriages within which to raise children. If a high-quality marriage is the optimal environment for responsible fathering, and for children's development, and if such marriages are threatened in contemporary society, then fathering programs and other community programs that wish to do primary prevention of nonresponsible fathering should take on the task of promoting these kinds of marriages in their communities—while not pulling back from services to the large number of fathers and children who are not in this situation.

An encouraging implication of a systemic, ecological view of fathering is that there are many pathways to enhancing the quality of father–child relations. Fathering can be enhanced through programs and policies that help fathers relate to their coparent, that foster employment and economic opportunities if needed, that change institutional expectations and practices to better support fathers, and that encourage fathers' personal commitment to their children.

NOTE

Portions of this chapter are taken from a report for the U.S. Department of Health and Human Services under contract HHH-100-93-0012 to the Lewin Group. A longer adaptation of the original report, without the implications section, is contained in the *Journal of Marriage and the Family* 60 (1998): 277-92.

REFERENCES

Ahrons, C. R., and R. B. Miller. 1993. The effect of the postdivorce relationship on paternal involvement: A longitudinal analysis. *American Journal of Orthopsychiatry* 63: 441-50.

Allen, W. D., and M. Connor. 1997. An African American perspective on generative fathering. In *Generative fathering: Beyond deficit perspectives,* ed. A. J. Hawkins and D. C. Dollahite. Newbury Park, Calif.: Sage.

Backett, K. 1987. The negotiation of fatherhood. In *Reassessing fatherhood: New observations on fathers and the modern family,* ed. C. Lewis and M. O'Brien. Newbury Park, Calif.: Sage.

Baruch, G. K., and R. C. Barnett. 1986. Consequences of fathers' participation in family work: Parent's role strain and well-being. *Journal of Personality and Social Psychology* 51: 983-92.

Becker, G. S. 1991. *A treatise on the family.* Cambridge, Mass.: Harvard University Press.

Belsky, J. 1984. The determinants of parenting: A process model. *Child Development* 55:83-96.

Belsky, J., and B. L. Volling. 1987. Mothering, fathering, and marital interaction in the family triad during infancy. In *Men's transitions to parenthood: Longitudinal studies of early family experience,* ed. P. W. Berman, and F. A. Pedersen. Hillsdale, N.J.: Erlbaum.

Blankenhorn, D. 1995. *Fatherless America: Confronting our most urgent social problem.* New York: Basic Books.

Bumpass, L. L. 1990. What's happening to the family: Interactions between demographic and institutional change. *Demography* 27: 483-98.

Bumpass, L. L., J. A. Sweet, and A. Cherlin. 1991. The role of cohabitation in declining rates of marriage. *Journal of Marriage and the Family* 53: 913-27.

Communitarian Network. 1997. *The Responsive Communitarian platform: Rights and responsibilities.* Washington, D.C.: Communitarian Network.

Cowan, C. P., and P. A. Cowan. 1987. Men's involvement in parenthood: Identifying the antecedents and understanding the barriers. In *Men's transitions to parenthood: Longitudinal studies of early family experience,* ed. P. W. Berman and F. A. Pedersen. Hillsdale, N.J.: Erlbaum.

Cox, M. J., M. T. Owen, J. M. Lewis, and V. K. Henderson. 1989. Marriage, adult adjustment, and early parenting. *Child Development* 60:1015-24.

Daly, K. J. 1995. Reshaping fatherhood: Finding the models. In *Fatherhood: Contemporary theory, research, and social policy,* ed. W. Marsiglio. Thousand Oaks, Calif.: Sage.

Day, R. D., and W. C. Mackey. 1989. An alternate standard for evaluating American fathers. *Journal of Family Issues* 10: 401-8.

De Luccie, M. F. 1995. Mothers as gatekeepers: A model of maternal mediators of father involvement. *Journal of Genetic Psychology* 156: 115-31.

DeMaris, A., and V. Rao. 1992. Premarital cohabitation and subsequent marital stability in the United States: A reassessment. *Journal of Marriage and the Family* 54: 178-90.

Doherty, W. J. 1990. Beyond reactivity and the deficit model of manhood: A commentary on articles by Napier, Pittman, and Gottman. *Journal of Marital and Family Therapy* 17: 29-32.

———. 1995a. Boundaries between parent and family education and family therapy. *Family Relations* 44: 353-58.

———. 1995b. *Soul searching: Why psychotherapy must promote moral responsibility.* New York: Basic Books.

———. 1997. The best of times and the worst of times: Fathering as a contested arena of academic discourse. In *Generative fathering: Beyond deficit perspectives*, ed. A. J. Hawkins and D. C. Dollahite. Newbury Park, Calif.: Sage.

Doherty, W. J., P. G. Boss, R. LaRossa, W. R. Schumm, and S. K. Steinmetz. 1993. Family theories and methods: A contextual approach. In *Family theories and methods: A contextual approach,* ed. P. G. Boss, W. J. Doherty, R. LaRossa, W. R. Schumm, and S. K. Steinmetz. New York: Plenum.

Dollahite, D. C., A. J. Hawkins, and S. E. Brotherson. 1997. Fatherwork: A conceptual ethic of fathering as generative work. In *Generative fathering: Beyond deficit perspectives*, ed. A. J. Hawkins and D. C. Dollahite. Newbury Park, Calif.: Sage.

Elder, G., J. Liker, and C. Cross. 1984. Parent–child behavior in the Great Depression: Life course and intergenerational influences. In *Life span development and behavior,* vol. 6, ed. P. Baltes and O. Brim. Orlando, Fla.: Academic Press.

Elder, G., T. Van Nguyen, and A. Caspi. 1985. Linking family hardship to children's lives. *Child Development* 56: 361-75.

Feldman, S. S., S. C. Nash, and B. G. Aschenbrenner. 1983. Antecedents of fathering. *Child Development* 54: 1628-36.

Furstenberg, F. S., and A. Cherlin. 1991. *Divided families: What happens to children when parents part.* Cambridge, Mass.: Harvard University Press.

Griswold, R. L. 1993. *Fatherhood in America.* New York: Basic Books.

Hawkins, A. J., S. L. Christiansen, K. P. Sargent, E. J. Hill. 1995. Rethinking fathers' involvement in child care. In *Fatherhood: Contemporary theory, research, and social policy*, ed. W. Marsiglio. Thousand Oaks, Calif.: Sage.

Hawkins, A. J., and D. C. Dollahite. 1997. *Generative fathering: Beyond deficit perspectives.* Thousand Oaks, Calif.: Sage.

Hetherington, E. M., and R. D. Parke. 1993. *Child psychology: A contemporary view.* New York: McGraw-Hill.

Ihinger-Tallman, M., K. Pasley, and C. Buehler. 1995. Developing a middle-range theory of father involvement postdivorce. In *Fatherhood: Contemporary theory, research, and social policy*, ed. W. Marsiglio. Thousand Oaks, Calif.: Sage.

Jones, L. 1991. Unemployed fathers and their children: Implications for policy and practice. *Child and Adolescent Social Work Journal* 8: 101-16.

Lamb, M. E., ed. 1987a. *The father's role: Cross-cultural perspectives.* Hillsdale, N.J.: Erlbaum.

———. 1987b. Introduction: The emergent American father. In *The father's role: Cross-cultural perspectives,* ed. M. E. Lamb. Hillsdale, N.J.: Erlbaum.

Lamb, M. E., J. Pleck, E. L. Charnov, and J. A. Levine. 1985. Paternal behavior in humans. *American Zoologist* 25: 883-94.

LaRossa, R. 1988. Fatherhood and social change. Family Relations 36: 451-58.

———. 1997. *The modernization of fatherhood: A social and political history.* Chicago: University of Chicago Press.

Larson, R. W. 1993. Finding time for fatherhood: The emotional ecology of adolescent–father interactions. In *Father–adolescent relationships,* ed. S. Shulman and W. A. Collins. San Francisco: Jossey-Bass.

Larson, R. W., and M. H. Richards. 1994. *Divergent realities: The emotional lives of mothers, fathers, and adolescents.* New York: Basic Books.

Levine, J. A., and E. W. Pitt. 1995. *New expectations: Community strategies for responsible fatherhood.* New York: Families and Work Institute.

Levy-Shiff, R., and R. Israelashvili. 1988. Antecedents of fathering: Some further exploration. *Developmental Psychology* 24: 434-40.

Lewis, C., and M. O'Brien. 1987. Constraints on fathers: Research, theory and clinical practice. In *Reassessing fatherhood: New observations on fathers and the modern family,* ed. C. Lewis, and M. O'Brien. Newbury Park, Calif.: Sage.

Marsiglio, W. 1991. Paternal engagement activities with minor children. *Journal of Marriage and the Family* 53:973-86.

———. 1995. Fathers' diverse life course patterns and roles: Theory and social interventions. In *Fatherhood: Contemporary theory, research, and social policy,* ed. W. Marsiglio. Thousand Oaks, Calif.: Sage.

McBride, B. A. 1990. The effects of a parent education/play group on father involvement in child rearing. *Family Relations* 39: 250-56.

———. 1991. Parent education and support programs for fathers: Outcome effects on paternal involvement. *Early Child Development* 67: 73-85.

McLoyd, V. C. 1989. Socialization and development in a changing economy: The effects of paternal job loss and income loss on children. *American Psychologist* 44: 293-302.

———. 1990. The impact of economic hardship on Black families and children: Psychological distress, parenting, and socioemotional development. *Child Development* 61: 311-46.

Ooms, T., E. Cohen & J. Hutchins. 1995. *Disconnected dads: Strategies for promoting responsible fatherhood.* Washington, D.C.: Family Impact Seminar.

Parke, R. D. 1996. *Fatherhood.* Cambridge, Mass.: Harvard University Press.

Patterson, C. J. 1992. Children of lesbian and gay parents. *Child Development* 63: 1025-42.

Patterson, C. J., and R. W. Chan. 1997. Gay fathers. In *The role of the father in child development,* 3d ed., ed. M. E. Lamb. New York: Wiley.

Pfannenstiel, A. E., and A. S. Honig. 1991. Prenatal intervention and support for low-income fathers. *Infant Mental Health Journal* 12: 103-15.

Phares, V. 1996. Conducting nonsexist research, prevention, and treatment with fathers and mothers: A call for change. *Psychology of Women Quarterly* 20: 55-77.

Pleck, J. H. 1997. Paternal involvement: Levels, sources, and consequences. In The role of the father in child development, 3d ed., ed. M. E. Lamb. New York: Wiley.

Pleck, E. H., and J. H. Pleck. 1997. Fatherhood ideals in the United States: Historical dimensions. In *The role of the father in child development,* 3rd ed., ed. M. E. Lamb. New York: Wiley.

Popenoe, D. 1996. *Life without father.* New York: Free Press.

Silverstein, L. B. 1996. Fathering is a feminist issue. *Psychology of Women Quarterly* 20: 3-37.

Simons, R., L. Whitbeck, R. Conger, and J. Melby. 1990. Husband and wife differences in determinants of parenting: A social learning and exchange model of parental behavior. *Journal of Marriage and the Family* 52: 375-92.

Snarey, J. 1993. *How fathers care for the next generation: A four-decade study.* Cambridge, Mass: Harvard University Press.

Thomson, E., T. Hanson, and S. S. McLanahan. 1994. Family structure and child well-being: Economic resources versus parent socialization. *Social Forces* 73: 221-42.

University of Minnesota Extension Service. 1994. *Dads make a difference.* St. Paul: University of Minnesota Press.

University of Minnesota Extension Service. 1997. *Parents forever.* St. Paul: University of Minnesota Press.

U.S. Bureau of the Census. 1994. *Household and family characteristics.* Current Population Reports, Series P20-483. Washington, D.C.: U.S. Government Printing Office.

Wolfe, A. 1989. *Whose keeper? Social science and moral obligation.* Berkeley: University of California Press.

4

Peer Marriage

Pepper Schwartz

Our generation has been the first to witness the emergence of "partnership" or "peer" marriages on a large social scale. Such marriages differ from their traditional counterparts in at least four key respects: men and women in these relationships regard each other as full social equals; both pursue careers; partners share equal authority for financial and other decision making; and, not least important, husbands typically assume far greater responsibility for child rearing than in the past. Many of us (including much of the feminist movement, of which I have been a part) tend to regard these marriages as a major social breakthrough, the culmination of an arduous, generation-long effort to redefine women's roles and to secure for women the same freedom and dignity that society has traditionally accorded to men.

Yet in recent years conservatives, particularly the adherents of the "pro-family" or "family values" movement, have increasingly called for a rejection of the peer marriage ideal and a return by society as a whole to the traditional role-differentiated model. Bolstering their case is a significant body of traditional social theory arguing for the superior stability of the role-differentiated marriage, in which the husband serves as sole provider and main figure of authority, and the wife bears the lion's share of responsibilities for child rearing and day-to-day household maintenance.

Contemporary concerns with marital and family stability are certainly warranted. In a society with a 50 percent divorce rate—in which a host of social pathologies can be traced directly to havoc in struggling single-parent homes—policymakers and theorists are right to place a high priority on measures aimed at keeping families intact. Yet it is far from self-evident that the road to greater marital stability lies in a return to tradition. Over the past generation, I would argue, broad changes in society, and in the expectations that men and women bring to the marital relationship, have undermined much of the original basis of the traditional model of marriage. In reality, as I will try to show here, peer marriage offers a new

53

formula for family and marital stability that may be both more durable and better adapted to the demands of contemporary culture than the older form. New data from studies that I and others have conducted support the notion that peer marriages are at least as stable as traditional unions and may in the long run prove more resilient vis-à-vis the special social pressures that marriages confront today.

MARITAL STABILITY AND MARITAL SATISFACTION

There is a close connection between marital stability and happiness or satisfaction in marriage—in both practice and theory. Even the most hard-headed theorists of the traditional model, such as sociologist Talcott Parsons or economist Gary Becker, have invariably sought to reconcile their advocacy of gender-based role differentiation with the possibility of marital satisfaction. To justify the traditional division of labor in marriage purely on the basis of men's and women's different biological aptitudes, historical experience, or cultural training is, after all, not a difficult theoretical task. But to posit happiness and mutual satisfaction as the outcome of such a union is another matter.

This is not to say that happiness was or is impossible to achieve under the traditional marital regime. Many people, especially when the larger culture supports it, find happiness in holding up their part of the marital bargain: women who like to be in charge of the kitchen, and men who want to bring home the bacon but do not want to cook it. In the past, and even today, this contract has worked for many people. Increasingly, however, it does not work as well as it used to. It did not work for me as well as it worked for my mother, and it didn't work for her all the time, either. The gender-based division of labor, so automatic for so much of history, increasingly fails to bring the promised emotional fulfillment that was supposed to be a major part of its contribution to family satisfaction and stability—emotional fulfillment that in today's world is increasingly vital to marital stability.

We may contrast the experience of my mother's generation with that of my own. Like so many women of her era, my mother traded *service* for *support*, a transaction with which she usually seemed content. She bore almost complete responsibility for raising her children and at the same time had full charge of household upkeep: cooking, cleaning, keeping my father's closets and drawers impeccably neat, and so forth. My father, not atypical of his generation, was a man who never packed his own suitcase for a trip. In return, he provided handsomely—beyond my mother's wildest dreams, since she had grown up in poverty and was forced to drop out of high school to support her ailing mother and sisters. Having met my father as a secretary in his fledgling law office, my mother was very grateful to have been pulled from destitution into a different social class. Later she could afford to finish high school and college, raise three children, and become a docent in an art museum. Her lifestyle with my father was something secure and in a sense wonderful, exceeding all her childhood expectations.

The arrangement worked well for my father also. He was not born to privilege. The eldest of five growing up on a farm in Indiana, he put himself through law school, transferring from the University of Chicago to night school at Loyola when times got rough. He scrambled to better himself and his family. He and his wife had the same goal: to achieve the means for the good life. They entertained clients and traveled.

But my father also expected my mother to do everything he told her to do. After all, his own father had been dictatorial; it was something a woman owed a man—even though, in my grandfather's case, his wife had purchased the farm for the family. No matter. Leadership at home was owed a man as part of his birthright. When my mother—an intense, intelligent woman—would occasionally resist an order or talk back, my father's response to her was scathing and uninhibited.

What was the bargain my mother willingly made? She had a husband who loved her, who created an increasingly luxurious environment, and who ordered her around and reminded her—almost incessantly—about how lucky she was to have him. Love and what my generation of women would call patriarchal control went hand in hand. On my mother's side, gratitude, deep resentment, and anger all came in a neat package. The marriage lasted fifty-five years, until my mother's death. Children were launched. The marriage could be declared a success. Nevertheless, under today's circumstances, I would expect such a marriage to survive ten years at best.

Today my mother would have had a chance at her own career, at which she had the talent to excel. She would have had a new identity as a human being with core rights and her own sense of entitlement. (Surely, she promoted mine.) She would have had a different standard of equality and different ideas about equity. She would probably not have thought it enough to have been rescued from poverty. She would have felt entitled to a different style of family decision making, and she would have had the options—and the cultural support—to demand more. But if my father had remained the same man he was when I was growing up, he would not have acquiesced. Under contemporary circumstances, the marriage most probably would have broken up—much to my own, my siblings', and probably my parents' disadvantage.

And that is one reason that I believe peer marriage—a marriage founded on the principle of equality and supported by shared roles and a greater chance of shared sensibilities—is an adaptation in the direction of greater family stability rather than instability. Indeed, in contemporary culture, a peer or partner relationship between spouses becomes pivotal in keeping marriages intact. It also offers new advantages to children, to which I will return in a moment.

We must be clear, however, that the mere existence of separate careers does not guarantee a peer marriage. Such a marriage also requires a comprehensive reconceptualization of the partners' roles. Dual incomes alone are insufficient to guarantee stability.

MONEY AND WORK

Much empirical research, some of it my own, indicates that labor force participation and achievement of high income by women destabilizes marriage. A number of studies, including the well-known Income Maintenance Study done out of the University of Michigan, found that when one raised the income of low-income women—hoping to stabilize families by reducing poverty—divorce increased substantially. Theorists have deduced that, under such circumstances, growth in income simply opens a new option for women to leave the relationship, an option that many of them exercise. Moreover, many studies show high-earning women with higher breakup rates. It is unclear whether high earnings make women less willing to tolerate unwanted behaviors or other disappointments on the part of their spouses, or whether men find women who are ambitious or aggressive (or who possess other traits consonant with career success) unsatisfying to be with in the long run. At any rate, the correlation is real enough.

Nor do couples necessarily adapt smoothly to equalization of income and status between partners. In *American Couples*, a study of six thousand married, cohabiting, and lesbian and gay couples, Phil Blumstein and I (1983) found that a partner's power rose in relation to his or her relative income as compared with that of the spouse or live-in lover, but not necessarily in the ways we would have predicted. Women's power rose and became more equal to their partners' when they had equal income, but only if they had a supportive ideology that allowed them to claim equal power. And power did not necessarily increase proportionally to the income differential. For example, more power did not release women from as much housework as one might expect. Higher-income career women did less, but not equivalently less, and their partners did not do proportionately more. (Male partners of high-earning women *did* feel their partners were entitled to do less housework, but they did *not* feel required to do more themselves!) Feminists may be inclined to despair: Are men so resistant to participation in household labor that nothing will induce them to pitch in appropriately?

Yet—and this is the key point—it remains to be seen whether the tensions we found are the permanent consequence of change or merely transitional pains that arise as couples, and society as a whole, grope for a new definition of the marital relationship. Many men are clearly uncomfortable with the weakening of the traditional male role as sole provider. Notably, there has been little effort—outside a small and probably unrepresentative "men's movement"—to reconceptualize the husband's role under these new economic circumstances. However, several changes are conspiring to move society as a whole beyond this sometimes painful transitional phase: transformations in the economy, in the attitudes of younger men, and in the cultural definition of marriage itself.

In the first place, in the contemporary economy female income has become an important ingredient of family prosperity (even, in many cases, a necessity). Economists have long recognized that household income has maintained stability in the United States over the past decades only through large-scale entry of women into the workforce. The two-income household, once an exception, is now the norm.

Furthermore, corporate restructuring and downsizing have intensified the trend. Women's labor force participation has become increasingly important for family stability in a society where job security is, for all but a few, a thing of the past. Men are now beginning to realize that their hold on continuous employment after age forty is, to say the least, shaky. By age fifty-five, less than half of all men are still fully employed. Women, having many of the skills necessary for a service-oriented society, stay employable longer and more steadily. Indeed, in our society, the non-wage-earning wife has become a symbol of exceptional male wealth and conspicuous family luxury—or of a major ideological commitment either to the patriarchal family or to a vision of the female as the primary parent.

There are signs that these new economic realities are beginning to affect attitudes among men in their twenties. Young boys today are increasingly growing up in families in which females are either the chief provider or an essential contributor to family income. Moreover, they understand their own economic futures as providers to be far from secure. Partly as a result, more and more young men are seeking in marriage someone to be part of an economic team rather than an exclusive parenting specialist. Just as women have in the past sought "a good provider," so, I predict, men will increasingly want to marry (and stay married to) a woman who can provide her share of economic stability.

But possibly the most important change has come in the subtle cultural redefinition of the marital relationship itself. In a society in which divorce is prevalent and the economic independence of both spouses is the rule, marital stability depends increasingly on factors of personal satisfaction and emotional fulfillment. The glue holding marriages together today is neither economic necessity nor cultural sanction but emotion. Marital stability in contemporary society increasingly depends on sustaining the emotional satisfaction of *both* partners. It is here that peer marriage shows its special advantages.

Under these new economic and cultural circumstances, the ability of men and women to participate in each other's lives—to build companion status—becomes essential to marital survival. Equality is a crucial ingredient of this form of intimacy. When women have validation in the outside world through career, and when couples can operate as a team on both economic and home issues, partners become more similar to each other and achieve greater emotional compatibility— or so I would hypothesize on the basis of my research with peer couples. With more outside experiences to bring to the marital community, the woman becomes a more interesting companion for the long run. Moreover, whatever competition or tensions may result from this new arrangement, women today probably need some of these career-related personality traits simply to stay competitive with the women men now meet in the workplace. This ability to "compete" was less important in a society where home and family were sacrosanct and a mother and wife—no matter how far she was from being a "soul mate"—was automatically protected from outside contenders for her spouse. However, that is not the society we live in anymore, nor is it likely to return. And even though income creates independence and therefore opportunities for separation, the recognition that spouses would lose their mutually constructed lifestyle if the marriage ended has its own stabilizing effect, as I have found in my interviews with dozens of peer couples (Schwartz 1995).

LOVE VERSUS MONEY

Of course, even today, if one were to analyze marriage in purely economic terms, the traditional model can seem to offer certain advantages over the peer arrangement. Gary Becker (1981) and others have contended that, at least during child-raising years, couples with the wife in a full-time mothering role tend to gain more income. And a few studies have shown that men with working wives have lower incomes than men with nonworking wives. Economically ambitious couples probably calculate correctly that one parent, usually the male, should be released from most parental duties to earn as much as he can; the payoff here will lie in enhanced family income and social status, in which both partners presumably will share.

But this approach fails to address the real problem at the base of today's shaky marital system—maintaining a high standard of emotional fulfillment. "Efficient" role allocation frequently leaves partners leading parallel and largely separate lives. Mom and Dad did that—each an expert in their separate spheres. It worked when there was less expectation that marriage should produce a soul mate and when Mom's tolerance levels were higher for the habitual carping at dinner. While this system did and does work for some, it tends to diminish emotional partnership. People in such "parallel marriages," financially secure, look at each other ten years later and say, "Why you?"—and they divorce, often with children still in primary grades.

SECRETS OF PEER SUCCESS

One key to the success of peer unions lies in *joint child rearing*—the creation of a male parenting niche in day-to-day family life. Indeed, I would go so far as to say that joint child rearing constitutes the secret of successful peer unions and a new pathway to marital and family stability in contemporary life. Joint child rearing cements a new intimacy between husband and wife and, research shows, builds a critical and difficult-to-sever tie between the two parents and the children.

Some theorists in the past have actually argued *against* a model of significant daily paternal participation in parenting, on the grounds that male involvement will erode the natural dependence of men on women and that men, resenting the extra burden, will ultimately leave (Crouter et al. 1987). Of course, a lot of men are leaving in any case. Certainly some studies, particularly among working-class men, show child care and household labor participation to be associated with lower marital satisfaction (Yogev and Brett 1985). Still, other researchers have found large numbers of men whose perception of shared participation correlates with greater marital satisfaction (Cherlin 1989).

On the woman's side, moreover, the picture is not at all ambiguous. Shared labor has a *major* impact on women's satisfaction in marriage; since more women than men leave relationships, this is a significant finding. A 1996 study by Nancy K. Grote (1996) and others showed that the more traditional the division of labor, the lower marital satisfaction was for women (though *not* for men). However, *both* men and women reported higher erotic satisfaction and friendship with one another when household labor, including parenting, was shared more equitably.

My studies and others (Schwartz 1994; White, Booth, and Edwards 1986) show several other important benefits to joint child rearing: First, the more men participate, the more attached they are to their children. Second, the more they parent, the more grateful wives are. Third, under joint parenting, it becomes harder for either the husband or the wife to consider leaving. Finally, unless the men are manifestly awful parents, children benefit from their father's attention, skills, and additional perspective. This extra parenting and contact with the father can represent a real boon for children.

While my study draws from interviews with only about one hundred couples, some research based on large data sets reinforces my findings. In *Bitter Choices: Blue Collar Women In and Out of Work*, E. I. Rosin (1987) shows that a substantial number of working-class women interpret the husband's help with children and housework as an expression of love and caring. A very interesting study (Morgan, Lye, and Condran 1988) found, among other things, that men who had the lowest divorce rates had the highest interaction with their sons around traditionally male games (e.g., football, baseball). Interestingly, the same was true of men who participated in similar activities with their daughters. Other studies have found a lower divorce rate among men who attended prenatal classes.

Still, one may argue that we are talking here about atypical men. Only a certain kind of fellow will participate in a prenatal class: peer men are born, not made. Yet that is not what I found in my research. Most men I interviewed in egalitarian marriages did not come to them by way of ideological motivation, nor were they married to women who described themselves as feminists. The usual road to peer marriage was happenstance. The four most common routes were as follows: (1) a serious desire on the part of the husband to father more, and more effectively, than he himself had been fathered (men in these situations were frequently wrestling with significant pain left over from paternal abuse, neglect, or abandonment); (2) a job that *required* shift work or role sharing and that, over time, greatly attached the father to the parenting role; (3) a strong-willed working

partner who presumed egalitarian marriage (men in these cases were mostly prepared to structure the marriage any way their wives—often not declared feminists—preferred to have it); (4) the experience of an unsatisfactory, highly traditional first marriage in which the wife was perceived as too emotionally
dependent during the marriage and too economically helpless after it was over
(men in these cases consciously selected a different kind of spouse and marital
bargain in the second marriage).

Were they happy with their new bargain? Most of these men expressed pride
in themselves, their wives, and their home life. Were these typical egalitarian
marriages? It is impossible to say. But these marriages, while not invulnerable,
looked more stable for their integration—in much the way traditional marriages
often appear: integrated, independent, and satisfied.

"NEAR PEERS"

Some of the most troubled contemporary marriages, I have found, are those, in
essence, caught between the old and the new paradigm—marriages that are neither
fully traditional nor fully peer. I called such couples "near peers," since they professed belief in equal participation but failed to achieve it in practice. I believe the
experience of such near peers may lie behind some of the frustrations that lead
conservatives and others today to declare, in effect, "We have tried equality and it
has failed." In reality, what many couples have tried is inequality under the label
of equality—an experience that has given equality, in some quarters, a bad name.

In near peer marriages, the wife typically devoted vastly more energy to the
children while holding down a job. Although the husband made certain contributions to child rearing and household upkeep and professed an eagerness to do
more, actual male performance fell short of the intended ideal, stirring the wife's
resentment. In most cases, near peer men still controlled the finances and exercised veto power over the wife. The wife, performing a full-time job outside the
home with little or no relief inside of it, was typically caught in a "slow burn" of
inward anger. Paradoxically, such women did not long for more equality, since
they assumed it would bring more of the same: increased responsibilities with no
substantial male contribution. These women felt trapped and overwhelmed, and
many of them, I found, would have been happy to leave the workforce if it were
financially possible. Furthermore, all their power—and much of their pleasure—
continued to reside in the mothering role. They loved their children, felt compromised at the inadequacy of parenting time, and, perhaps surprisingly, rarely considered that one answer might be greater paternal participation. In truth, many
such women were unwilling to surrender hegemony at home.

In such marriages, each spouse typically clings to his or her traditional powers
while simultaneously craving a more partnership-oriented relationship. The result
is emotional disappointment and conflict. Women in such relationships tend to

view egalitarian gender roles as oppressive—seeing more respect, security, and satisfaction in the role of full-time mother. Yet they simultaneously resent the husband's low participation and quasi-autocratic behavior, since they feel they have earned equality and crave it on an emotional level.

ROADBLOCKS AND SUGGESTED POLICY REFORMS

While I have found that many different routes lead to a stable peer marriage, achievement of such a relationship is not automatic, as the experiences of the near peers attest. Several barriers stand in the way.

In the first place, it is often hard to avoid role differentiation, especially when partners have been strongly socialized to one or the other role. For example, it is simply not in the couple's best interests for the "bad cook" to prepare dinner while the good one does dishes. Even though cooking can be learned—quite easily, in fact—the startup costs (bad meals for a while) stop most couples in their tracks. The better the homemaker-parent and the more outstanding the provider, the less likely there is to be taste for change.

Other inhibitors to peer marriages include the gender-based organization of jobs in the outside world (which affect evaluations of each partner's career prospects) and the overall pull of the status quo. Yet, in a sense, the biggest roadblock we face is our sense of the possible. Many women and men simply do not believe an egalitarian marriage is feasible—unless they happen to be in one. Even many who desire the peer model do not believe it can be achieved within ordinary working schedules. And most women expect significant male resistance and see a risk in asserting themselves, fearing that conflict with their husbands will lead to defeat and deeper resentment on their own part, or even divorce.

These are all reasonable cautions. The pleasure of sharing the day-to-day administration of home and family is not apparent to many men, especially those socialized to the older model. Nonetheless, today we find an increasing number of young men and remarried men actually yearning to be an involved parent. This represents a shift in ideology, a new view of "what is important in life."

However, women, too, need to change. Many women are used to being taken care of and are trained for submissive interaction with men. In effect, during courtship they set up many of the inequities they will complain about in marriage—and ultimately flee from. They want intimacy, yet they often establish conditions (e.g., maximization of mate income) that subvert family time and marital closeness.

In addition, several public policy reforms might assist in the formation of peer marriages and thereby help anchor families of the future. Such reforms might include classes on marriage and the family in high school, in which young men and women can learn a model of partnership, equity, and friendship; more pressure on employers to offer flextime and on-site child care, so that individuals are not penalized for their parenting choices; and after-school care in the public schools (until 6 P.M.).

There also needs to be more cultural support from the larger society. Most parents do not want to see their sons in the role of primary parent, do not want their sons' careers compromised, and still view a woman's work, including care for children, as unmanly. Moreover, most women are not encouraged to think of themselves as potential providers; only recently have they come to imagine themselves as fully committed to careers. I know there is a great split of opinion over whether young mothers should work at all, much less be encouraged to be responsible for their own economic welfare. But I would suggest that too much specialization in parenting and insufficient equality of experience may be more injurious in the long run than the difficulties involved when both partners juggle work and home.

CONCLUSIONS

We must recognize that there is no one form of marital organization appropriate for all couples. But I believe the profamily or family values movement has been needlessly antagonistic to feminist models of marriage. After all, the two sides in this dialogue share some important goals: we do not want marriages to break up unless they absolutely have to; we want children to be loved and cherished and brought to adulthood in an intact family if there is any way it can be accomplished without punishment to either the children or the parents; we want people to want to form lasting bonds that strengthen the extended family.

The big question is how best to accomplish these goals. I suggest that shared parenting and increased spousal satisfaction are the most effective routes to family stability. I think that newfound feelings about equity and emotional closeness are essential to modern marital durability. Peer relationships will be good for women, children, and families—and a great benefit for men as well. Peer marriage is not a feminist or elitist vision. It is a practical plan to lower the divorce rate. But to see how well it works, society needs to offer the cultural and structural support to permit both men and women to parent, to participate in each other's lives, and to have the time together that a strong relationship requires. Whether peer marriage will actually work better than traditional marriage is, at this point, a matter of conjecture. We do know, however, that traditional roles have failed to ensure stability. The new model is an experiment we can ill afford to ignore.

REFERENCES

Becker, Gary. 1981. *A treatise on the family*. Chicago: University of Chicago Press.

Blumstein, Phil, and Pepper Schwartz. 1983, *American couples: Money, work, and sex*. New York.

Cherlin, Andrew. 1989. *Marriage, divorce, and remarriage*. Cambridge, Mass.: Harvard University Press.

Crouter, A. Perry, H. Jenkins, T. Houston, and S. McHale. 1987. Processes underlying partner involvement in dual earner and single earner families. *Developmental Psychology* 23: 431-40.

Grote, Nancy. 1996. Children, traditionalism in the division of family, labor, and marital satisfaction: What's love got to do with it? Personal Relationships 3: 211-18.

Morgan, S. P., D. N. Lye, and G. A. Condran. 1988. Sons, daughters, and the risk of marital disruption. *American Journal of Sociology* 94, no. 1 (July): 110-29.

Rosin, E. I. 1987. *Bitter choices: Blue collar women in and out of work*. Chicago: University of Chicago Press.

Schwartz, Pepper. 1994. The shared parent. In *Peer marriage: How love between equals really works*. New York: Free Press.

———. 1995. *Love between equals*. New York: Free Press.

White, L. K., A. Booth, and J. N. Edwards. 1986. Children and marital happiness: Why the negative correlation? *Journal of Family Issues* 7: 131-47.

Yogev, and Brett. 1985. Perceptions of the division of housework and childcare and marital satisfaction. *Journal of Marriage and the Family* 47: 609-18.

5

Building a Sound Marital House

Kimberly D. Ryan, Sybil Carrère, and John M. Gottman

Jeff:	Hi, Monia.
Monia:	Hi. I'm glad you're home. I missed you today.
Jeff:	I'm glad to be home, too. I had an awful day at work. I think I'll go lie down in the study and read. (Jeff notices the breakfast dishes in the sink.) Why can't you ever clean up after breakfast?
Monia:	I stay at home with the kids, and then you come home and all you can do is criticize.
Jeff:	Well, I'm tired from working all day and want a little time to unwind from all the tension.
Monia:	Yeah, right, just go into your little study and hide. You're always trying to get away from the kids and me.

As you read through this conversation, it becomes clear that Jeff and Monia are upset with one another, but is their relationship at risk? Research from our marital laboratory at the University of Washington suggests that it could be if this discussion is typical of the couple's interactions. How is it that we are able to make this prediction? More generally, what is it that allows us to predict which couples will divorce and which couples will stay together, and why do some marriages fail while others succeed?

We have reached a point in our marital research, across three longitudinal studies, where we can predict with 88 to 94 percent accuracy those marriages that will remain stable and those marriages that will end in divorce (Buehlman, Gottman, and Katz 1992; Carrère et al. 2000; Gottman 1994). Moreover, we have discovered some of the common pathways that lead to marital dissolution. Although this understanding of what causes a marriage to fall apart is important, it only provides us with half of the picture. We also need to describe what couples can do to have a successful marriage. Recent findings in our laboratory indicate that stable, happy marriages are based on a series of marital processes and behaviors that are more than just the absence of dysfunctional patterns. Constructive activities can build a strong marital relationship and help the union withstand the stressful events and transitions that can destroy weaker marriages. This chapter will describe briefly the research being conducted in our laboratory and then present an overview of our research findings regarding both those processes that make a marriage dysfunctional and those that make a marriage work.

STUDYING MARRIAGE IN THE LABORATORY

We have been following 638 couples in our laboratory and in collaboration with Robert Levenson, Lynn Fainsilber Katz, Neil Jacobson, and Laura Carstensen to assess the stability of the marriages as well as marital satisfaction, health, and family functioning. We are studying six different cohorts: a newlywed group of 130 couples (for the past six years); a group of 79 couples whom we first saw when they were in their thirties (for the past fourteen years); two cohorts of 119 couples with a preschool child at the time of the first visit to our laboratory (for the past eleven and eight years, respectively); a group of 160 couples, half in their forties and half in their sixties the first time we contacted them, and half happily and half unhappily married; and a group of 150 married couples who were physically violent, distressed but not violent, or happily married (for the past eight years). We have collected much of the same marital assessment data across all of our various studies. The methods that we use in carrying out this research are outlined later.

In studying marriage, we have been particularly interested in how couples remember and talk about their relationship history, as well as how couples communicate and respond to one another when asked to problem-solve. One way we learn about a couple's sentiments about their relationship is through the use of the Oral History Interview, a semistructured interview that we have been using since 1986. During the interview, each couple is asked to respond to a series of open-ended questions about the history of their relationship. The couple is asked about the path the relationship has taken from the first moment the couple met through the dating period, the decision to marry, the wedding, adjustment to marriage, the highs and lows of the marriage, and changes in the marriage. The couple is also asked about their philosophy of marriage, by having the couple choose two marriages they know, one that they would describe as good and one that they would describe as bad. The interviewer then asks the couple to identify the qualities that make these marriages positive or negative. Finally, the couple is asked to describe their parents' marriages. This interview yields a wealth of information and tends to be enjoyable for both the couple and the interviewer. Marriages are composed of struggles, joys, tragedies, and hard work, and the Oral History Interview reveals the dynamics of the marital journey and provides a clear picture of a couple's identity and their feelings for each other.

Kim Buehlman (Buehlman and Gottman 1996) has developed a coding system for this interview that assesses nine dimensions of marriage:

1. *We-ness versus Separateness* indexes the degree to which a couple sees themselves as a unit or as individuals.
2. *Fondness and Affection* indicates the degree of these emotions each spouse has for his or her partner.
3. *Expansiveness versus Withdrawal* measures how large a role the marital partner and the marriage plays in each spouse's worldview, it is the "cognitive room" an individual allocates to the marriage and to their spouse.
4. *Negativity toward the Spouse* reflects the disagreement and criticism expressed during the interview by the husband and/or the wife.
5. *Glorifying the Struggle* taps the level of difficulty the couple has experienced to keep the marriage together and how they feel about the struggle.
6. *Volatility* indicates whether the couple experiences intense emotions, both positive and negative, in their relationship.
7. *Gender Stereotypy* is a measure of how traditional or nontraditional the couple's beliefs and practices are in their marriage.
8. *Chaos* is linked to whether the couple feels as though they have little control over what happens to them.
9. *Marital Disappointment and Disillusionment* tells us whether the couple feels hopeless or defeated about their marriage.

Couples are invited to participate in a fifteen-minute marital interaction laboratory session. During this visit, the couple are asked to identify and discuss problem areas that are an ongoing source of disagreement in their marriage. The entire marital interaction is videotaped, with the images of both spouses recorded on a single tape as a split-screen image for coding and viewing purposes.

Physiological measures are collected during the discussion period and synchronized with the videotape. The physiological measures of interest are interbeat interval (the time between the r-spikes of the electrocardiogram; the heart rate is 60,000/interbeat interval), pulse transit time (the time it takes for the blood to get to the fingertip), finger pulse amplitude, skin conductance, and activity (gross-motor movement). Several of our most recent studies have included ear pulse transit time and respiration. In our study of newlyweds, we were also able to measure the stress-related hormones (epinephrine, norepinephrine, and cortisol) and collaborated with Hans Ochs to collect blood assays of immune response as well.

After the marital problem-solving interaction, the couples are asked to view the videotape of their problem-solving session. During the replay of the marital discussion the couples are instructed to rate, in a continuous fashion using a rating dial, how positive or negative they were feeling during the conflict interaction. Physiological measures, video recordings, and data from the rating dial are synchronized and collected during this recall session. The observational data collected in our laboratory is then coded for affect and problem-solving behaviors.

Affect is coded using our Specific Affect Coding System (SPAFF; Gottman 1996). This coding system is used to index the affect expressed by the couples during the marital interactions. SPAFF focuses solely on the affect expressed. The SPAFF system draws on facial expressions (based on Ekman and Friesen's [1978] facial action coding system), voice tone, and speech content to characterize the emotions expressed by the couples. The emotions captured by this coding system allow us to see the range and sequencing of affect the couples use during their conversations and problem-solving interactions. The positive affects include humor, affection, validation, and joy. The use of these positive emotions turns out to have an important role in the marital stability of the couples. The negative affects can be very toxic to the relationship and include emotions such as contempt, criticism, belligerence, domineering, defensiveness, whining, and fear. Anger and sadness are two other important emotions indexed by the SPAFF system.

We have used three different observational systems to index problem-solving behavior by couples. In our early work, we used the Marital Interaction Coding System (MICS; Weiss and Summers 1983) to code problem-solving behaviors. However, the Couples Interaction Scoring System (CISS; Markman and Notarius 1987), developed in our laboratory, did a better job of disentangling the behaviors used in problem-solving sessions from the affect displayed. The Rapid Couples Interaction Scoring System (RCISS; Krokoff, Gottman, and Haas 1989) is the most recent version of the problem-solving coding system and was created to assess conflict resolution behaviors more quickly. RCISS uses a checklist of thirteen behaviors that are scored for the speaker and nine behaviors that are scored for the listener at each turn of speech. We use the speaker codes to categorize the couples into *regulated* and *unregulated* marital types. These codes consist of five positive codes (neutral or positive problem description, task-oriented relationship information, assent, humor-laugh, and "other positive"), and eight negative codes (complain, criticize, negative relationship issue problem talk, yes-but, defensive, put-down, escalate negative affect, and "other negative"). We computed the average number of positive and negative speaker codes per turn of speech and the average number of positive minus the negative codes per turn.

CASCADING TOWARD DIVORCE

In our early studies, we were particularly interested in predicting which couples would become dissatisfied with their marriage and choose to divorce. Moreover, we wanted to identify what was dysfunctional in these ailing marriages (Gottman 1994; Gottman and Levenson 1992). One of the early studies was conducted with seventy-three married couples who were first brought into the laboratory in 1983. The study revealed that couples who eventually divorced went through a series of predictable relationship stages and shared similar patterns of behavior and interaction.

The Cascade Model of Marital Dissolution

Identifying the different trajectories toward divorce or marital stability is difficult, particularly if one is carrying out a short-term longitudinal study, because divorce is a low base-rate event. In an effort to address this problem, Gottman and Levenson (1992) reasoned that if they could identify frequently occurring events that were also precursors of divorce, then they could use these events to study the processes associated with divorce. They posited that these high base-rate events formed a series of stages (the cascade) through which the majority of couples who eventually divorce would travel. The Cascade Model of Dissolution identified three high base-rate events (marital dissatisfaction, considering dissolution, and separation) and suggested that a decline in marital satisfaction would lead to consideration of separation or divorce, which in turn would lead to separation and ultimately to divorce.

The data from our early work supports the Cascade Model of Dissolution. Between 1983 and 1987, thirty-six of the seventy-three couples (43 percent) considered divorce, eighteen of the couples (24.7 percent) separated, and nine of the couples (12.5 percent) actually divorced. Our findings suggest that the Cascade Model accurately represents the modal course of marital dissolution. Couples who divorced were more likely to have separated than those who had not divorced. Moreover, couples who had separated were more likely to have considered dissolution when compared to those who had not separated. Finally, couples who considered dissolution were more likely to report marital dissatisfaction than those who had not considered dissolution.

A Behavioral Cascade: The Four Horsemen of the Apocalypse

Our observational data from the 1983 cohort of couples revealed that the way couples communicated with one another around emotionally charged issues was predictive of marital dissolution (Gottman 1994). The four behaviors of interest were criticism, contempt, defensiveness, and stonewalling. In coding *contempt,* we looked for any direct communication that involves a lack of respect toward the spouse, including any suggested superiority. *Defensiveness* was coded when a spouse presented him- or herself as an innocent victim in an effort to explain or excuse his or her behavior. *Stonewalling* is a withdrawal behavior that involves an active tuning out of the spouse in response to something aversive that the spouse is doing. Our findings suggest that couples at risk for marital dissolution descend through a series of behavioral stages (see Figure 5.1). In this behavioral cascade, criticism leads to contempt, which in turn leads to defensiveness and subsequently to stonewalling. Stonewalling is observed primarily in men, but it is associated with physiological arousal in both spouses (Gottman 1994).

Figure 5.1. A Behavioral Cascade: The Four Horsemen of the Apocalypse.

The Distance and Isolation Cascade: The Domain of Perception

Another series of signposts indexing the trail of marital instability emerged from
the questionnaires used in our research (Gottman 1993b). The growing distance
and isolation a spouse experiences in the marriage can be modeled as a series of
five stages (see Figure 5.2).

The Distance and Isolation Cascade begins with a flooding stage. During this
stage, an individual feels that his or her spouse's negative emotions are unexpected and so overwhelming that he or she must do whatever is necessary to escape from these emotions. Men typically experienced flooding at a lower threshold than women. Specifically, men experienced flooding in association with
criticism, but women were more likely to report flooding in association with contempt. The finding that men experienced flooding at a lower threshold was consistent with the observation that men are more likely to stonewall than women. In
general, we found that once flooding starts, the cascade toward loneliness led to
an emotional divorce within the marriage and ultimately to marital dissolution.
Flooding is also thought to be the first step in building a set of negative attribu-

tions about the marriage. These attributions may serve as a filter through which neutral or ambiguous behaviors by one's partner are interpreted as negative. We believe that it is these attributions that move couples to the second stage of the Distance and Isolation Cascade.

The second stage of the cascade is characterized by a perception that the marital problems have become severe. Once couples begin to think of their marriage as having severe problems, they are less likely to turn toward each other for support. It is this tendency to move away from one another that leads to the third stage of the cascade. During this stage, spouses report a desire to work out problems individually rather than as a couple. In the fourth stage, each spouse actually begins to create a separate life for him- or herself. As such, it becomes less likely that these couples will spend any significant time with each other. The fifth stage of the cascade is characterized by an increasing sense of loneliness within the marriage.

Figure 5.2. The Distance and Isolation Cascade: The Domain of Perception.

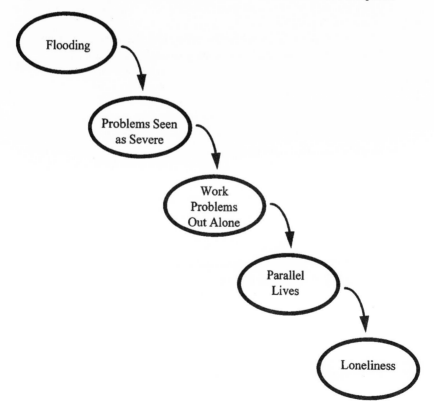

TYPOLOGIES OF DYSFUNCTIONAL AND FUNCTIONAL COUPLES

Nonregulated and Regulated Couples

We have found that the patterns of affective behaviors couples use with each other are at the root of dysfunctional marital processes. The "balance" theory of marriage (Gottman and Levenson 1992) suggests that each couple will find a balance, or a steady state, between positive and negative affect.

Nonregulated couples are those couples in which at least one spouse exhibits a greater number of negative problem-solving behaviors (e.g. complaining, criticizing, defensiveness, escalating negative affect) than positive problem-solving behaviors (e.g., neutral or positive problem description, assent, humor). In *regulated* couples, both spouses display significantly greater numbers of positive problem-solving behaviors than negative ones. Our work reveals that unstable couples had a positive to negative affect ratio of 0.8 to 1, while stable couples had a ratio of 5 to 1. This ratio of positive to negative affective behavior during the marital interaction discriminated between those couples who remained married and those couples who later divorced (Gottman and Levenson 1992).

The nonregulated and regulated couples differ from one another in many specific ways. When they were first brought into the marital laboratory in 1983, the nonregulated couples were generally less satisfied with their marriages. The rating dial data indicated that these nonregulated couples were more likely to experience the marital problem-solving discussion as a more negative encounter than the regulated couples. The wives in the nonregulated couples also exhibited greater arousal of the sympathetic nervous system (as indexed by heart rate and smaller finger pulse amplitude) than the regulated wives during this discussion. Arousal of the sympathetic nervous system is associated with stress and subsequent risk for disease (e.g., Cohen, Kessler, and Gordon 1995).

When Gottman and Levenson (1997) recontacted the couples four years later, they found that the nonregulated couples, as might be expected, had traveled a very different course in their marriages than the regulated couples. The nonregulated couples were less satisfied with their marriages and were experiencing poorer health than the regulated couples. We believe that the increased sympathetic arousal during the 1983 marital conflict sessions is indicative of the pattern of physiological arousal likely to be found in these maritally distressed wives and perhaps causally related to their reports of poor health in 1987.

The behavioral differences between the nonregulated and regulated couples during conflict and conflict resolution indicate that although all couples exhibit both positive and negative behavior, it is critical to the health of the marriage, as well as the physical health of the spouses, that couples employ more positive behaviors than negative in their interactions. The findings suggest that the greater the proportion of positive to negative affect in communication patterns and problem-solving behaviors, the more stable and healthy was the relationship. Indeed, the manner in which these couples approached conflict resolution discriminated between those couples who remained married and those who later divorced (Gottman and Levenson 1992).

Behavioral Differences between Nonregulated and Regulated Couples

The next step in understanding what leads some couples toward divorce and others toward marital stability was to further distinguish the behavioral differences between the nonregulated and regulated couples. To this end, Gottman (1993a) presented a typology of unstable, dysfunctional marriages and stable, functional marriages. Analyses revealed that unstable couples could be categorized into two distinct typologies: a *hostile* type and a *hostile/detached* type. The stable couples were of a validating type, a *conflict-avoiding* type, or a *volatile* type (Gottman 1993a). The behavioral differences among each of these groups was determined using the observational data that coded speaker and listener behavior in our 1983 cohort of married couples.

Unstable Marriages

The two groups of unstable marriages, hostile and hostile/detached, were characterized as having more negative than positive interactions. Hostile couples, in particular, exhibited high levels of conflict, and although these couples listened attentively to one another, they were also likely to express defensiveness during their interactions.

Chris: You never try to save any money. You just don't care that we're broke.
Terry: I do so save money. You just don't notice. Just the other day I told my friends I couldn't go out to lunch with them every Wednesday.
Chris: All right, but wait a minute—you didn't let me finish. I always find credit card receipts for CDs and things like that. Those are things we don't need and that we can't afford.
Terry: (Groan) Oh.

In contrast, couples who were both hostile and detached (the hostile/detached type) were less involved in listening to each other but would engage in reciprocal attacks on each other and bouts of defensiveness.

Karen: Don't you think we're doing a little better with our finances?
Miguel: Yeah.
Karen: What do you think?
Miguel: But I get tired of talking about our budget all the time.
Karen: Well, those are things people need to talk about. I'm sorry (sarcastic).
Miguel: If it's not pleasant, and the budget talk isn't pleasant, I don't want to talk.
Karen: Yeah, you're the only family I've got and damn it, if I have to keep all my problems to myself, I might as well live by myself.

Gottman (1994) proposed that hostile and hostile/detached marriages (nonregulated marriages) were those in which the spouses were unable to accommodate each other to find an adaptive pattern of interaction and thus stability. The partners in nonregulated marriages had mismatching patterns of conflict interaction that served to destabilize the relationship and move it toward dissolution. The unstable couples were also mismatched in their patterns of persuasion and influence, tending to be more negative in their interactions overall. Their conflict resolution patterns were less successful because one spouse's style of persuasion or influence was not consistent with the influence pattern used by the other spouse in the marriage (Cook et al. 1995).

Stable Marriages

Each stable couple type (the validating type, the conflict-avoiding type, and the volatile type) has a very different mix of behaviors but in all cases more positive behaviors than negative. Validating couples have many neutral moments, but like other stable marital couples, they have a high ratio of positive to negative behaviors. Validating couples were selective in their persuasion techniques and used positive emotions extensively. They tended to disagree, confront conflict, and then express support for their spouses. Our research indicated that they were more likely to try persuasion during the middle period of the fifteen-minute problem-solving interaction.

Sean: I'm worried we're not saving enough money. We seem to live hand to mouth.

Melissa: Uh-huh. So you'd like to save more. Well, I don't think we have a problem with finances, and I think it is important for us to be using the money we have now to fix up the house.

Sean: Well, you're right—we did need to replace the carpet, but you know how anxious I am when we don't have a healthy savings account.

Melissa: Yes, you are good about getting us to save, but I think you're wrong about our finances.

Sean: Um-hmm. I just would feel more secure if we had some savings.

Volatile couples are very expressive emotionally and have fewer neutral moments than the other stable couple types. These couples appear to have passionate, romantic marriages. While they frequently express negative emotions during marital interactions, they also laugh together and approach problems from a positive perspective. Volatile couples typically engage in persuasion throughout the problem-solving interaction, rarely giving up on their efforts to convince their spouse of the importance or correctness of their own perspective. Indeed, in volatile couples, both spouses work hard to persuade their partner, and both express more nonneutral emotions.

John:	I'm worried that we're not saving enough money.
Emy:	I don't agree. We do not have a problem with finances. You're wrong.
John:	No, you're wrong. I would feel more secure if we had some savings.
Emy:	"Reporting live from the scene of John and Emy's latest shoot-out. . . ." (both spouses laugh).

Conflict-avoiding couples, the third type of stable marriage, minimize the importance of disagreement in their marriages. When asked to talk about a problem in their relationship, these couples frequently begin the fifteen-minute marital conflict sessions by dismissing the problem and then proceed to discuss neutral topics for the remainder of the session. In general, these couples are more neutral in their interactions than the other stable couple types, and while they are likely to express their views on the conflict, they spend little time trying to persuade their partners or sway their partner's point of view.

| Josh: | Like money, for instance. We never get into arguments about what we're gonna do; we don't get into any arguments as far as a problem for both of us. I mean, we both would like to save money. |
| Anne: | It's not really a problem between us; it's a problem with the money. |

In general, our findings suggest more positive emotional communication patterns for stable couples in comparison to unstable couples. An examination of the various types of stable couples, however, reveals that functional marriages can come in very different forms. While some researchers have suggested that patterns of interaction in which there are escalating quarrels (volatile couples) or in which there is an avoidance of conflict (conflict-avoiding couples) can damage the marriage and lead to divorce (e.g., Raush et al. 1974), our research indicates otherwise. Each type of stable marriage has a different level of emotional expressiveness that is associated with a particular balance of rewards and costs, and all of these stable marriages have a balance of positive interactions that outweighs the negativity and serve to make the marriage successful.

In addition to using more positive affect in their interactions, the spouses in each of the three kinds of stable couples have similar patterns of persuasion. Cook et al. (1995) found that validating couples were able to influence each other in both positive and negative directions. Conflict-avoiding couples were only able to influence each other in the positive ranges of behavior, while volatile couples had influence on their partners' behaviors only in the negative ranges of behaviors.

Stable couples also reveal a propensity to act in positive ways during conflict interactions. Subsequent work by Gottman et al. (1998) also found gender differences in conflict resolution important in stable marriages. Marriages were more likely to last when husbands were able to accept influence from their wives and deescalate the conflict and when wives used softened start-up techniques in conflict situations. The use of positive affect and having matched patterns of influence and persuasion appear to be important components in conflict resolution, and both contribute to marital stability.

BUILDING A SOUND MARITAL HOUSE

Up to this point, we have focused almost primarily on the dysfunctional processes and behaviors that are active in dismantling marriages, discussing the functional processes that primarily serve to elucidate dysfunction processes. Our research suggests that certain forms of negativity, including criticism, contempt, defensiveness, and stonewalling, are particularly deleterious to one's relationship and predictive of divorce. But what of functional processes? What are these processes, and what role do they play in developing and maintaining marriages? In short, what is it besides the absence of negativity that makes a relationship successful?

While there is clearly no monolithic formula for building a satisfying relationship, key elements such as friendship, intimacy, and trust are considered important by most couples. The Sound Marital House theory, proposed by Gottman (1998), outlines some of the elements that we have identified in our marital laboratory as important in building and sustaining a functional marriage.

The Role of Positive Affect

The role of positive affect in marital processes has received scant attention in the marital literature (Coan et al. 1997). Our own work has sought to understand the relationship among positive affect, marital satisfaction, and marital stability. We have found the roots of functional marital processes in the patterns of affective behaviors couples use with each other. Satisfaction in marriage appears to be related to a high level of (or increase in) everyday positive affect and a low level of (or reduction in) negative affect, particularly during conflict. Our early research indicated that successful marriages have a greater ratio of positive emotion to negative emotion (5:1) compared with unstable marriages (0.8:1). In our research with newlyweds, the amount of positive affect used by a couple was shown to be predictive of both marital satisfaction and marital dissolution. In general, low rates of positive affect were associated with higher rates of marital dysfunction.

Gottman and Levenson (1997) recently developed a model to study the role of affect in predicting marital stability and divorce among the couples first assessed in our laboratory in 1983. The model identifies those affective behaviors predictive of divorce early in the relationship, occurring on average at 5.2 years, or divorce late in the relationship, occurring on average at 16.4 years. Four negative affective behaviors (criticism, contempt, defensiveness, and stonewalling) were associated with early divorce. Interestingly, though, later divorce was associated not only with the presence of negative affect but also the absence of positive affect during the initial marital assessment. These data suggest that the presence of positive affect during marital problem-solving interactions is associated with long-term stability. These two dimensions of affect are not just two sides of the same coin. The absence of negative emotional communication patterns during marital conflict does not mean that couples are using positive affect in their interactions.

When couples fail to employ positive emotions in their interactions, it reduces the feelings of warmth and support within the relationship and increases the sense of emotional detachment. Emotionally detached marriages are indicative of couples further down the distance and isolation cascade. Our findings suggest that without positive affect, couples may be able to sustain short-term relationships but that they will have a reduced chance of forming a lasting, long-term relationship with their partner. These findings are true even when little negative affect is present in the couple's marital communications and interactions. Marriages are unlikely to last unless positive affect is woven into marital communication.

A related finding comes from our research with newlywed couples. We assessed the influences of marital quality on immune function in the newlywed couples (Carrère, Gottman, and Ochs 1996). This research suggests that both the husbands' and the wives' use of positive affect during the marital conflict sessions are associated with the wives' enhanced immune function. A husband's use of positive emotions is also linked to his own enhanced immune function. The use of negative affect by the wife is associated with suppression of both her own immune response and the immune response of her husband. What is important to note about these health findings is the fact that both negative and positive marital emotion have an impact on health. This research is consistent with previous studies that demonstrate a link between the quality and stability of marriage and health outcomes (e.g., Berkman and Syme 1979; Burman and Margolin 1992; Friedman et al. 1995; Kiecolt-Glaser et al. 1994; Verbrugge 1979).

Clearly, positive affect plays an important role in developing a sound marital house, but how does one go about creating or strengthening positive affect? The development of a strong friendship in marriage that is characterized by interactions involving positive affect is a major accomplishment. It appears to be linked to one's knowledge of their partner, as well as a sense of fondness and admiration for that partner. Moreover, the everyday interactions between partners are also important. Across the mundane interactions occurring everyday, couples have numerous chances to move closer to one another, thus gaining intimacy, or to turn away, thus emotionally distancing themselves from one another. The culmination of these small but significant movements toward or away from one's partner is vital to the health of the relationship. These qualities make up the first three levels of the Sound Marital House (see figure 5.3). Gottman (1998) refers to these, from lowest to highest, as the Love Map level, the Fondness and Admiration system level and the Turning Toward or Turning Away system level. These three levels of the Sound Marital House form a foundation for the relationship, helping to establish a sense of friendship that fosters positive affect within the relationship.

Figure 5.3. The Sound Marital House.

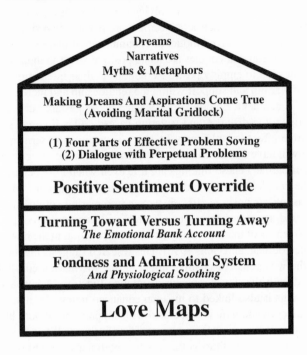

At the Level of the Love Map

In Gottman's (1998) view, a healthy marriage is one in which each member of the couple knows one another and continuously updates that knowledge. This first level involves creating a *Love Map,* or being able to map one's knowledge about one's partner—for instance, knowing who your partner's best friends are, knowing what your partner's current and past stresses are, knowing what times have been most special for your partner, and knowing what your partner's major aspirations and hopes in life are. Not only does such knowledge help establish a satisfying relationship, but our research indicates that marriages are able to weather hard times and to remain stable when couples prioritize knowing about each other's experiences, feelings, and concerns.

Our research with newlywed couples indicates that when both the husband and wife have extensive information about their partners' interests, feelings, and behaviors (expansiveness), stressors and transitions, such as the transition to parenthood, were less likely to have a negative impact on the marital relationship, and marital satisfaction was more likely to remain high (Shapiro and Walker 1997). It is remarkable to us that how a couple told the narrative story of their relationship during the Oral History Interview can so accurately predict the future of their marriage.

Buehlman et al. (1992) have also used the Oral History Interviews to predict the marital stability or marital dissolution of married couples with young children. Using a cohort of couples from the Midwest who had preschool children, Buehlman and her associates were able to predict with 94 percent accuracy those couples who would stay married and those couples who would be divorced at a two-year follow-up.

Stepping Up to the Level of the Fondness and Admiration System

As we have seen, predictors of divorce include the amount of criticism each spouse expresses toward their partner, the extent to which spouses are disillusioned about the marriage, and the extent to which spouses feel that the challenges of the marriage are outside their control (chaotic relationship). The Fondness and Admiration system falls at the far end of this continuum, which ranges from damaging to nurturing behaviors. We have learned that a couple's fondness and admiration for one another is vital in building a successful, long-term marital relationship. Indeed, the couple's expression of fondness and admiration for their partner has been shown to be predictive of marital stability (Buehlman et al. 1992).

Carrère and her colleagues (Carrère et al. 2000) predicted which couples would remain married or get divorced within the first six years of their marriage using the Oral History Interviews. Using just the marital attachment dimension, a dimension that taps into the connection, unity, and fondness that a couple have for one another, Carrère et al. were able to predict with 87.9 percent accuracy those couples whose marriages remained intact or broke up. These data revealed that husbands had displayed significantly more fondness and wives had expressed greater unity during the Oral History Interview in those couples who remained married. Couples exhibiting weak marital attachment were at higher risk for divorce than couples with strong marital attachment. Indeed, for couples who divorced, both spouses were shown to have demonstrated significantly more negativity and disillusionment with the marriage during this first interview. Couples who later divorced also indicated that they found their relationship to be chaotic, reporting that many of the problems and challenges of the marriage felt outside their control.

A couple's fondness and admiration for one another also serve to buffer them during stressful or transitional periods. For instance, in our newlywed sample, husbands and wives who expressed fondness for and unity with (we-ness) each other during the Oral History Interviews were more likely to maintain their level of marital satisfaction during the transition to parenthood (Shapiro and Walker 1997).

All of the findings reviewed so far underscore the importance of taking the time to learn about what is important to one's partner as well as the importance of expressing fondness and admiration for one's partner. These functional processes are predictive of marital stability. Indeed, the development of positive affect and a sense of attachment to one's mate are important if a couple is to build a sound marital house that is capable of withstanding life's challenges.

Moving Up to the Turning Toward versus Turning Away Level

Emotional interactions can be seen in one of two ways: involving an approach, a turning toward one's partner; or involving a moving away from, a distancing from one's partner. Common sense dictates that the use of positive emotions in one's relationship should lead to engagement and approach behaviors within that relationship. Our research supports this view. We found that the expression of positive emotions constituted moments of turning toward one's partner and that these everyday, mundane interactions set the stage for a more satisfying and successful relationship. Furthermore, our research suggests that anger, on its own, may also be a healthy form of approach and engagement. While the idea that anger constitutes a form of turning toward may seem counterintuitive, we have found that anger is not the corrosive emotion or destructive force some have suggested it to be (e.g., Hendrix 1988; Parrott and Parrott 1995). Our perspective is that it can have a positive long-term effect in marriage (Gottman and Krokoff 1989). Our own research does not show anger to be implicated in destabilizing the marriage (Gottman et al. 1998). Indeed, the research indicates that the amount of anger expressed by the newlywed couples in our study discriminated neither between divorce and marital stability outcomes nor between happily married or unhappily married couples (Gottman et al. 1998).

The negative emotions that are toxic to the well-being of a relationship are those that distance the members of a couple from one another: criticism, contempt, and defensiveness. These more corrosive negative emotions are predictive of divorce (Gottman 1994). In our newlywed study (Gottman et al. 1998; Gottman 1993b), we found evidence, replicating Gottman's (1994) findings, that contempt, belligerence, and defensiveness (high-intensity negative affect) displayed by both the husbands and wives were predictive of divorce. The expression of low-intensity negative affect by the wives (the sum of sadness, whining, anger [in conjunction with these other negative emotions], domineering, disgust, tension/fear, and stonewalling) was predictive of divorce; however, it did not reliably differentiate between satisfied and dissatisfied couples six years after the initial marital assessment.

It is interesting to note that psychophysiological research has delineated the physiological basis underlying the differentiation of these positive and negative emotions. This research indicates that left frontal brain activity increases during all of these emotional states involving approach toward the environment (e.g., joy, interest, anger) (Davidson et al. 1990; Fox 1991). The right frontal region exhibits a similar increase in activity during the expression of negative emotions associated with withdrawal from one's environment (e.g., disgust, contempt, sadness, distress, defensiveness) (Bell and Fox 1994; Davidson 1994; Dawson 1994).

Over the course of one's relationship, these turning-toward and turning-away behaviors establish a kind of "emotional bank account." When a couple engages in turning-toward behaviors, they add to this bank account, bolstering their emotional commitment. On the other hand, turning-away behaviors drain the relationship emotionally. Over the long run, turning-away behaviors are likely to lead to a sense of distance and isolation. This change is characteristic of marriages heading for divorce. Our research indicates that this increasing distance and isolation is the outcome of several factors. The first is a feeling of being flooded by the unexpected and overwhelming nature of one's partner's negative emotions. Second, there is an increasing perception of the marriage as having severe problems and a sense that it is more effective to work those problems out separately. Finally, as the sense of distance and isolation increases, couples begin to engage in social and recreational lives in parallel rather than together. In short, the trajectory toward divorce is one of increasing emotional toxicity and distance.

Positive Sentiment Override

Sentiment override is a concept first proposed in 1980 by R. Weiss, who suggested that reactions during marital interaction may be determined in part by a more global dimension of affection or disaffection for one's partner and one's marriage. We have extended Weiss's (1980) idea of sentiment override, suggesting that it had its basis in everyday, mundane, nonconflict interaction. In *positive sentiment override,* a spouse may say something with negative affect (as judged by observers) and still have it be received as a neutral message by the partner (as indicated by rating dial outcomes). In *negative sentiment override,* the opposite occurs: a neutral message (as judged by observers) gets received as if it were negative.

Notarius and his associates (Notarius et al. 1989) evaluated the impact of sentiment override in a study that examined a series of verbal exchanges and how couples evaluated these exchanges. Surprisingly, they found no evidence to support the idea that positive sentiment override helped buffer the effects of negative affect in couple interaction. However, they found evidence for the operation of negative sentiment override, with distressed wives having more negative views overall and being more likely to evaluate their partner's neutral and negative messages as negative. Distressed wives were also more likely than all other spouses to offer a negative reply when they evaluated their partner's antecedent message as negative.

In contrast to the work of Notarius et al., research by members of our own laboratory suggests that positive sentiment override plays a significant role in the everyday interactions of a couple (Hawkins 1997). The information collected during the Oral History Interview allowed us to assess marital attachment, which indexes spouses' thoughts and feelings about their partners and their marriages. As such, marital attachment reflects the global sentiments that spouses hold regarding each other and their relationship. These sentiments appear to act as a filter through which a partner's behavior is interpreted. Using the marital interaction data from the newlywed couples, Hawkins (1997) compared objective affect codes with the partners' rating of their spouse's affective behavior. Wives who scored very high on the marital attachment dimension of the Oral History Interview, indicating higher levels of positive sentiment override, rated their husbands' expression of anger as a neutral emotion, whereas the wives who scored low on marital attachment, indicating low levels of positive sentiment override, rated their husbands' expression of anger as a negative emotion. This suggests that while the expression of anger in and of itself does not predict marital success, the manner in which wives perceive their husbands' anger may determine the outcome of the interaction and discriminate between distressed and happily married couples. In functional marriages, wives are less likely to escalate a low-intensity negative affect, such as anger, to a higher level of negativity. Consequently, wives exhibiting positive sentiment override may be more capable of engaging in successful and productive conflict resolution.

Hawkins (1997) also found that the wives' perception of their husbands' humor was associated with marital attachment. Wives scoring high on marital attachment rated their husbands' expression of humor more positively than the wives who scored low. Moreover, our research indicates that in happy, stable couples, wives' use of humor reduced their husbands' heart rate significantly (Gottman et al. 1998). When husbands were physiologically soothed, they were more likely to stay engaged in the marital interaction and participate in successful patterns of conflict resolution.

As discussed earlier, we found that the Distance and Isolation Cascade indexed an increasing emotional detachment in the marriage as couples moved on a trajectory toward divorce (Gottman 1993b). The Distance and Isolation Cascade is thought to reflect a set of negative attributions that couples make about their relationship. These attributions include the belief that the negative emotions of the partner come out of nowhere (emotional flooding), the sense that the problems in the marriage are severe, the view that problems are best worked out individually rather than together, and a feeling of loneliness in the marriage.

These negative attributions may act as a kind of filter, not unlike negative sentiment override, through which the behaviors in the marriage are viewed. If so, there should be some association between the Distance and Isolation Cascade and marital attachment as measured by the Oral History Interview. Indeed, the individuals who are further along the cascade appear to be the same individuals with weak marital attachment. In our sample of newlyweds, those couples who scored low in marital attachment were the same couples in which the husbands felt lonely and flooded by their wives' emotions and in which the wives reported being lonely and leading separate lives from their husbands (Carrère and Gottman 1999).

Positive sentiment override is also important to the pivotal developmental changes that occur across a relationship (Shapiro and Walker 1997). One such change is the transition to parenthood. It is common for couples to experience some decline in marital satisfaction during this period in the relationship (e.g., Belsky and Pensky 1988; Raush et al. 1974). Shapiro and Walker (1997) used the marital attachment scores from the Oral History Interview to predict the course of marital satisfaction (Marital Adjustment Test; Locke and Wallace 1959) during the transition to parenthood. They hypothesized that the global sentiments couples held about each other and their marriages in general might act as buffers during this major life event.

The results indicated that wives who became mothers were more likely to experience a decline in satisfaction when compared with newlywed wives who did not become parents. There were no significant differences found between the newlywed fathers and newlywed men who did not become fathers. As expected, however, there was a significant relationship between marital satisfaction and marital attachment for the women going through the transition to parenthood. For these couples, marital satisfaction either remained the same or increased during this period.

The work from our laboratory suggests that sentiment override is important in shaping the perceptions spouses have about their partners' behavior. It also appears likely that the Oral History Interview taps the kinds of global sentiments spouses have about each other and the marriage. Research in our lab, and by others, indicates that husbands are likely to view their partners' behavior more benevolently or more disparagingly depending on sentiment override. Indeed, the kind of global sentiments that spouses hold about each other and their marriage is vital to the health of that marriage.

Effective Problem Solving and Dialogue with Perpetual Problems

Softened Start-up

The manner in which a conflict was started, and by whom it was started, also predicted the stability of the marriage. Negative start-up involves the escalation of conflict in which the neutral affect of one partner is followed by an expression of negative affect in the other partner. For example, a husband may make a neutral comment that is followed by a belligerent statement on the part of the wife. This concept is part of the negative start-up model that originated in the work of J. R. Patterson (1982) on coercive processes in families. In our newlywed study, we found that divorce was more likely to occur if wives frequently used negative start-ups. This is consistent with the female-demand/male-withdraw pattern described by Christensen and his colleagues (e.g., Christensen 1987; Christensen and Heavey 1990; Heavey, Christensen, and Malamuth 1995).

A related behavioral exchange is negative affect reciprocity, which is an individual's tendency to respond with negative affect following the expression of similar affect by one's spouse. Research in our laboratory (Gottman 1994) and in other settings (e.g., Margolin and Wampold 1981) has demonstrated the role of negative affect reciprocity in discriminating between happy and distressed couples. We were able to further refine the negative affect reciprocity model into two categories: negative reciprocity in kind and escalating negativity.

Negative reciprocity in kind is a kind of interaction in which a negative affect is reciprocated with a negative affect of the same intensity, such as anger being met with anger or sadness. The other type of negative interaction, *escalating negativity,* is a behavioral sequence in which a low-intensity negative affect is followed by a high-intensity negative affect, such as a wife's sadness being followed by her husband's contempt. We looked at these two patterns of negative reciprocity in our newlywed couples. Wives in unstable marriages were more likely to reciprocate low-intensity negativity in kind when compared with wives in stable marriages (Gottman et al. 1998).

Repair

During conflicts, efforts by the couple to repair an interaction and exit the cycle of negative communication are important. Lorber (1997) found that repair attempts took place on average about once every three minutes and that they were actually more likely to occur among distressed couples with high levels of negative affect than among nondistressed couples. However, distressed couples tend to be less successful in their repair attempts. This outcome is particularly problematic, given the finding from our own research that increasing negativity, or negative affect reciprocity, is more common in distressed marriages. It also appears that repair attempts during marital conflict interactions are more successful if the husband demonstrates positive global sentiments about the marriage. Lorber's (1997) results are compelling in that they suggest a significant and robust association between the husband's positive sentiment override and the success of repair attempts by the couple.

Deescalation

The escalation of marital conflict is more common in distressed and abusive relationships. On the other hand, the ability of a couple to deescalate conflict is important in developing and maintaining a functional marriage. Our research indicates that physiological soothing may be an important factor in determining marital stability and that the ability to soothe oneself and one's partner is related to one's ability to deescalate conflict.

Research by Gottman and Levenson (1988) indicates that men may be more emotionally flooded by negative affect in marital interactions and that they experience greater physiological arousal than do women. When this occurs, men are more likely to withdraw from the marital conflict. We wondered whether deescalation of marital conflict among the newlywed couples, especially by women, served to soothe their husbands physiologically and, as a consequence, played a functional role in the marriage.

It turns out that positive affect and deescalation among these happy, stable newlywed couples was associated with both physiological soothing of the husband by the wife and self-soothing by the husband (Gottman et al. 1998). The wife's use of humor in these satisfied, stable marriages soothed the husband's physiology, as did his own deescalation of emotion and his use of affection and validation during the marital interactions.

We also wanted to examine whether positive affect in the newlywed couples was generated randomly (noncontingent on a previous behavior) or whether it was primarily being used to deescalate marital conflict (Gottman et al. 1998). We found that positive affect was contingent and acted to deescalate negative affect only among couples who were later judged to be happy and stable. These satisfied, stable couples perhaps best displayed validation through the husbands' acceptance of the wives' influence—that is, responding to her negative affect by deescalating the conflict (Gottman et al. 1998).

Accepting Influence

In our study of newlywed couples, we found that couples in which the husbands escalated their wives' low-negative affect instead of accepting their wives' influence were more likely to seek divorce than couples in which the husbands accepted their wives' influence. However, negative escalation by the wives in these couples did not reliably discriminate between divorced or maritally stable couples, nor did it discriminate between unhappy and happy couples.

This same pattern was apparent in our sample of abusive couples. The husband's escalation of his wife's low-level negative affect indexed violent males' rejection of influence from their wives (Coan et al. 1997). This escalation by the husbands of their wives' low-level negative affect was a pattern of behavior that occurred significantly more often in violent husbands than in nonviolent husbands.

Perpetual Problems

While many problems can be resolved when couples use the effective conflict resolution strategies outlined earlier, some problems are intractable (Gottman 1998, Levinger 1980). These perpetual problems in the relationship are often the result of fundamental personality differences, or differences in preferences, interests, and lifestyle needs, between spouses and are generally not resolvable (Kelly and Conley 1987). For instance, differences in how much time one wants to spend together or apart from one's spouse or differences in the expression of emotion involve needs that are basic to each partner's identity and who they are as a person. It is these chronic problems that lead to most marital conflict, creating what we have coined "gridlock" in the relationship.

It is not uncommon for couples to face problems that have no solutions, and therefore it becomes important for couples to establish a dialogue around, or a kind of verbalized acceptance of, these issues. A dialogue does not seek a resolution but rather a regulation of the conflict. Indeed, the ability to regulate conflict was predictive of long-term marital success in our longitudinal work with couples (Gottman 1994). The idea of acceptance of one's partner sounds good, but how does one create this dialogue? What is it that allows a couple to regulate these perpetual problems and avoid gridlock in their marriage?

Our work suggests that the process of acceptance and regulation involves two important elements (Carrère and Gottman 1999; Gottman 1998). The first, discussed earlier, involves the use of positive affect in both day-to-day interactions as well as during conflict resolution. We theorize that continued positive affect is associated with the perception of the marriage as effective in making personal life dreams and aspirations come true. The second element involves the creation of a shared symbolic meaning within your relationship—in short, a meshing of a couple's individual life dreams. To develop and maintain a relationship in which there is positive affect and shared meaning, each spouse must first explore the symbolic value and meaning of their partner's position. This process allows each member of the couple to gain a more complete understanding of the emotions and ideas that underlie one's partner's dreams and expectations about life, marriage, and family.

Making Dreams and Aspirations Come True and Avoiding Marital Gridlock

The process of making dreams and aspirations come true for each member of the couple involves either tolerating and supporting each other's dreams or working to share in each other's dreams (Gottman 1998). Often couples do not discuss these dreams because they do not feel entitled to them. They may also have complaints when they feel that they have given up their dreams to adjust to the marriage. Moreover, when the feelings and needs associated with one's dreams are discussed, it is often within the context of ongoing conflict. In these situations, the symbolic meaning of the dreams is often not apparent or not discussed directly. Again, this is the result of partners, especially wives, believing that they are not entitled to their dreams. Unfortunately, partners often view their spouses' dreams as terrifying or dangerous to the relationship and may position themselves in opposition to these dreams. Ironically, it would appear that it is this fear of one's partner's dreams, the stifling of those dreams, and the conflict that ensues, that pose the greatest risk to a couple's relationship. Couples begin to feel that their dreams, and who they are as a person, are unacceptable to their partner. This leads people to become alienated from one another, viewing their partner's dreams as in opposition to their own. At this point couples often fear the influence of their spouse, whom they see as the "bad guy." This process of entrenchment and vilification is extremely detrimental to the development and maintenance of a functional marriage. Changing this process requires that couples talk about their dreams and their fears. This is often a hard task for couples, especially when couples are unaware that they have given up their dreams. Indeed, this realization may lead to feelings of disappointment, hurt, disgust, and anger. It is important for both spouses to address and take responsibility for their own feelings and to avoid blaming and/or deriding their partner. Exploring each other's dreams in a nonjudgmental and open fashion can help create a safe environment for the discussion of the relationship and its dynamics and a better understanding of one's partner.

Dreams, Narratives, Myths, and Metaphors

When we talk about dreams, narratives, myths, and metaphors, we are referring to the *symbolic meaning* of our ideas about emotion (meta-emotion), family rituals, marriage, and central symbols such as "home" and "holidays." These are the ideas that make a person an individual, with a rich and dynamic cultural history of his or her own. In the creation of a marriage and family, that culture merges with another person's personal culture to form, if successful, a new world of meaning. The couple's inability to integrate, respect, and support each other's personal cultures can lead to dysfunctional processes in the marriage.

The meanings that people give to daily rituals, roles, and dreams arise in large part from their experiences with their family of origin, peers, and community—for instance, the role(s) that an individual was asked to play in their family of origin (e.g., son, daughter, protector, mentor, friend) or the rituals associated with things such as weekends, holidays, religion, time with friends, helping others, and politics. Every marriage will have a mix of similarities and discrepancies across these various roles, rituals, and dreams.

Each level of the Sound Marital House is interconnected by these meanings and values. An understanding of what is meaningful to and valued by one's partner connotes knowledge of one's partner, which, as the reader will recall, is pivotal in building a Sound Marital House. When both members of a couple are able to integrate their individual dreams, narratives, myths, and metaphors to create a new, shared culture, they are in effect providing the glue that holds the elements in the Sound Marital House together in a healthy and functional manner.

REFERENCES

Bell, M. A. and N. A. Fox. 1994. Brain development over the first year of life: relations between EEG frequency and coherence and cognitive and affective behaviors. In *Human behavior and the developing brain*, ed. G. Dawson and K. Fisher. New York: Guilford.

Belsky, J., and E. Pensky. 1988. Marital change across the transition to parenthood. *Marriage and Family Review* 12: 133-56.

Berkman, L. F., and S. L. Syme. 1979. Social networks, host resistance, and mortality: A nine-year follow-up study of Alameda County residents. *American Journal of Epidemiology* 109: 186-204.

Buehlman, K. T., and J. M. Gottman. 1996. The oral history coding system. In *What predicts divorce: The measures*, ed. J. M. Gottman. Hillsdale, N.J.: Erlbaum.

Buehlman, K. T., J. M. Gottman, and L. F. Katz. 1992. How a couple views their past predicts their future: Predicting divorce from an oral history interview. *Journal of Family Psychology* 5: 295-318.

Burman, B., and G. Margolin. 1992. Analysis of the association between marital relationships and health problems: An interactional perspective. *Psychological Bulletin* 112: 39-63.

Carrère, S., K. T. Buehlman, J. Coan, J. M. Gottman, and L. Ruckstuhl. 2000. Predicting marital stability and divorce in newlywed couples. *Journal of Family Psychology* 14: 1-17.

Carrère, S. and J. M. Gottman. 1999. Predicting the future of marriages. In *Coping with divorce, single parenting and remarriage: A risk and resiliency perspective*, ed. E. M. Hetherington. Mahwah, N.J.: Erlbaum.

Carrère, S., J. M. Gottman, and H. Ochs. 1996. The beneficial and negative influences of marital quality on immune function. Paper presented at the Thirty-sixth Annual Society for Psychophysiological Research Meeting, Vancouver, British Columbia.

Christensen, A. 1987. Assessment of behavior. In *Assessment of marital discord*, ed. K. D. O'Leary. Hillsdale, N.J.: Erlbaum.

Christensen, A., and C. L. Heavey. 1990. Gender and social structure in the demand/withdraw pattern of marital conflict. *Journal of Personality and Social Psychology* 59: 73-82.

Coan, J., J. M. Gottman, J. Babcock, and N. Jacobson. 1997. Battering and the male rejection of influence from women. *Aggressive Behavior*.

Cohen, S., R. C. Kessler, and L. U. Gordon. 1995. Strategies for measuring stress in studies of psychiatric and physical disorders. In *Measuring stress: A guide for health and social scientists*, ed. R. C. Kessler, S. Cohen, and L. U. Gordon. New York: Oxford University Press.

Cook, J., R. Tyson, J. White, R. Rushe, J. M. Gottman, and J. Murray. 1995. Mathematics of marital conflict: Qualitative dynamic mathematical modeling of marital interaction. *Journal of Family Psychology* 9(2): 110-30.

Davidson, R. J. 1994. Temperament, affective style, and frontal lobe asymmetry. In *Human behavior and the developing brain*, ed. G. Dawson and K. Fisher. New York: Guilford.

Davidson, R. J., P. Eckman, C. Saron, R. Senulis, and W. V. Friesen. 1990. Approach-withdrawal and cerebral asymmetry: Emotional expression and brain physiology. *Journal of Personality and Social Psychology* 58: 330-41.

Dawson, G. 1994. Frontal electroencephalographic correlates of individual differences in emotion expression in infants: A brain systems perspective on emotion. *Monographs of the Society for Research in Child Development* 59(2–3): 135-51.

Ekman, P., and W. V. Friesen. 1978. *Facial Action Coding System*. Palo Alto, Calif.: Consulting Psychologists Press.

Fox, N. 1991. If it's not left, it's right: Electroencephalograph asymmetry and the development of emotion. *American Psychologist* 46: 863-72.

Friedman, H. S., J. S. Tucker, J. E. Schwartz, K. C. Tomilson, et al. 1995. Psychosocial and behavioral predictors of longevity: The aging and death of the "Termites." *American Psychologist* 50: 69-78.

Gottman, J. M. 1993a. The roles of conflict engagement, escalation, and avoidance in marital interaction: A longitudinal view of five types of couples. *Journal of Consulting and Clinical Psychology* 61(1):6-15.

———. 1993b. A theory of marital dissolution and stability. *Journal of Family Psychology* 7, no. 1: 57-75.

———. 1994. *What predicts divorce: The relationship between marital processes and marital outcomes*. Hillsdale, N.J.: Erlbaum.

———. 1996. *What predicts divorce: The measures*. Hillsdale, N.J.: Erlbaum.

———. 1998. A scientifically-based marital therapy. Unpublished manuscript. University of Washington.

Gottman, J. M., J. Coan, S. Carrère, and C. Swanson. 1998. Predicting marital happiness and stability from newlywed interactions. *Journal of Marriage and the Family* 60: 5-22.

Gottman, J. M., and L. J. Krokoff. 1989. The relationship between marital interaction and marital satisfaction: A longitudinal view. *Journal of Consulting and Clinical Psychology* 57: 47-52.

Gottman, J. M., and R. W. Levenson. 1988. The social psychophysiology of marriage. In *Perspectives on marital interaction,* ed. P. N. and M. A. Fitzpatrick. Clevedon, England: Multilingual Matters.

Gottman, J. M., and R. W. Levenson. 1992. Marital processes predictive of later dissolution: Behavior, physiology, and health. *Journal of Personality and Social Psychology* 63, no. 2: 221-33.

———. 1997. The role of positive affect in long-term marital stability. Unpublished manuscript, University of Washington.

Hawkins, M. W. 1997. Sentiment override: The effect of perception on marital conflict. Unpublished manuscript, University of Washington.

Heavey, C. L., A. Christensen, and N. M. Malamuth. 1995. The longitudinal impact of demand and withdraw during marital conflict. *Journal of Consulting and Clinical Psychology* 63: 797-801.

Hendrix, H. 1988. *Getting the love you want: A guide for couples*. New York: Holt.

Kelly, L. E., and J. J. Conley. 1987. Personality and compatibility: A prospective analysis of marital stability and satisfaction. *Journal of Personality and Social Psychology* 52: 27-40.

Kiecolt-Glaser, J. K., W. B. Malarkey, J. T. Cacioppo, and R. Glaser. 1994. Stressful personal relationships: Immune and endocrine function. In *Handbook of human stress and immunity*, ed. R. G. and J. K. Kiecolt-Glaser. San Diego: Academic Press.

Krokoff, L. J., J. M. Gottman, and S. D. Haas. 1989. Validation of a Rapid Couples Interaction Coding System. *Behavioral Assessment* 11: 65-79.

Levinger, G. 1980. Toward the analysis of close relationships. *Journal of Experimental Social Psychology* 16: 510-44.

Locke, H. J., and K. M. Wallace. 1959. Short marital-adjustment and prediction tests: Their reliability and validity. *Marriage and Family Living* 21: 251-55.

Lorber, M. 1997. Repair attempts in marital conflict. Unpublished manuscript, University of Washington.

Margolin, G., and B. E. Wampold. 1981. Sequential analysis of conflict and accord in distressed and nondistressed marital partners. *Journal of Consulting and Clinical Psychology* 49: 554-67.

Markman, H. J., and C. I. Notarius. 1987. Coding marital and family interaction: Current status. In *Family interaction and psychopathology: Theories, methods, and findings,* ed. T. Jacob. New York: Plenum.

Notarius, C. I., P. R. Benson, D. Sloane, N. A. Vanzetti, and L. A. Hornyak. 1989. Exploring the interface between perception and behavior: An analysis of marital interaction in distressed and nondistressed couples. *Behavioral Assessment* 11:39-64.

Parrott, L., and L. Parrott. 1995. *Becoming soul mates: Cultivating spiritual intimacy in the early years of marriage.* Grand Rapids, Mich.: Zondervan.

Patterson, J. R. 1982. *Coercive family process.* Eugene, Oreg.: Castalia.

Raush, H. L., W. A. Barry, R. K. Hertel, and M. A. Swain. 1974. *Communication, conflict, and marriage.* San Francisco: Jossey-Bass.

Shapiro, A. F., and K. Walker. 1997. Marital satisfaction: Predicting changes over the transition to parenthood. Paper presented at the biennial Meeting of the Society for Research in Child Development, Washington, D.C.

Verbrugge, L. M. 1979. Marital status and health. *Journal of Marriage and Family* 41: 267-85.

Weiss, R. L. 1980. Strategic behavioral marital therapy: Toward a model for assessment and intervention. In *Advances in family intervention, assessment and theory,* vol. 1, ed. J. P. Vincent. Greenwich, Conn: JAI.

Weiss, R. S., and K. J. Summers. 1983. Marital Interactional Coding System—III. In *Marriage and family assessment,* ed. E. Filsinger. Beverly Hills, Calif.: Sage.

6

The Role of Psychotherapy in Promoting or Undermining Marriage: A Call for Reform

William J. Doherty

Marriage can be the best and the worst of human relationships. Marital happiness is a primary source of psychological and physical well-being for adults and their children. Its opposite, marital distress, is an important health hazard associated with depression and reduced immune system functioning in adults and lower emotional and physical well-being in children. It is no wonder that the longest-running magazine column in the United States is titled "Can This Marriage Be Saved?" (Burman and Margolin 1992; Gottman and Katz 1989; Kiecolt-Glaser et al. 1993; Prince and Jacobson 1995).

These patterns pertain to the quality of intact marriages. Another large body of research attests to the destructive power of divorce for adults and children, albeit in some cases divorce is a constructive alternative to a destructive marriage. In addition to well-established links between divorce and mental health problems, long-term prospective studies have begun to document the effects of divorce on mortality. Adults who experience divorce more than double their risk of earlier mortality. And children who experience a parental divorce have their life expectancy shortened by an average of four years, according to a fifty-year longitudinal study. These effects of divorce on mortality are comparable to those of cigarette smoking. If we also consider the effects of marital conflict and distress in ongoing marriages, we have a major public health problem associated with contemporary marital relationships, a problem seen every day in the offices of psychotherapists (Dawson 1991; Cherlin et al. 1991; Doherty and Needle 1991; Tucker et al. 1996; Schwartz et al. 1995).

MARRIAGE IN PSYCHOTHERAPY PRACTICE

Therapists have a wide and deep connection with distressed married individuals and couples in the United States. The evidence for this assertion comes from two sources. First, large numbers of Americans see mental health professionals. Approximately 11 percent of the adult population use outpatient mental health services each year, according to the Mental Health Epidemiological Catchment Area study (Regier et al. 1993). A 1995 national survey of public opinion of mental health issues commissioned by the American Psychological Association found that nearly half (46 percent) of Americans reported that they or someone in their immediate family had seen a mental health professional at some point in their lives. Rates for divorced people were over 60 percent. Thirty-eight percent of those who had seen a therapist reported going to a psychiatrist; 37 percent, a psychologist; 7 percent, a social worker; 4 percent, a marriage counselor; and 2 percent, a school counselor (American Psychological Association 1995). It should be borne in mind, however, that the public does not appear to distinguish clearly among mental health professionals.

What kinds of services do these mental health professionals offer to their clients? According to evidence from a second national survey, this one of randomly selected private practice psychotherapists, "marriage and family therapy" services are offered by 81 percent of all therapists in the United States. This figure is second only to "individual therapy" on a list of fourteen professional services. And it is a safe bet that the other 19 percent of therapists are also treating marriage and family problems through working with individual clients only (American Association for Marriage and Family Therapy 1997).

THE IMPACT OF THERAPISTS ON MARRIAGE

Two significant problems arise with how psychotherapists deal with marriage problems in individual or marital therapy: inadequate training and therapists' individualistic orientation.

Training and Competence of Therapists

Given the high prevalence of marital therapy services, consumers would be surprised that most therapists have little or no academic training in marital therapy. Simmons and Doherty (1998) have documented that the accreditation guidelines for training programs in the largest "talking therapy" professions—psychology, social work, and professional counseling—have no course work or clinical training requirements in marital or family therapy. (Psychiatry also has none.) The obvious exception is the profession of marriage and family therapy, which, as an independent mental health discipline licensed in forty-one states, requires extensive course work and clinical training in this area. Furthermore, much of the optional training in "family therapy" in social work training programs focuses on parent–child therapy and not at all on marital therapy. (The two approaches are quite different.) Similarly, many child psychologists who work with parents in the context of children's needs have no training in working with marital issues separate from parenting.

If family (parent–child) therapy differs from marital therapy, individual psychotherapy differs even more. The extensive professional literature on marital and couples therapy indicates that this is a specialized and difficult form of psychotherapy, requiring unique interviewing skills and therapeutic strategies because of the presence of two individuals who have an intense, multidimensional relationship and frequently competing perspectives and goals (Crane 1996; Datillo 1998; Jacobson and Christensen 1996; Jacobson and Gurman 1995).

Most therapists working on marriage problems, then, are inadequately trained for this complex form of therapy. The results of a much-publicized *Consumer Reports* survey on the effectiveness of psychotherapy suggest that many therapists seeing couples are not doing a good job. In his article on this survey, Seligman (1995) reports that "marriage counselors" were the only group of professionals whose clients reported consistently lower than average improvement after therapy. Note that clients were asked to describe what kind of professional they saw, and there was no independent confirmation of the professional degree or license status of the therapists. Since "marriage counselors" can include a wide range of mental health professionals who claim expertise in the area, it is not surprising that this group received the lowest consumer ratings.

What happens when therapists are actually trained to work with couples? In contrast to the *Consumer Reports* survey that did not specify the training of the marriage counselors, Doherty and Simmons (1986) conducted a national survey of clients of therapists who hold credentials in marriage and family therapy; that is, they have a license in marriage and family therapy or equivalent course work and supervised clinical experience. The authors found that 77 percent of the respondents reported improvement in marital functioning. These findings are comparable to, and somewhat better than, the improvement rates found in controlled studies of marital therapy and individual psychotherapy (Bray and Jouriles 1995). We have reason to believe, then, that well-trained therapists can help married couples but that inadequately trained therapists are not helpful.

Therapists' Individualistic Orientation

Beyond these empirical studies documenting the sorry state of the training and practice of marital therapy in most psychotherapy professions, a number of scholars and social critics have raised concerns about how the individualistic orientation of much mainstream psychotherapy serves to undermine marital commitment. In other words, the problem may just not be lack of competence; there may also be an active, albeit unintended, undermining of marriage in the guise of promoting individual well-being (Bellah et al. 1985; Doherty 1995, 1997). In their groundbreaking book, *Habits of the Heart*, Robert Bellah and his colleagues (1985) placed psychotherapy at the center of the growing hegemony of individual self-interest in American society, in which "expressive individualism" supersedes notions of commitment to family and community. It's not that therapists do not care about relationships, according to the authors, but that they seem to believe that pursuing individual psychological well-being inevitably leads to family and community well-being. It's what I call "trickle-down psychological economics," the idea that if we concentrate on meeting our individual needs, we inevitably will be good for others in our lives.

In a prophetic discussion of the same issue two decades earlier, the sociologist Philip Rieff (1966) pointed out in *The Triumph of the Therapeutic* that therapists became the de facto moral teachers in the second half of the twentieth century, because psychology had supplanted religion as the main source of guidance about human living. Beginning with Freud, according to Rieff (1966), "the best spirits of the twentieth century have thus expressed their conviction that . . . the new center, which can be held even as communities disintegrate, is the self" (p. 5). I have argued elsewhere (Doherty 1995) that therapists, although claiming to be value free and morally neutral, have ended up promoting the prevailing mainstream American ethic of individual self-interest. In this implicit moral code, interpersonal commitments serve as means to the end of personal well-being, to be maintained as long as they work for us and discarded when they do not. The high-water mark of this moral teaching came in the 1960s and 1970s, when many contemporary psychotherapy leaders and teachers were trained. It was crystallized best by Fritz Perls (1969), the founder of Gestalt therapy, in his classic "Gestalt Therapy Prayer":

> I do my thing and you do your thing.
> I am not in this world to live up to your expectations,
> And you are not in this world to live up to mine.
> You are you and I am I,
> And if by chance we find each other, it's beautiful.
> If not, it can't be helped. (p. 4)

The continuing influence of this "prayer" can be seen in the wedding vow popular in California: the promise to stay married "as long as we both shall love." The following case illustrates how some therapists apply this ethic to working with people experiencing marital distress.

Monica was stunned when Rob, her husband of eighteen years, announced that he was having an affair with her best friend and wanted an "open marriage." When Monica declined this invitation, Rob bolted from the house and was found the next day wandering around aimlessly in a nearby woods. He spent two weeks in a mental hospital for an acute, psychotic depression and was released to outpatient treatment. Although he claimed during his hospitalization that he wanted a divorce, his therapist had the good sense to urge him to not make any major decisions until he was feeling better. Meanwhile, Monica was beside herself with grief, fear, and anger. She had two young children at home, a demanding job, and was struggling with lupus, a chronic illness she had been diagnosed with months ago. Indeed, Rob had never been able to cope with her diagnosis or with his own job loss six months later. (He was now working again.)

Clearly, this couple had been through huge stresses in the past year, including a relocation to a different city where they had no support systems in place. Rob was acting in a completely uncharacteristic way for a former straight-arrow man with strong religious and moral values. Monica was depressed, agitated, and confused. She sought out recommendations to find the best psychotherapist available in her city. He turned out to be a highly regarded clinical psychologist. Rob was continuing in individual outpatient psychotherapy, while living alone in an apartment. He still wanted a divorce.

As Monica later recounted the story, her therapist, after two sessions of assessment and crisis intervention, suggested that she pursue the divorce that Rob said he wanted. She resisted, pointing out that this was a long-term marriage with young children and that she was hoping that the "real" Rob would reemerge from his midlife crisis. She suspected that the affair with her friend would be short-lived (which it was). She was angry and terribly hurt, she said, but determined not to give up on an eighteen-year marriage after only one month of hell. The therapist, according to Monica, interpreted her resistance to "moving on with her life" as stemming from her inability to "grieve" the end of her marriage. He then connected this inability to grieve to the loss of her mother when Monica was a small child; Monica's difficulty in letting go of a failed marriage stemmed from unfinished mourning from the death of her mother.

Fortunately, Monica had the strength to fire the therapist. Not many clients would be able to do that, especially in the face of such expert pathologizing of their moral commitment. And equally fortunately, she and Rob found a good marital therapist who saw them through their crisis and onward to a recovered and ultimately healthier marriage.

This kind of appalling therapist behavior occurs every day in clinical practice. Consider these other examples:

- A counselor suggested that a newly married, depressed woman have a trial separation from her husband because an "unhappy" (but not conflicted) marriage was keeping her from feeling better. When she turned to her priest, he suggested that if her marriage problems were causing her depression, he could help her get an annulment.
- The anxious wife of a verbally abusive husband who was not dealing well with his Parkinson's disease was told at the end of the first therapy session in her HMO that her husband would never change and that she would have to either live with the abuse or get out. She was grievously offended that this young therapist was so cavalier about her commitment to a man she had loved for forty years and who was now infirm with Parkinson's disease. She came to me to find a way to end the verbal abuse while salvaging a commit-

ted marriage. When I invited her husband to join us, he turned out to be more flexible than the other therapist had imagined. He, too, was committed to his marriage, and he needed his wife immensely.

A final illustration: One of my students suffered serious postpartum depressions after the births of her two children. She told me that both of the therapists she had seen at different times challenged her about why she stayed married to a husband who did not understand her needs. (Her husband was befuddled by his wife's moods and sometimes became impatient with her, but he was not a mean-spirited man.) One therapist, in the first session, said in a challenging tone of voice, "I can't believe you are still married." Diane Sollee, executive director of the Coalition for Marriage, Family, and Couples Education, told me that people who had sought out counseling send her e-mail or phone messages such as this one every day.

These illustrations should not be dismissed as examples of random bad therapy or incompetent therapists. They stem from a pervasive bias among many individually oriented therapists against sustaining marital commitment in the face of a now-toxic relationship. From this perspective, abandoning a bad marriage is akin to selling a mutual fund that, although once good for you, is now a money loser. The main techniques of this kind of therapy are twofold: (1) walk clients through a cost–benefit analysis with regard to staying married—what is in it for me to stay or leave? and (2) ask unhappily married clients why they are staying married. If those questions and challenges yield what appears to be an irrational commitment in the face of marital pathology, as the therapist believed to be true for Monica, then the therapist falls back on pathologizing the reasons for this commitment or on outright recommending divorce. It takes extraordinary conviction to weather such "help" from a therapist.

In sum, contemporary therapy for marital difficulties poses two major problems: most practicing therapists are not well trained to do the work, and an unknown number of therapists undermine marriage by promoting an ethic of personal fulfillment narrowly construed.

COMMUNITARIAN PRINCIPLES FOR MARITAL THERAPY

The first plank in a communitarian platform for marital therapy would be for therapists to recognize and affirm the moral nature of marital commitment. This stance moves therapists beyond the guise of neutrality that masks a contractual, self-interested approach to marital commitment. Divorce, from a communitarian perspective, is sometimes necessary when great harm would be caused by staying in the marriage. Particularly in the presence of minor children, the decision to divorce would be akin to amputating a limb: to be avoided if at all possible by sustained, alternative treatments but pursued if necessary to save the person's life. Marriage is a fundamentally moral enterprise calling for love and sacrifice over a lifetime, not merely a lifestyle choice.

The second plank affirms that personal health and psychological well-being are also central dimensions of marriage and important goals of therapy. There is no inherent contradiction between emphasizing the moral nature of marital commitment and promoting the value of personal satisfaction and autonomy within the marital relationship. These moral and personal elements together define the unique power of marriage in contemporary life.

The third plank is that it is a fundamental moral obligation to seek marital therapy when marital distress is serious enough to threaten the marriage. We need a cultural ethic that would make it just as irresponsible to terminate a marriage without seeking professional help as it would be to let someone die without seeing a physician.

The fourth plank holds that promoting marital health should be seen as an important part of health care. We know the medical and psychological ravages of failed marriages for most adults and children. The health care system should support this kind of treatment as an essential part of health care, instead of regarding marital therapy as an "uncovered benefit."

The fifth plank concerns the importance of education for marriage and early intervention to prevent serious marital problems. We need a public health campaign to monitor the health of the nation's marriages and to promote community efforts to help couples enhance the knowledge, attitudes, values, and skills needed to make caring, collaborative, and committed marriage possible. A number of well-researched courses and programs in marriage education across the country can fill this need. We also need grassroots efforts among couples without direct reliance on professional leadership.

The sixth plank asserts that therapists should help spouses hold each other accountable for treating their spouse in a fair and caring way in the marriage. Although commitment is the linchpin of marriage, justice and caring are essential moral elements as well. A communitarian approach to marital therapy would incorporate feminist insights into gender-based inequality in contemporary marriages. It would be sensitive to how women are often expected to assume major responsibility for the marriage and the children and then are criticized for being overresponsible. When a husband declines to do his fair share of family work on the grounds that "it's not my thing," the therapist should see this as a cop-out from his moral responsibilities, not just as a self-interested bargaining position with his wife. Communitarians promote more than marital stability; they promote caring, collaborative, and equitable marital unions that are good for the well-being of the spouses as individuals.

PROPOSALS FOR REFORM OF MARITAL THERAPY PRACTICE

This section outlines several specific proposals, based on the communitarian principles outlined previously, for reform in the practice of marital therapy and, just as important, the reform of individual therapy that addresses marital problems.

1. *Caveat emptor: Create public awareness of the dangers of seeking help for marital problems from a typically trained therapist.* Even therapists who are competent in individual psychotherapy might be incompetent in marital therapy. We need documentation of the extent of incompetence and undermining of marriage that occurs in everyday therapy practice. One approach would be to secure funds for a national survey asking about people's experiences with therapists when marital problems are an issue. Following the survey, a media campaign could be conducted to raise public awareness, a kind of *Consumer Reports* approach to this problem. Data and anecdotes together can raise the consciousness of therapists and consumers alike.

2. *Encourage consumers to ask therapists to declare their value positions with regard to marital commitment.* Consumers can be given guidelines about how to interview a potential therapist, with questions such as "What are your values about the importance of keeping a marriage together when problems arise?" If the therapist responds only with the rhetoric of individual self-determination ("I try to help both parties decide what they need to do for themselves"), the consumer can ask whether the therapist holds any personal values about the importance of marital commitment. Consumers can then avoid therapists whose values differ from their own.

3. *Urge licensing boards to require training in marital therapy before permitting its practice.* The assumption now is that any generically trained therapist can work with couples. Even boards of marriage and family therapy currently do not require proof of supervised clinical experience in marital therapy, since state regulations generally refer to "marriage and family" therapy experience. It is possible to do only parent–child work and have no experience with couples. Therapists who wish to do marital therapy would have to retool.

4. *Expand graduate and postgraduate training opportunities in marital therapy.* The current level of professional incompetence will require many years to transcend, but universities and psychotherapy institutes should embark on a large-scale educational enterprise in the values, knowledge, and skills of marital therapy. This training should involve extensive face-to-face work with couples, not just dealing with marital problems during individual therapy, along with immersion in the extensive professional literature on marital therapy.

5. *Encourage professional associations of therapists to address how their members deal with marital commitment.* Most mental health professional ethics guidelines address only the well-being of individuals and are silent on the moral underpinnings of marriage and family bonds and the therapist's responsibility to promote the viability of such bonds. In both individual and marital therapy, the

therapist should be expected to inform clients about his or her value orientation toward marital commitment. Professional associations are not in a position to dictate value orientations to their members, but they can serve as catalysts for a searching professional discussion of whether the pendulum has swung from "save every marriage no matter how destructive" to "therapist-assisted marital suicide."

6. *Require payers of health care services to reimburse for the treatment of marital problems.* Many insurance companies and HMOs exclude marital therapy unless one of the partners has a psychiatric disorder. This policy is short-sighted in light of the evidence for the role of marriage in promoting health and the role of marital distress in precipitating and maintaining illness. Therapists reimbursed for marital therapy should meet minimum requirements for couples therapy training, beyond just having a mental health license.

7. *Place more emphasis on education and prevention of marital distress.* Therapists are trained to meet with people after they are in trouble. Well-researched marriage education programs have demonstrated that brief, skills-based educational programs for couples increase couple satisfaction, improve communication skills, reduce negative conflict behaviors including violence, and may prevent separation and divorce (Markman et al. 1993; Wampler 1990). Therapists should lend more of their efforts to work with couples "upstream" from the problems that lead to the need for therapeutic treatment. And they should support community-based initiatives to promote marital well-being, such as marriage mentor programs in religious settings (Parrott and Parrott 1995).

8. *Integrate clinical work with couples across different professions and different levels of intensity.* Not every mental health professional, primary care physician, or pastoral counselor can be expected to be an expert marital therapist. But each can work with marital issues at different levels of intensity, from supportive to psychoeducational to therapeutic, and refer the couple when they cannot benefit from less intensive help.

CONCLUSION

I believe that therapists are now reconsidering their approach to marital commitment. They have been entranced by a cultural mirage about what constitutes the good life in the twenty-first century, and they are beginning to rethink their ill-begotten moral neutrality in the face of disturbing levels of family and community breakdown. A communitarian critique and reformulation of marital therapy can point the way to a new kind of marriage covenant that views moral responsibility, sustained commitments, and personal fulfillment as a garment seamlessly sewn, not a piece of Velcro designed for ease of separation.

But more than moral sensitivity is required to do good marital therapy. We also need a commitment to standards of competence in this unique form of therapy practice, along with a commitment to public awareness and a reorientation of licensing boards and professional associations. People seeking help for their marital problems should not have to roll the dice to determine whether they get help from a skilled therapist who supports their marital commitment.

NOTE

Portions of this chapter are adapted from the author's article "How Therapists Threaten Marriage," *The Responsive Community* 7 (1997): 31-42.

REFERENCES

American Association for Marriage and Family Therapy. 1997. *Practice Strategies* 3: 1-12.

American Psychological Association. 1995. *Public opinion on mental health issues.* Washington, D.C.: Author.

Bellah, R. N., R. Madsen, W. M. Sullivan, A. Swidler, and S. M. Tipton. 1995. *Habits of the heart: Individualism and commitment in American life.* Berkeley: University of California Press.

Bray, J. H., and E. N. Jouriles. 1995. Treatment of marital conflict and prevention of divorce. *Journal of Marital and Family Therapy* 21: 461-73.

Burman, B., and G. Margolin. 1992. Analysis of the association between marital relationships and health problems: An interactional perspective. *Psychological Bulletin* 112: 39-63.

Cherlin, A. J., F. F. Furstenberg, et al. 1991. Longitudinal studies of effects of divorce on children in Great Britain and the United States. *Science* 252: 1386-89.

Crane, D. R. 1996. *Fundamentals of marital therapy.* New York: Brunner/Mazel.

Datillo, F. M., ed. 1998. *Case studies in couple and family therapy: Systemic and cognitive perspectives.* New York: Guilford.

Dawson, D. A. 1991. Family structure and children's health and well-being: Data from the 1988 National Health Interview Survey on Child Health. *Journal of Marriage and the Family* 53: 573-84.

Doherty, W. J. 1995. *Soul searching: Why psychotherapy must promote moral responsibility.* New York: Basic Books.

———. 1997. How therapists threaten marriage. *The Responsive Community* 7: 31-42.

Doherty, W. J., and R. H. Needle. 1991. Psychological adjustment and substance use among adolescents before and after a parental divorce. *Child Development* 62: 328-37.

Doherty, W. J., and D. S. Simmons. 1986. Clinical practice patterns of marriage and family therapists and their clients. *Journal of Marital and Family Therapy* 22: 9-25.

Gottman, J. M., and L. F. Katz. 1989. Effects of marital discord on young children's peer interruption and health. *Developmental Psychology* 25: 373-81.

Jacobson, N. S., and A. Christensen, eds. 1996. *Integrative couple therapy: Promoting acceptance and change.* New York: Norton.

Jacobson, N. S., and A. S. Gurman, eds. 1995. *Clinical handbook of couple therapy.* New York: Guilford.

Kiecolt-Glaser, J. F., W. B. Malarkey, et al. 1993. Negative behavior during marital conflict is associated with immunological down-regulation. *Psychosomatic Medicine* 55: 395-409.

Markman, H. J., M. J. Renick, et al. 1993. Preventing marital distress through communication and conflict management training: A 4- and 5-year follow-up. *Journal of Consulting and Clinical Psychology* 61: 70-77.

Parrott, L., and L. Parrott. 1995. *The marriage mentor manual.* Grand Rapids, Mich.: Zondervan.

Perls, F. 1969. *Gestalt therapy verbatim.* Lafayette, Calif.: Real People Press.

Prince, S. E., and N. S. Jacobson. 1995. A review and evaluation of marital and family therapies for affective disorders. *Journal of Marital and Family Therapy* 21: 377-401.

Regier, D. A., W. E. Narrow, D. S. Rae, R. W. Manderscheid, B. Z. Locke, and F. K. Goodwin. 1993. The de facto U.S. mental and addictive disorders services systems: Epidemiologic Catchment Area prospect 1-year prevalence rates of disorders and services. *Archives of General Psychiatry* 50: 95-107.

Rieff, P. 1966. *The triumph of the therapeutic.* New York: Harper & Row.

Schwartz, J. E., H. S. Friedman, et al. 1995. Sociodemographic and psychosocial factors in childhood as predictors of adult mortality. *American Journal of Public Health* 85: 1237-45.

Seligman, M. E. P. 1995. The effectiveness of psychotherapy: The *Consumer Reports* Study. *American Psychologist* 50: 965-74.

Simmons, D., and W. J. Doherty. 1998. Does academic training make a difference among practicing marriage and family therapists? *Journal of Marital and Family Therapy* 24: 321-36.

Tucker, J. S., H. S. Friedman, et al. 1996. Marital history at midlife as a predictor of longevity: Alternative explanations to the protective effect of marriage. *Health Psychology* 15: 94-101.

Wampler, K. S. 1990. An update of research on the Couple Communication Program. *Family Science Review* 3: 21-40.

7

The Task of Religious Institutions in Strengthening Families

Don Browning

A communitarian family policy aspires to balance the good of society with the good of families and their individual members. It holds that the well-being of families, individual family members, and society is best guaranteed when the health of each is promoted equally. This principle is easy to state but difficult to actualize in concrete circumstances.

In this chapter, I ask what churches and synagogues as institutions of civil society should do to promote family well-being. What should they do for the families they immediately influence, and how should they work to shape public policy? I pursue these questions in this order because of my conviction that the strength of a society flows outward from its voluntary institutions—religious and civil—to public institutions and their policies. I hold, however, that government programs, religious institutions, and other institutions of civil society should be complementary in what they do for families. The state, market, churches and synagogues, and other voluntary organizations play different roles in relation to families, but these roles should be appropriately coordinated.

The proposals of the Communitarian Family Task Force are guided by three normative ideas. First, although the various spheres of modern societies—government, business, religion, education, law, and the therapies—have unique responsibilities and privileges, they do not and cannot function independently from deeper ethical guidelines and constraints.

Second, family and local community should be allowed to exercise initiatives and natural capabilities in their spheres of immediate influence without undue interference from either government or market, even though both of these have their rightful role in supporting families and local communities. This concept is close to what the Roman Catholic tradition calls the "principle of subsidiarity"—an idea that can be given religious meaning even though it also has ancient philosophical roots.[1]

Third, an ethic of "equal regard" should guide both the inner lives of families and family public policy. Realizing that the idea of a family ethic of equal regard needs a definition,[2] I offer the following: this ethic means that a husband or wife should (1) treat the other with unconditioned respect (as an end and never as a means only) and (2) within this mutual respect work to enhance the well-being of the other. Concretely, the ethic of equal regard means that husband and wife should each in principle have equal access to the privileges and responsibilities of both public and private worlds, although this may be realized differently in specific households depending on individual interests and talents.

A familism guided by an ethic of equal regard is a "critical" familism—another term that requires definition. Critical familism is different from *naïve familism,* which generally is interpreted as placing family togetherness above other values such as equality between husband and wife, the well-being of children, and the flourishing of individual family members. *Critical familism* balances family cohesion with the ethics of equal regard. It does this by uncovering and critiquing distortions in power in families that block the realization of equal regard among members.

The equal regard family does not relinquish parental authority; instead, it uses this authority to promote equal regard, dialogue, and the raising of children to gradually grow toward adult relations of mutual respect with their parents and others. In the case of relations between families, the ethic of equal regard holds that each family has the moral obligation to respect and work for the good of all other families. In turn, each family has the right to be respected and have its good promoted by others.

CIVIL SOCIETY, RELIGION, AND STATE: TOWARD A CRITICAL MARRIAGE CULTURE

I affirm the emerging view that religious institutions are central to the health of civil society. Religious institutions are major wellsprings of philanthropic action and seedbeds of civic, religious, and familial virtues. In light of their importance, I make the following recommendations.

Churches and Synagogues Should Critically Retrieve Their Marriage and Family Traditions

First, churches and synagogues should play a leadership role in stimulating the dialogue that creates a new familism. In the judgment of the Communitarian Family Task Force, with few exceptions, religious institutions have not exercised this leadership in recent decades. To reclaim this role, they must retrieve their marriage and family traditions, even though they must do so critically. Religious institutions should examine their heritages, enter into dialogue with other denominations, work with secular institutions, survey the human sciences, and articulate a fresh vision of marriage and family—something close to what has been called critical familism.

In addition to the marriage theologies of various denominations, this recommendation also can be illustrated by what Catholics and Protestants variously have called the "first" or "little" church. The continuity between the official church and the church at home has been a constant theme throughout Christian history. Because the early church met in homes, sacred actions around common meals in the gathered ecclesia were imitated in private home life. The importance of domestic rituals is even stronger in Judaism. When home rituals and the liturgies of church or synagogue reinforce each other, family life is made more cohesive and integrated more completely into the wider community. When these rituals or devotions are followed by free discussion between parents and children, they give rise to the reflective or critical assimilation of family traditions.

Evidence indicates that home-based rituals are extremely important for the creation of family cohesion. Family rituals at the dinner table, before bed, and on trips correlate with the effective communication of family traditions.[3] Rituals are important as well for families with a primarily secular identity. In these families, rituals may consist of carefully planned beginnings and endings to meals, family meetings, and other shared and regularly scheduled family activities.

Religious Institutions Should Cooperate with Other Institutions in Helping Families

Second, religious congregations should join with other parts of civil society to foster a critical marriage and family culture. In some instances this cooperation might entail partnerships with the state. In establishing these cooperative ventures, religious institutions must simultaneously seek to maintain their unique identity while striving to respect the separation of church and state. They can do this by searching for the points of analogy between their specific goals and the state's concern with the common good. The state, for instance, should be guided by an ethic of justice for individuals and families analogous to the ethic of equal regard promoted by religious institutions. Government also should abide by the principle of subsidiarity that respects the initiative and responsibility of families yet supports them when they need help.

Some cooperation between religious and public institutions already exists: witness the cooperation between churches and public health institutions. Catholic Charities and Lutheran Social Services both receive some state support. Note also the cooperation between churches and other institutions of civil society such as the Red Cross, a model that could be expanded and applied more directly to family issues. For example, a complex cooperative project involving church, state, and other voluntary organizations can be found in recent efforts to expand the idea of a Community Marriage Policy. This program was first used to organize common marriage policies among local Protestant churches but has now been expanded in some communities to include judges, justices of the peace, and secular marriage counselors.[4] I say more about this policy later.

Public institutions should not become isolated from the energies and positive cultures of specific religiocultural traditions. Sociologist James Coleman argues that Catholic high schools provide better education than public schools because they receive more support from parents and church.[5] As societies organized around extended families have disappeared, Coleman believes that market, corporation, and government have expanded their influence on society, including schools. Catholic schools are succeeding, he argues, because they are an exception to this trend; they represent the values of families and their churches. Coleman urges us to abandon the idea that schools are solely agents of the state. Rather, they should more nearly reflect the values of the family and local community, including religious institutions.[6]

The view of the Communitarian Family Task Force is sympathetic to Coleman's but somewhat different. We do not believe that family and church should dominate public schools. We hold that families, religious institutions, market, and government each has its rightful expertise and authority for influencing the values and purposes of schools. Hence, each of these spheres should conduct an intense dialogue about the direction of public schools and what they teach about marriage and family. This dialogue should result in developing new educational approaches to marriage and family life—approaches that have continuity with, but may not be identical to, the basic values of particular local families, traditions, and churches.

Some proposals by William Bennett and Senator Dan Coats in their Project for American Renewal illustrate how state and civil society, including religious institutions, can cooperate. Coats and Bennett have been mildly critical of programs that gave welfare for families to the states. They also reject the idea of centering social programs for families mainly in the federal government. They call, instead, for funneling government support directly to the institutions of civil society, including the churches. They argue that these institutions are the conveyors of civic virtue, do most of society's moral education, and need to be revived to provide some of the cultural and institutional supports needed by families. They propose allowing individuals to give $500 of their tax liability to worthwhile nongovernmental charities that help poor families.[7] They recommend demonstration grants for programs that match welfare families with religious communities that offer moral guidance and help. To encourage savings by poor families, demonstration grants would be provided for family deposits to be matched by churches, foundations, and corporations. Funds would be made available for predivorce counseling.

It is not my intention to advocate these particular programs but rather to show that such proposals exist and deserve careful evaluation as possible ways for civil society, religious institutions, and the state to cooperate. Furthermore, I use them to illustrate the meaning of subsidiarity—the way large units of society such as government can support family and local communities without taking over the functions these smaller institutions perform best. Such cooperation also illustrates a dialogical view of authority—that is, how family, local community, state, and market can work together in creating a critical family culture.

Ecumenicity and Critical Familism

Third, churches must join with other churches and synagogues to create a new critical marriage culture. Seventy-five percent of all marriages, even today, are performed in synagogues and churches. This figure suggests that churches still have a significant role in marriage and should therefore work together in proclaiming and implementing a marriage and family culture.

But how can this happen? Michael McManus recommends that churches cooperate in adopting something like the Roman Catholic Church's coordinated program of premarital and marital support called the "Common Marriage Policy."[8] It has been adopted by the vast majority of Roman Catholic dioceses in the United States. Because of this common policy, Catholic churches have a unified front on marriage issues. Young Catholic couples confront a common set of expectations and a common culture about what it takes to prepare for and thrive in family relations. This common policy has five components:

1. A six-month minimum preparation period
2. The administration of the new premarital questionnaires that have been tested for their capacity to predict marriages likely to end in divorce (PREPARE, the Pre-Marital Inventory, or FOCCUS)
3. The use of lay leadership and "mentoring couples" with the engaged and newly married
4. The use of marriage instruction classes (weekend workshops, evenings for the engaged in the homes of mentor couples)
5. Engagement ceremonies held before the entire congregation

McManus proposes bringing together Catholic, evangelical, and mainline Protestant churches (I would add synagogues) to create a "Community Marriage Policy"[9]—an ecumenical and interfaith common marriage policy that would help congregations across denominations to develop a united stance on marriage and family. Such a united front could help churches and synagogues counter the individualism and impatience of couples and parents who expect ministers to perform marriages on demand without careful preparation. The common elements McManus proposes look much like the Catholic model, but he suggests shorter waiting periods to adapt to more liberal customs among some denominations. Although the model needs further refinement, early reports suggest it is an idea moving in the right direction.

Youth and a Critical Marriage Culture

Fourth, churches and synagogues should take the lead in preparing youth for a critical familism. Large portions of society have retreated from guiding and inspiring youth in the areas of marriage and family. Many churches do not do adequate marriage preparation with engaged couples; they do even less with youth and teenagers. Churches have yielded leadership in these areas to public education, at both the college level and below.

As churches have retreated from sex, marriage, and family education, secular courses, often at the college level, have taken their place. A recent authoritative review of college textbooks by Professor Norval Glenn of the University of Texas has revealed that most of these texts are devoid of historical knowledge of the family, overly optimistic about the successes of alternative family forms, neglectful of children, and uninformed about new research on the benefits of marriage.[10] They tend to ignore evidence showing that married people are mentally and physically healthier, have more wealth, have much more sex, and are generally far more content with life than those who are not married.[11] Churches and synagogues should not only be concerned about this state of affairs but develop better alternative educational resources.

Religious institutions should be aware that there are very few adequate educational resources addressing issues of marriage and family in secondary schools.[12] Sex education courses aim primarily to prevent disease and out-of-wedlock births.[13] Setting aside the question of their effectiveness in realizing these goals, they say little about marriage or family except to promote an attitude of tolerance for different family forms. One of the most competent sex education programs (designed by Marian Howard of Emory University) is not about education for marriage but about the delay of sexual activity until "maturity."

Existing educational programs emphasizing preparation for family life either are deficient in their use of religious resources or fail to present an adequately critical view of marriage, as do most fundamentalist religious programs. We members of the Communitarian Family Task Force believe that religious institutions should use the powerful new video technologies to teach their religious traditions, the best insights of the new marriage education programs (PREP, PREPARE/ENRICH, etc.), and realistic understandings of the economic, legal, and medical aspects of marriage.[14]

Addressing Family Pluralism from a Center

Fifth, churches and synagogues should develop theologies and programs that give priority to promoting the health of intact families while also helping other family forms. The cultural and social forces that are disrupting families are relentless, and high rates of family disruption are likely to continue in the foreseeable future. While family dissolution is often advisable in cases of violence, abuse, and addiction, religious institutions should recognize that many families could function well together if they had better supports.

Much can be done to mitigate strains on disrupted families, be they never-married single parents, the divorced, or stepfamilies. Finally, we must recognize the advent of families with gay and lesbian parents and families consisting of heterosexual parents with gay or lesbian children. Although churches hold a range of positions about the nature and moral status of homosexual practice, almost all churches, conservative or liberal, wish to minister to these families.

Religious institutions should imitate those churches and synagogues that simultaneously and aggressively prepare people for stable and fulfilling marriages yet support and assist alternative family forms. For example, there is a burgeoning white Pentecostal church in the western suburbs of Chicago that has, in addition to its strong emphasis on marriage and opposition to divorce, a highly popular twelve-week postdivorce support program.[15] Many African American churches have such complex ministries. The Shiloh Baptist Church, located in the poorer section of Washington, D.C., has a complex approach. It has delicately balanced programs designed to increase the number of intact families, while through its Family Life Center, it also reaches out to disrupted families in the community.

Churches, Synagogues, and the Balance of Work and Family

Sixth, religious institutions should address one of the major sources of strain on families: the tensions between family needs and the demands of paid work. Mothers have joined fathers in the workforce, the average workweek has been extended, parents spend less time with children (the "parenting deficit"), and married couples spend less time with each other. Clearly, it takes time and energy to create an equal-regard family with parents guiding children into an ever-deepening dialogue with them, their faith traditions, and the wider society. The Communitarian Family Task Force proposes a model not exceeding a total sixty-hour workweek for a mother and father with young children. The compensated working hours could be divided between husband and wife as thirty-thirty, forty-twenty, or twenty-forty. Evidence indicates that the happiest families are those in which both husband and wife have some paid employment, share household chores and child care,[16] and work less than two full-time positions.[17] Churches, in their theologies of work and leisure, should support such arrangements.

If the equal-regard family is to become a reality within the context of modern work demands, however, it will need to gain the skills of intersubjective communication (the ability to see and feel issues from the partner's point of view) required to define what is just and equitable. Church-sponsored day care centers, support groups for working parents, church-sponsored baby-sitting networks, church-sponsored nursing support for parents of sick children—dozens of programs are possible. But more fundamental than any of these is a theory that sanctions the balance of work and parenting and the development of the communicative skills required to iron out the practical arrangements of everyday life.

Religious Institutions and Divorce

Seventh, religious institutions should do more to address the reality of divorce. While religious groups differ on the question of divorce, they all have tended to be either cautious or genuinely restrictive about this issue. Despite trends in secular society toward the easy acceptance of divorce, churches and synagogues should continue to be conservative in their attitudes on the dissolution of marriage. However, this view does not necessarily mean an absolute prohibition of divorce.

The Communitarian Family Task Force recommends four strategies that local churches can use to address the reality of divorce. First, prevention is the best cure. The best divorce prevention is extensive marital preparation of the kind envisioned by the task force's proposal for a Community Marriage Policy and its suggestions for early church-based and school-based education for marriage and family.

Second, both church-based and secular marriage counseling should begin with a humane bias toward preserving marriages. One of our team on the task force has written with reference to both the counseling pastor and the secular psychotherapist: "As therapists, we are moral consultants, not just psycho-social consultants. We should not try to impose our beliefs on undecided clients, but we can advocate in an open manner when appropriate."[18] Counseling that presents theological and moral reasons for the importance of preserving marriage is entirely justifiable as long as it is not coercive, does not override the decision-making integrity of the individuals involved, does not suppress important dynamic and communicative issues that the couple should face, and does not ignore abuse, violence, and addiction. The idea that divorce is generally not good for children and that couples not involved in physical and mental violence may be able to learn to communicate and love one another again must be taken seriously in the counseling of churches.[19] Recent social science research by Paul Amato and Alan Booth (1997) in their acclaimed *A Generation at Risk* indicates that only one-third of all divorces are preceded by high conflict of the kind destructive to children. This raises the question as to whether the less destructive remaining two-thirds might have avoided divorce had they found the proper help.[20]

Third, synagogues and churches should love, minister to, and sustain the divorced and their children. In spite of what worshiping communities do to discourage them, divorces will occur, although we hope with less regularity. Churches and synagogues must also make a special effort to support children of divorced parents, whose experience of the divorce may be quite different from that of their parents and whose journey through childhood may be different from many other children. The religious communities that simultaneously promote a marriage culture, discourage a divorce culture, and advance a culture of care for the divorced, remarried, and their children[21] are the ones that make full use of their theological traditions to hold authentic ideals together with a charitable sense of human weakness. Furthermore, these congregations help disrupted families create the networks—what sociologists call "social capital"—necessary for the support and enrichment of all families, especially those disrupted by transitions. Finally, churches and synagogues, even at the local level, should join the national discussion about whether our divorce laws should be revised. (For further discussion on that issue, see chapters 10–13 in this volume.)

Churches, Synagogues, and Fathers

Eighth, churches and synagogues should do more to address the growing absence of fathers from their children. If the movement toward father absence is to be abated, nearly every aspect of civil society must address it and religious institutions should take the lead. There is much to learn from black churches about restoring responsible fatherhood. The ten-thousand-member Apostolic Church of God on Chicago's South Side routinely and vigorously addresses father absence and discusses the positive contributions to children that fathers make. Another nearby church does all these things but with more consciousness of African themes. This church has rites-of-passage ceremonies for both teenage boys and girls that combine African themes and Christian meanings in defining adult male–female relations. It has an "adopt-a-school" program in which adult males relate to a neighborhood school, give courses on "responsible living," and help guide male students away from gangs and sexual involvement and toward their studies.

CRITICAL FAMILISM, RELIGION, AND PUBLIC POLICY: BEYOND VALUE NEUTRALITY

Churches and synagogues should become involved in public policy beyond the natural confines of their memberships and immediate communities. The Communitarian Family Task Force holds that public policy should not and cannot maintain "value neutrality" on family matters. Furthermore, family issues cannot be solved strictly through technical and economic interventions by state and market. A critical familism is first a result of cultural visions—indeed, religiocultural visions—that come from the institutions of civil society, especially churches and synagogues. Nonetheless, economic measures from both state and market are also important for families.

The Economic Support of Families

First, religious institutions should explicitly support several economic strategies that can help families. The tax structure, for one thing, should be far more family-friendly than it is. If the child exemption on federal income tax returns had kept pace with its value when first enacted in 1948, it now would be equivalent to $8,200 rather than its current $2,500.[22] We members of the task force applaud the recent adoption by Congress of a $500 per child tax credit. But it may need to be more. The 1991 report to the president of the National Commission on Children recommended a refundable tax credit of $1,000,[23] and William Mattox of the Family Research Council has called for a $1,500 credit.[24] We also support the earned income tax credit for poor families, which is generally believed to have contributed to the stability of low-income working parents. Finally, the so-called marriage tax penalty—the fact that married couples often pay considerably more in taxes than they would if single—is both a real and symbolic assault on the social value of marriage and should be removed.[25] (See also the discussion of this issue in chapter 9.)

Then there is the issue of welfare. The task force agrees with those who argue that government's first obligation, at this moment in history, is to strengthen the institutions of civil society—churches, clubs, community organizations, voluntary service organizations—to carry more of the welfare system for families. But, at the same time, government must be involved in welfare to assure consistency, sufficient funding, and universality of some very fundamental programs.[26]

In this chapter, I will not debate whether such goals should have been realized in a revised national welfare plan or through one administered by each of the fifty states, as established by the 1996 welfare reform. Instead, I am concerned about an issue in workfare, whether administered by states or by the national government. In keeping with proposals that married couples with young children should not work in wage employment more than a total of sixty hours a week between them, the Communitarian Family Task Force proposes that single welfare parents with young children not be required to work over twenty-five to thirty hours per week, roughly five to six hours a day.[27] Even this time should be undergirded with state-supported child and medical care. The idea of thirty-hour working weeks for single parents and sixty-hour working weeks for married parents has been tried with success. For two decades, from 1930 to 1950, W. K. Kellogg ran his corn flakes plant in Battle Creek, Michigan, on a six-hour day. Recent research based on interviews with older employees reveals a high level of employee satisfaction with the arrangement.[28]

New welfare reform efforts should raise this model to public consciousness. A critical familism rewards family formation, gives social supports to those seeking gender equality, encourages paternal responsibility, discourages family welfare dependency, equips people for work, supports them with child care and medical care, and makes these policies as consistent as possible throughout the various states.

A Family-Friendly Workplace

Second, churches and synagogues should urge policymakers to promote a family-friendly workplace. Some people advocate minimizing work strains with tax reductions that lower the need for families to have two incomes, thereby giving parents more time with their families. Many commentators argue that these proposals simply support the nineteenth-century model of an industrial family with its wage-earning father and domestic mother. President Clinton tried to solve family–work strains with proposals such as better job conditions for parents, more flextime, an extension of the Family and Medical Leave Act (1993), twenty-four hours a year for parents to keep school appointments and take children to doctors, portable family insurance, health insurance for poor families, compensatory time off in lieu of overtime pay, and new federal child care programs.[29] These proposals acknowledge women's desire to work and the realities of the postmodern family. The task force supports both strategies—tax breaks and supports for family-friendly work conditions.

But these strategies do not go far enough. To implement the sixty-hour workweek, state and market must cooperate in creating the new twenty- and thirty-hour a week positions necessary for families to arrange the right combinations. These jobs should provide retirement and medical benefits. This raises the need for a basic universal health plan. I do not presume to settle here the best way to provide universal, cheap, and equitable health coverage for all workers, whether employed twenty, thirty, or forty hours a week. But to create flexible work arrangements that give parents sufficient time with their children, some such system of health care is required.

Child Care

Third, although there is a need for more and better care for the children of employed parents, some of the proposals that the Communitarian Family Task Force advocates should mitigate that need. If parents limit their employment outside the home to sixty hours each week, fathers and mothers will have more time for child care. If the tax breaks listed earlier went into effect, couples will work fewer hours, have more time for child care, yet be able to afford better quality care because their overall income will improve.

Nonetheless, government initiatives to stimulate the development of more affordable quality child care are necessary. Government should invest in training and upgrading child care workers, stimulate the development of minimum standards of care, encourage child care provisions in parent's place of employment, and offer more flextime and home-based employment. Government operated child care facilities eventually may be necessary but should not be the country's first approach to meeting the needs of families.

State-Supported Marriage Education

Fourth, public policy should provide for marriage and family education. As noted earlier, the state is already participating in marriage education, mainly through university-level courses on the family and elementary and high school sex education classes. Much of this instruction is deficient on marriage and family, and some is directly misleading. Although marriage and family life should not be reduced completely to simple public health issues, at this level alone the state has every right to promote marriage and family education. Other countries, such as Australia, sponsor marriage and family education courses. Sometimes these programs function through existing institutions of civil society. They emphasize communications skills, conflict resolution, and parenting skills.[30] At the level of junior high and high school education, such programs would not be addressed to couples but would emphasize education in intersubjective communication skills that, later in life, would prove important for sustaining marriage and family.

Mothers, Fathers, and Public Policy

Fifth, religious institutions should support public policies that help both mothers and fathers with the new challenges they face. We members of the Communitarian Family Task Force advocate measures that go beyond finding ways to force deadbeat fathers to support their children. We agree that measures should be used to garnish wages, use federal and state income taxes to collect delinquent payments, and compel responsibility by canceling auto or professional licenses. But such policies, although necessary, are basically punitive.

The state should become a moral and financial partner of the initiatives in civil society to promote better fatherhood. Take, for instance, Charles Ballard's widely recognized National Institute for Responsible Fatherhood and Family Development, which receives some state support. Ballard's program is designed to reunite fathers with their children, help fathers support their children financially, and foster in these men an attitude of respect for former girlfriends or wives. Counselor-educators (called "sages") visit alienated fathers in their homes, help establish paternity, and model responsible fatherhood themselves.[31] Other programs receive moral support from government even though they get no direct financial help. The National Fatherhood Initiative was founded during the autumn of 1994 with bipartisan support from Democrats Al Gore and William Galston as well as Republican William Bennett. It addresses the growing absence of fathers from their children by distributing information on the importance of fathers and the social costs of father absence.[32] Ken Canfield's National Center for Fathering is an older hands-on program with considerable grassroots impact.[33] Both organizations have more general audiences than Promise Keepers, and their messages are less laden with the language of a particular religious tradition. Both programs work intensively with religious organizations.

The situation of mothers in contemporary society has been very different from that of fathers. Fewer mothers have fled families but may instead feel trapped by them. Even today many women feel that they must choose between paid employment or time with their infants, a choice that often leads mothers to leave the workforce and fall behind in job and career advancement. This predicament has led economists Richard and Grandon Gill to propose what they call a Parental Bill of Rights.[34] Just as American men were given the GI Bill to help them make up for lost career time after serving in the armed forces during World War II, so should parents who take time to care for their children receive child care payments, modest annual child allowances, job training, education, and other protections so that the years spent caring for their infants will not cause long-term financial, job, and career losses. The authors estimate that this Parental Bill of Rights would cost citizens no more than $200 per capita in 1990 dollars.

Divorce and Public Policy

Sixth, religious institutions should back the revision of divorce laws. Since the advent of no-fault divorce in the late 1960s and early 1970s, the marriage contract has become weaker than most business contracts. In many states, it can be broken unilaterally, and the dissenting partner has little recourse. From a both a philosophical and theological perspective, the Communitarian Family Task Force holds that marriage agreements should be more like covenants—that is, binding agreements between a husband and wife, between them and the wider society, and, for the religious, between these two individuals and a transcendent power as they conceive it. Such multidimensional agreements should not be broken with ease. In reality, marriages should be conceived as both contracts and covenants. The system recently enacted in Louisiana that gives couples the option of choosing no-fault marriage contracts or more binding covenant marriages is a sound and noncoercive way to reestablish the legal seriousness of marriage.

The members of the task force do not agree as to whether the present system of no-fault divorces should be rejected completely by the several states. We do agree, however, that in cases in which couples with children want divorce by mutual consent, they should undergo required counseling on parenting after divorce and on the potential impact of the divorce on the children. Furthermore, couples should be required to develop a long-term financial plan to cover the children's needs until they are eighteen and in some cases older. This plan would have to be accepted by the court before the divorcing couple could begin dividing property between them.[35] (See also the discussion of a "children-first" legal principle of property division in the event of divorce in chapter 14.)

Some members of the task force believe that the assignment of fault may not be necessary if waiting periods, required counseling, and long-term financial plans for child support are part of the proposal. However this is decided, we believe that marriage, even before the law, increasingly should be seen as a public covenant vital for both individuals, children, and the common good.

The Media, Public Policy, and Civil Society

Seventh, the institutions of civil society and churches should join with government and the market to launch a critique of media images of marriage and family. The emphasis should be on providing criticism and well-grounded evaluations, not censorship. Nor should criticism be voiced in ways that obscure the good that educational television can do and the positive images that some programs and movies convey. But critiques of the unhealthy aspects of the media should be relentless, should come from many different voices, and must be heard.

From one perspective, the media are an expression of the overflow of cost–benefit, individualistic, and consumption-oriented patterns of the market that increasingly pervade our society. We are not against the market, but we do believe that the rational-choice and ethical-egoist motives of the market can and should be restrained by an ethics of equal regard for persons within and outside of families. This applies as well to a responsible critique of the family images found in movies, television, popular music, and popular journalism.

Rather than portraying the media, however, as single-mindedly seditious,[36] the task force follows Kay Hymowitz's analysis of the dialectical relation of the media and social attitudes.[37] She points out that the values governing marriage and family have changed due to a variety of economic and cultural trends. The media, she explains, do not by themselves create these changes, but they exploit and exacerbate them. Furthermore, to sell movies, TV series, and consumer products, the media use shock and excitement to create interest and viewing addiction to the more titillating aspects of these changes. They give a stamp of normality to behavior and conditions once thought to be immoral and still deserving of analysis and moral criticism.

Censorship is not the answer. A new critical familism is the answer. But this familism and marriage culture should be supported by multiple voices critiquing and sometimes boycotting the media—voices no longer afraid of the charge of moralism. So far, the groups willing to do this are few in number. Such criticism is generally limited to the important reality of violence; addressing family and marriage issues seems to be more difficult.[38] More needs to be done on both questions. The kind of criticism we have in mind is found in a long document by Roger Cardinal Mahony, archbishop of Los Angeles, in which he publicly urges the entertainment industry to "adopt general guidelines for the depiction of violence, sex, family, and the treatment of women."[39] Recent steps taken to adopt an industry-administered rating system that will later be reinforced by the parent-controlled V-chip may help.[40] Watchdog organizations such as the National Institute on Media and the Family should be encouraged.

But until a new artistic sensibility informed by a critical familism emerges, these suggestions will inevitably constitute partial measures. Just as Secretary of Health and Human Services Donna Shalala challenged Hollywood to live up to its creative potential by inventing stories not featuring people smoking cigarettes, so too should multiple voices challenge the media to tell more truthful and positive stories about human love, sexuality, marriage, and families.

CONCLUSION

There is no single cure for the family crisis in society. There is no magic bullet. I have listed over a dozen strategies that religious institutions, voluntary associations, the government, and the market should take in cooperation with one another. The power of these strategies will become apparent not when viewed in isolation from one another but when they become orchestrated into a new gestalt—a new critical familistic culture with accompanying social supports.

NOTES

This chapter was adapted, with extensive suggestions from the members of the Communitarian Family Task Force, from chapter 11 of *From Culture Wars to Common Ground: Religion and the American Family Debate,* by Don Browning, Bonnie Miller McLemore, Pamela Couture, Bernie Lyon, and Robert Franklin (Louisville, Ky.: Westminster/Knox, 1997). This is the summary book of the eleven-book Religion, Culture, and Family Series produced by a research project located at the University of Chicago and financed by a generous grant from the Division of Religion of the Lilly Endowment, Inc.

1. For a discussion of the Aristotelian roots of the concept of subsidiarity, see *From Culture Wars to Common Ground,* 238-44, 363. For a more proximate source of subsidiarity in Roman Catholic thinking, see Pope Leo XIII, "Rerum Novarum," *Proclaiming Justice and Peace:Papal Documents from Rerum Novarum through Centesimus Annus* (Mystic, Conn.: Twenty-Third Publications, 1991; originally published in 1894).

2. The philosophical and theological grounds for the ethic of equal regard is extensively developed in the introduction and chapters 4, 5, and 10 of *From Culture Wars to Common Ground.* Chapter 8 also gives a discussion of the concept of subsidiarity and demonstrates how both American Roman Catholicism, the thought of evangelical Ralph Reed, and the social philosophy of Senator Daniel Patrick Moynihan all have been influenced by this idea.

3. William Doherty, *The Intentional Family* (New York: Addison-Wesley, 1997).

4. As reported by Judge James Sheridan and Michael McManus at the "Smart Marriages: Happy Families" conference on July 10, 1997, Washington, D.C.

5. James Coleman, "Schools, Families, and Children" (Ryerson Lecture, University of Chicago, 1985), 9-18.

6. Ibid., 18.

7. Dan Coats, "Can Congress Revive Civil Society?" *Policy Review* (January–February 1996): 27.

8. Michael McManus, *Marriage Savers: Helping Your Friends and Family Stay Married* (Grand Rapids, Mich.: Zondervan, 1993), 131.

9. Ibid., 267.

10. Norval Glenn, "The Textbook Story of American Marriages and Families," Publication No. W.P. 46 (New York: Institute for American Values, May 1996).

11. Linda Waite, "Does Marriage Matter?" *Demography* 32, no. 4 (November 1995): 483-504.

12. One of the best videos for high school education for marriage and family is prepared and distributed by the American Bar Association. It brings legal perspectives on marriage together with insights from the new psychoeducation movement. See *Partners: An Interactive Televised Course* (Chicago: ABA Family Law Section, 1996).

13. Few careful studies of the values clarification approach to sex education show it to be successful. This is an approach in which teachers take no stand on moral issues. Decisions are left to students about how to use information. See Barbara Dafoe Whitehead, "The Failure of Sex Education," *Atlantic Monthly,* October 1994, 55-80.

14. For information on PREPARE, write PREPARE/ENRICH, P.O. Box 190, Minneapolis, Minnesota 55440-0190; and on PREP, write Professor Howard Markman, PREP, Inc., 1780 South Bellaire Street, Suite 621, Denver, Colorado 80222.

15. Paul Numrich, "A Pentecostal Megachurch on the Edge," in *Congregations and Family Ministry,* eds. Bernie Lyon and Archie Smith (Louisville, Ky.: Westminster/Knox, 1997).

16. Rosemary Barciauskas and Debra Hull, *Loving and Working: Reweaving Women's Public Lives* (Bloomington: Indiana University Press, 1989).

17. Rosalind Barnett and Caryl Rivers, *She Works/He Works: How Two-Income Families Are Happier, Healthier, and Better Off* (New York: HarperCollins, 1996).

18. William Doherty, *Soul Searching* (New York: Basic Books, 1995), 33. See also Don Browning, *The Moral Context of Pastoral Counseling* (Philadelphia: Westminster, 1976), and Bonnie Miller-McLemore, "Will the Real Pro-Family Contestant Please Stand Up? Another Look at Families and Pastoral Care," *Journal of Pastoral Care* 49, no. 4 (Spring 1995): 61-68.

19. Michelle Weiner-Davis, *Divorce Busting* (New York: Simon & Schuster, 1995).

20. Paul Amato and Alan Booth, *A Generation at Risk: Growing Up in an Era of Family Upheaval* (Cambridge, Mass.: Harvard University Press, 1997), 220.

21. The Willow Creek Community Church, a megachurch in the northern suburbs of Chicago, is an example of a church with a strong marriage culture that promotes intact families but also has a wide range of services for the divorced, single parents, stepfamilies, and singles.

22. *Free to Be Family* (Washington, D.C.: Family Research Council, 1992), 35.

23. *Beyond Rhetoric: Report of the National Commission on Families* (Washington, D.C.: U.S. Government Printing Office, 1991), xxi.

24. William Mattox, "Government Tax Policy and the Family," paper presented at "The Family, Civil Society, and the State," a conference sponsored by the American Public Philosophy Institute, June 21–22, 1996, Washington, D.C.

25. *Free to Be Family,* 34-43; Nick Rave, "Married Couples Feel Jilted by Uncle Sam," *Chicago Tribune,* March 17, 1995, C6.

26. John DiIulio, "Government Welfare to Support Families—the Right Way," paper presented at "The Family, Civil Society, and the State," a conference sponsored by the American Public Philosophy Institute, June 21–22, 1996, Washington, D.C.

27. Proposals for part-time work for welfare single parents have been advanced by David Ellwood, *Poor Support: Poverty in the American Family* (New York: Basic Books, 1988), 135-37; and Pamela Couture, *Blessed Are the Poor* (Nashville, Tenn.: Abingdon, 1991), 178-184.

28. Benjamin Kline Hunnicutt, *Kellogg's Six-Hour Day* (Philadelphia: Temple University Press, 1996).

29. Alison Mitchell, "Clinton Prods Executives to 'Do the Right Thing,'" *New York Times,* May 17, 1996, C 4; Alison Mitchell, "Banking on Family Issues, Clinton Seeks Parents' Votes," *New York Times,* June 25, 1996, C19.

30. Margaret Andrews, "Developing a National Strategy of Marriage and Family Education," address given to the International Conference on the Family, University of Melbourne, July 1994; see also "Moving Counseling to Community Agencies," *Threshold: A Magazine about Marriage Education* 49 (December 1995):3.

31. Brochure provided by the National Institute for Responsible Fatherhood and Family Development, 2. To contact, write the National Institute for Responsible Fatherhood and Family Development, 8555 Hough Avenue, Cleveland, Ohio 44106-1545.

32. Taken from a brochure titled "Creating a Father-Friendly Neighborhood: 10 Things You Can Do" (Lancaster, Pa.: National Fatherhood Initiative).

33. For information, write the National Center for Fathering, P.O. Box 413888, Kansas City, Missouri 64141.

34. Quoted from Richard Gill and Brandon Gill, "A Parental Bill of Rights," *Family Affairs* 6, no. 1-2 (Winter 1994): 1.

35. These suggestions were, to my knowledge, first put forth by Mary Ann Glendon, *Abortion and Divorce in Western Law* (Cambridge, Mass.: Harvard University Press, 1987), 93-95. Later they were affirmed by Elaine Ciulla Kamarck and William Galston, *Putting Children First: A Progressive Family Policy for the 1990s* (Washington, D.C.: Progressive Policy Institute, 1991), 30.

36. Michael Medved, *Hollywood vs. America: Popular Culture and the War on Traditional Values* (New York: HarperCollins, 1992).

37. Kay S. Hymowitz, "'I Don't Know Where This Is Going': What Teenagers Learn about Marriage from Television and Magazines," Council on Families in America Working Paper (New York: Institute of American Values, 1995).

38. An excellent program sponsored by Family and Community Critical Viewing Project is unfortunately limited to violence. See *Taking Charge of Your TV: A Guide to Critical Viewing for Parent and Children.* For this pamphlet and information on an extensive list of resources, write Family and Community Critical Viewing Project, 1724 Massachusetts Avenue, N.W., Washington, D.C. 20036-1969.

39. Roger Cardinal Mahoney, *Film Makers, Film Viewers: Their Challenges and Opportunities* (Boston: Daughters of St. Paul, 1992).

40. Mark Caro and Steve Johnson, "Foes of New TV Ratings Worry about 'Forbidden Fruit' Factor," *Chicago Tribune,* December 23, 1996, A1, A4; Richard Morin, "Confronting Sex and Violence on TV," *Washington Post National Weekly Edition,* December 23, 1996, 38.

8

Turning the Hearts of Parents to Children: A Mother's Meditation on the Role of the Church

Enola G. Aird

It was a Sunday morning, and our family had gotten up a bit later than usual to get ready for church. We were not late yet. But if we didn't hurry, we were going to be. My gentle proddings of the children and my husband to move things along were not getting us out the door quickly enough.

After repeated reminders to pick up the pace, I began to raise my voice. "Why," I cried, "can't you children get up, shower, eat, and get yourselves dressed and ready quickly without my yelling at you?" "And why"—I turned to my husband, Stephen, my decibel level increasing—"can't *you* be more helpful?" And on I went, making our time of preparing for worship most unpleasant.

As is too often the case, Stephen and I had to rush off after church to different places, so we had to drive separate cars. Not surprisingly, the children chose to ride with their dad.

As I made my lonely way to church, hurrying so that I would make it in time to ask my family's forgiveness before the service began, I reflected on the irony of losing my temper in my zeal to get us to our house of worship.

And I reflected anew on questions that had been on my mind for some time. As a member of the Episcopal Church, I wanted to know what my church and other churches were doing to offer concrete help to mothers and fathers as they struggle day in and day out to deal with the small and large stresses of raising their children. Are churches equipping parents to build strong and healthy relationships with their children in the face of the intensifying forces pulling families apart? What more could churches be doing to help parents meet the challenges of raising moral and spiritually grounded children in this relentlessly individualistic and materialistic culture?

IN SEARCH OF CHURCH-BASED HOME BUILDERS

I had set out months before to find some answers to these questions, and the events of my hurried life on that Sunday—and on the many other days on which I have not acted toward my family in keeping with the faith that I profess—made the project all the more urgent.

Looking back, I realize that my pleas were being met with the natural resistance that comes from bodies, minds, and spirits exhausted from a week of getting up before the sun, rushing off to work and school from one activity to another—classes, sports, music lessons, Cub Scouts, horseback riding, choir rehearsals, homework—not to mention the endless rounds of meetings and phone calls and hours in front of the computer. But that Sunday, I was focusing only on getting us up and out to church.

Pressures on parents have increased dramatically in recent years. The challenges of earning a living in our competitive times, a growing emphasis in our culture on the values of the market over spiritual values, and the chaos of our busy lives have all conspired to leave parents with relatively little time, energy, and patience to spend with their children, and even less time to preserve and pass on vital family stories, rituals, and traditions. Parents face stiff competition from television and other formidable new technologies in carrying out the primary mission of parenting: teaching values to shape their children's morality.

The church is in a unique position to help parents meet the moral challenges of raising children today. The basic work of the church is to help people live lives in accordance with the requirements of their faith. Most are connected to religious institutions, and one of the most common reasons young adults return to faith communities after dropping out is for the sake of their children.[1]

How are churches responding to parents' growing needs for help in guiding and strengthening their relationships with their children? The answer is that churches are doing more than might be expected—but less than they could and should be doing. In particular, church leaders in the mainline Protestant churches do not have the same passion for and commitment to these matters that they have for the more politically charged issues in the church today.

This chapter recounts highlights of what I have found so far in my search for promising responses by churches to the needs of parents and families. It is not intended to be an exhaustive study. It is, in part, a series of reflections from a mother in the pews, sharing some of what I have been able to learn about encouraging developments in the church for parents and the vocation of parenting. It is also a mother's plea to the leaders of the mainline Protestant church to turn more intentionally and aggressively to the task of helping parents to build strong families. Finally, it is a call to mothers and fathers in the church to join in the work of helping shape a renewed vision of the spirituality of the family and to press for the changes in the mainline churches that will help bring that vision to life.

A NOTE ABOUT HEADLINES

If you just get your news from the daily papers, you would probably think that the major family issues facing the mainline Protestant churches have to do with sex. News reports about the recent national conventions of major Protestant denominations have focused primarily on the churches' deliberations and debates about matters of sexual morality.

High on the meeting agendas of the annual national conventions of Presbyterians, the United Church of Christ, and Episcopalians, for example, have been such issues as the blessing of same-sex unions, the ordination of homosexuals, and the sexual standards to be applied to heterosexual clergy. These are the convention topics that have made the headlines.[2]

The vocations of parenting and family building have not been highly visible on the agendas of these churches. For example, when the leaders of the Episcopal Church met in national convention in July 1997, they adopted a Children's Charter that lays out a new vision for ministry to children, with profound implications for ministry to parents and families as well. Yet, when the headlines were written, it was the convention's actions with respect to sexual matters, not the church's initiatives on children and families, that led the news.

Why the news of the Children's Charter did not lead the headlines is a question not only for the popular media but for the church as well. This one-sided impression of the mainline church's family ministry is due in part to the media's preoccupation with sex, but it also points to the need for the mainline church itself to be more intentional in reaching out to parents and to the broader community to make it resoundingly clear that the concerns of parents are, in fact, vital concerns for the church. Most important, parents need to be prime movers in the effort to make parenting and family life top priorities within the mainline church.

PROMISING SIGNS

Unfortunately, there is something to the one-sided press reports. The mainline denominations have been preoccupied by a narrow, controversial slice of family-related issues, leaving parenting and other family-building matters relatively low on the list of priorities.

Still, there are encouraging signs,[3] and I want to highlight a few initiatives that offer hope for mothers and fathers who want the church to play a more active role in helping them carry out their parental and family obligations.

To Be Seen, Heard, and Nurtured: Children and Parents in the Episcopal Church

The Children's Charter of the Episcopal Church speaks in eloquent terms of the church's mandate to nurture and minister to children and to develop children's capacities to minister. The charter calls on the church to:

> receive, nurture and treasure each child as a gift from God . . . to give high priority to the quality of planning for children and the preparation and support of those who minister with them . . . to nurture and support families in the caring for their children, acting in their children's best interest, and recognizing and fostering their children's spirituality and unique gifts . . . and to foster community beyond the family unit, in which children, youth and adults know each other by name, minister to each other, and are partners together in serving Christ in the world.[4]

In adopting the charter, the Episcopal Church acknowledged that by adhering to a "seen and not heard" attitude toward children, it had for too long excluded children from full participation in the life of the church. It admitted its failure to include children in key aspects of church life, urging all Episcopal congregations across the country to "respond to Christ's mandate to care for and respect all children."[5]

All dioceses of the church are being urged to study and adopt the Children's Charter as a guide to developing new ministries to children. Study guides and resource materials have been developed and disseminated to diocesan offices in the church, and the process of sharing the Charter with local congregations has begun. An October 1998 national conference on implementing the charter brought together more than four hundred Christian educators to share strategies for implementing the charter. Much of the conference focused on the important work of including children fully in the worship and congregational life of the church and on outreach to, and advocacy of, children in need. The idea is to give children in the church equal rights to participate in all aspects of church life and in the governance in the church.

Although the Children's Charter is a long way from full implementation, it issues an important invitation to members of the church to see children in their proper light—as treasures from God who come to us bearing their own unique gifts and talents and who are entitled to our care, support, and nurture.

By urging members of the church to go against the tide of the popular culture in which children and youth and adults are growing further and further apart to forge new bonds with the children in our homes, in our neighborhoods, and in our churches, the charter makes progress.

Even though the charter calls on the church "to nurture and support families in caring for their children," few Episcopal churches have so far used the charter as a springboard for launching parent and family support ministries.[6]

The charter nevertheless opens the door to possibilities for a deeper ministry to parents and families. A *Charter Study Guide* adds substance to the call to the church to "nurture and support families" by urging congregations to consider what assistance parents, godparents, and members of the church require to keep the promises they make at the moment of baptism, when they vow to "be responsible for seeing that the child is brought up in the Christian faith and life," "to help the child grow into the full stature of Christ," and to "do all in [their] power to support the [newly-baptized] in their life in Christ."[7]

Implementation of the charter in the congregations of the church will require profound changes, because churches will have to look carefully at all that they do with respect to children and their families to ensure that they are living congregational lives in the full spirit of the charter.

For one thing, churches will need to work harder to make baptism more than just a celebratory event. Too many children are baptized after a perfunctory preparation, and, too often, neither they nor their parents are seen again after the big day. The charter should remind us that baptism is in fact just the beginning of a lifelong relationship of nurture between the baptized child and his or her parents, the godparents, and the community of faith into which the child is baptized. This renewed vision of a lifelong relationship with the child and family begun at baptism means that the church must necessarily find creative ways to nurture and strengthen the relationship between parents and children on a continuing basis through concrete parent and family support ministries.

It remains to be seen whether the Children's Charter will actually be implemented in a majority of congregations within the Episcopal Church. Nevertheless, it holds promise as a vehicle for mothers and fathers in the church to work to expand the church's ministry to those engaged in the vocations of parenting and family building.

THE "FAMILY PERSPECTIVE" IN THE ROMAN CATHOLIC CHURCH

The United States Conference of Catholic Bishops, writing in a 1993 *Pastoral Message to Families*, declared:

> What you do in your family to create a community of love, to help each other grow, to serve those in need is critical, not only for your own sanctification but for the strength of society and our church. It is a participation in the work of the Lord, a shar-

ing in the mission of the church. It is holy. . . . As Christian families, you not only belong to the church, but your daily life is a true expression of the church. . . . We need to enable families to recognize that they are a domestic church.[8]

The Catholic Church, responding to the call of Pope John Paul II to families to be "churches in miniature," has for many years been working to give new meaning to the concept of the domestic church or the "church of the home" by introducing into all levels of the church a "family perspective."

This "family perspective" contemplates a paradigm shift in which all programs of the church are reviewed to assess their impact on families and in which the primary focus is on the development of ministries and missions that ease the burdens on families and help lift up parents, children, and elders in the living out of their vocations within the context of family life. A central goal is to help parents come to see their daily work as vocation and themselves as ministers.

In its pastoral message, the National Conference of Catholic Bishops reminded the families of the church that the family is "our first community and most basic way in which the Lord gathers us, forms us, and acts in the world."[9] The bishops described how the early church expressed this reality by referring to the Christian family as the "church of the home." The message urged today's clergy to work with parents to recover a sense of the sacred in their everyday lives—and thus end the disconnect that all too often exists between what is taught in the institutional church and what is done in day-to-day, rough-and-tumble family life.

The bishops acknowledged that "official structures [within the church] sometimes make it difficult to have dialogue with families,"[10] and they urged diocesan agencies to create ways for families to communicate with church leaders about their concerns and needs. They also directed dioceses to see that the institutions of the church examine the extent to which their policies and programs help or hinder family growth and to work to change those policies that "make it difficult for families to assume their rightful place as a church of the home."

The National Conference of Bishops, in partnership with the National Association of Family Life Ministers (NAFLM), has developed a wealth of resources designed to promote the family perspective in Catholic parishes across the country. NAFLM has prepared guides for preaching with families in mind to help homilists apply scriptural references to concrete family joys and challenges. It has published a variety of manuals on how to minister from a family perspective, serving as a clearinghouse for information on a wide range of models and strategies for advancing the idea of the domestic church.[11]

Even with all the theological and practical work that has been done in the Catholic Church to promote the idea of the church of home, progress has been slow. Writing in 1995, Gerald Foley, author of *Family Centered Church: A New Parish Model*, said that "the U.S. bishops declared 1980–90 as the decade of the family, when all other church ministries were to take a back seat to family ministry, a commitment they renewed for the decade of the 1990s. The response was discouraging. . . . [T]he silence in most parishes has been astounding."[12]

Nevertheless, many churches have responded to the call and have begun to make some changes that can turn theories into realities. For example, the Ministry of Moms Sharing (MOMS)[13] is a mother's ministry created by Sister Paula Hagen, O.S.B., in 1986, with groups in twenty-six states and in Ecuador. The MOMS program seeks to equip mothers to discover a sense of the sacred in their daily life and work. MOMS leads mothers "through an experience of peer ministry, self-discovery, mutual support, and prayer" to help them appreciate and live out their calling to the vocation of motherhood. Through MOMS, mothers learn that they are engaged in a vital ministry—that of shaping the bodies, minds, and spirits of God's most precious gift: the gift of children. Working together, mothers learn how to develop family practices and traditions that reveal the holiness of their daily lives—even in the midst of the dirty laundry, the shrieking children, the surprises and disappointments that each day brings.

At Holy Spirit Church in Louisville, Kentucky,[14] the focus is on helping mothers see that there is a blessedness in their family stories—no matter how imperfect and complicated they may be. The church helps families create rituals that sanctify their daily activities. Whether it be a service of blessing for an expectant couple, the blessing of a new home, services of welcome for families new to the church or departing families, birthdays, anniversaries, or special family occasions, large or small, the church seeks to be present to the family to help lift them up as they carry out their vocations in the home and in family life. Days are set aside to honor parents, children, grandparents, and other extended family members. The church sponsors support groups through which mothers and fathers identify family needs and, with the church, fashion appropriate pastoral responses. Family activities in church always include child care and food is always served. A parish nurse makes regular visits to the homes of parishioners with new babies, to the sick and shut-in, and the elderly. The church issues regular bulletins with creative ideas on how families can use their time together to build up their home churches.

In New Orleans, a Diocesan Family Life Office has taken the lead in promoting "family friendliness" in the diocese.[15] Parish life committees have been convened to review church programs and schedules in light of the family perspective—assuming that a central goal of the church is to serve and support the home church and not the other way around.

As one example, through a program called Elizabeth Ministries, several parishes in the diocese offer support to the families of newly baptized children from the time of baptism through preschool, with frequent communications sent to the home, regular calls, and drop-in visits.

The family perspective is taking hold slowly in diverse parishes of the Catholic Church, providing valuable models for other churches seeking to provide nurture and support to help build the church of the home.

"Caring Couples": One Form of Nurture and Support in the United Methodist Church

Imagine a church with a family ministry that includes a serious effort to re-create the vital extended family supports that existed before families in the United States became so highly mobile and fragmented. The Caring Couples Network is a relatively new, but important, part of the United Methodist Church's efforts to build up the domestic church.[16]

The Caring Couples Network offers an innovative and inspiring model for nurturing couples and families. Through the network, a local church creates a circle of care and support around a couple and family, providing friendship, fellowship, and opportunities to share life experiences and wisdom.

The Caring Couples Network combines "mentoring couples" with training and skill development and networking with community agencies and professional consultants to provide a package of what might best be described as family-building resources to "partner couples." "Caring Couples" are couples who have been married long enough to have had their marriages tested, who are committed to Christian values and to growing in their own marriages, and who are willing to share their experiences with other couples and families. The Caring Couples serve as mentors to younger, less experienced couples.

Each Caring Couples ministry is tailored specifically to the needs of the community in which it does its work. After completing their training, the Caring Couples ascertain the needs of the other couples they are to serve and develop the mix of resources that in their view best responds to the needs of those they are mentoring.

The Caring Couples team consists of couples, consultants (who work in various human service disciplines in the community), and the pastor. The mission of the Caring Couple is to pray with, be supportive of, and nurture the younger couple or family. The consultant's task is to link the members of the network to the broader resources of the community, to provide and arrange access to appropriate training for developing skills in the couples and families (choosing from the array of available resources now in the field to build skills and strengthen relationships within families), and to make referrals, when necessary. The pastor identifies, recruits, encourages, and supports Caring Couples, helps identify those who will be mentored, facilitates links between the parish and the community, and supports the caring couples ministry through preaching, teaching, and other aspects of parish life.

The focus of the network is on couples, but for couples with children, the whole family may benefit. As the *Caring Couples Handbook* makes clear:

> The purpose of the network is to encourage the health of marriages in order to maintain the quality of living for spouses and children. . . . The spousal relationship directly impacts the health of all relationships in the family. . . . Committed Christian couples shape family values and provide real-life examples that demonstrate God's intentions for families.[17]

So, in addition to offering support to young couples and help to couples in crisis, Caring Couples can offer continuing fellowship and nurture to couples with children of all ages—from the birth of children through the birth of grandchildren.

One of the key features of the Caring Couples ministry is its flexibility and adaptability.

> The primary emphasis of the Caring Couples Network is on strengthening engaged and married couples, but other family situations are also of concern to the network. Post-marriage situations result from the death of a spouse or divorce. There are also situations that might be termed quasi-marriage, such as couples living together with no intention of getting married. The Caring Couples Network may want to consider these situations as part of its ministry.[18]

A church may, therefore, choose to use the Caring Couples ministry to reach out to and "evangelize" nonmarried couples. In this way, the church can help provide much-needed guidance, support, and parenting wisdom and show compassion and love to unmarried and single parents in the congregation, while at the same time holding up a vision of marriage as the preferred and morally right relationship for expressing love between a man and a woman and for raising children.

Promoting Family Strength: The Church of Jesus Christ of Latter-day Saints

I dialed the 800 number listed on the back of a booklet entitled *Family First*, prepared and distributed by the Church of Jesus Christ of Latter-day Saints. Within twelve hours, I received a call from a missionary and within four days I received a personal visit from three members of the church.

The church is well known for its creative, thought-provoking public service advertisements promoting the importance of family and healthy family living. The advertisements are a small part of a comprehensive family ministry within the church that includes a very efficient rapid response network for people who want to know more about how they can strengthen their family lives.

In 1995, the First Presidency and Council of the Twelve Apostles of the Church of Jesus Christ of Latter-day Saints issued a "Proclamation to the World" on the subject of family. This document set forth the church's view on marriage and family life, declaring that "husband and wife have a solemn responsibility to love and care for each other." It further stated:

> Parents have a sacred duty to rear their children in love and righteousness, to provide for their physical and spiritual needs, to teach them to love and serve one another, to observe the commandments of God and to be law-abiding citizens wherever they live. . . . Husbands and wives—mothers and fathers—will be held accountable before God for the discharge of these obligations.

This powerful commitment to family grows out of the strongly held belief that families are eternal. As one of the members who came to visit me put it, "Married couples are married and families are sealed to each other in covenant 'for time and all eternity.' That is why we work so hard to build strong families."

In the Church of Jesus Christ of Latter-Day Saints, parents bear the primary responsibility for nurturing the faith of their children and for teaching them how to live in accordance with their faith. The institutional church exists to support the family in its growth and development. Church services and Sunday school place a great emphasis on sharing lessons about parenting and family communication and teaching the faithful how to use the principles of Christian living to build stronger family relationships. Home teachers, members who are given responsibility for ministering to a small group of families, make monthly home visits to teach and to attend to the pastoral needs of the families in their charge. The church also provides a variety of social service ministries to address special needs of families in the church.

The Proclamation on the Family and church teaching is supported and supplemented by a variety of written and video resources and materials made available to members of the church and the public at large under the heading of "Family First" and "Family Answers." These resources are designed to help families build lives based on "unity and love" and encourage families to conduct weekly Family Home Evenings, special times set aside for families to come together for study, prayer, and reflection on different aspects of family life.

A "Family Home Resource Book" is available to help families plan their time together and to learn what the church considers to be vital family-building lessons about faith, living and growing as a family, loving and reaching out to neighbors, and celebrating special family occasions. Representatives of the church are on call to help families as they work to implement the suggestions included in the Family Home Evening Resource Book and related materials.

The Church of Jesus Christ of Latter-day Saints, through its public service advertisement ministry and its Proclamation to the World, has issued an important challenge to churches in the United States to attend to the needs of the families in their pews. Reading the proclamation, Gordon B. Hinckley, the president of the church, said, "[W]e warn that the disintegration of the family will bring upon individuals, communities, and nations the calamities pretold by ancient and modern prophets."[19]

At the start of a new century, mainline Protestant churches, especially, would be well-advised to articulate their own time-honored values about family and to engage the parents and families of their churches in a sustained dialogue and outreach to strengthen their families.

REVIVING THE CHURCH OF THE HOME: RENEWED PURPOSE AND STRENGTH FOR FAMILIES

None of the programs described in this chapter gives a perfect answer to the questions that I posed at the outset. But each one gives me hope that we may be on the verge of a radical redefinition of what it means to be a church, a redefinition that will, in turn, breathe new life into what it means to be a mother, a father, a child, and a family.

Marjorie J. Thompson, a Presbyterian minister, has written:

There is a misperception all too common in the church that real spirituality is the purview of monks, ministers, and missionaries. Culturally, we are in the habit of separating the sacred from the secular—an indication, no doubt, of the extent to which we have segregated God from the mainstream of ordinary life. What, after all, makes something sacred? Simply that it is set apart to honor God, or is recognized as revealing the divine nature. God's presence makes all things, including time and space, holy; and God is present always, everywhere. All of life is holy when we recognize God's presence in it. Even the most commonplace moments of ordinary existence can be celebrated as sacred. . . . Holiness is not an antiseptic state of isolation from the ordinary world. It is absolutely practical and concrete. Holy people are immersed in the dirt and sweat of real life where light and darkness contend with real consequences, for that is where God is at work.[20]

The notion of the domestic church finds expression not only in the Catholic Church but among Protestant denominations as well. It is a concept as old as the church itself. The household church, so much a part of Jewish tradition, helped give form to the early Christian church. The earliest church gatherings for prayer and worship took place in the homes of believers.

The idea of the home as a place of prayer, worship, spirituality, and faith formation is a vital part of our Judeo-Christian heritage. Yet, according to Dr. Joseph Leonard of the Office of Family Ministries at the National Conference of Churches, the idea of the domestic church is still a "flickering vision" for much of the contemporary Protestant community.

I embarked on this project with a modest goal. I wanted to identify good parenting and family-building programs and resources for churches. I have come to the conclusion, however, that the answer for parents and families in the mainline denominations does not lie in having the church provide more programs. Although they can help, these programs need to be a part of something much grander in scope and scale.

That grander vision lies with the church helping parents and children and families rediscover the sacredness of family relationships and family life. In this vision, the institutional church does more than provide supportive programs for families. It lifts up families and helps them realize a vision of family life as a holy life and a vision of family members as engaged in sacred vocations.

What a difference it makes to think of families as engaged in a sacred vocation and the home as a domestic church. This vision carries the potential to change the way mothers and fathers and sisters and brothers who profess the Christian faith actually treat one another each day.

If we see ourselves as being in a sacred place and space in our homes and in our relationships with the members of our family, then our daily interactions must necessarily change. If we truly believe these things, then we will work harder to treat each other with a greater degree of reverence, respect, love, and care.

This is the point I missed on that fateful Sunday when I yelled at my family for being too slow in preparing for church. It would not have occurred to me to raise my voice at my children and my husband in the church sanctuary, no matter how hurried I felt. So the idea of home as church and parenting as holy work holds great promise for changing for the better the way those of us who profess to be Christians run our families.

Changing for the better, of course, is easier said than done. But it is surely the church's job to help believers live out on Mondays through Saturdays the beliefs that we profess on Sundays.

I never felt the presence of God more strongly in my life than when I gave birth to my two children. Those early days were filled with joy and wonder. I understood intuitively the sacred bond between a mother and child, between parents and children. As time has passed and the pressures of getting through each day have grown, I have often lost sight of the sacred nature of my relationship with my family. This is where I believe that the church can be of the greatest help to me and to my fellow mothers and fathers in the pews.

Far too many Christians have lost a sense of the sacredness and spirituality of everyday life. The central challenge for the church today as life becomes more and more chaotic for families is to help its people realize anew that church is where the people are, not where the building is—that ordinary, everyday family life is holy. It is time for the mainline church to breathe new life into the idea of the "church of the home."

The call to raise up the domestic church represents a fundamental challenge to today's institutional church. It demands that the church make revolutionary changes in many of its ways of doing business. In particular, it demands that the church discard its building-centered view in favor of a family-centered view, helping us focus on the blessedness of everyday family life with all of its sloppiness, frustrations, challenges, pains, and joys. It demands that the clergy recognize and affirm and equip parents and family members as genuine ministers of the church. And, in the greatest of all challenges to the church in the United States, it demands that the church reverse its lurch toward an increasing emphasis on the individualism that characterizes the larger culture and that represents the greatest threat to reclaiming the tradition of the family as domestic church.

And here parents and families have a revolutionary role to play. As Gerald Foley has put it:

> They can call us away from our attention to the individual leading us to a greater awareness of relationship-building and intimacy. In our world of independence and autonomy, a sense of the family as an interrelated system reminds us of the futility of ministering pastorally to individuals. In a church which stumbles over social justice awareness, families with a sense of mission teach us greater concern for all our

brothers and sisters. For a church long suspicious of experiential knowledge, emphasizing truths learned instead from theologians, families remind us that God is present in and through our unpredictable relationships with one another.[21]

The notion of home as church calls on parents and families to assume responsibilities that are at once empowering and frightening. It means that parents who are part of the Christian community have to answer tough questions about how we are spending our time and energy (often on work instead of home). We have to decide for ourselves which we really value more—material or spiritual things? We have to assess whether we are really teaching our children the difference between right and wrong—as judged by our actions, not our words. We have to choose whether we want our families to be collections of unconnected individuals seeking to fulfill their own personal desires or family members seeking to fulfill their responsibilities to one another.

Tough questions, yes. But no one in the mainline church can see more clearly than parents the need for looking at our daily lives and our relationships with those in our family in a whole new way. The church can help, but it will not do so without the informed and persistent prodding of those of us in the pews.

What more can the church do to help? Elizabeth Barrett Browning wrote, "Earth's crammed with heaven, every common bush afire with God; but only he who sees, takes off his shoes." The church can summon all its passion to help us see that Earth is, indeed, crammed with heaven, and it can bend all its efforts to helping us live that way each day. The church can do this only if it makes this issue as important as the more politically charged issues that have, until now, been preoccupying it.

POSTSCRIPT: "AS FOR ME AND MY HOUSE . . ."

Sunday mornings at our house are not as hectic as they used to be. We are making some progress on weekdays, too. Inspired by what we have learned about the "domestic church" and the notion of "ordinary holiness," our family has embarked on a new adventure. We have constituted ourselves as a "home church" and are eagerly pursuing our new vocations. We try to take that vision of family as church with us everywhere we go, from our waking up to our lying down. It has tended to slow us down just a little bit, and it has made us set aside more time to be together—for prayer and reflection on the subject of family.

As I know my children can attest, our new perspective does not make us anywhere near perfect or any better than any other family. But it has given us a profound sense of gratitude. It has made it harder for us to take things—even little things— for granted. Paul Hogan, the Australian actor, once said in an interview that Americans treat life as though it is a dress rehearsal for something else. Trying to see ourselves as a church has made our family less inclined to treat our lives as dress rehearsals and more inclined to treat each day as though it really matters.

NOTES

1. Eugene C. Roehlkepartain and Peter C. Scales, *Youth Development in Congregations: An Exploration of the Potential and Barriers* (Minneapolis: Search Institute, 1995), 57.

2. See, for example, Kenneth L. Woodward, "Sex, Morality, and the Protestant Minister," *Newsweek*, July 28, 1997; Kenneth L. Woodward and Anne Underwood, "A House Divided," *Newsweek*, July 14, 1997.

3. The last five years have seen a dramatic increase in the number and variety of publications and resource materials focused on parenting and family development and intended for use by churches. A growing number of churches are offering parenting and family relationship courses that help strengthen communication skills, share stress management strategies, and offer other helpful tools for building stronger families. Among the many resources now at the churches' disposal are these:

- *Active Christian Parenting: Practical Skills for the Preschool to Preteen Years* offers practical parenting skills and helps parents make stronger connections between their faith and the everyday work of parenting, based on *Active Parenting* by Michael Popkin (1995); write Augsburg Fortress, Box 1209, Minneapolis, Minnesota 55440; or call (800) 328-4648.
- *Building Shalom Families for the 1990s and Beyond*, by Wendy Nortup with James and Kathleen McGinnis (1994), a six-session program offered for parents by the Parenting for Peace and Justice Network, focuses on communication and conflict resolution, family meetings, promoting stewardship instead of consumerism within the family, celebrating diversity, and bringing peace into a violent world. Contact Institute for Peace and Justice, 4144 Lindell Blvd., St. Louis, Missouri 63108; (314) 533-4445. See also *Building Shalom Families: Christian Parenting for Peace and Justice*, James and Kathleen McGinnis (1986), also from the Institute for Peace and Justice.
- *It Takes More Than Love*, by Dick Hardel and Roland Martinson, a project of Lutheran Social Service Ministries, helps parents identify their family's assets, approach parenting from a value-centered perspective, and nurture children and prepare them to enter the larger community. Call the Augsburg Youth and Family Institute, (612) 330-1624.
- *Stones of Promise: Celebrating the African American Family*, by Joseph Crockett, Carolyn Johnson, Barry Scott, and Mary Love (1972), offers a way for families to work intergenerationally to understand their past and present as a way of building for the future. The program provides a vehicle for members of families to talk about their family history, heal old wounds, and covenant about how they will live their lives together going forward. Cokesbury Video, Nashville, Tennessee, 1993.
- *The Family Wellness Program*, by Virginia Morgan Scott and George Doub, helps parents and children learn together about the challenges of building a healthy family and provides coaching in the skills that can improve relationships within the family. The program aims to teach families about healthy patterns and the skills necessary to maintain those patterns from day to day. The basic Family Wellness workshop consists of

six two-hour family sessions that deal with parenting as leadership, defining children's roles in the family, describing adult relationships, handling change and stress, problem solving, and passing on values to children. Through the program, families—parents and children—are quite intentionally brought together to talk about the central purpose of family: to help every person in the family be his or her own person, but at the same time live cooperatively with others in the family. Family members learn and talk about the basic skills needed to fulfill that purpose: speaking up, listening, negotiating. And, most important, family members engage in role plays (switching sides at times) to strengthen these skills. The Family Wellness experience helps parents and children build the family team by establishing shared understandings and heightening their sense of family mission. Contact Family Wellness Associates, P.O. Box 7869, Santa Cruz, California 95061.

4. A Children's Charter for the Episcopal Church, Resolution 1997-B005, Adopted by the 72nd General Convention of the Episcopal Church, 1997.

5. *An Emerging Study Guide for a Children's Charter for the Church*, Office of Children's Ministries, Rev. Howard K. Williams, 2.

6. The people with whom I talked (Merlyn Byrne, Diocese of Minnesota, and Robb Bruce, Episcopal Church Office of Children's Ministries) could point to only one church that, in responding to the charter's mandate, has expanded its outreach to help support parents in the work of Christian education and formation at home: St. Mary the Virgin Church in San Francisco. Note: Candle Press, at (303) 337-6852, produces a variety of family-focused resources targeted to families within the Episcopal Church.

7. *The Book of Common Prayer,* 302 and 303.

8. Follow the Way of Love: A Pastoral Message of the United States Catholic Bishops to Families on the Occasion of the United Nations 1994 International Year of the Family, National Conference of Bishops, November 17, 1993, 8 (available by calling [800] 235-8722).

9. Ibid., 8.

10. Ibid., 26.

11. See, for example, Kehrwald Leif, ed., *Family Perspective: Workshop Manual for Interministry Teams* (Meridien, Conn.: National Association of Catholic Family Life Ministers, 1991); *Preaching with Families in Focus: Scripture Reflections* (Meridien, Conn.: National Association of Catholic Family Life Ministers, 1997); *Linking Parish and Home: Helpful Hints for Implementing a Family Perspective in Ministry* (Meridien, Conn.: National Association of Catholic Family Life Ministers, 1994).

12. Gerald Foley, *Family-Centered Church: A New Parish Model* (Kansas City, Mo.: Sheed & Ward, 1995).

13. The contact for MOMS is Sister Paula Hagen, (904) 733-1630, ext. 22.

14. The contact at Holy Spirit Church is Michael Hamilton, (502) 893-3982.

15. The contact for the New Orleans Diocese is Paula Stuckart, (504) 861-6248.

16. On the Caring Couples Network, see *Christian-Based Counseling with Couples: Caring Couples Network*, CCN, an audiotape featuring Richard Hunt, 1997 Coalition for Marriage, Family, and Couples Education (CMFCE) Annual Conference, available from the Resource Link, (800) 241-7785. The United Methodist Church, through its Office of Discipleship Resources, provides a wealth of materials designed to advance the concept of the domestic church. Contact Mary Jane Pierce Norton, director, Family Ministries, General Board of Discipleship, P.O. Box Nashville, Tennessee 37202-0840.

17. Richard and Joan Hunt, *Caring Couples Network Handbook* (Nashville: United Methodist Church, Discipleship Resources, 1996), 6.

18. Ibid., 64.

19. The First Presidency and Council of the Twelve Apostles of the Church of Jesus Christ of Latter-Day Saints, "A Proclamation to the World."

20. Marjorie Thompson, *Family: The Forming Center: A Vision of the Role of the Family in Spiritual Formation* (Louisville, Ky.: Westminister/John Knox Press, 1989), 13.

21. Foley, *Family-Centered Church,* 13.

9

A Comprehensive Approach to Removing Marriage Penalties

C. Eugene Steuerle

Sitting in the jury box those few days, I couldn't help but think about how our legal system—taxes, transfers, Census measures—would treat this particular household. The man was suing a company that he claimed entered his premises illegally and seized some goods that belonged to him, his wife, and his daughter. Only it wasn't his premises; it was the apartment of a friend. And not all the goods were his; some belonged to the constant stream of temporary occupants of this household. And he was not formally married, or so claimed his sister, who occasionally lived in the same household. And his daughter was living in another city.

This household is not all that unusual. Each of us today knows many households whose members have permanent or temporary relationships with other adults, whether in dormitories, nursing homes, rental apartments with friends, convents, or homes of parents or children. The Census Bureau tells us that male and female "cohabiting" partners alone have risen to 8 percent of all households, but this is clearly an understatement. A significant share of these households would never report this information to Census, IRS, or any other agency.

The definition of a household is important for more than counting purposes. In particular, U.S. government programs tend to base taxes and transfers on how the "household" or tax unit is defined. Small changes in definition, however, can have large consequences for individuals. In many cases, these tax and transfer systems have been built around stereotypes of the family that ignore the existence of many modern household arrangements and unintentionally provide strong disincentives to marriage and work.[1] In my own research, I have found the following:

- Someone earning annual wages between one-quarter of the minimum wage and three times the minimum wage often faces a combination of explicit and implicit tax rates of 70 percent (e.g., see figure 9.1).[2] Until very recently, these high rates applied mainly to traditional, nonworking, welfare recipients who would both lose welfare benefits (through an implicit tax rate on income) and pay direct taxes on their wages if they worked. Today they apply to a significant portion of those working at moderate wages, although the full social implications probably will not be felt until the system has matured.[3]

- This same set of tax rates imposes very high penalties on marriage—or not divorcing—especially in low- and moderate-income families. What happens is that the tax rate that normally applies to single low- and moderate-income workers—usually ranging from 15 to 30 percent for the combination of Social Security and income taxes—jumps to 70 percent or so when they marry low-income heads of household. Essentially the new married partner's earnings are now added to the measure of household resources when government phases out benefits. People engaged in cohabitation or serial relationships, of course, avoid this large bump up in effective tax rate.

These large marriage penalties reflect the crazy quilt of tax and expenditure policies that directly affect the family.[4] It is a quilt woven with a piece of thread here and a string there; most important, it has no overall pattern or shape. If the reasons for these developments were pernicious, they would probably be easier to deal with, but they are primarily the unintended consequences of what at first appear to be reasonable goals. For example, military and foreign service pensions grant an extra benefit or protection for widows and widowers, a worthwhile goal.

Figure 9.1. Incremental Tax Rate on Additional Earnings (Without Work Expenses) Sample: All AFDC Households

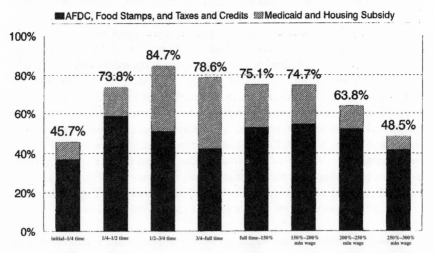

Bars show the proportion of increased earnings that would be lost due to taxes and changes in benefits from the indicated programs over the long-term under 1996 EITC rules. Sample weighted by (household weight) * (change in earnings). *Source:* Linda Giannarelli and C. Eugene Steuerle, "The True Tax Rates Faced by Welfare Recipients," in *National Tax Association, Proceedings of the Eighty-Seventh Annual Conference,* 1995.

To limit costs, however, they often take away the benefit if the widow or widower remarries someone with sufficient earnings. The consequence is a marriage penalty on those who remarry rather than cohabit with a new partner.

The Congressional Budget Office estimates that 26.8 million couples pay additional income tax simply because of marriage (while 21.5 million receive marriage bonuses).[5] But this is only the tip of the iceberg. An extraordinary array of marriage penalties also arise from the high rate at which welfare and other expenditure programs reduce benefits in the presence of a spouse with earnings. Because penalties are built into so many tax and transfer programs, almost every couple is faced with potential rewards from divorce or nonmarriage at some point or another, and many partners with marriage bonuses will one day pay tax penalties if their incomes become more equal.

Warnings are in order: this is not a simple tour, and it requires branching off at times to explain some related policies affecting the family. For example, giving benefits to married couples is sometimes favored as a means of compensating for the costs of raising children, but providing adjustments for children is a much more direct way of achieving that goal.[6] The area is fraught with technical complexity, which is one reason few elected officials understand when or how they are creating marriage penalties. It's not enough simply to be against marriage penalties if one doesn't understand what causes them in the first place. Finally, because of conflict among legitimate principles, this "family" issue breaks down conventional wisdom of what it means to be a liberal or conservative, if such labels have any meaning in this context. Both Democrats and Republicans, left and right, share responsibility for the large historical increase in the size of these penalties.

My own view is that we should make substantial efforts to reduce marriage penalties because they violate traditional notions of fairness, and they weaken the natural tendency to rely on marriage as an institution for mutual support. Furthermore, they tend to subvert citizens' allegiance to a government of laws: those who manipulate taxes and transfers through marriage decisions come to view the law as expressing few values or norms; those who value the law but pay penalties as a consequence come to view it as unfair. I consider this as a special problem in poorer communities where government subsidies for not marrying have become a major source of financial support for the community itself.

Somewhat reluctantly, I also raise the issue of whether marriage for religious purposes should automatically imply marriage for purposes of the state. I say "reluctantly" because the legal support of marriage as a social institution was designed partly to protect spouses. But this was in a world where the state generally encouraged, or was neutral toward, marriage for almost everyone—not in a world where it penalized marriage for substantial portions of the population. I also say "reluctantly" because conflicting principles imply no clear-cut righteous answer, even though a large tax on moral commitment cannot help but have moral implications.

To remove most marriage penalties, as I will demonstrate, requires reconsideration of practically the entire shape of our transfer and tax systems. This tail literally would wag the dog, or, perhaps more precisely, one can't take the tail somewhere without bringing along the whole dog. Independently from my own views, most of this chapter will pull together, for what I believe the first time, a fairly comprehensive analysis of what causes marriage penalties throughout the expenditure and tax systems and the pros and cons of alternative methods to remove or reduce them.

REQUIRED CONDITIONS FOR CREATING MARRIAGE PENALTIES

Now let us turn more precisely to the conditions under which marriage penalties arise. Except for the income tax, which is a special case that will be discussed later, I do not believe that these conditions have been specified elsewhere in the literature. For those considering the reduction or elimination of marriage penalties, a technical understanding of these conditions is crucial if they wish to do more than merely tinker with the transfer and tax system.

Marriage penalties or bonuses will arise in almost any tax or expenditure system meeting the following two conditions: (1) a tax (or subsidy), explicit or implicit, assessed on the basis of household or family resources[7] and (2) different marginal or incremental tax (or subsidy) rates at different levels of resources. *Explicit* taxes are those that derive from quite visible tax rate schedules, as in the income tax. *Implicit* taxes are those that derive from the "phase-out," claw-back, or elimination of some benefit as resources increases. Resources may include income, wealth, or consumption (or even the addition of a new "breadwinner" in the case of some widow's and widower's benefits), but in most programs household income is the base on which the phase-out of benefits is assessed. The *marginal* or *incremental tax rate* refers to the tax imposed on an additional dollar of resources, not the average rate on all resources. The increased cost in taxes of a rise in income, say, from $10,000 to $10,001 is the marginal tax rate.[8]

Some believe that taxing or subsidizing on the basis of the household (condition 1) should involve marriage penalties—imposing higher taxes or fewer benefits on a married couple than on two single individuals with the same combined income as the couple. The argument is that there are economies of scale in households because of shared facilities and goods. One TV may be enough for two people, one person may be able to prepare a meal for two just as easily as for one, and so on. Thus, sharing is a process that adds economic benefit over and above the money income that individuals receive. Through the process of sharing, the household effectively achieves economies of scale in consumption.

One way this plays out is through adherence to providing benefits or taxes according to a "poverty" scale. Because of the way that they were constructed, most poverty scales imply that a couple needs only about one and a half times the income of a single person to avoid poverty. Suppose a program would be designed to cover exactly the cost of poverty. Then if two people married, they would get only three-fourths of the benefits they would receive if they remained as single individuals and cohabited.

If taxes or benefits had no effect on behavior and we were trying to treat all households equally on their ability, then it is correct, technically, that the household sharing goods and services would have greater ability than an equal-size, equal-income grouping of people not sharing. The problem with using this argument to justify marriage penalties is not that there are no economies of scale from sharing. There are, and, indeed, these gains reinforce other natural instincts to engage in mutual support.

Economies of scale, however, apply to almost all sharing arrangements—dormitories, old age homes, movie houses, and cohabitation. Yet, in practice today, marital vows of allegiance are the only type of arrangement that is taxed. At one point welfare programs tried to determine whether there were cohabiting partners, but they have largely abandoned this effort because of the intrusion involved and the difficulty of providing adequate proof.

In those communities where marriage is no longer the norm—and these communities are growing—this natural social incentive to achieve economies of scale in living arrangements does not disappear but merely is converted into forms that avoid the marriage contract. (Recall the household involved in the jury trial noted at the beginning of this chapter.) For example, adult males in marriage-discouraged communities often still live with someone, only now they are more likely than before to stay with their mothers, with other relatives or friends, or in serial relationships rather than with a spouse or with their own children. The tax and transfer systems say that these males deserve significantly lower levels of taxation and higher levels of support than males with equal incomes who marry. If they are fathers, it tells them that they can support their children better by remaining unmarried.

The economies of scale argument can be turned on its head. Since sharing can increase the effective well-being of individuals even with no nominal increase in their nominal income, society might want to subsidize it rather than tax it. A similar efficiency argument lays behind some of the subsidies offered for education and other income-improving activities.

MARRIAGE PENALTIES: A CLASSIC
LIBERAL–CONSERVATIVE COMPROMISE

Marriage penalties are a classic example of the type of liberal–conservative compromise that has dominated policymaking for several decades. The primary (although not only) problem arises in a modern welfare state that attempts to provide a variety of benefits to households but then wants to limit costs by confining eligibility (thereby creating conditions 1 and 2). Note, however, that marriage penalties do not derive from more traditional government programs that provide benefits to the community on a more universal basis, such as defense, primary and secondary education, highways, or even Medicare. These programs may be good or bad, efficient or inefficient, but they do not involve the separating out and labeling of groups by economic status. None of these programs create marriage penalties because the individual gets the same benefits whether married or not.

It is usually through the way in which specific expenditures and taxes are targeted that penalties arise. Liberals, wanting social programs to be as progressive as possible, often try to concentrate whatever benefits are available at the bottom of the income distribution. Conservatives, wanting to limit the cost to government, also want to limit the benefits. Both motives, progressivity and budget containment, are honorable. The compromise usually used to achieve these goals, however, is to phase out benefits quickly as income (or wealth) increases in the household. This effort attempts to achieve "target efficiency" by maximizing help to the poor for the lowest stated expenditure cost.

To tax experts, phase-outs are implicit taxes with almost identical economic effects as explicit taxes.[9] Their effects, however, are often hidden (see box 9.1). The main justification for putting these income phase-outs in expenditure programs rather than a direct tax like the income tax is that with less universal programs, the additional tax is assessed only against the beneficiaries of the program itself. For the most part, however, most government policymakers have little idea of how all these systems combine together.

Since each new expenditure and tax subsidy program tends to have its own unique, built-in phase-out, households in America (and in most developed countries) literally face dozens of tax systems, both big and small, most of which arise out of subsidy programs. The Joint Committee on Taxation recently identified twenty-two provisions in the income tax alone that resulted in a taxpayer's marginal tax rate differing from the statutory tax rate.[10] For example, if I lose $0.50 of a benefit when my income goes up by $1, the effective tax rate from that benefit program alone is 50 percent. Now start to think about all of the multiple programs in the expenditure and direct tax systems that are phased out—welfare, food stamps, housing allowances, earned income tax credits, Medicaid, child credits, educational assistance, personal exemptions, eligibility for participation in individual retirement accounts, exclusion from the minimum tax, and so on. The 1997 tax legislation, small by historic standards, added several new phase-outs all by itself. It is not hard to see why so many households in all income ranges, but especially those with low incomes in welfare programs, face tax rates of 50 percent, 70 percent, or even 100 percent for some of their income.[11]

These high tax rates affect not only extra income earned through work. They affect any income introduced into a benefit-receiving household through marriage. Some examples are presented in table 9.1 and figure 9.2.[12] One of the worst cases involves a low-income single head of household earning about $10,000 a year—exactly the situation to which recent welfare reform encourages heads of

Table 9.1. Marriage Penalty for a Single Mother with Two Children Who Receives Some Public Assistance and Marries a Single Worker

Example 1: Single Mother Not Working and a Single Minimum Wage Worker

	Before Marriage	After Marriage	Marriage Penalty
Earnings	$10,300	$10,300	$0
TANF Benefits	$4,668	$0	$(4,668)
Food Stamps	$3,751	$3,700	$(52)
Medicaid	$4,564	$2,414	$(2,149)
EITC	$0	$3,656	$3,656
Income Tax	$(525)	$0	$525
Social Security Tax	$(788)	$(788)	$0
Total Income*	$21,970	$19,282	$(2,688)

Example 2: Single Mother Not Working and a Single $8/hour Worker

	Before Marriage	After Marriage	Marriage Penalty
Earnings	$16,000	$16,000	$0
TANF Benefits	$4,668	$0	$(4,668)
Food Stamps	$3,751	$2,332	$(1,420)
Medicaid	$4,564	$2,412	$(2,149)
EITC	$0	$2,799	$2,799
Income Tax	$(1,380)	$0	$1,380
Social Security Tax	$(1,224)	$(1,224)	$0
Total Income*	$26,379	$22,321	$(4,058)

Example 3: Single Mother Working Half-Time at Minimum Wage and Single Minimum Wage Worker

	Before Marriage	After Marriage	Marriage Penalty
Earnings	$15,450	$15,450	$0
TANF Benefits	$598	$0	$(598)
Food Stamps	$3,736	$2,464	$(1,273)
Medicaid	$4,564	$2,414	$(2,149)
EITC	$2,060	$2,915	$855
Income Tax	$(525)	$0	$525
Social Security Tax	$(1,182)	$(1,182)	$0
Total Income*	$24,701	$22,081	$(2,640)

Example 4: Single Mother Working Full-Time at Minimum Wage and Single $8/hour Worker

	Before Marriage	After Marriage	Marriage Penalty
Earnings	$26,300	$26,300	$0
TANF Benefits	$0	$0	$0
Food Stamps	$2,680	$0	$(2,680)
Medicaid	$2,414	$0	$(2,414)
EITC	$3,656	$630	$(3,026)
Income Tax	$(1,380)	$(1,320)	$60
Social Security Tax	$(2,012)	$(2,012)	$0
Total Income*	$31,658	$23,598	$(8,060)

* Income = after tax earnigs + TANF + Food Stamps + Medicaid + EITC. Assumes 1997 rules for all programs except for TANF. Assumes TANF rules are the same as 1996 AFDC rules in the median benefit state. Note this table does not include housing subsidies.
Source: Eugene Steuerle, THE URBAN INSTITUTE

Figure 9.2. Marriage Penalty for Single Mother with Two Children Who Receives Some Public Assistance and Marries a Single Worker

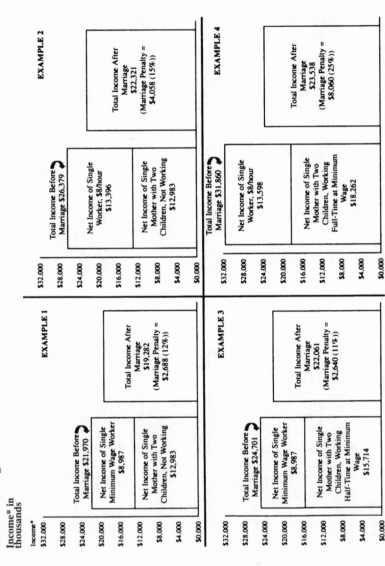

*Income = after tax earnings + TANF + Food Stamps + Medicaid + EITC. Assumes 1997 rules for all programs except for TANF. Assumes TANF rules are the same as 1996 AFDC rules in the median benefit state.   Source: C. Eugene Steuerle and Gordon Mermin, The Urban Institute.

households to move. Such an individual does succeed in moving out of traditional welfare (defined as Aid to Families with Dependent Children or its replacement, Temporary Assistance to Needy Families) but still receives a variety of other supplements, such as food stamps and earned income tax credits. The problem is that if this benefit recipient now marries a single person earning $20,000 a year, their combined income would fall by almost 30 percent, or close to $9,000, because of the marriage alone! What happens is that the income of the new partner, normally taxed at a rate of about 15 to 30 percent through federal and state income taxes and Social Security tax, is suddenly taxed at a rate of 70 percent or more simply because it is combined with the income of the benefit recipient to force further phase-out of income assistance.

Confirming this analysis with a sample of representative taxpayers, Dickert-Conlin and Houser find that the net gain to separating for the median married poor family was 16 percent of income. Similarly, they find that the median loss in income from marriage is equal to 12 percent of unmarried income for all poor single women with children. However, while their estimates include most taxes and transfers, the marriage penalties would be even larger if programs such as Medicaid and housing assistance were included.[13]

These programs may explain in part why the literature on fatherhood reports that in many low-income families and neighborhoods, fathers feel little sense of accomplishment in staying around to marry and raise children in a traditional family structure. Government in effect has declared that working fathers in low-income, two-parent families are a liability.[14] Whatever the changes in cultural standards or mores that may have led to this situation, the government has created enormous barriers to responsible fatherhood (whether of one's own children or stepchildren) in the context of marriage. The total income of those communities and housing complexes dominated by income assistance, children born out of wedlock, and the absence of married couples would fall significantly if individuals in these communities would marry in patterns closer to national averages. In these communities, government has effectively pronounced that marriage is a foolish exercise—even though marriage is traditionally a principal route out of poverty.[15]

These penalties in expenditure programs are not all confined to programs to provide income assistance. Take the case of some widows' and widowers' benefits. Policymakers treat the widow or widower as a welfare-type recipient who no longer "qualifies" as needy if she or he marries someone who has her or his own source of income. Examples here include benefits for widows and widowers of career military and foreign service personnel. The effect is the same—a large tax on marriage.

THE TRADITIONAL MARRIAGE PENALTY ISSUE: THE DIRECT INCOME TAX

While here I am emphasizing the marriage penalties arising out of many subsidy and tax programs, Congress in recent years has turned its attention mainly to a moderate subset of all the marriage penalties it has created. Members of Congress and many students of the individual income tax often associate marriage penalties only with the progressive rate schedule in that tax and with its requirement for joint filing in the case of married couples. These features of the American income tax meet the two conditions that create marriage penalties or bonuses. In effect, the progressive rate schedule often requires an individual's income to be taxed at a different rate depending on whether that individual is taxed as a single person or as part of a joint return.[16]

While this chapter addresses marriage penalties arising from multiple tax and subsidy systems, the history of the income tax is relevant for understanding the fixes that are often proposed today.[18] Before 1948, taxpayers filed as individuals, so in most states there were no marriage penalties or bonuses arising from the rate schedule (no condition 1).[19] Between 1948 and 1969, there were no penalties arising from the marriage of two single individuals but for a different

---

Box 9.1. Conflicting Principles: The Case of the Income Tax

Conflicting principles in the income tax are often demonstrated through the following example.[17] An income tax cannot simultaneously meet the following three principles: (1) equal taxation of all households with equal income, (2) progressivity as defined by increasing tax rates as income increases, and (3) neutrality toward marriage as defined by equal taxation of individuals whether married or not. Note that the first principle essentially establishes condition 1 (defined earlier) and the second principle is one way of setting up condition 2. The inherent logic is that if an individual's taxes or benefits depend on his or her marital status, then marriage penalties or bonuses will be created.

Take a tax system that contains only the following progressive element: an exemption or the nontaxation (a zero tax rate) on the first $10,000 of earnings of an unmarried or single individual. Now consider how this system is to treat couple A, whose earnings are from one worker earning $50,000, and couple B, which has the same total earnings, but one worker earns $40,000 a year and the second $10,000.

If the system is to be neutral with respect to marriage for couple A, then it should carry over into the marriage exactly the one $10,000 exemption it had before marriage (one partner had no earnings to which an exemption would apply; the other partner had a $10,000 exemption). If the system is to tax equally all married couples with the same income, then couple B should also get only one $10,000 exemption, or else it would pay less tax than couple A. However, if couple B gets only one $10,000 exemption, then it will pay more tax than it did before marriage, when each member of the couple got a $10,000 exemption, or $20,000 in total.

Although the income tax is more complicated (i.e., it has multiple rates rather than just one zero rate and one positive rate), its penalties arise in a similar manner. Some individuals are forced to have a smaller exempt amount, as well as some income taxed in higher brackets, than if they were unmarried.

reason.[20] Although there was joint filing as a household by this time, the 1948–69 period also entailed what was called "income splitting." Essentially individuals were allowed as married couples to "split" their income equally and then be taxed as if they were each single individuals. This effectively allowed them to file with an assumed share of income that would minimize total tax burden, although it simultaneously created marriage bonuses in almost all married households with two earners.[21]

After 1969, Congress turned its concern toward single individuals who paid more tax than married individuals who had equal earnings but split their income with a spouse. It abandoned complete income splitting and gave married couples a tax treatment that effectively divided their income roughly as if it were about 70/30 (70 percent earned by one spouse, 30 percent by the other) or 80/20. What this meant was that couples with more equal income splits such as 50/50 paid marriage penalties even while those with less equal splits approaching 100/0 still got marriage bonuses.

With some exceptions, these conditions still apply today. There is no real formula or principle defining where an income split should lead to a marriage penalty or bonus, and the crossover point tends to vary by the total income of the household. As noted earlier, Congress has also added an earned income tax credit that phases in and phases out, and it has phased out many income tax benefits, ranging from eligibility for individual retirement account deductions to personal exemptions. Like income-conditioned expenditures, these types of provisions do create marriage penalties, but they cannot be analyzed in the traditional income tax framework because they meet condition 2 through a different type of tax rate structure—one where the marginal rate on additional income falls as income rises.

OPTIONS FOR REMOVING OR REDUCING MARRIAGE PENALTIES

To reduce or eliminate marriage penalties essentially involves addressing *either* of the two conditions—household filing or multiple rates—that create the penalties. Several approaches or options are possible, and sometimes they can be combined.[22]

Flattening of the Combined Tax Rate Schedule

No, this isn't a pitch for or against supply-side economics. But the consequences of a variable rate schedule must be recognized. Tax reform in 1986 attempted to get at the problem of marriage penalties partly by flattening the income tax rate schedule in a way that did not reduce overall progressivity. By evenly taxing all sources of income and removing deductions and tax shelter opportunities—that is, by offsetting the benefits of rate reduction for each income group with fewer tax preferences—this reform was able to maintain progressivity while reducing and flattening statutory rates. Congress has since been moving in the opposite di-

Box 9.2. How Income Splitting Works in a Progressive Rate Structure

> In a progressive rate structure, the tax rate on each additional dollar of income is at least as high as on any previous dollar of income. A simple structure, for instance, might tax the first $10,000 of the earnings of a single individual at a zero rate, the next $15,000 at a 10 percent rate, and any remaining income at a 20 percent rate.
>
> Take the case of a couple in which each individual starts out by filing as a single individual under this schedule. The higher earner would always pay an average tax rate as high or higher than the lesser earner in a couple. Why? For every dollar they had in common, they would pay the same rate, whereas the extra earnings of the higher earner would always face a rate as high or higher than any rate paid on the lesser amounts of income. If a share of that extra income can be "split" evenly with a spouse, then it would always move "down," falling into the same or lower rate schedules.
>
> For example, take the simple rate structure described earlier and apply it to two individuals, one with $20,000 of earnings and the second with $30,000, and income split of 60/40 (the higher earner has 60 percent of their combined income). Treated as single individuals, each would pay $1,000 on their first $20,000 of earnings, and the higher earner would pay an extra $1,500 on the additional $10,000 of income (between $20,000 and $30,000). The combined burden would be $3,500.
>
> If they are allowed to split their income 50/50, each will be treated similarly to having $25,000 of earnings as a single individual, and the tax burden on each would be $1,500. (In practice, one gets the same result exactly with a joint rate schedule with bracket widths twice as wide as that for a single individual: in our example, the couple together would see tax rates of 0 percent on the first $20,000 of income, 10 percent on the next $20,000, and 20 percent thereafter.) The combined tax under income splitting would be only $3,000, and they get a marriage bonus.
>
> Suppose, on the other hand, that they are required to file a joint return that effectively treats their income as if it were earned 100/0; then their income would be taxed as if all the income ($50,000 in the example) were earned by one person, nothing by the other. (In practice, this is achieved with a joint rate schedule that is identical to the single schedule.) This leads to a total tax burden of $6,500, and the couple in the example would face a large marriage penalty. Current law provides treatment that is somewhere between the 50/50 and the 100/0 split, but not in any consistent fashion.

rection with the income tax by reducing the tax base and raising tax rates in budget agreements during the 1990s. Still, as noted earlier, the income tax is not the main problem when it comes to marriage penalties.

Complete elimination of variable rates would mean that income would face the same tax rate whether it was combined in marriage or not. The principal application would be in transfer programs, not the income tax. As a practical step, one could try to limit the combined marginal tax rate for low- and moderate-income individuals moving out of welfare programs to around 30 or 40 percent rather than the 70 percent (sometimes 100 percent or more) rate they now often face. Then, when they moved into the income or Social Security tax systems, they would again face a similar combined rate (in general, the 15.3 percent Social Security tax plus a 15 percent bottom rate bracket in the income tax). The marriage would be penalized much less, and it would matter less how the income was split as long as each person faced the same tax rate inside or outside marriage. As explained later, it is possible to use this method to flatten the rates only in the lower and middle classes and use some other method to deal with higher-income individuals. This would allow the tax system to retain a fair amount of progressivity.

Note that a true flattening of tax rates at low-income levels requires a wide variety of legislative and administrative action. It requires reconsideration of almost every income-conditioned tax and expenditure program on the books. Today, however, these programs often do not even share administrative records, and their administrators have little idea how they overlap. It requires abandonment of the liberal–conservative compromise placing so much stress on progressivity and measured (although not always real) budget saving within *every* income-related program, taken one at a time. Given changes that could simultaneously be made in other features, such as the level of minimum benefit and the direct income tax rates at higher income levels, it is unclear whether overall progressivity would be reduced by this type of effort alone. Nonetheless, Congress cannot seek phase-outs every time it deals with an individual expenditure or tax subsidy program without playing havoc with marriage penalties.

Income Splitting

Rather than trying to reform the system by flattening tax rates, one could try to work on the conditions under which family or household filing is required. One of the older methods of doing this in the income tax was to allow income splitting. To repeat: Income splitting effectively taxes married couples as if each were an individual filing a single return and having exactly the right share (one-half) of the couple's total income so as to minimize tax liability. Returning to the days of income splitting would deal mainly with marriage penalties arising from the direct income tax rate schedule that applies to the middle- and upper-income classes.

Unfortunately, income splitting eliminates only those marriage penalties arising from a rate schedule where rates are always successively as high or higher at higher levels of income. But our two conditions demonstrate that marriage penalties can also occur when rates fall as income increases. Because of all the phase-outs and implicit tax schemes Congress has adopted, the real tax system now imposes such a rate structure on a large portion of the population. Thus, when one moves through the phase-out ranges of the earned income tax credit, food stamps, Medicaid, the itemized deduction limitation, the IRA contribution limit, and so forth, marginal tax rates fall rather than rise.

Take the simple case of the welfare recipient who considers marriage. Even with split income and individual filing, marriage still can introduce income that reduces or removes eligibility for welfare payments. Assume a welfare/tax structure that provides to unmarried adults $5,000 of benefits at zero income, no tax and no benefits at $10,000 of income, and a tax of $1,000 at $20,000 of income. Before marriage, a couple with $0 income for one partner and $20,000 for the other would get benefits of $5,000 and taxes of $1,000, for a net benefit of $4,000. If they marry and split their income, then each is treated as having $10,000 of income. They then get no benefits and pay no taxes, for a net benefit of $0. True, income splitting applied to the progressive rate schedule part of the income tax did reduce the couple's income tax slightly, but that only slightly offset their loss of other benefits. The net income of the couple still fell dramatically because of the marriage itself.

Still another issue is that income splitting in the income tax would increase marriage bonuses for households in which income is not split very evenly. This raises the cost of action. A compromise here is to limit income splitting, say, to the first $50,000 of income and, of course, use that technique only with the income tax.

Income splitting is not a way of dealing with efforts of parents to raise children, since the marriage bonuses go to both those with and without children. Where adjustments are desired because of the cost of raising children, they can be achieved through child credits and dependent exemptions without giving additional bonuses to all married couples. Put another way, if the goal is to give parents some reduction in tax or increase in expenditures because of the presence of children, spousal adjustments are a poorly targeted device.

Mandatory Individual Filing

For income tax purposes, Congress could return to the days of mandatory individual filing. While it still might be easy to move around property income to achieve income splitting through the back door, that is not true for earnings from work, which, with the increase in the number of two-earner couples, is the dominant concern today—unlike a few decades ago. Community property state rules are also no longer considered to be a major issue because of a change in legal interpretation; individuals are no longer allowed to split their income and file as single individuals to avoid marriage penalties under the current income tax.

With respect to phase-outs and welfare programs, however, pure individual filing could mean that the nonworking spouse of a millionaire might be entitled also to welfare benefits. An intriguing possibility here, and one that I increasingly favor, is that wage subsidies like the earned income tax credit accompany the worker and not the family and that child credits or subsidies accompany the child. Canada is currently experimenting with such an approach with respect to wage subsidies, although eligible recipients are limited to those already on welfare.[23] I recognize that some high-income families would then get a credit or subsidy. But high-income individuals and households could still more than pay for any small subsidy through the overall progressivity of the tax and transfer system.

Worrying about whether someone paying millions of dollars in tax gets a small subsidy here or there is simply not worth the trouble. On average, higher-income families can be made to pay for these changes through an explicit tax rate structure. The standards applied to different expenditure programs are simply not consistent. Thus, we now have programs that allow high-income individuals to benefit from the much larger and more expensive social security or Medicare programs or from public school education, yet progressivity is not removed in these systems that do not have benefit phase-outs. The rich simply pay more than their share of taxes to support these systems. Put another way, progressivity is determined by the net benefit and tax structure, not by the benefit structure in one or even several programs.

My main concern here is with trying to address issues related to parenthood, marriage, and work among low- and moderate-income individuals. If subsidies were applied at low wage levels on an individual basis, they would not create the current strong incentives for absent parents (mainly fathers) and lack of marriage in low-income communities. The trick again is that once a program is aimed at the individual, marriage can have no effect on benefits or taxes paid. This type of reform could significantly change the environment of those communities. Take an example: if a single mother earning $10,000 a year received a wage rate subsidy such as the earned income tax credit on an individual basis, she would not lose it if she married someone with income of his own. Similarly, if a low-earning male married into a family, he would still be eligible for any wage rate subsidy that was available for low-income workers living with dependent children. With individually based programs, his earnings would not affect her credit, and her earnings would not affect his.

Optional Individual Filing

Mandatory individual filing would partially "pay" for the removal of income tax marriage penalties by removing marriage bonuses as well. An alternative is *optional individual filing,* a procedure that allows married couples either to garner marriage bonuses, or, when there are penalties for joint filing, to avoid them by filing as separate individuals. Optional filing increases administrative costs in deciding how to file, as the taxpayer often must calculate taxes two different ways to see which is cheaper. When options are put into place in several areas—for example, choosing between regular IRAs or Roth IRAs—the combination of options that have to be considered rise in an exponential fashion. Revenues also fall and costs rise when individuals can optionally choose the best system to apply to themselves.

Unfortunately, many taxpayers are already in a world of optional individual filing. The main difference is that the benefit now is granted only to those who are able or willing to treat the act of marriage as the option by which to trigger filing status. Putting optional individual filing into the statutes would simply extend those benefits from unmarried couples to married couples. Then the discretionary act triggering the lower tax burden would switch from avoiding marriage to filing an alternative type of return. Many states already allow optional individual filing for state income tax purposes. They often avoid the increased complexity of two calculations, however, because they are really systems based on the taxation of the individual, not the household, and, hence, joint filing is almost always an inferior option.

Special Subsidies for Second Earners

In 1981, Congress adopted a special subsidy for second earners by exempting from tax a small percentage of the income of the lesser-earning spouse of a married couple. This subsidy was removed in 1986 because of its complexity and because the flattening of the rate schedules had removed many marriage penalties in the income tax. One of the difficulties of this method was that it was not very efficient, it gave subsidies to some families who already had marriage subsidies, and it did not target benefits to cases where marriage penalties were the worst.

A COMPREHENSIVE APPROACH

In my view, taxing a large share of marital commitments makes little sense in any society, much less one searching for ways to revive or foster community (or communitarian) spirit among its members. After all, the primary feature of community is to share, and the most basic form of sharing is between two people or within a family. Admittedly, the research in this field does not *prove* that removal of marriage penalties would have a significant effect on behavior.[24] It would not, for instance, by itself reverse the sexual revolution. But the empirical research is not good at detecting the influences of policy on long-term social norms, as opposed to whether slight variations in tax rates result in behavioral variations among individuals *at a point in time*. These social effects take place over very long periods and often do not show up in the statistical studies that are made across individuals at a point in time or that follow some individuals for a few years.

Although the marriage penalties within the income tax have been around since 1969, moreover, we have only recently moved to a society where the very large marriage penalties from income assistance and wage subsidy programs have been extended well into the middle class and beyond the stereotypical poor, nonworking, welfare recipient. It is doubtful that the long-run influences of any of these conditions have yet to be fully experienced by society. As an aside, it is interesting that policymakers seem willing to accept evidence that high marginal rates influence behavior negatively at the top but not at the bottom of the income distribution.

Independently from whether marriage penalties will significantly affect behavior in a narrow sense, I believe they have a corrosive effect on society and especially on those low-income communities where the penalties are so high that average societal rates of marriage would significantly reduce the total income of the community. Marriage penalties violate almost everyone's sense of fairness because they penalize only that type of sharing done through moral and legal promises. These penalties further discourage responsible fatherhood and motherhood. Finally, where there are economies of scale, one can turn the argument on its head. That is, if economies of scale are a way of improving economic well-being by stretching the value of each dollar further, then one shouldn't want to discourage gains from economies of scale any more than one should want to discourage other income-improving behaviors, such as education.

What all this implies in practical terms is that to deal with marriage penalties in a thorough manner, Congress almost inevitably has to reconsider the entire range of explicit and implicit taxes it has imposed on income. Most of the hidden taxes it has adopted over the years would need to be reconsidered, pulled into an integrated whole, and, where appropriate, replaced by direct, explicit taxes.

Gradually over time, a combination policy that I increasingly have come to favor would not only replace implicit with explicit taxes but would also contain some of each of the following elements:

- *Reduce combined marginal tax rates on low- and moderate-income individuals so that they did not rise much above the rate that applies to middle- and higher-income individuals* (in this latter case, ranging today from about 30 to 45 percent). Politically, I would justify this last reform on the basis that we should consider tax disincentives as important or more important for low and middle income taxpayers as for upper income taxpayers.[25] Movement to this type of rate, however, would entail more universal benefits than under current law and less concentration of benefits at the very bottom. One could achieve this end without reducing real benefits in existing programs for low-income individuals if a portion of the revenues that derive from economic growth were used to reduce the tax rates applying mainly to these low- and moderate-income families.
- *Use the direct tax rate schedule as the primary means to establish overall progressivity, and abandon the complicated effort to put "progressivity" into everything government does.* This requires recognition that each new phase-out introduced is simply another tax rate schedule added onto the existing system.
- *Within the income tax, apply income splitting to lower- and some middle-income ranges.* For example, if a single individual got a standard deduction

of $3,000, a couple would receive a standard deduction of $6,000. If the single individual faced a tax rate of 15 percent for the first $30,000 of income, a couple would face a tax rate of 15 percent for the first $60,000 of income.[26] Recalling our earlier discussion, this means that the couple would never face a higher tax rate if married than if single, at least for income up to that level.[27]

- *For income over and above the levels to which income splitting would apply, use mandatory or optional individual filing.* For a given rate structure, this approach would be both less expensive and retain a higher degree of progressivity than income splitting at all levels. Although optional filing is more complex, the complexity would be limited if it applied only at higher income levels.

- *If income splitting is unacceptable at any income level, enact mandatory or optional individual filing at lower and middle-income levels.* While more complex than needed at those income levels, it would still be preferable to current law.

- *Grant some subsidies, such as low-wage supplements like the earned income tax credit, on the basis of individual, not household, earnings.* One could still limit the total credit to their supporting children. Although not without cost, this change would remove one of the largest sources of penalties discouraging low-income men from marrying and supporting children.

Let me again be clear that the issue of how to make adjustments for children for the most part is a separable issue. Marriage bonuses, for instance, do nothing for single heads of households with children, while providing extra benefits for those who no longer are raising children. Therefore, family adjustments for children can be targeted more directly through changes in such devices as the child credit that was first made available in 1997 tax legislation for 1998 and beyond. Nonetheless, we must note that this credit, along with a related child and dependent exemption, are currently more complex than required and are among the multitude of programs that have phase-outs that need to be addressed because of the marriage penalties they create. While a very important family issue, adjustments for children are not addressed in this chapter but elsewhere.[28]

As I have indicated, it is not clear to me that policymakers fully comprehend how to achieve changes of this scale and magnitude. Incremental changes here and there may reduce marriage penalties little, and they may be more than offset by new marriage penalties introduced every time there is some new phase-out or implicit income tax introduced. The momentum for change may have to come from acceptance of a broader principle. For example, a law might limit the combined marginal tax rate facing a low- or moderate-income worker to no more than the tax rate applying to the highest income individuals. To implement that goal, however, would also require years of effort to coordinate administrative structures in all the government's many programs, converting the crazy quilt of family policy into a more consistently designed overall pattern.

As long as policymakers are not able to deal with the issue in any comprehensive way, perhaps some private consideration ought to be given to examining the consequences of allowing marriage for religious or moral purposes without legal marriage being an automatic consequence. This is a matter that needs to be considered carefully and wisely, for a variety of issues—especially those dealing with spousal rights—must be given substantial consideration. Nor, given the conflict of legitimate principles, is it a matter on which anyone can be righteous. Still, consideration of an option on this level might highlight the nature of the problem and the dilemmas that current law has established. A primary goal in all the alternatives I have suggested is to find a pragmatic way to remove from families—particularly, low-income families—the moral quandary of having to reduce the family support they can give each other and their children if they marry.

NOTES

1. See Eugene Steuerle, Edward M. Gramlich, Hugh Heclo, and Demetra Smith Nightingale, *The Government We Deserve* (Washington, D.C.: Urban Institute Press, 1998).

2. *Explicit* tax rates are those that can be seen directly in the tax rate schedule of income and Social Security taxes; *implicit* tax rates, as discussed in more detail later, are those that derive from a loss of benefits as income increases.

3. See Eugene Steuerle and Linda Giannarelli, "The True Tax Rates Faced by Welfare Recipients," in National Tax Association, *Proceedings of the Eighty-Seventh Annual Conference, 1995* (n.p.: Author, 1996), 123-29.

4. Still another source of marriage issues arise with spousal benefits in Social Security. As it turns our, these provide a "marriage bonus" that is much more generous for the spouse of a rich person than the spouse of a poor person and is independent of any child-raising performed by the family. This particular design of spousal benefits contributed significantly to two lesser-known facts about Social Security: it provided greater net transfers (benefits over and above taxes paid) to the rich than the poor over most of its history; and it continues to provide significantly higher benefits to families with one earner than to families with two earners when they earn the same total family income and pay the same total Social Security tax. See Eugene Steuerle and Jon Bakija, *Retooling Social Security for the 21st Century: Right and Wrong Approaches to Reform* (Washington, D.C.: Urban Institute Press, 1994), 207-15.

5. See Congressional Budget Office, *For Better or Worse: Marriage and the Federal Income Tax* (Washington, D.C.: U.S. Government Printing Office, June 1997), 13.

6. For decades after World War II, families with children were made to bear higher and higher portions of the total tax burden, as family adjustments such as the dependent exemption did not keep pace with economic growth. While my research here was partially instrumental in the creation of two offsets—child tax credits in 1997 and increases in the dependent exemption in 1986—a typical middle-income working family with children still bears a much larger share of the tax burden than it did a few decades ago. See Eugene Steuerle, "The Tax Treatment of Households of Different Size," in *Taxing the Family,* ed. Rudolph G. Penner (Washington D.C.: American Enterprise Institute, 1983). See also

Eugene Steuerle, "Taxation of the Family," Statement before the Committee on Ways and Means, United States House of Representatives, April 15, 1997.

7. A rare exception is when the government removes potential penalties by assuming conditions at least as good as, if not better, than individual filing. This was the case with income splitting in the income tax, discussed later.

8. Also, note that while we will confine our examples later to those provisions that tax or take away something from households as their resources increase, it is possible to create marriage penalties in less common, pure subsidy systems that never phase out, as long as they meet our two basic conditions.

9. The purest example of hiding a tax system in an expenditure program comes from an expenditure that is universally available, except at higher income levels. If a phase-out rate applies to everyone's income, it operates just as if it were part of the income tax. One proposal that came close to this condition was President Bush's proposal to create an almost universal health credit that would phase out quickly once a family moved above poverty-level income. If the phase-out were explicitly put as a tax rate in the income tax instead, it could have achieved almost the same end, but if done that way, the proposal would have appeared much more expensive and explicit tax rates of near to 100 percent would have formally shown up in the income tax rate schedule. With a phase-out rather than a direct tax rate, the cost of the proposal appears smaller and no additional tax rates are revealed.

10. These differences included some phase-ins and floors, as well as the phase-outs on which most our attention is directed here. See Joint Committee on Taxation, "Present Law and Analysis Relating to Individual Effective Marginal Tax Rates" (Washington, D.C.: U.S. Government Printing Office, 1998).

11. As an aside, one reason that meaningful income tax reform is so hard to achieve is that most proposals only deal with the direct income tax, while ignoring the dozens of other income tax systems we now have. What does it mean, for instance, to have a "flat" tax or a "consumption" tax if only one of the many "income taxes" is being flattened or converted to a consumption base?

12. Examples are taken from C. Eugene Steuerle, "The Effects of Tax and Welfare Policies on Family Formation," in *Strategies to Strengthen Marriage: What Do We Know? What Do We Need to Know?* papers presented at a Family Impact Seminar Roundtable Meeting, June 23–24, 1997, Washington, D.C.

13. See Stacey Dickert-Conlin and Scott Houser, "Taxes and Transfers: A New Look at the Marriage Penalty," *National Tax Journal* 51, no. 2 (June 1998): 175-217.

14. See Eugene Steuerle, Edward Gramlich, Hugh Heclo, and Demetra Smith Nightingale, *The Government We Deserve* (Washington, D.C.: Urban Institute Press, 1998), 40-43.

15. See Greg Duncan, Richard Coe, and Martha Hill, "The Dynamics of Poverty," in *Years of Poverty, Years of Plenty,* ed. Greg Duncan (Ann Arbor, Mich.: Institute for Social Research, 1984).

16. There was a brief period of time, before the days when transfer systems were large, when most marriage penalties did arise out of the progressive income tax rate schedule and its standard deduction (which may be considered for this purpose as nothing more than part of the rate schedule—that part which taxes some initial levels of income at a zero rate).

17. See Congressional Budget Office, *For Better or Worse.*

18. For a longer discussion of the history behind income tax marriage penalties, see Congressional Budget Office, *For Better or Worse.* See also Joint Committee on Taxation,

"Present Law and Background Relating to Proposals to Reduce the Marriage Penalty Tax," *Highlights and Documents,* January 28, 1998.

19. An exception was in community property states where a married individual could lower liability effectively by treating income as if earned by a spouse. In those states, there was a marriage bonus to many couples.

20. A new head of household rate schedule for single individuals with dependents would create some marriage penalties.

21. The changeover from individual filing was forced on Congress partly by complications created by community property states in the absence of universal income splitting. In those states, income was essentially divided equally between the partners in marriage, so that individual filing by married couples in those states effectively created the same situation as income splitting. Unfortunately, in the days of individual filing, this meant that couples in community property states had a distinct advantage relative to couples in other states. By adopting joint filing and income splitting, Congress extended to all couples the benefits previously enjoyed only by those in community property states See Michael J. McIntyre and Eugene Steuerle, *Federal Tax Reform: A Family Perspective* (Washington, D.C.: Finance Project, 1996).

22. For another discussion of some proposals to reduce marriage penalties in the income tax see, "Reducing Marriage Taxes: Issues and Proposals," Joint Committee on Taxation, May 1998. This report addresses only those penalties arising in the income tax and does not get at penalties in expenditure programs.

23. The experiment goes under the name of the "Self-Sufficiency" Project.

24. See for example, James Alms and Leslie Whittington, "Til Death or Taxes Do Us Part: The Effect of Income Taxation on Divorce," *Journal of Human Resources* (Spring 1997); James Alms and Leslie Whittington, "Income Taxes and the Timing of Marital Decisions," *Journal of Public Economics* 64, no. 2 (May 1997); James Alms and Leslie Whittington, "The Rise and Fall and Rise . . . of the Marriage Tax," *National Tax Journal* 49, no. 4 (December 1996). See also Stacy Dickert-Conlin, "Taxes, Transfers and Family Structure: Are They Related?" Department of Economics and the Martin School of Public Policy, University of Kentucky, April 1996; and Robert Moffitt, "Incentive Effects of the US Welfare System: A Review," *Journal of Economic Literature* 30, no. 1 (March 1992).

25. Advocates of purer forms of supply-side economics will note that a more even set of marginal rates goes against the movement toward a "head tax," in which the highest tax rate applies to the first dollars of income so that marginal rates can be moved toward zero as income increases. However, even most advocates of a flat rate tax do not argue for movement toward a head tax.

26. For example, one could double, for couples, the income level at which the 15 percent rate bracket ends.

27. One would need to eliminate the separate schedule for heads of household if the goal were to remove marriage penalties in the presence of children. This chapter has not dealt in depth with this other source of complication. As indicated in the text, however, adjustments for children generally should be made through child credits and exemptions, not through attempts at income splitting (which is what the head of household schedule does). Since heads of household tend to be poorer on average than other households, these adjustments for children may need to be raised to avoid any tax increase if the head of household schedule is eliminated.

Chapter Nine

28. See Eugene Steuerle, "The Tax Treatment of Households of Different Size," in *Taxing the Family*, ed. Rudolph G. Penner (Washington D.C.: American Enterprise Institute, 1983); and Eugene Steuerle, "Taxation of the Family," statement before the Committee on Ways and Means, U.S. House of Representatives, April 15, 1997, and Eugene Steuerle, "Child Credits," statement before the Finance Committee, U.S. Senate, August 7, 1995.

Part Two

Making Divorce a Less Popular
Response to Marital Difficulties

10

Marriage as a Precommitment

Elizabeth S. Scott

Much of the recent call for reform of family law has a somewhat punitive tone. Family values advocates focus on divorce and the instability of modern families as an important source of our social ills and argue that the values of tolerance and privacy must be subordinated to children's welfare.[1] Some seem to believe that the only prospect for salvaging the American family and preserving the future of our children is for the state to restrict divorce, reinstituting fault and coercing unwilling spouses to remain married, despite their selfish desire to escape. Those who oppose these restrictions on divorce object on two grounds: (1) the restrictions will not be effective as a means of enhancing family stability or promoting children's welfare, and (2) in a liberal society, the state should not be in the business of imposing oppressive constraints on individual freedom.[2] Since the issue is framed in this way, this conflict appears to be yet another battleground in the "culture war,"[3] in which one group in society seeks to impose its values and preferences on the rest. Not surprisingly, liberals tend to oppose the restrictions, and conservatives (and some communitarians) tend to be more supportive.

A different approach to promoting marital stability is one in which the law's role is to assist couples to achieve their goal of lasting marriage.[4] Most people enter marriage aspiring to a lifelong relationship[5] and view the success of their marriage as important to a good life. Marriage vows are more than rhetoric, and Elizabeth Taylor—who married seven times—does not represent "the life well lived." Many people also expect to have children and plan to live as a family with their spouse and children. Moreover, most people who marry recognize that they are giving up some freedom but also believe that by investing in the marriage, their own welfare will be promoted; indeed, the expectation is that both parties will be better off through the commitment than they would be otherwise.[6]

As divorce statistics reveal, for many people the commitment and optimism with which they enter marriage does not last. Life presents stresses and temptations, and decisions are made that weaken or destroy the bond between spouses. Gradually (or suddenly), the marriage succumbs. The original commitment is "nonbinding"[7] under the current no-fault divorce regime and can be readily set aside. Not only are there few legal restraints to provide disincentive to divorce, but under current law, the couple may not be permitted to undertake voluntarily a more binding commitment through restrictions on divorce.

I will argue in this chapter that divorce law reform should build on the aspirations with which many people enter marriage, by providing couples with the means to reinforce their commitment to the marital and family relationships that they are undertaking. From an ex ante perspective, the voluntary reinforcement of the marital commitment through restriction on divorce serves two important functions. First, the restrictions can serve as precommitment mechanisms, which discourage each spouse from pursuing transitory preferences that are inconsistent with the couple's self-defined long-term interest in lasting marriage. Second, each spouse, knowing that the other's commitment is enforceable, receives assurance that his or her investment in the relationship will be protected. In contrast, if marriage is a relationship that can be easily terminated at any time by either party, trust will be impaired and investment will be tentative. Allowing couples entering marriage to undertake a greater commitment to the relationship than the law currently encourages or allows would have a direct effect on the decision to divorce and indirect effects on attitude toward and behavior in marriage.

A roadmap for the rest of the chapter may be helpful. Through a description of a pattern of marital conduct leading to divorce, I will show the value of enforceable precommitments in assisting spouses (and people generally) to achieve their long-term goals, a benefit that is enhanced in the marital context because the commitments are mutual. I then suggest that current divorce law undermines commitment by assuming that commitment is antithetical to personal freedom. To the contrary, basic contract principles demonstrate that freedom to commit extends our ability to fulfill our ends. Next I explore some restrictions on precommitment that are important because of unique attributes of marriage. Then, turning to policy, I propose several precommitment measures that could be implemented either through contract or through alternative marital regimes. The second approach is embodied in covenant marriage statutes, such as those that have recently been enacted in Louisiana and Arizona.[8] These options allow couples to choose a legal commitment that for many people approximates more closely than does current law their psychological commitment to marriage.

WHY COMMITMENT IS IMPORTANT

Causes of Marital Failure

Modern family law provides individuals with greatly expanded freedom to pursue their personal goals for "the good life." A review of divorce statistics over the past generation might lead one to conclude that enduring marriage is not part of the typical life plan for most Americans.[9] Yet, as I have suggested, survey evidence consistently shows that most young people aspire to a lasting marriage and that most people entering marriage expect that the relationship will last a lifetime.[10] How does it happen, then, that so many marriages fail? The causes of marital failure surely are varied. The marriage may simply be a terrible mistake from the outset, because one or both spouses has inadequate or erroneous information about the other (or about themselves); once the information is gained and weighed, the relationship becomes untenable.[11] Sometimes marriages fail because one or both spouses have changed so fundamentally over time that the couple is incompatible and no longer shares the same values and goals.[12] A more mundane pattern is surely just as common: many marriages fail because the initial commitment is hard to sustain. Over time, the spouses may be diverted from their goal and make choices based on immediate preferences that are inconsistent with their objective of lasting marriage, choices that either gradually or suddenly can lead to divorce.

My focus is on the third pattern of marital failure, which requires further clarification. The fact that a person has a stable belief that marriage will be rewarding over a lifetime does not mean that he or she will always act consistently with that goal. The long-term rewards of the relationship sometimes seem remote and incompatible with immediate desires and preferences. In most marriages, even successful ones, both spouses will be tempted to engage in selfish or uncooperative behavior, which reflects current preferences that may be transitory but that undermine the stability of the relationship. There are obvious examples: immersion in career at the expense of family, pursuit of other relationships, disputes over family finances and children, withdrawal, boredom, and so forth. A pattern of uncooperative behavior can cause retaliation, estrangement, and erosion of the marital commitment and ultimately can lead to the breakdown of the relationship.

Precommitments in Everyday Life

This account suggests that many marriages fail because people tend to make choices based on immediate desires that are inconsistent with their long-term plans and preferences. Described in this way, the failure of marriage is analogous to other situations in life in which individuals make choices based on transitory preferences that temporarily dominate and undermine the fulfillment of their long-term goals. A commitment to a healthy diet to lose weight, moderate use of alcohol, completion of a project, or saving money for a new home can involve sacrificing pleasures that, at a particular moment, may represent the more compelling choice than adherence to the long-term goal. The tendency to make decisions that are inconsistent with long-term preferences is generally attributed by psychologists and economists to a tendency to discount the future, so that long-term preferences are devalued when balanced against short-term desires. A familiar corrective to the problem of inconsistent preferences in everyday contexts involves the use of precommitment mechanisms.[13] Precommitments are self-management strategies designed to penalize the short-term choice that the decision maker wants to avoid (eating the cake) or to reward adherence to her long-term goal (losing ten pounds). Through the use of enforceable penalties or rewards, she reinforces her initial commitment to her goal and reduces the likelihood that she will be diverted by temporarily attractive temptations.[14] Thus, the dieter may remove fattening food from the house (making it more difficult to succumb to temptation) or create a reward (a new dress) if she achieves her goal.

Precommitments as Restrictions on Divorce

Although the parallels initially may seem a little strained, restrictions on divorce can function in a way that is roughly analogous to precommitments in other contexts, reinforcing the initial commitment to the marriage and discouraging inconsistent choices. Most directly, the restriction will tend to affect the unhappy spouse's decision about divorce. Suppose, for example, that the couple agrees before marriage to a three-year mandatory waiting period before divorce. This barrier imposes a substantial cost on the decision to exit the marriage and thus reduces the likelihood that divorce will take place unless the costs of remaining in the marriage are substantial (or the benefits minimal).[15] In other words, as the unhappy spouse makes a choice between continued marriage and divorce, the precommitment shifts the calculus in favor of remaining in the marriage. Predictably, decisions to divorce will be less common and more carefully made.

More subtly but perhaps more importantly, precommitments that impose restrictions on divorce can promote stability in marriage by influencing the couple's attitude about the kind of relationship that they have undertaken, which in turn may affect their behavior in marriage. The decision by the couple to undertake a binding commitment signals the seriousness with which each enters the marriage. Moreover, at least indirectly, the knowledge that exit will not be easy can encourage cooperation and assist each spouse to resist the temptation to pursue his or her short-term self-interest.[16] In a marriage bounded by precommitment, the original cooperative intentions may be less likely to be forgotten because the relationship cannot be readily abandoned if it becomes unsatisfactory. This may influence the parties to protect the marriage by avoiding behavior that could lead them to confront the costly decision to divorce. Such a conception of marriage might be expressed as follows: "We have made a commitment to this marriage and we're not getting out of it easily. Since we're in for the duration, we might as well make the best of it."

Contrast this response with that of parties to a marriage in which in the midst of the stresses of life, divorce is always an option. The stability and survival of the marriage is dependent on sustained continuous satisfaction with the relationship compared to the alternatives with less mitigation for temporary fluctuations in commitment. With low barriers to exit, the likelihood is greater that the resolve and cooperative intentions of the newly married couple will fade and that one or the other spouse will decide to end the marriage.

Mutual Commitment and the Benefits of Contract

In the context of marriage, restrictions on divorce not only function as self-management strategies but also establish reciprocal obligation between the spouses. Whether a couple enters a formal contract or chooses a marital regime that restricts divorce, the parties benefit, not only because they themselves will be more likely to conform to a course of conduct in marriage that fits with their goals, but because they know that their spouse is also bound in the same way.

In this regard, it is useful to consider the benefits that contracting offers in other contexts, benefits that are relevant to marriage as well.[17] In other legal settings, parties enter contracts when they need the cooperation of others to achieve their own goals. Through a contract, each party gives up some future freedom because both parties predict that the joint benefit produced by the agreement will be greater than the combined benefit that each could achieve on his or her own.[18] The legally enforceable contract allows each party to rely on the other's future cooperation, and to be assured that his or her own performance will not be wasted because the other decides to defect. Without the assurance provided by enforcement, parties may believe that cooperation would be beneficial, but each will be reluctant to invest effort and resources.[19]

The benefits of mutual commitment apply in the context of marriage as well. By restricting her or his own freedom, each spouse gains greater assurance of the commitment of the other and greater confidence that the relationship will endure through good and bad times. This sense of security promotes a level of trust in the partner that fosters substantial investment in the marriage, in terms of time, energy, emotions, and resources. Indeed, the kind of interdependence that is often associated with a successful marriage may only be possible with the level of trust that is conditioned on a binding commitment.[20] Contrast this with the situation in which each partner knows that the other is free to leave if the marriage becomes unsatisfying. Neither will be inclined to make a wholehearted commitment to the relationship, because each knows that he or she cannot rely on the security of the personal investment. Under these circumstances, marriage becomes a more limited and less stable relationship as each partner protects him- or herself against future disappointment.

THE CONSTRAINTS ON COMMITMENT UNDER NO-FAULT DIVORCE LAW

In general, the law has come to deal with family members as separate individuals with individual rights, rather than as a group with interdependent and inseparable interests—a trend that (some) liberals applaud and communitarians re-gret.[21] Two dimensions of the modern legal regime regulating divorce are thought in an undifferentiated way to reflect this trend. The first is a policy of maximizing the freedom of each spouse to pursue his or her personal ends, a pol-icy that is reflected in rules facilitating an efficient "clean break" upon divorce. The second dimension is the movement toward private ordering in divorce, a trend reflecting the view that the law should be a neutral framework for the mar-ried couple to work out the terms of their relationship and its termination—the growing acceptance of premarital agreements is part of this trend. These two de-velopments (freedom maximization and private ordering) are related in that they both reflect the law's moral neutrality and disinclination to prescribe family roles. It is clear, however, from our earlier discussion of contract, that they are quite different, in that a contractual framework provides the means to freely choose to *restrict* one's future freedom in pursuit of one's personal ends. In prac-tice, probably because the principle of freedom maximization has been so cen-tral to the no-fault reform, there has been a reluctance to give couples the free-dom to undertake binding commitments that restrict divorce.[22] Thus, for example, it is unclear whether a premarital contract restricting divorce is cur-rently enforceable.

Maximizing Individual Freedom and No-Fault Divorce

The enthusiasm for maximizing individual freedom by making divorce easy has waned in recent years, but this norm continues to shape the rules for termination of marriage. No-fault law itself in most states gives each spouse the ability to ter-minate the marriage quickly and unilaterally.[23] Moreover, a clean-break policy pervades the postreform legal regime, driven by a goal of allowing the former spouses to get on with their lives. Thus, lump-sum property settlements and re-habilitative alimony are preferred to arrangements that result in continued in-volvement between parties. Until recently, even financial responsibilities toward children of the marriage seemed to be subject to this policy, with lax enforcement of child support obligations after divorce.[24] The rules cumulatively express a vi-sion of marriage as a relationship that is easily set aside when it becomes unsat-isfactory—even when the couple has children—so that the parties may be free to quickly get on with their lives. It is a vision that is inconsistent with the under-standing of marriage held by many people—that of a relationship of mutual com-mitment and obligation.

Private Ordering and Premarital Agreements

The aspect of the trend toward private ordering in divorce that is most relevant for my purposes involves the legislative and judicial acceptance of the use of premarital agreements.[25] Currently, premarital agreements providing for distribution of property and spousal support are generally enforced, although courts intervene paternalistically far more than in the commercial context, and provisions about custody or child support are unenforceable.[26] Typically, couples execute antenuptial contracts when one or both of them want to protect assets from the claims of the other upon divorce or death. Since the mid-1980s, more than twenty states have enacted statutes based on the Uniform Premarital Agreement Act (1983),[27] which seeks to promote routine enforcement of these agreements under general contract principles. Thus, enforcement is conditioned on whether the premarital negotiation process is fair, not on whether both parties are happy with the outcome when the agreement is enforced.[28]

Courts have been lukewarm toward premarital contracts in which the couple seeks to reinforce their commitment to one another by restricting divorce,[29] a response that is curiously inconsistent with the liberal premises of modern regulation of marriage. As I have suggested, this view may reflect the pervasive importance attached to individual freedom in the no-fault era. In fact, as the discussion of contracting suggests, individual autonomy is enhanced when spouses are able to bind themselves to promote their mutual ends by voluntarily agreeing to modest restraints on divorce.[30]

Currently, the social and legal climate is changing again as the costs of maximizing the freedom of adults to leave marriage and family are becoming ever more apparent. This climate is likely to be more hospitable toward precommitment contracts between couples, and it seems probable that courts will enforce these agreements more routinely than is currently the case. Even under current law, the barriers to judicial enforcement are more psychological than doctrinal. For example, nothing in the language of the Uniform Act, the basis of modern regulation, presents any doctrinal impediment to precommitment contracts.[31]

This point leaves us with many questions unresolved, however. Should these contracts be distinguished from other contracts because of the distinctive nature of the marriage relationship? If so, what limitations on freedom of contract are needed? Finally, are contracts between spouses the best way to assist couples who want to reinforce their marriage?

RESTRICTIONS ON THE FREEDOM TO PRECOMMIT

That the law should provide a means for couples to voluntarily undertake a serious commitment when they marry has considerable appeal as an initiative to promote family stability. A policy of total legal neutrality toward couples' choices or rejection of precommitments may not be desirable, however. Precommitments carry unique risks in the marital context, and their use must be limited and monitored, lest they do more harm than good. The cautionary observations that follow set the stage for the proposals in the next section regarding legal policies to facilitate beneficial precommitments.

Decision-Making Biases in the Premarital Context:
Over- and Undercommitment

Individuals who are about to marry may tend to be influenced by emotional and cognitive biases that could distort decision-making in this setting. Both parties may be overly optimistic in calculating the prospects for successful and lasting marriage. Moreover, thinking about divorce in this context may generate discomfort and be avoided on that account. Researchers suggest that individuals seek to reduce cognitive dissonance when they are confronted with two inconsistent facts or events.[32] Furthermore, decision makers generally tend to overvalue vivid experiential data that can be readily called to mind and to discount remote, abstract information.[33] In the warm glow of the premarital context, the possibility of divorce or even of serious conflict in the marriage may seem like a distant possibility.[34] In general, the period before marriage is not optimal for making decisions about divorce because of predictable cognitive error.[35]

The effect of these cognitive biases on decision-making about marital precommitment is not easy to predict. Optimism could lead some couples to see no need for precommitment. If this reaction is widespread, the mechanism would simply not be used much—a response that might be characterized as "undercommitment." Other couples may view the adoption of precommitments as an opportunity to affirm their confidence in the success of the marriage and for each future spouse to signal their commitment to the other. This response might be quite common, given the evidence that most couples entering marriage know about the high divorce rate but reject the possibility that their own marriage will fail.

The upshot of the latter response may be "overcommitment," a more onerous restriction on divorce than most observers would conclude was rational under the circumstances. Thus, the couple might agree never to divorce or create a prohibitive fine to be imposed on the spouse who ends the marriage. This is not a problem, of course, if the precommitment functions as predicted, reinforcing the stability of a mutually beneficial relationship. It is a serious problem, however, if the failure of the marriage does not derive from the pattern of behavior on which the precommitment model is based. Earlier, I suggested that some marriages fail because they are mistakes from the outset, because the parties lack adequate information. Others fail because the personal identity, values, and preferences of one or both of the spouses change so dramatically that the long-term interest of either or both is seriously undermined by remaining in the marriage. For both of these categories of marital failure, prohibitive barriers to divorce seriously infringe on the individual's pursuit of his or her ends. Thus, legal regulation is necessary to ensure that precommitments impose only moderate obstacles to divorce.[36]

Other Constraints and Cautions: Protecting Vulnerable Spouses

Sometimes, precommitments that are moderate in most cases may be unacceptable because of the conduct of one spouse and the resulting vulnerability of the other. In cases of spousal abuse, for example, obstacles to divorce may increase the harm to the victims, and exemption should be readily available. In general, any precommitment that insists on continued cohabitation or even direct association is risky and should be unenforceable. Procedures should be readily available to expedite spousal and child support upon separation in cases involving dependent spouses and minor children. That is not to say that mandatory delay before final divorce or remarriage cannot be prescribed, under conditions in which financial support for a dependent is provided.

Caution is required on other grounds as well. A precommitment that is likely to have a differential impact on the spouses because of different marital roles is undesirable. Thus, monetary penalties—includes those affecting spousal support—are problematic unless the spouses have equal assets and earning capacity, which in most marriages will not be the case.[37] The homemaker spouse, for example, would be systematically disadvantaged by this type of precommitment, because it presents her with a greater barrier than it poses for her husband. Furthermore, since the ultimate policy goal of promoting marital stability is to enhance the welfare of children, only precommitments that serve that objective are acceptable. Thus, precommitments withholding access to visitation or child support, or otherwise undermining children's security, should not be enforced.

LEGAL POLICY PROPOSALS FACILITATING PRECOMMITMENT

How can the law facilitate the efforts of couples entering marriage to strengthen their relationships—without creating harmful effects that outweigh the benefits that precommitments may provide? In this section, I will suggest some useful precommitment mechanisms, focusing particularly on the benefits of a mandatory waiting period before divorce or remarriage as the optimal precommitment. I will then examine two means by which couples could adopt precommitments— through premarital contracts or through alternative legal regimes.

Beneficial Precommitment Restrictions

After the cautionary warnings of the last section, it may seem that precommitments are attractive in theory but that in practice most restrictions on divorce are too problematic. The following precommitments offer the prospect of enhancing marital stability and do not suffer from the disabilities discussed.

Family Property Trusts and "Supersupport"

Although monetary penalties may often be problematic, an agreement that all or most marital property will be held in trust during the minority of the couple's children will serve a dual function of discouraging divorce and providing for the financial security of children if divorce occurs. Similarly, provisions for high levels of child support (which cannot be reduced based on future family claims[38]) impose the responsibilities of marriage on the divorced spouse, making freedom from family less attractive. Many spouses, anticipating their role of parents, assume that they will want to act in the best interest of their children and readily accept that the role carries serious responsibilities they expect to fulfill. Thus, ex ante, this restriction is one that many would willingly undertake. For most parents, it is only in the midst of the divorce that they perceive their children's interest as being in conflict with their own.

Marital/Predivorce Counseling and Mediation

A period of prescribed psychological counseling before a divorce petition can be filed may assist the couple to examine the stresses that have undermined the stability of the marriage. Moreover, counseling can help the dissatisfied spouse probe the nature of his or her dissatisfaction and to clarify whether the desire to leave the marriage reflects transitory or stable and settled preferences. Requiring custody mediation presents a very minor hurdle to the divorce itself, but it offers benefits for reducing conflict in future family relations.

Mandatory Waiting Periods before Divorce or Remarriage

A mandatory waiting period of some substantial duration before divorce (perhaps two or three years) is the optimal precommitment, in my view, because it serves several functions. First, a mandatory period of delay serves well the standard precommitment purposes. It creates a barrier to divorce that makes leaving the marriage more costly, and at the same time it defines the relationship as one that is not easily set aside, subtly influencing the spouses attitudes and behavior. Beyond this, an extended waiting period promotes better decision-making. The spouse who is unhappy in the marriage can more accurately assess whether her or his decision reflects long-term interest or transitory intense preferences. In general, time is a good tool for making better decisions and avoiding cognitive errors.[39] Finally, a waiting period undermines the ability of a spouse quickly to establish a new family, a step that may dilute interest in children of an earlier marriage.

What about Fault?

Fault-based divorce law served a little noticed precommitment function that was sacrificed in the movement toward no-fault divorce. It signaled that neither spouse was free to leave the marriage unless the other had committed a grievous offense. Many of the modern critics of no-fault divorce law argue for a return to fault grounds—although not on precommitment grounds. Should fault be reintroduced as a precommitment?

In some regards, fault would seem to serve quite well as a precommitment. Some parties would choose to provide that certain fault grounds are a basis for excusing performance. Including a provision in a premarital agreement reminds the spouses of the kind of behavior that is unacceptable and undermines the relationship. It thus may influence marital behavior in a direction that stabilizes the relationship. Fault grounds certainly create barriers that restrict divorce.

In many regards, however, fault grounds do not function well as precommitments. First, the modern understanding of the dynamics of divorce suggests that although the failure of some marriages can be attributed solely to the behavior of one spouse, in most cases the responsibility cannot be so clearly assigned. Marriage is a complex web of reciprocal interactions; a failing marriage may involve a pattern of misconduct and retaliation that is impossible to sort out and evaluate. Furthermore, some of the troublesome aspects of fault grounds that lead to the no-fault reform should invoke caution before these restrictions are embraced as precommitments. The proving of fault undermined the integrity of the judicial process and surely undermined the parties' future relationship, an important concern if the objective is to promote the welfare of children whose lives currently are disrupted by family instability. In general, I would be hesitant to reintroduce fault as a precommitment.

Premarital Agreements and Alternative Marital Regimes

Couples entering marriage could undertake precommitments through two means. The first is through a premarital agreement, either through open negotiation or through the adoption by the couple of a standard form contract. The second means involves creating alternative marital regimes, so that couples as they enter marriage can consider and choose a level of commitment. While both approaches offer benefits, the latter, as I conceive it, offers benefits as a way to promote children's welfare.

Premarital Agreements

As I suggested earlier, no doctrinal innovation is needed for courts to routinely enforce precommitment agreements under ordinary contract principles. As in other contract settings, defenses against enforcement would include fraud, duress, and unconscionability; courts also would have the authority to refuse to enforce contracts that are against public policy.[40] Although the couple's freedom to design precommitment agreements is most fully protected if they can freely negotiate terms, the risks of contract formation and enforcement in the context of marriage that were described earlier can be mitigated through the use of standard form contracts. Form contracts can offer the couple the benefit of reflective consideration and accumulated experience about the effectiveness of various restrictions and about costs and contingencies that the couple may not anticipate. In short, a form contract will include the most effective and beneficial precommitment terms and will reflect the constraints and protections that were discussed earlier.

Premarital precommitment contracts offer benefits only if couples contract, and most couples do not execute premarital agreements. Thus, the utility of this means of promoting marital stability is likely to be quite limited unless couples are actively encouraged to enter these agreements. This encouragement could come through educational programs, advertising, or premarital counseling. The state could encourage precommitment contracts more actively by providing forms to couples when they obtain a marriage license, with advice about the benefits that the contract may offer. More active encouragement would involve incentive schemes such as tax benefits to couples who execute an agreement that involves substantial commitment. Finally, a couple could be legally required to choose from a menu of standard form contract provisions ranging from little to serious precommitment. This, of course, is the functional equivalent of requiring couples to select from alternative marital regimes.

Alternative Marital Regimes

Couples entering marriage could be invited to select from a menu of marital regimes the one that corresponds to their plans and purposes; their choice would determine the obligations and restrictions that marriage entails. Thus, couples whose commitment is somewhat tentative might choose marriage as currently defined—the "easy exit" plan. Couples whose commitment is deeper would opt for marriage with greater restrictions on exit and would be bound by rules about divorce that embody some or all of the recommended precommitments, such as a waiting period and counseling.[41] The conversation that the couple would be required to have as they decided which marital regime to choose would have two desirable effects. First, it would require them to consider together the type of relationship that they wanted undertake more carefully than they otherwise might. It would also require each to reveal information to the other about the seriousness of her or his commitment.

The recent covenant marriage statutes that have been enacted in a few states represent a version of this approach.[42] For example, the Louisiana statute invites couples contemplating marriage to choose between alternative commitment options. One is the standard no-fault rule, while the other allows divorce only after a two-year separation or on fault grounds. Couples are free to choose the commitment option that best corresponds with their mutual goals for the relationship. The statute also requires couples choosing covenant marriage to undergo counseling to assure that they understand the meaning of the commitment they are about to undertake.

Covenant marriage statutes are revolutionary among recent reform proposals directed at no-fault divorce law in that the commitment is not imposed by the state but chosen by the parties. In my view, the commitment options provided under these statutes are not optimal, because they include fault grounds. Nonetheless, covenant marriage statutes represent the first step toward an approach to reform of no-fault divorce law that can be understood as treating restriction on divorce as a precommitment undertaken by the couple entering marriage, to assist them to achieve their goals for a lasting relationship.

CONCLUSION

Under a precommitment approach, many of the rules that restrict divorce and protect the welfare of children could be quite similar to reforms directed toward enhancing family stability that other reform advocates have proposed (except that I do not favor a return to fault grounds). The restrictions are justified on a different basis, however, from that which supports much of the "family values" reform initiative of recent years. Whereas most critics of no-fault divorce law criticize its liberal premises, I am persuaded that the current no-fault regime caricatures liberal principles and that, for the most part, restrictions on divorce fit quite comfortably in a liberal framework. Of course, some individuals marry without commitment and then have children without a sense of responsibility. For those individuals, restrictions on divorce may continue to be an exercise of the state's coercive power. I am confident, however, that many people contemplating marriage and parenthood cannot be described in this way. They enter marriage committed to its success and determined to fulfill responsibly their role as parents. For this group, restrictions on divorce are not "government intrusion into the fundamental rights of individuals"[43] but precommitment measures that assist them in fulfilling their own hopes and goals for a good life.

Perhaps the important lesson is that liberals and communitarians (or conservatives) have a far greater basis for agreement about divorce law reform than the current debate would suggest. In contrast to other divisive social policy issues such as abortion, homosexuality, or pornography, there is no great value clash about the worth of enduring marriage among those who are most affected by its regulation. The goals, values, and preferences that many individuals hold for themselves fit comfortably in a family values framework. Liberal principles support reforms that assist individuals to achieve their personal ends. In the context of marriage, those reforms strengthen marital and family stability, the core of the communitarian agenda.

NOTES

1. Council on Families in America, "Marriage in America: A Report to the Nation" in *Promises to Keep: Decline and Renewal of Marriage in America,* ed. D. Popenoe, J. Bethke Elshtain, and David Blankenhorn (Lanham, Md.: Rowman & Littlefield, 1995), 2.

2. The debate over the proposed reform of divorce law in Michigan to reinstitute fault grounds for parents of minor children has raised these themes. See J. Loven, "Michigan Lawmakers' Attack on No-Fault Divorce Part of National Trend," Associated Press Political Service, February 16, 1996; "House Passes Most of Divorce Reform Package, " Associated Press Political Service, September 12, 1996; P. Luke, "Divorce Bill Only Creates Other Woes," *Grand Rapids Press,* May 26, 1996.

3. Other battlegrounds include conflicts about homosexuality, abortion, and pornography.

4. I developed some of the ideas in this chapter in two earlier articles: "Rational Decisionmaking about Marriage and Divorce," *Virginia Law Review* 76 (1990): 9; and "Rehabilitating Liberalism in Modern Divorce Law," *Utah Law Review* (1994): 687. See also E. Scott and R. Scott, "Marriage as Relational Contract," *Virginia Law Review* 84 (1998): 1225.

5. This fact is mentioned in passing by family values advocates but is not seen as presenting an opportunity for policy reform. Council on Families in America, *Marriage in America,* 7.

6. Survey research supports that young people contemplating marriage have the aspirations described in the text. See the sources discussed in note 10.

7. Carl Schneider describes marriage as a "nonbinding commitment," although he was not the first to use the phrase. See his "Moral Discourse and the Transformation of American Family Law," *Michigan Law Review* 83:1848, citing N. O' Niell and G. O'Niell.

8. *Louisiana Revised Statutes* 9 (1998): 272-75 and 9: 307; *Arizona Revised Statutes* (1998), section 25-901.

9. L. J. Waite, "Does Marriage Matter?" presidential address to the Population Association of America, April 1995.

10. Survey data indicate that most people expect and intend that their marriage will be a lasting relationship, even though they are aware of the fact that the divorce rate is high. See Lynn Baker and Robert Emery, "When Every Relationship Is Above Average: Perceptions and Expectations of Divorce at the Time of Marriage," *Law and Human Behavior* 17 (1993): 439, which describes a study indicating that 100 percent of individuals about to marry reject the likelihood of their own divorce. Surveys of young people indicate that they are optimistic about their own marriages. A *Glamour* magazine survey indicates that 89 percent of male college students and 95 percent of female students surveyed believed they would have only one marriage; "How College Women and Men Feel Today about Sex, Aids Condoms, Kids: A Campus Report," *Glamour,* August 1987, 261, 263. A survey of high school seniors found that 85 percent believed that they would be married to the same person for life; Arland Thornton and Deborah Freedman, "Changing Attitudes toward Marriage and Single Life," *Family Planning Perspectives* 14 (1982): 297, 300. Moreover, many people seem to believe that divorce is too readily available. A Roper poll in 1982 found that a majority of those polled thought that divorce laws should be stricter. Herbert Jacob, *Silent Revolution: The Transformation of Divorce Law in the United States* (Chicago: University of Chicago Press, 1988), 83, citing General Social Surveys, 1972–82 (Chicago: National Opinion Research Center, July 1982). Other surveys indicate that most people find the care and support of family life to be important to a sense of well-being. See Mellman and Lazarus, *Mass Mutual American Family Values Study* (Washington, D.C.: Mellman Group, 1989), who say, "Most Americans want to have a happy marriage, have children, and have relationships in the home based on mutual love and respect" (8).

11. A significant percentage of the marriages that end in divorce do so in the first seven years. It seems likely that many of these marriages are based on inadequate information, and perhaps they follow a short relationship. In general, youth at the time of marriage is correlated with marital instability. Gay C. Kitson and Helen J. Raschke, "Divorce Research: What We Know, What We Need to Know," *Journal of Divorce* (Spring 1981): 1, 12-13.

12. Derek Parfit, the moral philosopher, examines the ethical implications of changing personal identity over time in "Later Selves and Moral Principles," in *Philosophy and Personal Relations,* ed. Alan Montfiere (London: Routledge & Kegan Paul, 1973), 137; see also Derek Parfit, *Reasons and Persons* (Oxford: Clarendon, 1984).

13. A voluminous literature examines the phenomenon of inconsistent preferences and the tendency of decision makers, through weakness of will, to make choices that are inconsistent with optimal plans, despite a constant ordering of preferences. Most analysis has focused on the use of precommitment strategies to preclude future inconsistent preferences. See R. H. Strotz, "Myopia and Inconsistency in Dynamic Utility Maximization," *Review of Economic Studies* 23 (1955–56): 165, which is a classic early account of this phenomenon, arguing for precommitment. A rich interdisciplinary literature in economics, psychology, and social theory has explored this subject. George Ainslie, a psychologist, focused on the precommitment strategies as mechanisms for controlling impulsive behavior. See George Ainslie, "Specious Reward: A Behavioral Theory of Impulsiveness and Impulse Control," *Psychological Bulletin* 82 (1975): 463, 476-80. Thomas Schelling, a political economist, has described precommitment strategies from everyday life, such as weight loss clubs and smoking clinics. See Thomas Schelling, "Self Command in Practice and in a Theory of Rational Choice," *American Economic Review* 74 (1984): 1, 6-7; Thomas Schelling, *Choices and Consequences,* 83-112 (Cambridge, Mass.: Harvard University Press, 1984). Jon Elster, a social theorist, has explored the effect of weakness of will on the capacity for perfectly rational behavior, which would take all future preferences into account. Precommitment strategies are rational responses to imperfectly rational behavior. See Jon Elster, *Ulysses and the Sirens: Studies in Rationality and Irrationality,* 36-47 (Cambridge: Cambridge University Press, 1979). For a discussion of academic interest in the problem of inconsistent preferences and the use of precommitment strategies, see Scott, "Rational Decisionmaking," 40-42.

14. Thus, the dieter may make a bet with a friend, remove all sweets from the house, create a system of fines, join an expensive health club, or set aside money for an elegant outfit when she reaches her goal. Schelling (see note 13) has enlivened the discussion of precommitment strategies with many illustrations from everyday life.

15. Social psychologists who study decision making about divorce conclude that the decision is typically made through a cost–benefit calculus, in which the individual compares divorce with continued marriage. Marital stability is a function of the attractions of the marriage and the barriers around it and an inverse function of the attraction of alternatives. With legal barriers to exit (e.g., delay and the costs of the legal process) reduced, a decision based on a temporarily strong short-term preference is facilitated. In theory, at least, if barriers to exit exist, inhibiting a decision to divorce of this kind, the value attached to leaving the marriage may diminish over time, and the value of lasting marriage may reassert itself. See George Levinger, "A Social Psychological Perspective on Marital Dissolution," in *Divorce and Separation: Context, Causes, and Consequences,* ed. George Levinger and Oliver C. Moles (New York: Basic Books, 1979) 37-60.

16. For a discussion of how the existence of a long-term contractual relationship promotes cooperation, see R. Scott, "Conflict and Cooperation in Long Term Contracts," *California Law Review* 75 (1987): 2005.

17. See generally R. Scott and D. Leslie, *Contract Law and Theory* (Charlottesville, Va.: Michie, 1993).

18. This, of course, is the familiar principle of joint utility maximization.

19. The enforceable contract solves the familiar prisoners' dilemma problem. Each party needs the cooperation of the other to achieve her or his objectives. The optimal solution for each individual would be to maintain her or his freedom and be able to rely on the other's cooperation. Of course, neither would agree to this. Thus, each party voluntarily relinquishes some freedom to obtain the other's cooperation.

20. Milton Regan argues that family roles based on fixed status facilitate the reliance and vulnerability that enables individuals to establish the trust necessary for intimacy. He suggests that contractual relationships do not permit the kind of commitment that would allow trust to develop. See his *Family Law and the Pursuit of Intimacy* (New York: New York University Press, 1993), 89-97, 148-52. In my view, this response reflects a narrow conceptualization of contract.

21. For a discussion of this trend and the communitarian response, see Scott, "Rehabilitating Liberalism."

22. See Theodore F. Haas, "The Rationality and Enforceability of Contractual Restrictions on Divorce," *North Carolina Law Review* 66 (1988): 879. However, even under traditional law, some courts upheld contractual restrictions on remarriage. See S. Williston, *A Treatise on the Law of Contracts,* section 1741 (Rochester, N.Y.: Lawyers Cooperative, 1990). In *Cowan v. Cowan,* the court upheld a contract provision restraining marriage until minor children were adults, with $10,000 forfeiture. 75 NW D. 920 (Iowa 1956). Ironically, because of the emphasis on individual liberty under the no-fault regime, some courts may be less inclined to enforce parties' private contracts restricting divorce today.

23. Only two states require both spouses' consent to obtain divorce on breakdown grounds. See the discussion of this trend in Scott, "Rational Decisionmaking," 14-21.

24. In 1982, David Chambers argued, somewhat ruefully, that short-term child support was on the horizon. See "The Coming Curtailment of Compulsory Child Support," *Michigan Law Review* 80 (1982): 1614. However, as the economic impact of divorce and generally of living in single-parent families has become more apparent, Congress and state legislatures have established more effective mechanisms for enforcement of child support orders. The 1984 Child Support Enforcement Amendments (42 USCA, sect. 651) condition state receipt of federal welfare funds on the establishment of expedited nonjudicial processes to issue support orders for recipients on public assistance and require states to establish rebuttable child support guidelines. The amendments also provide for automatic wage withholding for obligors in arrears and mechanisms for locating absent parents. The Family Support Act of 1988 (PL 100-485; 42 USCA, sect. 1305) mandates that after January 1, 1994, states receiving federal welfare funds must provide for immediate automatic withholding by employers of legally due child support payments. The statute also orders the Department of Health and Human Services to set standards for state performance in determining paternity of children receiving Aid to Families with Dependent Children (AFDC) support services and provides for the use of genetic tests of paternity (sect. 111). The Child Support Recovery Act of 1992 (18 USCA, sect. 228) authorizes interstate imposition of fines and imprisonment for nonpayment of child support and mandates restitu-

tion after conviction. Some states withdraw professional and drivers' licenses from delinquent obligors. See Massachusetts Code MGLA 119A, section 16.

25. The trend is also evident in the judicial response to separation agreements and in the enthusiasm for child custody mediation.

26. Thus, premarital agreements may be set aside not only if the court concludes that the execution of the contract was tainted by duress, misrepresentation, unconscionability, or some other defect that would result in refusal to enforce any contract, but also if enforcement results in hardship or inequity. The later would not be a basis for setting aside a commercial contract.

27. 9B U.L.A. 371 (1983).

28. Under section 6 of the act, defenses against enforcement include lack of voluntariness and unconscionability in execution. See generally I. Ellman, P. Kurtz, and E. Scott, *Family Law: Cases, Text, Problems,* 2d ed. (Charlottesville, Va.: LEXIS Law, 1998), P09-10; *Teacher's Manual Update* (1994).

29. Some courts, as mentioned earlier, have enforced these agreements; see note 22. Of course, premarital agreements that do not explicitly restrict divorce may sometimes make divorce more costly for one party or the other. Consider, for example, the spouse who gives up a life of luxury under the agreement.

30. Paternalistic intervention may be justified to prohibit couples from binding themselves excessively. A contract never to divorce, for example, comes close to self-enslavement.

31. Section 3 of the Uniform Premarital Agreement Act authorizes the parties to contract with regard to "any other matter, including their personal rights and obligations, not in violation of public policy."

32. See Leon Festinger, *A Theory of Cognitive Dissonance* (Stanford, Calif.: Stanford University Press, 1957); Leon Festinger, *Conflict, Decision and Dissonance* (Stanford, Calif.: Stanford University Press, 1964).

33. This bias, one of several that can contribute to cognitive error, is known as the *availability heuristic.* See Amos Tversky and Daniel Kahnemann, "Judgment under Uncertainty: Heuristics and Biases" in *Judgment under Uncertainty: Heuristics and Biases,* ed. D. Kahnamann, P. Slovic, and A. Tversky (Cambridge: Cambridge University Press, 1982). It explains why prospective car buyers who have had one experience with a "lemon" will weigh that more heavily in choosing a car than *Consumer Reports* recommendations. It probably also explains why previously divorced persons are far more likely to consider premarital agreements.

34. Unless, of course, one of the parties has been through a divorce. See note 33.

35. For a full discussion of how cognitive biases may distort decisionmaking in the marital context, see Scott, "Rational Decisionmaking," 62-70.

36. Anthony Kronman has argued that the state is justified in paternalistically refusing to enforce a contract not to divorce, because such a contract is analogous to self-enslavement. See "Paternalism and the Law of Contract," *Yale Law Journal* 92 (1983): 763.

37. Monetary penalties that are fixed amounts are also problematic in that it will be hard to predict at the time of marriage how much of a burden on divorce will be imposed by the fine. A $50,000 fine on the party who initiates might be trivial or prohibitive depending on the couple's financial circumstances.

38. Currently, responsibility for a new wife and children can constitute "changed circumstances" and serve as the basis for reducing child support to children of an earlier marriage. See Ellman et al., *Family Law,* 565-67.

39. This commonsense observation is supported by experimental research; see W. Edwards, "Remarks Delivered at Symposium on Legal Implication of Cognitive Error," University of Southern California, February 1985. This is the premise of the Home Solicitation Sales Act, which allows a "cooling-off" period to purchasers from door-to-door salespersons. See generally, Byron D. Sher, "The 'Cooling-Off' Period in Door to Door Sales," *U.C.L.A. Law Review* 15 (1968): 717, 734-35.

40. For example, contracts never to divorce would fall in this category.

41. There might well be more than two options with different precommitments, although it would not be desirable to make things too complicated.

42. See note 8.

43. Description of Michigan legislation restricting divorce by Mary Schroer, state legislator, in J. Lovern, "House Passes Most of Divorce Reform Package," Associated Press Political Service, September 12, 1996.

11

The Law of Marriage and Divorce: Options for Reform

William A. Galston

My topic is the law of marriage and divorce. This issue is not, as many suppose, like a switch with only two positions—where we are now, and where we were forty years ago. Over and over again I find myself in situations where it is assumed that if I'm uncomfortable with the way things are today, it must be because I want to return to the way things were for our parents. This is not my intention, and it is not a result I could accept. If I were to be persuaded that the only alternatives to current laws and practices are the marital and gender relations of the 1950s, I would conclude that we should live with what we now have. I am in that respect (as in many others) a good child of my generation, married to a law professor who has worked full-time outside the home at least as long as I have.

My belief is that the scope of realistic choices before us is far greater than the "switch" metaphor implies. My hope is not to restore a vanished past but rather to extend the sphere of debate, both within the liberal camp and more generally, so that a wider range of options can be considered on their merits.

There are contrasting views, within the scholarly community and among citizens, concerning the current status and future course of the law of marriage and divorce in the United States. Some differences involve questions of how to assess and interpret data. Other differences concern the basic values at stake. Still others revolve around the nature of law itself.

Two different conceptions of law are at work in society today. One way of looking at the law is that it creates a set of permissions and prohibitions, incentives and disincentives that shape behavior in the ways that economists have taught us to understand. Another way of looking at the law is that it represents the moral voice of the community, that it is an effort by the people to declare what it believes, what it values, what sorts of things it seeks to encourage or discourage on moral grounds.

Questions inevitably arise concerning the relationship between those two basic functions of law. What happens when the effort to project a certain moral voice comes at great cost as measured in the standard calculus of incentives or disincentives? Conversely, what happens when a more economistic, incentive-based approach comes at great cost to a society's moral self-conception? These sorts of issues are very much at stake in discussions of the law of marriage and divorce.

SOME BASIC FACTS

A standard view among scholars is that the rate of divorce in the United States has been rising steadily and inexorably since the Civil War.[1] If you fly high enough over the data, this view is roughly right. Closer up, a somewhat different picture emerges. The rate of divorce in 1960 was no higher than in 1940, and barely higher than in 1920. By 1980, however, the rate of divorce was two and one-half times its 1960 level. Since 1980, the rate of divorce has stabilized somewhat below its peak, at a level that is the highest in the entire industrialized world. If these rates continue, about half of all first marriages undertaken today will end in divorce.[2] The divorce rate for second and subsequent marriages is even higher, vindicating (in the drab language of social science) Samuel Johnson's dictum that remarriage represents the triumph of hope over experience.

The number of children newly and directly touched by divorce each year has more than doubled in the past generation to about one million annually. This is what we would expect, because almost three-fifths of all divorces involve minor children. More than 40 percent of all children of divorce living with their mothers have not seen their fathers even once during the past year. Only 17 percent see their fathers as often as once a week.[3] Recent research has confirmed that custodial mothers and their children experience significant postdivorce income declines (on the order of 25 to 30 percent), while noncustodial fathers experience a nontrivial increase.[4]

Why should we care about these facts? Let me offer three reasons: first, the effects of divorce on children; second, its consequences for women who have made long-term commitments to "traditional" marriages—consequences measured not just in income but also in social status and standing; and third, the moral message that the current legal code of marriage and divorce sends to society as a whole.

Such concerns are being articulated by a broad public. In 1993, a survey suggested that 94 percent of Americans agree (and 78 percent *strongly* agree) that children suffer when their parents divorce. In the spring of 1996, a *Los Angeles Times* survey on the state of American values probed (among other things) attitudes toward marriage and divorce. Nine percent of respondents indicated that the law of divorce should be made easier, while 42 percent said that it should be made harder. In a *Miami Herald* survey taken in 1986, 80 percent of the respondents indicated that they believed that divorce is now so easy to get that people don't work hard enough to stay married. (Intriguingly, when the researchers talked to kids age thirteen to seventeen, 79 percent said that divorce is too easy, and 72 percent opined that divorced adults don't try hard enough to stay married.) And in a *Time*/CNN survey conducted in July 1997, 45 percent of respondents identified marriage not being taken seriously by couples as the "main reason" for the increase in divorce. (By contrast, only 7 percent thought that changes in women's and men's earning power was the principal cause.) While we cannot and should not draw policy inferences from survey data alone, such studies at least identify areas of public concern that policymakers should take seriously.

Does divorce per se make a difference to children? The conventional wisdom a decade ago was that to the extent that negative effects on children could be observed, they were the consequences of two variables, neither of which had to do with the divorce itself: the level of predivorce conflict in the family and postdivorce income loss. We now know that although these variables are significant, they are not the whole story. The work of scholars such as Frank Furstenberg, Andrew Cherlin, Nicholas Zill, Sara McLanahan, and Gary Sandefur (scholars, by the way, who do not agree with my policy prescriptions) has converged on the following finding: correcting for predivorce conflict and income loss, divorce has an independent negative effect on children. Affected areas include high school performance and dropout rates, college attendance and graduation, labor force attachment, crime, depression and other psychological disorders, suicide, out-of-wedlock birth, and the propensity to become divorced in turn.[5] (Some evidence, as yet inconclusive, indicates that the experience of divorce diminishes trust and the ability of the children of divorce to form stable attachments, whether in marriage or elsewhere.) There is a general consensus among these researchers that while children from high-conflict marriages are better off if their parents divorce, kids from lower-conflict marriages are not.[6]

The most recent work by Cherlin, Lindsay Chase-Lansdale, Kathleen E. Kiernan, and Christine McRae has further advanced our understanding. Like previous studies, their results show that children of divorced couples are significantly more likely to experience educational and emotional problems as adolescents and young adults. But unlike many earlier studies, their data and methodology are able directly to account—and correct—for levels of disruption in intact families, and it refutes the oft-repeated view that the apparent effects of divorce are reducible to conflict inside the home prior to divorce.[7]

What accounts for changing divorce rates over the past generation? In my judgment, three variables are key. First, enormous economic changes have occurred since 1960—the surge of women into the paid workforce and the decline of male salaries, both absolutely and relative to women. Second, cultural change has also been marked. Daniel Yankelovitch has written about what he calls the "affluence effect," the value shifts stemming in large measure from widespread prosperity. As compared to 1960, we place less value on things such as obligations to others, restraint, and sacrifice and more value on things such as individualism, personal choice, self-expression, and self-realization.[8]

These economic and cultural changes have had, most agree, a significant effect on patterns of marriage and divorce. The question is whether they are the whole story. During the past generation, there has also been a very significant change in a third variable: the law of divorce. As recently as 1969, every state had some version of a fault-based system. The first no-fault law was signed with a ringing endorsement statement in 1970 by Governor Ronald Reagan of California. By 1974, forty-five states had moved in that direction. By 1985, every state had done so.

The movement from a fault to a no-fault system turned out in practice to be a shift from divorce by mutual consent to divorce by unilateral fiat. Unilateral, nonconsensual no-fault is now the norm rather than the exception. Indeed, in forty states, divorce after a separation of one year or less at the initiative of one party is possible, regardless of the opposition of the other party. As Herma Hill Kay, a principal backer of the pioneering California no-fault reform ruefully observed in 1990, two decades after the first no-fault law went into effect, "Divorce by unilateral fiat is closer to deserting than to mutual separation. Unlike divorce based on mutual consent, unilateral divorce is apt to produce unexpected emotional distress and financial dislocation that exacerbates the upheaval accompanying family breakdown."[9]

This outcome—essentially unchecked unilateral divorce—was contrary to the reformers' hopes. A prime motivation of early no-fault legislation was not to loosen the system, recent research shows, but rather to reduce the incidence of divorce by substituting a court determination of marital breakdown for fault-based grounds that were readily faked by collusive spouses. The new approach failed in part because there was little support for the costly and intrusive system of family courts that were supposed to make substantive judgments about the condition of individual marriages.[10]

Recent scholarship suggests that in addition to the influence of economic and cultural change, these legal changes themselves had measurable effects on rates of divorce. For example, a careful fifty-state study by the University of Maryland economist Amanda Honeycutt finds that children with ten years' exposure to liberal divorce laws were about 10 percentage points less likely to be living with both biological parents in 1980 than were children who were never exposed to unilateral no-fault.[11]

These findings have an important bearing on a broader debate about law. One thesis is that the economic and cultural variables are the drivers and that law is simply an effect, what social scientists call a *dependent variable*. The contrary thesis, for which I believe there is accumulating evidence, is that the law of marriage and divorce not only reflects but also shapes our society. Law creates incentives, and incentives affect behavior. Over time law can help change culture, both directly (through its moral voice) and indirectly, as changed behavior helps create changes in understanding and belief.

There are some theoretical reasons to believe that this is so: (1) the "investment effect"—diminished incentives to work hard on processes of mutual adjustment and compromise if an arrangement can be canceled at will by one party[12]; (2) the "demonstration effect"—the effect of one's conduct on others, or the tendency of the statistical norm to become the moral norm; and (3) the "destigmatization effect." I recall very clearly when I was growing up in the 1950s and early 1960s that if you had been involved in a divorce, your political prospects were jeopardized. We have reached a point now where it seems to make no difference whatsoever. (Witness the recent leadership of the Republican party—including its 1996 presidential candidate.)

Beyond these theoretical considerations, there is the matter of simple consistency in our understanding of law across its various domains. It is amazing how many people who believe (rightly) that the changed behavior mandated by civil rights laws helped over time to shift underlying racial attitudes deny that any such consequences can flow from changes in the laws of marriage and divorce.

FROM FACTS TO POLICY

During the past generation, Americans have encouraged, or at least tolerated, the development of a new regime of divorce law that has favored adults over children and economically advantaged spouses, usually male, over economically dependent spouses, usually female. There is a widespread belief that the time has come to ask ourselves whether we have struck the right balance and, if not, to redress it in a reasonable way—in a manner that requires individuals to assume greater responsibility for the interpersonal and social costs of their actions.

This is a fair and appropriate question. After all, the family is a social issue, not just a matter of individual rights and opportunities. It is a profound mistake to see marriage as simply a relationship between individual human beings, severed from its broader context of social relationships and effects.

Society has an interest in marital stability. The social costs of divorce extend well beyond its impact on children to include such things as legal expenses, investments in child support enforcement, and public programs that try (inadequately) to compensate for diminished family capabilities. These costs are concerns that can legitimately shape divorce law. Within broad limits, the question of how they are to be balanced against other concerns (including personal autonomy) is a matter the people must decide.

Empirical evidence shapes, but cannot fully determine, this decision. For example, Cherlin and others have pointed out that the majority of children of divorce manage to escape serious educational and emotional problems, and they conclude that we should therefore be wary of sweeping changes in divorce laws. But the policy conclusion does not follow from the empirical premise. After all, the majority of cigarette smokers don't get lung cancer. That doesn't stop us from strengthening laws and regulations to reduce smoking. Trade-offs among individual and social goods should be made in the shadow of the facts as we know them, but the process of social choice inevitably involves contestable judgments about how much of some things we care about should be sacrificed for gains along other dimensions of value.

While Americans continue to debate the appropriateness of specific means—law, public policy, civil society, cultural and moral suasion—for strengthening marriage, we may be in the process of reaching a rough and ready agreement about ends: first, to reduce the number of divorces, particularly those involving minor children; second, when such divorces are unavoidable, to mitigate their negative consequences for children and their custodial parents; and third, to restore a more nearly level playing field and more nearly adequate protections for women who have chosen to make traditional marriages for extended periods.

In this section I will focus on the first of these goals. With regard to the second and third, on which I have written elsewhere,[13] I will make only some brief remarks.

If we are interested in mitigating the consequences of divorce for children and custodial parents, then we will create a more reliable regime of child support awards and enforcement, work much harder to create incentives for the ongoing involvement of both parents in the upbringing of their children, get much more serious about the enforcement of visitation rights, and give judges discretion to take steps such as excluding the family home from the property settlement for an extended period. (My personal preference is an exclusion until the children leave home to go to work or college. That is a radical proposal, admittedly; I'd be satisfied with something less as a first step.)

With regard to fairness for women in long-term "traditional" marriages, I think there is much to be said for reconsidering the retreat from long-term alimony and also for taking fault into account more regularly and significantly in property settlements, whether or not we choose to do so in other respects.

Now let me return to my principal focus: reducing the number of divorces. Let me put some options on the table as starkly as possible.

During the 1970s, we lurched from one extreme to the other, from a fault-based regime to one in which divorce could reflect the unilateral decision of one party to the marriage. My first question is, Why not a middle ground? Why not no-fault by mutual consent? This approach ought to be especially attractive to those people who objected to the "hypocrisy" of the previous system in which spouses colluded to trump up faults. What that collusion suggests is that the two parties in fact agreed that the marriage was at an end and should be ended in law. Why not mirror that with a consensual no-fault regime?

Second question: What if mutual consent is absent? I'm neither a lawyer nor a legislator, but let me make three separate suggestions. The question of how they may be labeled and combined is one that requires further reflection.

First, states should consider returning to what I call an updated fault system. By "updated," I mean a fault system that takes into account things that we've learned in the past generation about spousal abuse and other issues.

Second, judges should be given greater discretion to distinguish between circumstances of higher- and lower-intensity conflict between parents. It would be interesting to think about legal mechanisms and standards that might allow that difference to be taken into account more fully.

Third, in cases in which mutual consent, fault, and high-intensity conflict are absent, there should be longer waiting periods—years rather than months—before a divorce can be awarded. (This is the system that prevails in most European countries.)

STATES AS LABORATORIES OF DEMOCRACY

The brief history I offered at the beginning of this chapter showed that we lurched very rapidly—in all fifty states in a very short period—from one regime of divorce laws to a very different system. The speed and extent of that change was almost certainly a mistake. It would be an equally risky venture for all fifty states to lurch in another direction simultaneously. Although the current state of the evidence is suggestive, it is incomplete; we must allow for the possibility of unanticipated consequences flowing from well-intentioned proposals for reform.

For this reason, it would be best for a handful of states to take the lead in experimenting with new approaches to marriage and divorce. We should carefully monitor the consequences of those changes for a statistically relevant period—say, five or six years. Only then should we decide how to move forward on a broader front. This model of reform has been employed in a number of other social policy areas; it would serve in this instance as well.

There are signs that just such a "natural experiment" may be under way. In the summer of 1996, divorce law reformers in Louisiana achieved a surprising success—a new law that passed the state house and senate with only one dissenting vote. Rather than imposing a single standard on all couples, it gives them a choice between the existing no-fault system and "covenant marriage," which reinstates fault-based divorce updated to take into account our improved understanding of spousal abuse. Not only may couples at the threshold of marriage exercise this choice, but also couples already married under the existing no-fault regime have the option of switching to the covenant.

A recent *Time*/CNN poll helps explain why the Louisiana approach succeeded while efforts to revise no-fault have failed in so many other states. Fifty percent of the respondents thought that it should be harder than it now is for married couples to get a divorce. For couples with young children, that figure rose to 61 percent. But when asked whether "the government" should make it harder, 59 percent said no. Americans, it seems, want greater marital fidelity—but not at the

cost of coercive reductions in personal liberty.[14] The Louisiana reforms succeeded in part because they went some way toward reconciling the apparently antithetical goods of liberty and enforced fidelity.

While the passage of the Louisiana law produced astonished reactions in many
quarters, it was not exactly a bolt from the blue. For years, social scientists have
discussed ways that individuals can try to protect themselves against short-term
temptations that may conflict with long-term interests. (The classic example is
Ulysses binding himself to the mast against the Sirens' call.) Legal scholars such
as the University of Virginia's Elizabeth Scott argue that new forms of premarital agreement can create strong incentives for couples to remain together and to
make the emotional investments needed for satisfying long-term marriages.[15] In
the past two years, bills introduced (but not passed) in Illinois, Washington, and
Indiana proposed variations of covenant marriage aimed at differentiating between "marriages of commitment" and "marriages of compatibility."

The very existence of this choice in Louisiana is bound to make for some interesting—perhaps awkward—premarital conversations. The law's supporters
say that couples would have to consider their compatibility more carefully than
heretofore and that disagreements about the standard for divorce may ward off
potentially weak marriages that are likely to dissolve. Detractors fear that this
choice could open the door to a kind of emotional blackmail ("If you really loved
me, you'd agree to marriage for life") that could trap individuals in situations
against their subsequent judgment and long-term interests.

This new Louisiana law may help restore balance and fairness to a system that
at present gives little weight to important individual and social interests in
strengthening marriage. Still, no one really knows what its results will be. What
percentage of couples contemplating marriage will chose the covenant option?
What percentage of already-married couples will switch to a covenant marriage?
Will the rate of divorce in that state slow down? Will the impact of the law be
stronger for couples with children? Will it make a measurable difference, for
good or ill, on reported rates of spousal abuse?

Because we don't know the answers to these and many other questions, we
should take advantage of the fact that Louisiana is willing to serve as a laboratory
of democracy. Rather than criticizing this experiment prematurely, it makes more
sense to watch carefully and learn from its results. Experiments of various kinds
should be encouraged, not strangled, in other states as well. If we are willing to be
patient and profit from diverse, carefully evaluated experiences, the next generation of legal reform can produce results that better balance important social values
while minimizing the unintended consequences that so often bedevil public policy.

NOTES

1. For example, see Andrew J. Cherlin, *Marriage, Divorce, Remarriage* (Cambridge,
Mass.: Harvard University Press, 1992), 20-24.

2. Ibid., 24. The low end of scholarly estimates is 44 percent; the high end is 64 percent.

3. For these and other troubling statistics, see Frank F. Furstenberg Jr. and Andrew J. Cherlin, *Divided Families: What Happens to Children When Parents Part* (Cambridge, Mass.: Harvard University Press, 1991), 34-39.

4. Richard R. Peterson, Social Science Research Council, "A Re-Evaluation of the Economic Consequences of Divorce," paper presented at the 1994 Annual Meeting of the American Sociological Association. On the basis of a reanalysis of Lenore Weitzman's data, Peterson shows that women's standard of living postdivorce drops 27 percent on average — a significant decline, but far short of the 73 percent Weitzman reported. The average increase for men is about 10 percent.

5. In addition to the previously cited works by Cherlin and Furstenberg, see Nicholas Zill, Donna Ruane Morrison, and Mary Jo Coiro, "Long-Term Effects of Parental Divorce on Parent–Child Relationships, Adjustment, and Achievement, in Young Adulthood," *Journal of Family Psychology* 7, no. 1 (1993): 91-103; Sara McLanahan and Gary Sandefur, *Growing Up with a Single Parent: What Hurts, What Helps* (Cambridge, Mass.: Harvard University Press, 1994).

6. For a particularly clear statement of this consensus, see Furstenberg and Cherlin, *Divided Families,* 71-72.

7. Andrew J. Cherlin, Kathleen E. Kiernan, and Lindsay Chase-Lansdale, "Parental Divorce in Childhood and Demographic Outcomes in Young Adulthood," *Demography* 32, no. 3 (August 1995): 299-318; Chase-Lansdale, Cherlin, and Kiernan, "The Long-Term Effects of Parental Divorce on the Mental Health of Young Adults: A Developmental Perspective," *Child Development* 66 (1995): 1614-34; Cherlin, Chase-Lansdale, and Christine McRae, "Effects of Divorce on Mental Health through the Life-Course," Hopkins Population Center Papers on Population, WP 97-1 (February 1997).

8. Daniel Yankelovitch, "How Changes in the Economy Are Reshaping American Values," in *Values and Public Policy,* ed. Henry J. Aaron, Thomas E. Mann, and Timothy Taylor (Washington, D.C.: Brookings Institution, 1994).

9. Stephen D. Sugarman and Herma Hill Kay, eds., *Divorce Reform at the Crossroads* (New Haven, Conn.: Yale University Press, 1990), 8.

10. See especially J. Herbie DiFonzo, *Beneath the Fault Line: The Popular and Legal Culture of Divorce in Twentieth-Century America* (Charlottesville: University Press of Virginia, 1997), chap. 6.

11. Amanda Honeycutt, "Marriage, Divorce, and the Impacts on Children: Using State Laws to Identify Causal Relationships," Ph.D. dissertation, Department of Economics, University of Maryland, 1997), chap. 3.

12. See Allen M. Parkman, *No-Fault Divorce: What Went Wrong?* (Boulder, Colo.: Westview, 1992), chap. 5.

13. Galston, "Divorce American Style," *The Public Interest* 124 (Summer 1996): 12-26.

14. Reported in *Time,* July 14, 1997.

15. Elizabeth Scott, "Rational Decisionmaking about Marriage and Divorce," *Virginia Law Review* 76, no. 1 (1990): 9-94.

12

The Misguided Movement to Revive Fault Divorce

Ira Mark Ellman

There is some movement in America today to revisit no-fault divorce reforms. Some would eliminate unilateral no-fault divorce altogether; others would restrict it with lengthened waiting periods.[1] Still others argue that fault should remain relevant in allocating marital property or in fixing awards of spousal support.[2] Of course, the American divorce law has always varied among the states. About half, concentrated especially (but not exclusively) in the West, have pure no-fault laws. In the remainder, concentrated especially in the South and Northeast, no-fault reforms have always been hedged, typically by variations on the same rules these latter-day reformers now propose. So the reform proposal made in one state may resemble a rule that has long been the law of another. But this latest crop of reformers seek to enlarge both the hedges and the number of states that have them. So far they have failed. As of this writing, there has been no retrenchment from no-fault, and opponents have reason to hope that the fad will pass before doing any real damage.[3] But it has surely caught enough attention to put defenders of no-fault to the task of explaining their position.

These current reformers have their historical counterparts. Lawrence Friedman's histories tell us that the fault-divorce laws amended by the no-fault reforms of the 1970s were themselves enacted in response to the campaign of nineteenth-century reformers.[4] In 1816 President Timothy Dwight of Yale University complained that the rising divorce rate "is dreadful beyond conception" and threatened to make the entire state of Connecticut "one vast brothel." A successor, President Theodore Woolsey, wrote a book in 1869 denouncing Connecticut's divorce laws as "immoral." He argued that "petitions for divorce become more numerous with the ease of obtaining them," concluding that lax divorce laws have caused the disintegration of the family.[5] Woolsey would be heartened by today's movement. He went from Yale to the presidency of the New England Divorce Reform League in 1881, published a new edition of his book in 1882, and saw his New England league grow into the National Divorce Reform League in 1885. Their campaign suc-

ceeded in getting some tough new divorce laws that imposed a six-month wait before divorce decrees became absolute, a two-year ban on remarriage of the plain-
tiff in the divorce action, and a lifetime ban on remarriage by the defendant, unless
judicial permission was obtained.

The durability of fault's appeal is not surprising. It has always attracted those
who focus on the law's moral message. Those who believe marriage is a responsibility to be met see divorce as a failure whose losses should fall on the blameworthy. The movement to no-fault divorce was in part a repudiation of that conception of marriage and divorce, a repudiation that some recent writers question.[6]
But it was also—in equal measure, at least—a concession to the practical difficulties of using the law to implement this moral vision. Can the law really identify the blameworthy in marriage? And even if it sometimes can, would the required process cause more harm to more divorcing parties than the no-fault
alternative? Some recent writers attack these last propositions, largely by suggesting that the harms caused by no-fault are greater than may have initially been
appreciated.[7] But the available data suggest that stricter divorce laws will be no
more effective today in preventing divorce than when President Woolsey lobbied
for them. Indeed, a careful examination suggests that not only do most of the ills
no-fault critics attribute to modern divorce law have their source elsewhere, but
others may not even exist.

Some clarification of terms may be helpful in distinguishing among the variations on no-fault divorce that one finds today among the American states. The
classic form of fault divorce, under which a marriage could not be dissolved
without proof that one of the spouses was guilty of marital misconduct, was re-
pudiated in every American state by the late 1970s. Perhaps half the states repealed fault grounds for divorce entirely, replacing them with a no-fault system
allowing either spouse to terminate the marriage unilaterally. Most of the rest
simply added a no-fault ground to their existing fault statute, offering litigants
their choice. Many states in both groups specified that a no-fault divorce could
only be granted after the spouses live apart for some minimum period of time,
ranging from six months to three years. Typically, no analogous waiting period
was imposed on divorces granted on fault grounds, in those states that retained
such grounds.[8] In some states the waiting period is less when the divorce is not
contested.[9] A small handful of states never allowed unilateral divorce but still
joined the no-fault reform by allowing the divorce without any showing of fault
if both spouses consent. All these different state laws are typically called "no-
fault" because all of them allow divorce without any showing of misconduct,
even if they have a waiting period, require both spouses' consent, or also offer
them the choice of fault grounds.

One can in principle adopt a no-fault position with respect to ending the marriage but not with respect to fixing the financial consequences of the dissolution.
Most American states today exclude consideration of fault in the allocation of
marital property, but they divide about equally on whether marital misconduct

can be considered in determining whether, or in what amounts, alimony should be allowed.[10] One might label states that exclude consideration of marital misconduct in both property and alimony determinations *pure no-fault* or *true no-fault*. In these states the law provides no financial incentive to raise misconduct claims. This is the law of about half the states. The other half I would call *part-fault*, for while they make divorce available without a misconduct showing, they allow its consideration in alimony or even in property allocations. The traditional law that applied before the no-fault reforms can be called *true-fault* or *full-fault*, to reflect the fact that it both required a misconduct showing to end the marriage and also allowed consideration of fault in fixing alimony awards, and perhaps in allocating property.[11] There are today no full-fault states.

It is also useful, I believe, to distinguish among four different kinds of arguments offered by critics of no-fault divorce. This overview is far too condensed even to describe any of these arguments fully, much less to rebut them. I will give particular attention here to one set of arguments, those that urge waiting periods for no-fault divorces as a way to reduce the incidence of divorce. I have previously addressed some of the other arguments elsewhere, at greater length.[12]

NO-FAULT DIVORCE: AN OVERVIEW OF THE DIFFICULTIES WITH THE CRITICS' CLAIMS

No-Fault Divorce Laws Cause Divorce

Some opponents of pure no-fault divorce believe that no-fault provisions are a cause of rising divorce rates and that revision of the divorce laws will therefore help reverse that trend. With that goal in mind, some propose imposing a waiting period of a year or more before divorce will be granted, at least for couples with minor children. Even longer waiting periods, up to five years, have been urged before allowing a unilateral no-fault divorce, and some would bar them altogether.[13] Would such proposals work to reduce marital breakup? At one level the claim that the divorce laws affect the rate of divorce seems necessarily true. If divorce were entirely barred, as it was in Ireland until very recently, then there would be no divorces at all.[14] And so it also seems plausible to think that if divorce were allowed but more difficult to obtain, then the divorce rate would decline. The obvious problem, however, is that while legal barriers can affect the rate of formal divorce, it is far less clear they can affect the rate of actual marital demise. This point suggests that waiting periods might increase the lag between breakup and formal divorce in individual cases, but they have no long-term effect at all on overall divorce rates. In that case, the new laws would only increase the proportion of couples who have ended their marriage in fact, but not in form.[15] That result offers few societal advantages while creating many individual problems, as we will see later in this chapter.

There are many reasons to think that the law is a minor player in affecting divorce rates. The U.S. divorce rate has been climbing steadily since 1860.[16] President Woolsey's Divorce Reform League was alarmed by the jump in the number of divorces from 9,937 in 1867, to 25,535 in 1886, proportionately far greater than the increase in population.[17] Despite the league's political successes, however, the rate kept climbing: by 1900, more than 55,000 divorces were granted each year.[18] There was a very large jump in the divorce rate during World War II, followed by a decline to prior levels and an uncharacteristic period of stability during the 1950s.[19] The climb then resumed, and by the mid-1960s, it had become very steep. The divorce rate was 2.1 per 1,000 people in 1958, grew to 2.9 by 1968, and peaked at 5.3 in 1979.[20] That is, the divorce rate began climbing more than a decade before the no-fault movement began and peaked at about the time no-fault was adopted nationwide. Since then it declined, first to 5.0, where it held steady through 1986, and more recently to 4.5 per 1,000 — 15 percent lower than in 1981.[21] Indeed, recent analyses of 1988 data suggest that 43 percent of marriages end in divorce, not more than 50 percent, an estimate that is frequently heard.[22] I do not intend to argue that the fifteen-year decline in divorce rates since 1981 was caused by the preceding decade's nationwide adoption of no-fault laws, since that inference would be as unwarranted as some that fault proponents have made. But in light of this history, I am not surprised that repeated efforts by researchers in this area have been unable to find any evidence that no-fault reforms yield an increase in divorce rates. A recent review concludes that the "consensus among researchers and informed commentators" is that "divorce law reforms had little or nothing to do" with the rising divorce rates of the 1960s and 1970s.[23] These findings are even less surprising if one understands that the law prior to the no-fault reforms allowed divorce by mutual consent in practice, even though it did not in form.[24] So even under the old fault laws, when marriages ended in fact, divorce usually followed, even though there might be some delay. For that reason, one would not expect no-fault reforms to have much long-term impact on the divorce rate; their main impact would instead be to reduce the time lag between marital breakdown and formal divorce.

Of course, it is true that divorce rates are higher today than in the 1960s. The long-term historical pattern of rising divorce rates "is a widespread phenomenon in western societies"[25] despite their varying divorce laws. Indeed, divorce laws vary within the United States as well. At the time they first adopted no-fault reforms, many states imposed the very kinds of waiting periods that reformers now urge, and while some later shortened or abandoned them, others did not. At least three states never allowed unilateral no-fault divorce at all.[26] But although marked regional variations in divorce rates are evident in the United States, they are entirely unrelated to regional patterns in divorce laws: the two regions most resistant to pure no-fault laws, the South and the Northeast, have the highest and lowest divorce rates, respectively.[27] Cultural patterns, in contrast, have clear effects on divorce rates: Some religious groups have far lower divorce rates than others, and interfaith marriages, which have increased, have higher divorce rates than intrafaith marriages.[28] And while there have been no legal changes that could plausibly account for the last decade's decline in the divorce rate, two demographic changes are suggestive: a rise in the median age of first marriages, and the aging of the baby boom generation, which has had a higher divorce rate than other cohorts but has now probably completed most of its divorces.[29] Even seasonal variations in divorce rates seem easier to show than variations associated with legal regimes.[30] So it seems unlikely that lengthening the waiting period before a divorce decree is issued, or barring unilateral no-fault divorces, would have any important impact on divorce rates.[31]

Some might argue that long waiting periods are nonetheless worth trying, on the grounds that they surely would do little harm. Fault rules, however, have historically been a minefield of unintended consequences, and I suspect that here as well the damage they would cause would far outweigh any benefits, even if a few marriages remained intact because of them. What damage? Consider first a proposal to require couples with minor children to wait two or three years before they can obtain a consensual no-fault divorce.

Imagine the Smith couple, married seven or eight years, in their early thirties, with a four-year-old child. For whatever reason, they don't get along. Maybe the marriage didn't work from the start, and perhaps they had their child in the mistaken belief it would solidify their marriage but discover instead that child rearing causes them yet more interpersonal conflict. So after several years of difficulties, they mutually decide to divorce. One of them moves out, and they consult a lawyer, who tells them they must wait three years. Perhaps the lawyer can obtain a legal separation for them, establish a division of their property, a custody arrangement, and child support obligations, but the divorce itself must wait. Proponents of the waiting period apparently believe that couples made to wait might change their minds, reunite, and live happily—or at least functionally—ever after. They apparently think that many couples with children divorce casually, without thinking much about what they are doing, and that they therefore will stay together if we just make them think about it some more. None of this seems to have much application to the Smiths, and their story seems more likely to me than that of the impetuous parents that waiting period proponents seem to have in mind. So if the waiting period really works to delay the divorce, its main effect on couples like the Smiths is to prevent their remarriage. This important point is masked by the very language we use. What we call a waiting period for divorce is really a waiting period for remarriage, for remarriage is the only thing that is truly delayed. Do we want this result? For what purpose? Do waiting period proponents want the Smiths to avoid establishing new relationships or to cohabit without marrying? I find this particularly puzzling because remarriage of the parent with primary custody may well be beneficial for the child, as well as for the parents.[32]

So the imposition of a waiting period for consensual no-fault divorce would be quite problematic, if in fact it worked as intended. I take solace, however, that here, as with so many government programs, we can say that while the law may be stupid, at least it won't work. Everything we know tells us that waiting periods will hardly delay remarriage at all. The reason is a troublesome policy problem confronting waiting period proponents: They don't really want to impose a delay on the spouse who is badly mistreated in the current marriage. For that reason, jurisdictions with lengthy waiting periods typically apply them only to no-fault divorces, while retaining fault grounds for divorce that, if proven, allow much earlier dissolution. The result, of course, is that couples who agree on divorce also quickly agree on some fault ground that they can present to the court so as to avoid the waiting period.

Consider, for example, some recent data from England, which requires two years' separation before a mutual-consent no-fault divorce can be granted (and five years' separation before a unilateral no-fault divorce is ordered). The result: there are very few no-fault mutual consent divorces. Where wives are the petitioner, 76 percent of divorces were granted on grounds of adultery or "unreasonable behavior"; only 19 percent on two years' mutual separation and 5 percent on five years' unilateral separation. Among the 30 percent of divorces in which the husband was the petitioner, fault grounds were less dominant but still accounted for a clear majority of all decrees.[33] Similar patterns are found in the American statistics as well as in other British data.[34] That is, where long waiting periods are imposed for consensual no-fault divorces, but not for fault divorces, couples who want to avoid the delay do so easily by cooperating in an uncontested fault divorce. What this means is that the primary consequence of imposing waiting periods for no-fault divorces is the revival of the sham "fault" proceedings that were common under the old fault regimes, in which the spouses collude in presenting the fault grounds necessary to obtain the quicker decree.[35]

A further detail in these recent British data is even more interesting: both husbands and wives were even less likely to wait the two- (or five-) year period if they had children under sixteen: the percentage who instead relied on fault grounds increased 6 percent among petitioning wives and 11 percent among petitioning husbands (46 percent of whom charged their wives with adultery). Indeed, the younger that the youngest child was at the time of divorce, the more likely were the parents to avoid the waiting periods and petition instead on fault grounds.[36] The parents apparently knew something that the law's draftsmen did not: that once a marriage fails, prolonging the divorce process is unlikely to be good for the children, particularly if the divorce is likely to exacerbate parental conflict.[37]

What, then, of a common companion proposal, an even longer waiting period—five years has been suggested—before a unilateral no-fault divorce is allowed?[38] Would problems be avoided if a wait were imposed only on unilateral no-fault divorces? Consider the Mitchells, whose story is told in two Missouri appellate decisions.[39] They are not so different from the Smiths, except that Mrs. Mitchell was not ready to give up on the marriage and wouldn't consent to divorce. Mr. Mitchell thought their "marriage was irretrievably broken [because] for three years he has felt that he no longer loves his wife." His emotional neglect of her leaves no doubt of the accuracy of this self-report; indeed, the court's detailed review of the marriage's deterioration would persuade anyone but Mrs. Mitchell that it was dead. Neither spouse seems particularly nasty, however, and one has the impression they were mismatched from the start.[40] But Mr. Mitchell, who now wants to call it quits, could find no objective flaw in Mrs. Mitchell's conduct adequate to satisfy Missouri's fault provisions, the most flexible of which required the petitioner to show that the respondent's behavior was such that the petitioner could not "reasonably be expected to live with the respondent." Mr. Mitchell's alternative was a unilateral no-fault divorce, but Missouri's very hedged no-fault provision required two years' separation before that could be granted. While the Mitchells had separated twice, the most recent separation had not yet been two years in length. Mrs. Mitchell's appeal was thus successful in blocking the divorce decree.

Of course, Mr. Mitchell refiled five months later, once two years had passed, and the trial court again granted the decree. But Mrs. Mitchell appealed again, arguing that in reckoning the length of the separation period the trial court should not have counted the portion of the separation that occurred prior to the previous appellate decision. This claim was rejected, and Mr. Mitchell finally had his divorce. Perhaps impressed with the pointlessness of this exercise, later Missouri decisions seem more willing than *Mitchell* to find that the spouses' deteriorated relationship is itself a sufficient basis for concluding that a petitioner has met the burden required by the "reasonably be expected to live with" provision.[41] Such interpretive flexibility would presumably be unacceptable to recent no-fault opponents who urge a five-year waiting period, since it offers an easy way around the requirement they wish to impose. Imagine, then, the Mitchell's case decided under the regime they urge. Several years of marital difficulties and short separations being inadequate to end the marriage over Mrs. Mitchell's objection, Mr. Mitchell, after moving out for the last time, must wait five more years for divorce—while Mrs. Mitchell presumably waits for him to return. Will denying Mr. Mitchell the right to remarry during this time drive him back to Mrs. Mitchell? No one reading the court's opinion could think that likely, nor would they believe it necessarily the best result for Mrs. Mitchell or her children. And surely a five-year wait followed by divorce would not help them. Mrs. Mitchell needs to rebuild her life, and sooner is better than later, especially for her children.[42]

Making Mr. Mitchell wait five years to remarry will seem pointlessly vindictive to many, although fault proponents may not agree. Even they should pause, however, to consider that while the law can keep Mr. Mitchell from remarrying, it is unlikely to keep him celibate. What then happens when he develops a close relationship with Mrs. Smith? The enforced wait means he cannot legally commit himself to her and her child. Perhaps they will cohabit in any event—and perhaps produce a nonmarital child during that time. While that is surely not the result that waiting period proponents intend, it may be the result they achieve. Their effort to protect Mrs. Mitchell will thus burden Mrs. Smith.

And consider further whether requiring long waiting periods for a unilateral divorce will in fact help the Mrs. Mitchells of this world. Change our story a bit. Consider Mrs. Mitchell's sister, Mrs. Jones. She is unhappy in her marriage because Mr. Jones is an insensitive, domineering bully who psychologically mistreats both her and their child. Mr. Smith would be a far better husband for her, and they would like to marry. But Mr. Jones, who has no immediate interest in remarrying, gets in his last licks at Mrs. Jones by refusing to cooperate with her in obtaining a consensual divorce. So now the only way Mrs. Jones can avoid waiting five years before marrying Mr. Smith is to assume the burden of proving Mr. Jones's fault. But his nasty, demeaning conduct, though real enough, is not so simple to prove in a contested proceeding—and perhaps Mrs. Jones also worries that he might defend with proof of an adulterous act between her and Mr. Smith. Surely adultery is also misconduct under the fault law and would be an effective defense under classic fault regimes.

So Mrs. Jones has a dilemma. Should she incur the cost of a contest over his fault, in the hope she can prevail—and prevail soon enough to make the effort worthwhile? Or should she perhaps try to induce Mr. Jones's agreement to a quicker consensual no-fault divorce, by offering to accept a reduced share of their marital property? This is probably not the scenario that waiting period proponents have in mind, but it is surely one that their proposals are likely to produce. Fans of fault often make the mistake of thinking that fault laws protect the innocent. They do not. They protect the person who does not care about delaying the divorce, at the expense of the person who does—and who may have very good reasons for wanting out. That is why the "bargaining chip" rationale for these rules doesn't work: no matter how we design them, it is inevitable that in many cases they will give bargaining leverage to the wrong spouse. We can achieve the goal of protecting the financially vulnerable spouse far more effectively by the direct strategy of reforming the law of alimony than by the indirect one of hoping that the imposition of a waiting period will allow the financially vulnerable spouse to negotiate a better deal.[43] That is why reform of the alimony laws is the American Law Institute's recommendation.

It is dangerous to fashion a divorce law with only one vision of how marriages break up—for example, that unilateral no-fault divorces are all sought by men who are deserting their loyal wives. There are many different stories, but a rule imposing waiting periods, or barring unilateral divorces, will apply to all the cases, not just the ones the reformer had in mind. In fact, available data suggest that today, in contrast to the case in the fault era, most divorces are instigated by wives rather than by husbands.[44] On reflection, this fact is not surprising. Of course, an important cultural change has occurred over the last several decades: divorce no longer carries with it the stigma that it once did. But that is surely not the only factor explaining the great increase in the willingness of wives to end their marriages. It must also be important to note that while divorce is difficult financially, it is in fact *less* difficult for women today than it was during the fault era. It is not only that far more women are already employed in the labor market than was then the case, although this may be the single most significant change. But it is also true that the law of divorce is financially more hospitable to women today than it was then, in two ways. First, in the majority of common-law states, a significant reform of marital property laws took place contemporaneously with the advent of no-fault. These states moved from the traditional common law title system, under which divorced wives typically had no entitlement to share in property acquired during marriage from their husband's earnings, to equitable distribution, which recognized such an entitlement. Second, while much attention is focused today on the difficulty of collecting child support, there is no question that the divorced mother is far more likely to receive a meaningful amount of child support today than she was in 1960. In short, it seems likely that an important reason for the increase in divorce rates is that women, being financially less dependent than they once were on maintaining their marriage, are far less willing to stay in an unhappy marriage.[45]

There is an important point here: the goal of deterring divorce may be in tension with the goal of treating divorcing parties justly. If most divorces are instigated by wives, than the best strategies for deterring divorces will be ones that affect the choices wives make.[46] We probably would reduce divorce rates if we discouraged women from entering the labor market, relaxed efforts to collect child support for divorced custodial mothers, and repealed the equitable distribution reforms of marital property laws. Surely no one would seriously suggest such changes. Indeed, the current proposals of the American Law Institute (ALI) to breathe life into the law of alimony (see the final section of this chapter) may do further justice at the price of yet higher divorce rates.

In sum, I am skeptical that very many people now casually destroy their happy marriages or that the introduction of prolonged waiting periods would be likely to preserve many unhappy ones.[47] Its effect will rather be to increase the number of marriages that are, at any given time, legally intact but factually dead, to keep many victims of failed marriages from building new lives for themselves and their children, and perhaps to increase the proportion of children born out of wedlock.

Fault Divorce Rules Are Needed to Deter Selfish and Bad Marital Behavior

Some no-fault critics are less concerned about deterring divorce than deterring bad marital behavior. They are therefore less interested in abolishing no-fault grounds for divorce or imposing lengthy waiting periods than in making marital fault a factor in allocating marital property or awarding alimony. They believe such fault-based financial rules will improve marital conduct. Because I have addressed these claims elsewhere, my comments here will be very brief.[48]

We have already seen that the goal of deterring divorce and the goal of deter-ring bad marital behavior might call for different rules, forcing the policymakers to choose between these purposes. For example, a rule that punishes bad marital behavior by rewarding the "innocent" spouse with a larger share of marital prop-erty may encourage that spouse to terminate the marriage, so that the price of a rule meant to deter bad behavior could be an increase in the number of divorces.[49]

Whether fault-based alimony or property allocation rules would in fact have a salutary effect on marital behavior is, of course, a key question for proponents of such reforms. In this overview, perhaps one point bears emphasis. If one has in mind the suppression of truly bad behavior, like interspousal violence, then di-vorce law seems neither the simplest nor the most effective available tool. The be-havior one seeks to suppress is already a violation of the criminal law and action-able in tort, and in some states the tort claim can even be joined with the dissolution action. Undoubtedly, more could be done to improve these remedies. But the claim that the violent actor undeterred by these sanctions will nevertheless cease that violence to avoid its consideration at divorce—a divorce he may not yet even contemplate—seems rather implausible, at least to me.[50] So I wonder whether the deterrence point is not meant to be different. Perhaps some would like to use the divorce law to deter conduct other than physical violence—conduct that the criminal and tort law do not reach. If that is the point, one is likely to face a se-rious problem in defining the targeted behavior and in establishing a social con-sensus about the need to suppress it. Recall our story of Mr. Jones's bullying and Mrs. Jones's adultery: One might start out classifying both kinds of conduct as of the sort we wish to suppress. Should both then be penalized in this case? How are they weighed against one another? Is the court to consider both spouses' stories of the marital back and forth, perhaps over many years, to determine their relative blameworthiness and its dollar value? No system of this kind can lead to pre-dictable and consistent results—as is indeed confirmed by the experience in those states that still allow it.[51] One cannot systematically shape marital behavior with a legal rule of unpredictable application. If the goal is to reach beyond the tort and criminal law, this problem is inevitable, for predictable application requires clear definition of the culpable behavior; and if the behavior were easily defined, it would already be actionable in tort, if not a violation of the criminal laws—unless there is no societal consensus that the behavior is sufficiently bad to justify pun-ishing without the need first to inquire into the nuances of the marital relation-ship.[52] But if the consensus is insufficient to punish the behavior under one legal rubric, it ought be insufficient under another as well.

No-Fault Divorce Yields Unjust Outcomes

This view is closely allied with the deterrence view just surveyed, for it is an al-ternative rationale for the same rule—to allow consideration of fault in allocating marital property or setting alimony awards. The difference is that this rationale is

based not on a goal of shaping marital conduct but on the belief that consideration of fault is necessary to do justice between divorcing parties. I would expect
most people to start with this intuition. How, indeed, could anyone oppose the
idea that blameworthy conduct ought to be punished, or should at least be cause
for imposing on the actor an obligation to pay compensation to those harmed by
it? And one cannot talk about blameworthy conduct without talking about fault.
Most people are therefore left unsatisfied by a system of divorce that does not
permit the court to examine the marriage for such blameworthy conduct and adjust the financial consequences of the dissolution accordingly. Writers who support this view want the law to provide "the rhetoric and the remedies for addressing good and bad marital conduct and abuses of trust in intimate
relationships."[53] They want the law to allow the aggrieved to tell their story and
to obtain vindication and compensation.

In assessing this argument, one must first note that in fact it is hardly clear that
persons divorced in pure no-fault systems actually believe the system's exclusion
of fault brought about some injustice. Indeed, the level of satisfaction with the
substantive results seems reasonably high (and higher, on average, for women
than for men).[54] More important, however, the problem with this argument is no
different than the problem with the more instrumental rationale for fault rules that
we have just considered: the meaning of the aggrieved's "story," as even this
view's proponents understand, "is inherently contextual."[55] And therein lies the
rub, for even those sympathetic to fault concede "prudential considerations about
the law's ability to comprehend the meaning of a given marriage and to regard
certain kinds of behavior as blameworthy."[56] Violations of even the clearest marital understandings, such as the commitment to sexual fidelity, cannot possibly be
evaluated apart from the context of the entire marital relationship. Individual decision makers will inevitably react differently to similar stories, while the financial incentives created by the rule ensure that some story will be told in nearly
every divorce. So the problem, once again, is not the goal of the fault rules but
their consequence. The rule does not buy justice but rather the injustice of unpredictable and arbitrary results, and at a price of heightened transaction costs.
The loser will often be the financially dependent spouse who feels compelled to
settle for a thinner financial package than she (or he) would get under a less discretionary no-fault system, for fear that the judge will be sympathetic to her husband's (or his wife's) story. I have elsewhere concluded that these concerns are
sufficiently serious to preclude not only fault claims at divorce[57] but also interspousal tort claims for emotional distress.[58]

Of course, some kinds of misconduct are sufficiently egregious, sufficiently vi-
olative of social norms, sufficiently *bad*, that no story need be told. Physical violence is the preeminent example.[59] For this limited kind of fault, the question is
not whether the law should recognize it but where. Vindication and compensation
are available through the criminal law and the tort law. Do we want the divorce
law to offer an additional remedy because it will recompense harms the tort law

won't recognize? That seems unlikely.[60] Because we want to allow double recovery? That seems hard to defend. Because we prefer compensating marital misconduct by allowing the divorce judge unrestrained discretion to make any adjustment he or she deems appropriate to the financial remedies otherwise allowed at divorce, as compared to the tort law's rules of damages and proof? That seems at best a complex battle cry. Indeed, it would seem that any serious proponent of using the divorce law to provide compensation for spousal violence would have to offer some set of principles by which the validity of the claims are to be judged and the damages gauged. I know of no set of divorce fault rules that attempt this task, but if any did it is hard to imagine how they could look much different than the usual rules that govern claims for battery. If that is true, then the only real issue here is a procedural one, not a substantive one: the proponent of the divorce law remedy is in the end reduced to arguing that the victim of spousal violence ought to be able to join his or her tort claim to the divorce action, and not be required to bring it separately. Well, perhaps. There are procedural complications,[61] and there is the question of whether there really are benefits from thus encouraging more tort filings and, if so, whether they are worth the price of so complicating the divorce trial. But in any event, that question is a minor footnote to the question of fault divorce.

No-Fault Divorce Reflects Amoral Thinking and Leads to "No-Responsibility" Divorce

There is a body of writing that seems at once sympathetic to the concerns of fault proponents yet is also equivocal. Because these writers respect the limits of legal rules and are keenly aware that the law reflects cultural mores as well as being a source of them, this thread of thought seems sometimes to lament more than condemn no-fault, treating it as a symptom of broader social ills. Among the most thoughtful of these writers are Carl Schneider and Mary Ann Glendon, and their observations are far too rich to do them justice in this overview.[62] An important theme of their writing is the extent to which American no-fault divorce has been accompanied by cultural changes that discourage moral discourse about family relations, that focus on individual fulfillment more than mutual commitment, that emphasize marriage's potential for happiness and deemphasize its obligations, and that value individual independence and disparage mutual interdependence. One can be sympathetic to many of their points and still support no-fault divorce, for any number of reasons.[63] Unfortunately, however, some of these observations have been made with phrases easily converted into slogans by others with less nuanced views. An example that is particularly misleading is the suggestion that no-fault divorce means "no-responsibility" divorce.[64]

Of course, it does not. Even before any no-fault reforms, fault was not the basis for imposing child support obligations, and it is the children of divorce with whom these no-fault critics usually claim to be most concerned.[65] Nor is fault necessary or even desirable as the basis for establishing postdivorce responsibilities toward a former spouse. While American law has admittedly not always been firm on this last point, today clear models are available for laws that exclude fault while taking seriously the idea that marriage can be the source of durable financial obligations between spouses that survive its dissolution. One important model is offered in the ALI's work on family dissolution, in the chapters on marital property and compensatory spousal payments that the institute has now provisionally approved.[66] (Its work on child support should soon follow.) So let us now move to that topic.

THE FUTURE OF NO-FAULT DIVORCE

When I think about why people are concerned about no-fault divorce, I tend to doubt they really believe the law is responsible for causing marriages to fail. I suspect instead that their real concern is that people can walk away from their marriages with no continuing responsibility to their family. What they are against, to repeat the slogan, is "no-fault, no-responsibility" divorce. Well, of course. Who isn't? But is that slogan a fair description of no-fault?

This particular slogan is usually attributed to Mary Ann Glendon.[67] Interestingly, while Glendon certainly used it,[68] she just as surely appreciated that "freer terminability of marriage by no means connotes freedom from economic responsibilities toward former dependents."[69] While she is concerned that American law seems at times to have been "careless" about "assuring . . . responsibility for the economic casualties of divorce," she views these defects as the result of "accident" more than "design" and appreciates that no-fault divorce systems need not be so careless. On this as on many things, I find Glendon's observations insightful. In considering how to think about what reforms should be made in American divorce law, her observation has it just right. The law must recognize and enforce the responsibilities that arise both from marriage and from the procreation of children.

What does that mean? As must certainly be clear by now, I am skeptical of the law's ability to regulate or even affect the intimate relations of marital partners, and I am doubtful that it is productive or right to attempt to do so. And because this is precisely what the law of marital fault is all about, I remain a strong believer in no-fault divorce. But having said that, I must also emphasize that I am not skeptical about the law's ability to define and enforce the financial responsibilities that arise from marriage, and I just as strongly believe in the importance of having the law perform this role. If we are really concerned about the children of divorce and about fair treatment of financially dependent spouses, that is where our focus needs to be.

In the United States, the enforcement of child support is hardly a new theme. Indeed, it has become nearly an obligatory chant in the political process. But for all the attention that enforcement has received, the substantive law of child support remains inadequate. As we have studied the matter for our work in the ALI project, my coreporters and I have become convinced that the theory underlying the setting of child support guidelines is confused and that in consequence the guideline amounts employed by most American states are usually too low. I can say little more now, because the subject would take me too far afield from this chapter's focus, and also because our work on child support is still tentative and has not yet received ALI approval.

But on property allocation and alimony, the ALI's work is largely completed.[70] Let me then summarize some central features relevant to our concerns. The most innovative thing that the ALI has done is propose the replacement of alimony with a set of entitlements, presumptively arising in certain defined kinds of cases, that are called *compensatory payments*. To understand why we have done this and what changes its adoption would effect, I have to back up a little bit to explain why the concept of alimony needed such revitalization.

Alimony was originally a remedy of the English ecclesiastical courts developed at a time when complete divorce was available only by special legislative action and gender roles in marriage were rigid and unquestioned. The husband had a legal and customary duty to support his wife. This duty continued after divorce because there was no divorce in the modern sense but only legal separation. When judicial divorce became available in the eighteenth and nineteenth centuries, alimony remained a remedy even though its initial justification—the duty of the husband to support his wife—no longer applied because the parties were no longer married. In short, the traditional explanation for alimony was put in doubt long ago, when absolute divorce was allowed, and was undermined completely by modern reforms rejecting gender roles.

Some imagined that fault concepts could supply the missing rationale. One explanation for alimony offered early in the fault era was that the duty to support one's wife could not be extinguished by the husband's own misconduct. Following that rationale, some jurisdictions allowed alimony claims only by "innocent" wives divorcing "guilty" husbands—an approach still followed by North Carolina until very recently. This idea worked best, of course, in the traditional fault system under which every divorce necessarily has a guilty and an innocent spouse (since otherwise no divorce would be granted). As soon as one accepts that divorce might be allowed where neither party is "guilty," as under the traditional ground of incompatibility, it becomes impossible to explain the husband's continuing support duty on the basis of his own misconduct. Indeed, most jurisdictions in the fault era, concerned about women's financial dependency, in theory allowed claims even by guilty wives,[71] although in practice they undoubtedly fared less well. Claims by guilty wives were eventually allowed by the English ecclesiastical courts as well, from their concern that the wife might otherwise "be turned out destitute on the streets or led into temptation," the assumption being that women were limited to domestic skills and could not support themselves by employment.[72] So while misconduct continued to have a kind of wild-card impact on alimony awards in states that allowed its consideration, everyone could see that it could provide no general explanation for why we have that remedy. Of course, however, alimony was not abolished. The instinct that the doctrine of alimony was necessary kept it alive, even though the law had no theory to explain it.

Unease over the continuing validity of the traditional rationale for alimony affected decisions early in the modern regime of no-fault divorce. These decisions granted only limited-duration alimony to women who had been homemakers in long-term marriages. These courts expressed the view that alimony's principal purpose was to provide short-term transitional assistance to such women. The inability to articulate any basis for an indefinite continuation of the husband's support obligation, and the conviction that where possible divorce should effect a "clean break" between the marital partners, combined to push the courts in this direction. The result was buttressed by the expectation that the homemaker would develop marketable skills sufficient to afford her an acceptable living standard, at least when combined with her share in the equitable distribution of their accumulated property, an entitlement that was then relatively new in many common-law states. Of course, experience demonstrated the defects in the expectation that long-term homemakers could smoothly move into the labor market and thereby maintain something close to their accustomed living standard, and the "clean break" philosophy is not the vision of alimony one finds today in most appellate opinions. At least in long-term marriages, one instead finds a widespread view that marital dissolution should not dissolve all financial ties between the former spouses if the result would be a significant disparity in the spouses' postdissolution financial standing. A similar intuition encourages awards in marriages of shorter duration as well, in which there are children of the marriage who are still young and will be primarily in the care of one spouse.

But this apparent consensus exists only in very general terms, and there is still no dominant theory to explain the alimony award. The prevailing statutory formulation allows the court to grant alimony (or "spousal support," as it is commonly now called) to the spouse who is in need. Neither the statutes nor the cases, however, explain why a needy person's former spouse should be liable for his or her support rather than the needy person's parents, children, or society as a whole. The result is that the meaning of "need"—the most fundamental issue created by such statutes—is hopelessly confused. Some opinions find an alimony claimant in "need" only if unable to provide for her basic necessities; others find need if the claimant is unable to support himself at a moderate middle-class level; still others find need when the claimant is unable to sustain the living standard enjoyed during the marriage even if it was lavish. There can be no principled basis for choosing among these definitions of need without an explanation for imposing the obligation to meet it. In fact, "need" is often used in the law as a conclusory term whose only meaning is that a court has found the spouse entitled to an award of alimony.

It is therefore not surprising that research studies find that trial court decisions on alimony vary widely, even within the same jurisdiction. Some decisional variation would be expected in even a perfect system, because trial courts must have discretion in these matters to deal appropriately with factual variations that no statute can comprehensively anticipate. But it seems clear that the variation arises at least in part because trial courts apply different principles as often as they face different facts. As a consequence, decisions are very difficult to predict. This unpredictability affects the negotiations that settle the great majority of cases.[73] Finally, the unpredictability and unreliability of the alimony remedy has often led lawyers for one spouse to frame claims on the other spouse's postdivorce earnings flow in marital property terms, rather than within the alimony system that should be the proper forum for them. This creates a set of difficulties of its own that I cannot address here without leading us too far afield from our main topic.[74] The conclusion drawn by the ALI, however, is that the modern law's failure to express any systematic theory of alimony creates serious difficulties for the law of marital property as well as for the law of alimony. A central task of the ALI principles, therefore, was to develop a justification and approach to the law of alimony that would support a set of rules that will operate more consistently, more reliably, and more predictably.

As previously observed, need, the most common criterion for an alimony award under existing law, simply does not work as a central explanatory concept for alimony, and under current law it is invoked by courts largely as a conclusion rather than as an explanation. The ALI concluded that the solution did not lie in refining our understanding of need but in abandoning it. A unifying concept must be sought elsewhere. The ALI principles therefore refocus the alimony inquiry from need to *loss*. The result is not entirely revolutionary. A spouse found in need under existing law is usually a spouse on whom the marital dissolution imposes a loss that seems unfairly disproportionate. That is, the sense that one spouse has an obligation to meet the other's postdissolution needs arises from the recognition that the need results at least in part from an unfair distribution of the financial losses arising from the marital failure. The payment's true justification is therefore to provide a remedy for an unfair loss allocation, not to relieve need, and need is not therefore an eligibility requirement for the award. The spouse who incurs a disproportionate financial loss from the dissolution will often seem in need, but even in those cases the degree of need will vary. That is why no single standard of need appropriately decides all alimony cases. Chapter 5 of the ALI principles thus characterizes the remedy it recognizes as *compensation for loss* rather than relief of need and employs the term *compensatory payment* (instead of *alimony* or *spousal support*) to emphasize this conceptual change.

By grounding compensatory awards on a principle of loss, the ALI achieves a conceptual reformulation that helps explain many prevailing practices, even while revising others. The categories of compensable loss recognized in the draft bear a close relationship to the kinds of fact patterns that most often support alimony claims in existing law. At the same time, the shift to *loss* as the primary explanatory concept allows development of rules of adjudication that are more predictable in application than are rules grounded on a single but ill-defined goal of relieving need. Perhaps equally important, reconceptualizing the award's purpose as the equitable allocation of a joint loss changes it from a plea for help to a claim of entitlement, thereby making the award's availability more certain. Let me be very concrete for a moment and describe the most important sections of the ALI draft, the ones that apply in the case of the intermediate or longer-term marriage, especially one with children. First I want to explain just what kind of remedy arises in such cases under the ALI formulation, and then return to the no-fault rationale for that remedy.

The provisions I now describe are contained in topic 2 of chapter 5 of ALI's principles. They apply to the long-term spouse, especially one who has been the primary caretaker of the marital children. Whenever the duration of the marriage or of the child care period exceeds a specified minimum duration, and the claimant's earning capacity at divorce falls below a specified percentage of the other spouse's, a claim arises. The ALI leaves the precise choice of threshold values up to the local jurisdiction adopting its system, although it provides some guidance about what the reasonable range of choices would be. The point is that wherever in this range the local jurisdiction chooses to be, the applicable rule will create what is, in effect, a presumption that the financially dependent spouse who crosses that threshold is entitled to an award—a compensatory payment. The amount of the award is set under a system that is essentially identical in operation to the child support guidelines. A presumption arises that the amount of the claim is a particular percentage of the difference between the spouses' postdissolution incomes, and the applicable percentage increases with the duration of the marriage or child care period. If the marriage is long enough, the percentage will top out at a level somewhere between 40 and 50 percent of the income differential, depending on just how the local jurisdiction has chosen to implement the ALI recommendations. The term for which the payments continue is also set under a presumption that makes that term proportional to the duration of the marriage. If the marital duration and the age of the obligee are high enough, the duration becomes open ended.

Let me offer a specific example taken from the published ALI draft.[75] It is a marriage dissolved after eighteen years, during fifteen of which the wife has been the primary caretaker of the couple's children, who are fifteen and eleven at the time of divorce. The husband is a plumber earning $5,000 monthly; the wife attended a junior college, has worked occasionally as a teacher's aide in a nursery school, and at the time of divorce can find regular work paying $750 monthly. Under the particular implementation of the ALI principles that the draft assumes in setting out this example, the applicable guideline would call for an award to the wife of $1,700 monthly for seven and half years, with an additional year and half entitlement to $765. This will be the result unless the trial judge makes a finding on the record that the case presents a set of unusual facts justifying the conclusion that such an award would work a substantial injustice. Child support is of course calculated separately, but under the ALI system, the child support award would be based on the incomes the spouses will have after the compensatory payments are made.

This example assumes a relatively restrained implementation of the ALI recommendations. Other implementations also consistent with the recommendations could yield a higher award or one of longer duration. In either case, I do not believe the precise figures are revolutionary, even if more generous than many courts would now order. They are not revolutionary, however, because they are similar to what some courts have already done in some similar cases. The importance of the ALI reform lies not in the numbers but rather in the numbers' reliability and predictability. For while many courts would reach a similar result under current law, others from the same jurisdiction will not, and many potential claimants will therefore settle for less rather than take the risk that they would lose if they pursued more in litigation. The important difference, in other words, is between the presumption of entitlement created under the ALI principles and the appeal to the trial judge's discretion and goodwill that the claimant must make under current law.

I believe this move away from trial judge discretion is essential to any serious effort to place the financially dependent spouse in an acceptable position at the termination of a long-term marriage. In this respect, both the problem and the remedy with alimony are the same as they were with child support in 1980, when we began replacing judicial discretion with guidelines. But this reform can only work in a no-fault system: guidelines cannot take fault assessments into account and are pointless if the trial judge has discretion to adjust the guideline amounts to reflect his or her assessment of the spouse's relative blame for the marriage's demise. The movement to guidelines for compensatory payments (alimony) thus requires us to accept, once and for all, that neither the obligor's fault nor the obligee's innocence are the basis of the obligation.

I want to say more, in the context of our specific hypothetical case, about why it is right that a claim for compensatory payments not depend on a finding of the husband's guilt or the wife's innocence. But to get there I first want to continue my analogy to child support. It seems obvious to most of us that marital misconduct should play no role in setting child support amounts. Yet consider, for example, the father who says he never wanted the child but was duped into the conception by the mother's misrepresentations to him concerning her use of birth control. There have been a number of cases considering such a defense to a child support claim, all agreeing that it fails. Now if you believe that father's story, there is surely a real sense in which he is "innocent," but *of course* he still must pay because the child support obligation is not based on assessments of blameworthiness. The father must pay because past events have had irreversible present consequences. Those events have produced a situation in which there is a human being with claims to financial assistance, and the father was an essential actor in those events; it is therefore right for the law to insist he share the responsibility for their consequences. In reaching this result, the law does not pretend to address every aspect of the parent–child relationship. Parenting has many obligations and joys associated with it, not all of which are within the law's capacity to affect. We cannot assure the father that he will maintain a close emotional bond with his child, nor can we assure the child that the father will be a source of emotional support. The law's role is necessarily incomplete. But that provides no basis for declining to intervene where it can, and surely it can enforce the father's obligations of financial support.

I would like to suggest that the proper analysis of our hypothetical alimony claim is not as different from this child support example as many may assume. The chief difference is this: the obligation to provide postmarital financial support for a financially dependent spouse does not arise from the marriage alone, the way that the child support obligation arises from conception and childbirth alone. The child's dependence arises with his or her existence, and so it becomes irreversible at the outset. The dependence of the financially dependent spouse does not arise with the marriage vows but takes longer to develop. However, as a marriage lengthens, the parties assume roles and functions with respect to one another. Each molds the other, and the molds gradually set and harden. The precise timing will vary with the couple, and observers may not agree precisely either. But the basic process seems nearly inevitable, and few would urge a different analysis in the usual marriage of, say, thirty-five years. When adults share enough of their life together, they mold one another just as surely as parents create a child. We do not need to inquire into blameworthiness for the marriage's ultimate breakdown to conclude that the parties' situation at the end of their marriage is the consequence of both their acts and properly considered their joint responsibility. But, of course, the situation does not change suddenly at the close of the thirty-fifth year; it develops gradually over time. So then does the obligation that arises from the relationship. In most cases marital duration alone may provide the measure of the resulting obligation—an obligation that is not ended abruptly at divorce. One might sensibly argue that financial losses are not the only ones that arise when a marriage breaks down: either or both spouses may feel a loss of emotional attachment, of personal intimacy, of all the daily contributions once made by the other spouse to the life's functioning. But once again the law's inability to address every potential loss does not justify its failure to address the financial loss.

One final thought on this analogy: it is dependent, in another important way, on a no-fault approach to marital termination. I do not believe the law can base the imposition of a legal obligation on the duration of the relationship from which it arises, unless the law allows the parties free exit from that relationship.

CONCLUSION

I have attempted, in this chapter, to show several things. First, I have reviewed the enormous pile of data showing that the divorce laws have little if any impact on the divorce rate. Second, I have argued that the imposition of waiting periods will cause more harm than good. Third, I have reminded us that the law's role in divorce is necessarily circumscribed: pragmatics and principle both suggest it is a mistake to attempt to try to harness the law to regulate the personal conduct of marital partners, and it is precisely such regulation that is the only function that fault rules could serve. Fourth, I have urged that the definition and enforcement of financial obligations are, in contrast, a familiar, defensible, and *effective* use of the law, but one in need of reform. Fifth, I have given you a thumbnail description of such reforms, as embodied in the current proposal of the American Law Institute—reforms that would create more predictable and more reliable remedies than does current law to protect the financially dependent spouse when an intermediate or long-term marriage ends. I believe these reforms would do far more than would any revival of fault to make the consequences of marital dissolution more just. Finally, I have pointed out that such reforms of the rules governing the financial consequences of divorce depend in important ways on maintaining a system of no-fault divorce, for it is only within the rubric of no-fault that it will be possible to design and to justify a consistent and predictable system of compensatory payments.

NOTES

This chapter grew out of a paper presented at a conference sponsored by the Communitarian Network, whose support I acknowledge with thanks. I also benefited from the comments of Kate Bartlett, Grace Blumberg, and Steve Sugarman, who read an earlier draft of this chapter on very short notice. Portions of the chapter are adapted from Ira Ellman and Sharon Lohr, "Marriage as Contract, Opportunistic Violence, and Other Bad Arguments for Fault Divorce," *University of Illinois Law Review* 719 (1997).

1. One can find these proposals in magazines of political commentary—see, for example, William A. Galston, "Divorce American Style," *The Public Interest* 124 (1996): 12— as well as in the state legislatures—see "No-Fault Divorce Is under Attack," *New York Times,* February 12, 1996, A10.

2. This was a major arena of debate in the American Law Institute's current study of the law of marital dissolution. The chief reporter's draft, which adopted a pure no-fault system, ultimately prevailed, but only after a spirited debate at the ALI's May 1996 annual meeting, during which two motions to reinsert fault in these financial awards were defeated. The chief reporter's position is set forth in the draft, American Law Institute, *Principles of the Law of Family Dissolution* (Proposed Final Draft No. 1, 1997). The ALI publishes complete transcripts of its annual meetings; for a summary of the portion of the proceedings devoted to the debate on the "Family Dissolution" draft, see *Family Law Reporter* 22 (1996): 1339.

3. Current reform proposals have not all favored the revival of fault. The New York State Bar appointed a Task Force on Family whose report, issued August 19, 1996, recommended that New York amend its restrictive rules and allow, for the first time, unilateral no-fault divorce.

4. Lawrence M. Friedman, *A History of American Law*, 2d ed. (New York: Simon & Schuster, 1985), 204-7, 498-504.

5. The quotations are taken from ibid., 207, 500.

6. See, for example, Carl Schneider, "Marriage, Morals, and Law: No-Fault Divorce and Moral Discourse," *Utah Law Review* 2 (Spring 1994): 503, who argues that the movement away from thinking of marital failure in these terms has certain moral costs that have not always been appreciated.

7. Margaret F. Brinig and Steven Crafton, "Marriage and Opportunism," *Journal of Legal Studies* 23 (1994): 869; and Martin Zelder, "The Economic Analysis of the Effect of No-Fault Divorce Law on the Divorce Rate," *Harvard Journal of Law and Public Policy* 16 (1993): 241. Two articles go so far as to suggest that no-fault divorce has produced an increase in spousal violence: Brinig and Crafton, "Marriage and Opportunism," and Lynn Wardle, "Divorce Violence and the No-Fault Divorce Culture," *Utah Law Review* 1 (1994): 741. Indeed, Brinig and Crafton claim empirical support for their proposition. There are serious methodological flaws in their study, however, and a more careful analysis of available data finds no such relationship; see Ira Mark Ellman and Sharon Lohr, "Marriage as Contract, Opportunistic Violence, and Other Bad Arguments for Fault Divorce," *University of Illinois Law Review* 719 (1997).

8. See, generally, Ira Mark Ellman, Paul Kurtz, and Elizabeth Scott, *Family Law: Cases, Text, Problems,* 3d ed. (Charlottesville, Va.: Michie, 1998), 228-29.

9. See, for example, *Marriage of Mitchell,* 545 S.W.2d 313 (Mo. App. 1976).

10. See American Law Institute, *Principles of the Law of Family Dissolution* (Tentative Draft No. 2, 1996), 17-27. As of this writing, the successor to this volume, *Proposed Final Draft No. 1,* was in press. I will nonetheless refer to the 1996 version when, as in this case, reference to particular page numbers is appropriate. The relevant portions of the ALI work are also contained in Ira Mark Ellman, "The Place of Fault in a Modern Divorce Law," *Arizona State Law Journal* 28 (1996): 773.

11. The traditional fault law held sway at a time when many, if not most, American common-law states still adhered to the traditional common-law marital property system. Under that system, the question of whether misconduct could be considered in the allocation of property would not arise, because there was no allocation of property: all property went to the spouse who held legal title to it. That was typically the breadwinner-husband, unless he had made a gift of property to the wife.

12. See Ira Mark Ellman and Stephen Sugarman, "Spousal Emotional Abuse as a Tort," *Maryland Law Review* 55 (1996): 1268; and Ellman, "The Place of Fault," 773.

13. Michigan has been a particular battleground over such proposals; see "No-Fault Divorce Is under Attack," at A10. See also Galston, "Divorce American Style," 11.

14. Perhaps that would not be true if foreign divorces were recognized, but of course the refusal to recognize foreign divorces could be part of a truly rigorous anti-divorce reform.

15. In Ireland, for example, 6 percent of all marriages were in fact defunct, with the parties living separately, in 1986, before recent divorce law reforms. See Michele Dillon, *Debating Divorce: Moral Conflict in Ireland* (Lexington: University Press of Kentucky,

1993), 167. This was also the consequence under the prereform Italian divorce laws, as commemorated in the movie *Divorce Italian Style*.

16. See Ellman et al., *Family Law*.

17. Friedman, *A History of American Law*, 502.

18. Ibid.

19. Ibid.

20. Interestingly, the overall marital dissolution rate—the number of marriages ending by *either* divorce or death, per one thousand existing marriages, remained quite stable between 1860 and 1970: it was 32.2 at the beginning of this period, and 34.5 at the end. See Lawrence Stone, *The Family, Sex and Marriage in England, 1500–1800* (New York: Harper & Row, 1977), 56. It thus seems that the average marital duration may not have been that much longer even when divorce rates were lower. It was not until the mid-1970s that more American marriages ended in divorce than in death.

21. Divorce statistics are gathered by the Centers for Disease Control and Prevention, National Center for Health Statistics, and their most recent data, as available at this writing, are for the twelve months ending in April 1995. *Monthly Vital Statistics Report* 44, no. 4 (October 4, 1995).

22. Robert Schoen and Robin M. Weinick, "The Slowing Metabolism of Marriage: Figures from 1988 U.S. Marital Status Life Tables," *Demography* 30 (1993): 737, 742.

23. Martin Richards, "Divorce Numbers and Divorce Legislation," *Family Law* 96 (1996): 151. Research supportive of this conclusion includes H. Elizabeth Peters, "Marriage and Divorce: Informational Constraints and Private Contracting," *American Economic Review* 76 (1986): 437, 447 ("The unilateral divorce rule is found to have no relationship to the probability that a woman becomes divorced"); Gary Stanley Becker, *A Treatise on the Family* (Cambridge, Mass.: Harvard University Press, 1981), 228-29 ("The change to no-fault divorce does not appear to have had a lasting effect on the divorce rates in California"); Alan H. Frank, John J. Berman, and Stanley F. Mazur-Hurt, "No-Fault Divorce and the Divorce Rate: The Nebraska Experience—An Interrupted Time Series Analysis and Commentary," *Nebraska Law Review* 58 (1979): 1, 22 ("The major finding of this study [is] that the change in Nebraska's divorce law from a system based on fault to one based on the irretrievable breakdown of the marriage did not significantly influence the frequency of divorce"); Robert Schoen, Harvey N. Green, and Robert B. Mielke, "California's Experience with Non-Adversary Divorce," *Demography* 12 (1975): 223. Thomas B. Marvell, in "Divorce Rates and the Fault Requirement," *Law and Society Review* 23 (1989): 543, found evidence for an effect of no-fault reforms on divorce rates in some states but not in others, but he could identify no plausible explanation for this difference. One possibility is that the divorce rates of some no-fault states were inflated by migratory divorces from neighboring states that were late converts to no-fault. Marvell also found regional differences in the impact of no-fault laws, as well as differences associated with his classification of the kind of no-fault law enacted, that he could not satisfactorily explain. Marvell concluded that the methodological difficulties are sufficient to preclude any clear answer to the question of whether enactment of no-fault laws increased divorce rates. One possible explanation for the variations he found among states, but which he did not investigate, are differences in preform laws. It would not be surprising, for example, to find more evidence of an impact of the no-fault reforms in a state like New York, which previously allowed divorce only on grounds of adultery, than in a state that previously allowed

divorces on grounds of mental cruelty that were flexibly applied when functionally un-contested. Such a result would be plausible even though New York adopted a relatively cautious approach to no-fault, compared with some western states that both began and ended the reform process in a different place. Note that this explanation does not imply that no-fault reforms caused any increase in the rate with which New Yorkers actually ended their marriages, but only in the rate with which New York courts granted divorce decrees. That is, one would not be surprised to find that the postreform increase in New York divorces would be accompanied by a corresponding decrease in New York annulments (which surely did take place) and in divorce decrees granted to New Yorkers by the courts of other states.

One study that departs from what is otherwise the general consensus is Paul A. Nakonezny, Robert D. Shull, and Joseph Lee Rodgers, "The Effect of No-Fault Divorce Law on the Divorce Rate across the 50 States and Its Relation to Income, Education and Religiosity," *Journal of Marriage and the Family* 57 (1995): 477. This study contains two fatal and surprisingly obvious methodological flaws, however. It compares the average divorce rate in each state over the three years preceding its enactment of no-fault divorce with that state's average rate over the three years following the enactment. One expects to find a temporary surge in divorces in the years immediately following enactment of no-fault, however, for two reasons. First, some parties postpone filing for divorce in anticipation of the change, thus shifting some divorce decrees from the years immediately preceding enactment to the years immediately following it. Second, no-fault reforms generally reduce the time lag between the filing and the decree, with the result that the number of decrees in the years immediately following the reform are swelled with several years' worth of cases that had been in the pipeline. The rate comparison used in this study thus emphasizes the expected but transitory effects of the legal change. The second flaw arises from the difficulty of making this rate comparison during a time period in which divorce rates are rising in any event. The study attempts to control for this problem by comparing the rate rise it detects during the six-year period bracketing the legal reform with the rate rise found in each state over a randomly chosen six-year period that does not include the change in law. The silent but essential premise of this control technique, however, is that the base rate of increase is identical during both six-year periods. That premise, however, is clearly false. The study itself reports that 78 percent of no-fault reforms were enacted during the 1970s and an additional 10 percent in the 1960s. However, as is well known in the field, the national rise in divorce rates was extraordinarily steep between 1968 and 1979. One could as easily claim that attending high school causes a rise in male testosterone levels, as evidenced by the fact that the change during this four-year period is so much steeper than the change during any randomly chosen four-year period on either side of the high school years.

24. Ellman et al., *Family Law,* 191-98. If the real difference between fault and no-fault is a difference between divorce by mutual consent and divorce by unilateral consent, and if transaction costs are not high under either regime, then one would expect, under the Coase theorem, no difference in the number of divorces, although there should be a difference in the terms of divorce. For a more complete explanation of this, see Zelder, "The Economic Analysis," 241; Becker, *A Treatise on the Family,* 226-27; Elisabeth Landes, "The Economics of Alimony," *Journal of Legal Studies* 7 (1978): 35, 36-39.

25. Richards, "Divorce Numbers," 151.

26. They are New York, Tennessee, and Mississippi. See Ellman et al., *Family Law,* 216.

27. In 1986 the no-fault West and the fault-oriented South had almost indistinguishable divorce rates of 5.6 and 5.5, respectively, while the mixed Midwest had a rate of 4.4 and the more fault-oriented Northeast a rate of 3.6. National Center for Health Statistics, *Monthly Vital Statistics Report* 38, no. 2, "Advance Report of Final Divorce Statistics 1986" (1989).

28. Evelyn L. Lehrer and Carmelle Chiswick, "Religion as a Determinant of Marital Stability," *Demography* 30 (1993): 385. Mormons have significantly more stable marriages than non-Mormons do. Catholic upbringing (as distinguished from current Catholic religious affiliation) does not have much effect on the probability of divorce, for persons born after 1930. See William Sander, "Catholicism and Marriage in the United States," *Demography* 30 (1993): 373.

29. Between 1970 and 1993, the median age at first marriage increased from 20.8 to 24.5 for women, and from 23.2 to 26.5 for men. See "Divorce Me Not," *Numbers News* (May 1995); also at http://www.demographics.com:80/search/nn/NN386.htm. The relatively higher divorce rate for the baby boom generation can be seen by looking at the divorce rate broken down by age range: the baby boomers are a divorce "bump" that has moved through the divorce statistics over the past two decades. See Peter Uhlenberg, Teresa Cooney, and Robert Boyd, "Divorce for Women after Midlife," *Journal of Gerontology* 45 (1990): S3, S5.

30. The divorce rate is ordinarily below average in October through December, perhaps because people try to make it through the holidays, and then goes up in February and March, apparently inflated by the deferred winter divorces. June is the usual peak month for divorces, although it is not clear why. Paula Mergenbagen DeWitt, "Breaking Up Is Hard to Do," *American Demographics* (October 1992): 52, 56.

31. Galston, "Divorce American Style," 12, 22, suggests a one-year waiting period for mutual consent divorces and a five-year waiting period for unilateral no-fault divorces. While there is evidence that some cases are dropped during such waiting periods (e.g., Frank et al., "No-Fault Divorce," 80, n.329), it is not certain that this translates into a reduction in divorces, since the cases may be refiled later. However, two British researchers have concluded that "a minority of couples would use such a period in order to rethink, perhaps to seek help, and in a few instances to re-establish married life together. . . . [V]ery few decisions to divorce are taken impetuously although our research does demonstrate that minds may change"; Gwynn Davis and Mervyn Murch, *Grounds for Divorce* (Oxford: Clarendon, 1988), 155.

32. Remarriage of the custodial parent is usually the single event most likely to improve her economic status and thus that of her child. See, for example, Greg J. Duncan and Saul D. Hoffman, "Economic Consequences of Marital Instability," in *Horizontal Equity, Uncertainty, and Economic Well-Being,* ed. Martin David and Timothy Smeeding (Chicago: University of Chicago Press, 1985), 427, 437. If the child is young, the custodial parent's remarriage also offers the possibility of establishing a parental bond between child and stepparent, possibly an important advantage, especially because, remarriage or not, the likelihood is that emotional bonds with the noncustodial natural parent are likely to fade; see Lye, Klepinger, Hyle, and Nelson, "Child Living Arrangements and Adult Children's Relations with the Parents," *Demography* 32 (1995): 261.

33. John Haskey, "Divorce Statistics," *Family Law* 26 (1996): 301, who reports 1994 data from England and Wales.

34. When Ohio required a two-year separation before a consensual no-fault divorce would be granted, only 12.6 percent of the divorces were granted on no-fault grounds, as couples apparently chose to present evidence of other bases rather than wait. Robert E. McGraw, Gloria J. Sterin, and Joseph M. Davis, "A Case Study in Divorce Law Reform and Its Aftermath," *Journal of Family Law* 20 (1982): 443, 464 (presenting 1978 data). Some evidence indicates that even a one-year wait is too long for a great number of couples. When Wisconsin, for example, reduced its required separation period from five years to one year, the number of couples relying on that ground only increased to 8 or 9 percent, from 3 or 4; 86 percent of all divorces were still granted on grounds of "cruel and inhuman treatment." Alan H. Frank, John J. Berman, and Stanley F. Mazur-Hart, "No Fault Divorce and the Divorce Rate," *Nebraska Law Review* 58 (1979): 1, 47, n.180. See also British Law Commission, "Facing the Future: A Discussion Paper on the Ground for Divorce," *Law Commission* 170 (1988), also reporting that three-fourths of British divorces were granted on fault grounds such as adultery, desertion, or the other spouse's unreasonable behavior, rather than on the two years' separation.

35. It is, of course, hard to tell what proportion of the claims of fault were contested. While the 1994 British data do not report on that fact, they do indicate that the time between the petition and the granting of the divorce decree was on average a little bit shorter for divorces based on separation periods than for fault divorces. For example, looking at all couples in which the wife was the petitioner, that interval was less than a year in 78 percent of the divorces based on adultery, 75 percent of those based on "unreasonable behavior," but 86 percent of those based on two years' separation. This gap perhaps suggests that fault was in fact contested in a small proportion of the decrees based upon adultery and unreasonable behavior.

36. Haskey, "Divorce Statistics," 302.

37. Perhaps the most important recent findings on divorce are those contained in Andrew Cherlin, Frank Furstenberg, et al., "Longitudinal Studies of Effects of Divorce on Children in Great Britain and the United States," *Science* 252 (1991): 1386. Using longitudinal data on large sample of children from both United States and England, the researchers concluded that five years after divorce, one can discern relatively little negative impact of it on the children. This study is notable for separating out the effects of the divorce itself from the effects of the family dysfunction that may have led to it. Simple comparisons between the outcomes of children of divorced parents and those of children of intact families tell us little about the effect of *divorce*, since one cannot assume that had they only refrained from formal divorce these families would have functioned similarly to other families that in fact stayed intact.

38. Galston suggests five years. See "Divorce American Style," 22.

39. *Marriage of Mitchell*, 545 S.W.2d 313 (Mo. App. 1976), and 581 S.W.2d 871 (Mo. App. 1979).

40. A high school graduate "on the business line," Mrs. Mitchell testified that she read no books or newspapers but did "thumb through magazines." As described she had few interests apart from children. Mr. Mitchell was a few hours short of a college degree in economics and appeared to have a white-collar job at General Motors.

41. See Ellman et al., *Family Law,* 184-85.

42. Remarriage is probably Mrs. Mitchell's most promising option for improving her standard of living. See Duncan and Hoffman, "Economic Consequences," 427, 437. About 75 percent of all divorced women eventually remarry (Andrew Cherlin, *Marriage,*

Divorce, Remarriage [Cambridge, Mass.: Harvard University Press, 1989], 29), but the probability of their remarrying would seem to decline with the additional wait. In 1985, for example, the remarriage rate per one thousand divorced women varied in this way for some selected age ranges: under age twenty-five, 264; twenty-five to twenty-nine, 184; thirty-five to forty-four, 80; forty-five to sixty-four, 29. See Uhlenberg et al., "Divorce for Women after Midlife," S3, S5.

43. I may share responsibility for giving currency to the bargaining chip idea (see Ira Mark Ellman, "The Theory of Alimony," *California Law Review* 77 [1989]: 1, 7-8), but I was preceded by Lenore J. Weitzman, *The Divorce Revolution: The Unexpected Social and Economic Consequences for Women and Children in America* (New York: Free Press, 1985), 26-28, and M. Fineman, "Implementing Equality," *Wisconsin Law Review* (1983): 789, 801-2. The earliest instance of the observation that I know of is the seminal article by Robert Mnookin and Lewis Kornhauser, "Bargaining in the Shadow of the Law: The Case of Divorce," *Yale Law Journal* 88 (1979): 950, 952-54, 968-69 (noting that no-fault laws eliminated the bargaining chip of resisting divorce). Of course, the point here is not that the bargaining chip doesn't exist but that fault rules on grounds for divorce do not allocate it in any systematically defensible way.

44. It is not easy to really determine whether wives or husbands are instigating most of the divorces. The spouse who files the first papers in court may not be the one who really brought about the divorce. Also, of course, many divorces are truly mutual decisions. However, Gallup's interviews of divorced women seems to detect a shift from the fault era (1970), when most said their husbands were the primary initiators of the divorce, to the no-fault era (1988), by which time more than half of divorced women reported that the separation was their idea. See DeWitt, "Breaking Up Is Hard to Do," 53. A very careful study of a representative sample of couples with at least one minor child who filed for divorce in 1986 in Maricopa County (Phoenix) Arizona, interviewed both husband and wife at three times: within eight weeks of the divorce filing, one year after, and three years after. The following question was asked at each time: "Which one of you was the first to want out of the marriage, you or your ex?" While there was a slight tendency of both husbands and wives to be more inclined, as time went on, to view themselves as the "dumper," the answers at all three interview occasions were remarkably consistent: Husbands said that wives were the first to want out 62 to 63 percent of the time; husbands, 31 to 34 percent of the time, and "mutual," 4 to 6 percent. Wives' answers were quite similar: wives, 62 to 67 percent; husbands, 26 to 29 percent; and mutual, 8 to 9 percent. Answers to another survey question suggested that while both husbands and wives were more likely to blame their spouse than themselves for the marital failure, it was also the case that husbands and dumpers were more likely to blame themselves than were wives or dumpees. Sanford L. Braver, Marnie Whitley, and Christine Ng, "Who Divorced Whom? Methodological and Theoretical Issues," *Journal of Divorce and Remarriage* 20 (1993): 1.

45. This argument is, of course, inconsistent with the claim that no-fault divorce hurt women financially. But that claim, made famous by Lenore Weitzman's book, *The Divorce Revolution* (1985), has in any event been put in serious doubt. Stephen Sugarman has shown that Weitzman's own data do not support this claim; see "Dividing Financial Interests at Divorce," in Stephen D. Sugarman and Herma Hill Kay, *Divorce Reform at the Crossroads* (New Haven, Conn.: Yale University Press, 1990), 130, 132-34. More recently, Weitzman has conceded that her published figures are not supported by her data, and blames errors by her computer assistants. She made this concession in response to a care-

ful analysis by Richard R. Peterson of her raw data, which he found in an archive at Radcliffe. See Peterson, "A Reevaluation of the Economic Consequences of Divorce," *American Sociological Review* 61 (1996): 528; Lenore Weitzman, "The Economic Consequences of Divorce Are Still Unequal: Comment on Peterson," *American Sociological Review* 61 (1996): 537; Peterson, "Statistical Errors, Faulty Conclusions, Misguided Policy: Reply to Weitzman," *American Sociological Review* 61 (1996): 539. In any event, it is also important to note that Weitzman's work was all done in California, a community property state. The great majority of American states followed the common-law approach to marital property during the fault era, and they all shifted to equitable distribution during the same general time frame in which they moved to no-fault divorce. Weitzman's California data would not have reflected this shift, which gave most women a far *greater* entitlement to share in accumulated property than they had during the fault era.

46. I am indebted to Sandy Braver for making this point in one of our many conversations about divorce policies.

47. One might think that couples with children would be particularly unlikely to destroy their marriage casually. But Zelder ("The Economic Analysis," 243), who agrees that no-fault did not raise divorce rates generally, purports to show that it did increase the divorce rate among couples who spend proportionately more of their resources on their children than do other couples. Zelder explains his result with a bargaining theory based on the treatment of children within marriage as a public good. If children are a public good within marriage, then the spouse who wishes to continue the marriage cannot induce the other to forego divorce by offering to transfer some of that benefit. In marriages in which the benefits of children are a large proportion of the marital benefits, he therefore expects that no-fault reduces the bargaining leverage of the party wishing to remain married. He predicts more divorces for these marriages under fault divorce rules, which (unlike no-fault) require the spouse who wishes to divorce to induce the other spouse's consent. Zelder's theoretical explanation seems contrary to the intuition that spouses who place relatively greater value on their children are more likely to wish to preserve the marital relationship, at least if they believe their children are better off if the marriage remains intact. In addition, the theory fails to consider the effects of custody rules at divorce on the parties' relative bargaining positions. In a marriage in which the children are a large percentage of the benefit realized by the parties, termination of the marriage will yield the greater loss to the party who does not receive primary custody. If wives can usually expect to receive primary custody of the children at divorce, husbands who value access to their children would be less inclined to terminate their marriage. Thus, when custody rules are also considered, Zelder's theory suggests that men are the primary losers in no-fault divorce, which is contrary to his own suggestion, ("The Economic Analysis," 260), as well as to the nearly unanimous view of other commentators hostile to no-fault. (It is consistent, however, with the finding that women today initiate most divorces, reported earlier at n. 44.) I note that Zelder's regression found only marginal significance (at the 0.1 level) for his no-fault dummy*relative child wealth term. Given his n of 12,559 observations from a survey following six thousand households, it would not be surprising to discover that this modest significance would disappear if multi-collinearity and dependence were considered. See the discussion of these problems in Ellman and Lohr, "Marriage as Contract."

48. The most developed argument along these lines is offered by Brinig and Crafton, "Marriage and Opportunism," 869. They argue that no-fault encourages "opportunistic behavior" in marriage, since such behavior brings the actor no financial penalties; they pur-

port to demonstrate, as an example of this thesis, that there are higher rates of domestic violence in no-fault states than in part-fault states. Their empirical demonstration is deeply flawed, however, and their theoretical arguments make implicit assumptions about the law that are inaccurate. See Ellman and Lohr, "Marriage as Contract." For another piece sympathetic to the Brinig and Crafton thesis, see Lynn Wardle, "Divorce Violence and the No-Fault Divorce Culture," *Utah Law Review* (1994): 741, although I am not certain whether he argues that the cultural features he objects to are caused by no-fault divorce laws or whether the no-fault divorce laws have caused these cultural features. His target, in any event, is the big picture of social attitudes of which no-fault divorce is just one part.

49. Whether such a rule would really increase the number of divorces, as compared to a no-fault property allocation, is difficult to know. Under the no-fault allocation, perhaps the "guilty" spouse would be more likely to file for divorce. On the other hand, we might believe the guilty spouse realizes some devilish satisfaction from his or her marital misconduct and would be pleased to continue the marriage on those terms. In that case, a no-fault rule might preserve the marriage at the expense of leaving the misconduct unpunished.

50. If fault divorce laws actually worked in practice as their proponents envision, by penalizing truly blameworthy conduct and no other conduct, and if such laws really did provide additional deterrence, then one might expect to find lower rates of spousal violence in fault states. That is the claim made, at least, by one pair of fault law proponents. See Brinig and Crafton, "Marriage and Opportunism." This study is flawed, however, by a defective measure of spousal violence and numerous errors in the classification of state laws. A more careful examination of available data in fact finds no such relationship between no-fault divorce laws and the incidence of spousal violence. See Ellman and Lohr, "Marriage as Contract."

51. For examples of the arbitrary variation one finds in the application of such fault rules, see the American Law Institute, "Principles of the Law of Family Dissolution," chap. 1, topic 2, "Reporter's Note b, Discretion and Fault" (Proposed Final Draft, 1997).

52. This point is made in Ellman, "The Place of Fault."

53. Barbara Woodhouse and Katharine Bartlett, "Sex, Lies, and Dissipation: The Discourse of Fault in a No-Fault Era," *Georgetown Law Journal* 82 (1994): 2525, 2527. This piece is a back and forth in which Woodhouse is the voice for fault. Oddly, in arguing for consideration of fault in alimony and property allocation, Woodhouse uses as her main example a case in which the misconduct in question resulted in the dissipation of marital assets—precisely the kind of economic fault that even no-fault states in principle consider. See Ellman, "The Place of Fault," 773. This approach follows consistently from an understanding of no-fault divorce as excluding claims for injury to the person, including emotional harms, while still ensuring that neither spouse is denied his or her fair share of the assets accumulated during marriage. See Milton C. Regan Jr., "Market Discourse and Moral Neutrality in Divorce Law," *Utah Law Review* (1994): 605, 630; American Law Institute, "Principles" (Tentative Draft No. 2, 1996), 18-20, 239-65, 298-99. It is true that the particular decision from which Woodhouse borrows her hypothetical rejected the wife's dissipation claim, on grounds that the expenditures were made with her consent at a time when the marriage was still intact; *In re Marriage of O'Neill,* 563 N.E.2d 494 (Ill. 1990). But the rigorously no-fault ALI principles explicitly reach the opposite result on the same facts, precisely because of the husband's deceit, which is also emphasized in Woodhouse's discussion (ALI, "Principles", sect. 4.16, illustrations 11 and 12). The ALI can take this

position because the claim is one for waste of marital assets, not one for personal harms caused by the other spouse's misconduct. Woodhouse's example is thus not at all the "hard case" she portrays it as (2540), but rather an easy case for allowing consideration of "fault."

54. I know of no research specifically addressed to the question of whether divorcing parties in pure no-fault jurisdictions see the exclusion of marital misconduct from the process as a source of injustice. However, 1986 data from Phoenix, Arizona, a pure no-fault jurisdiction, taken from a random sample of divorcing couples with at least one minor child, found that both spouses were more satisfied than unsatisfied with the provisions of their divorce, in surveys taken both one year afterward and three years afterward. One year after divorce, wives reported themselves significantly more satisfied than did husbands with the custody, visitation, property division, and "other financial provisions" of their divorce decree (defined as everything other than child support and property division), while there was no significant difference between men and women in their evaluation of the child support provisions. Three years after divorce, the satisfaction gap between men and women on the custody and visitation provisions increased, but the women became less satisfied than the men with the "other financial provisions." See Virgil L. Sheets and Sanford L. Braver, "Gender Differences in Satisfaction with Divorce Settlements," *Family Relations* 45 (1996): 336. One can only speculate on what caused both these shifts, but it seems unlikely to be a delayed conclusion that the exclusion of fault was unjust.

55. Woodhouse and Bartlett, "Sex, Lies, and Dissipation," 2539.

56. Regan, "Market Discourse," 636; see also Schneider, "Marriage, Morals, and Law," 552-53.

57. Ellman, "The Place of Fault."

58. Ira Mark Ellman and Stephen Sugarman, "Spousal Emotional Abuse as a Tort?" *Maryland Law Review* 55 (1996): 1268. For doubts about the adequacy of tort remedies for marital misconduct, see Milton L. Regan, *Family Law and the Pursuit of Intimacy* (New York: New York University Press, 1993), 142-43; for some discussion of why tort remedies are preferable to employing fault rules at divorce, see American Law Institute, "Principles" (Tentative Draft No. 2, 1996), 17-60.

59. Woodhouse agrees; "Sex, Lies, and Dissipation," 2540.

60. That is, the tort law already recognizes physical violence as actionable, as well as other egregious conduct. See Ellman and Sugarman, "Spousal Emotional Abuse as a Tort?" Some may think that more claims would be allowed or pressed if they could be brought under the divorce law. *If* that were true, however, an additional question arises: Is it in fact a good idea to facilitate the bringing of these additional claims? There are reasons for doubt. See ALI, "Principles," 34-35, 37.

61. One important complication is that in most states, there is a right to jury trial for the tort claim, but not in the divorce action. Should the joined tort claim thus be tried by the judge? Wisconsin disfavors joinder to this reason, but allows it to parties willing to waive the jury trial; *Stuart v. Stuart,* 421 N.W.2d 505 (Wis. 1988) (also holding that the prior divorce action does not bar the subsequent tort claim). This seems a sensible result that preserves the jury for the party determined to have it, while also protecting the divorce action from the disruption of the joined jury trial. New Jersey recently adopted a vague and rather discretionary rule that allows but does not seem to require the family court judge to try the tort claim in a bench trial under the divorce court's "ancillary jurisdiction," when it concludes that its resolution is intertwined with issues of child welfare decided at divorce,

while allowing it to sever the tort claim for separate trial by jury when it is convinced that "vindicating a marital tort through the jury process is the dominant interest in the matter"; *Brennan v. Orban,* 678 A.2d 683 (N.J. 1996).

62. See Schneider, "Marriage, Morals and the Law," 503, and the earlier works of his cited therein, and Mary Ann Glendon, *Abortion and Divorce in Western Law* (Cambridge, Mass.: Harvard University Press, 1987) and Glendon, *The Transformation of Family Law: State, Law, and Family in the United States and Western Europe* (Chicago: University of Chicago Press, 1991).

63. Indeed, Schneider himself has said that "no-fault divorce was inevitable" given prevailing cultural views and that in light of them, "I cannot see how the law can turn back from no-fault divorce in any truly substantial way" ("Marriage, Morals and the Law," 551). He also provides a good summary of many of the reasons why one may in the end prefer no-fault divorce, despite its association with the cultural trends he otherwise seems to lament (551-55).

64. See text at nn. 60-62.

65. For example, see Galston, "Divorce American Style."

66. ALI, "Principles" (*Proposed Final Draft No. 1,* 1997).

67. See, for example, Galston, "Divorce American Style,"12.

68. See Glendon, *Abortion and Divorce in Western Law,* 104-5.

69. Ibid., 105.

70. ALI, "Principles" (*Proposed Final Draft No. 1,* 1997).

71. Well-known commentators of the era argued that "a guilty wife may starve as quickly as an innocent one," from which he concluded that the husband has a lifetime obligation to keep his wife from need until the obligation was assumed by another. Chester G. Vernier and John B. Hurlbut, "The Historical Background of Alimony Law and Its Present Statutory Structure," *Law and Contemporary Problems* 6 (1939): 197, 199.

72. John Eekalaar and Mavis Maclean, *Maintenance after Divorce* (Oxford: Clarendon, 1986), 9, 14.

73. As a general matter, settlement is more likely when the parties have similar expectations of the likely outcome of litigation than when their expectations differ significantly. Evidence indicates that clear rules encourage settlement, suggesting that the highly discretionary rules traditionally employed in divorce make parties less likely to settle, perhaps because the difficulty of predicting the result of litigation makes it more likely the parties' lawyers will have different predictions. See John Griffiths, "What Do Dutch Lawyers Actually Do in Divorce Cases?" *Law and Society Review* 10 (1986): 135, 161, n. 24. An alternative hypothesis observes that highly discretionary rules of adjudication also make the parties less confident of their predictions. Their uncertainty increases the bargaining advantage in the negotiations of the party who is more able, financially or emotionally, to bear the risk of an unfavorable outcome. This consequence of discretionary rules is thought unfortunate by writers who have considered them. See Robert H. Mnookin and Lewis Kornhauser, "Bargaining in the Shadow of the Law: The Case of Divorce," *Yale Law Journal* 88 (1979): 950.

74. For more on this subject, see ALI, "Principles" (*Proposed Final Draft No. 1,* 1997), especially topic 1 of chap. 1.

75. This example, specifically is taken from the facts that follow track illustration 6 of section 5.06.

13

Morality, Fault, and Divorce Law

Milton C. Regan Jr.

Several people in recent years have expressed concern that marriage is losing its moral significance. They fear that marriage tends to be regarded less as an important commitment and more as but one way of achieving individual happiness that can be abandoned without moral stigma. This portrait is consistent with Lawrence Friedman's (1990) suggestion that American culture places supreme value on the ability of the individual to make choices that do not foreclose the possibility of changing one's mind at a later time. At the same time, however, other observers maintain that the ideal of "companionate" marriage is more powerful than ever—that individuals believe that marriage should be a union of soul mates who attend to the deepest needs of one another (see, e.g., Riessman 1990). As Elizabeth Scott has observed, surveys indicate that most people profess devotion to the idea that marriage should last a lifetime (see chapter 10 in this volume). These two perspectives on the current state of marriage are not necessarily inconsistent. Those who seek deep communion in marriage may be unwilling to settle for anything that falls short of their aspirations. High rates of both divorce and remarriage may attest to a tension between short-term behavior and long-term goals.

Reinforcing the idea that marriage involves a substantial commitment may help individuals realize their aspirations by enhancing their willingness to persevere in the face of momentary disappointment. As Scott reminds us, the path from intentions to achievements is littered with obstacles that may deflect us from reaching our long-term destination (see chapter 10; also Scott 1990). To the extent that culture provides no support for surmounting those obstacles, many of us may fail in a task that we regard as critically important.

It is easy to identify numerous cultural influences that seem to exalt short-term gratification. Popular culture, advertising, global economic changes, some variants of the therapeutic ethic, and consumerism all can make commitment seem perilous and unattractive. Given the historic prominence of law in American society, however, it is not surprising that many critics focus on law as a culprit in draining marriage of normative significance. It is interesting that critics tend not to focus on marriage law—the prerequisites for getting married or the extent to which the law regulates partners in an ongoing marriage. They focus rather on divorce—the law dealing with the *end* of marriage. This reflects awareness that the terms on which one is permitted to leave a relationship say much about the vision of that relationship in the cultural imagination. Critics suggest that the ease with which divorce can be obtained and the absence—indeed, prohibition—of any consideration of fault in most divorce cases convey the message that marriage is primarily a private matter. They maintain that this legal regime signals that the state is neutral about whether spouses stay together and that the behavior of the parties is their own business. As such, it reflects the decline of "moral discourse" in family law (Schneider, 1985).

The most useful approach to the role of law in family matters posits not simply that neutrality is a bad idea and that the state should take a moral position regarding marriage. Rather, it is that the state cannot really be morally neutral in any meaningful sense. Ostensible neutrality is itself a moral position. The idea that marriage is primarily of private and not social concern rests on a host of normative assumptions about the nature of individual autonomy, the relationship between state and citizen, and the obligations that arise from intimacy, to name only a few considerations. As Lawrence Lessig (1995) has noted, law inescapably sends messages about the social meaning of activity. Divorce law is no exception.

Thus, as William Galston (see chapter 11 in this volume) reminds us, law works not simply by creating incentives and disincentives or by directly penalizing or rewarding behavior. It also inevitably serves as an agent of socialization by expressing moral norms about social life. Without doubt, law cannot be effective for long if it varies too widely from deep-seated attitudes and sentiments. At the same time, however, family law deals with powerful impulses, passions, and emotions. An influential strand of Western thought traditionally has regarded those forces as currents to be channeled and restrained rather than merely accommodated (see, e.g., Schneider 1988). Those who are concerned about the lessening moral significance of marriage therefore are warranted in directing at least some attention to law in general and divorce law in particular.

If we believe that law cannot help but express moral norms about marriage, the question then is what those norms should be. I believe that we can identify at least one basic norm that would garner widespread support: that marriage should represent a significant commitment to another person. This norm reflects the view that how spouses act toward one another is a moral matter, a question of social, not purely private, concern. It rests both on appreciation of the benefits that a stable long-term relationship brings to the partners within it, as well as awareness of the crucial role that marriage plays in the upbringing of children.

It might seem natural to look to the language of fault as a vehicle for promoting this moral conception of marriage. Finding fault is an intrinsically normative exercise. In the context of marriage, it signals that there are certain standards of behavior for spouses and that we will hold individuals accountable for violating them. If we are concerned about a decline in willingness to make moral judgments in public life, using fault to disfavor culpable parties in financial awards at divorce would seem a welcome effort to strengthen social norms. Furthermore, one might argue that relying more on fault as a condition for obtaining a divorce also would reinforce the view that marriage is an important commitment that should be abandoned only in serious circumstances.

I want to suggest, however, that reliance on fault has the potential to undermine, rather than enhance, our ability to use law to express the moral gravity of marriage. I will make this point by examining two ways in which law might seek to communicate a message about the gravity of marriage. First, we might make divorce more difficult, especially in instances in which one spouse desires a divorce but the other does not. Second, we might impose greater financial responsibilities at the time of divorce. The latter option must be constrained by notions of economic fairness, but we can still be attentive to the kinds of messages that different financial rules will send about marriage. If we look closely at both these proposals, we will see that reliance on fault is not the only way to communicate a moral message about marriage. Indeed, we may, in fact, be more effective in sending such a message if we reduce, rather than increase, reliance on the language of fault.

MORAL MESSAGES AND DIVORCE REQUIREMENTS

Elizabeth Scott has suggested that we might enhance appreciation that marriage is an important commitment by imposing greater waiting periods before divorce, on the order of two to three years (see chapter 10). Couples might agree contractually to such a provision at the time that they enter into marriage, an approach that Scott finds particularly appropriate for couples without children. Alternatively, law might offer a menu of standard contracts from which couples might choose. Those with a lesser degree of commitment might prefer the ability to divorce with relative ease, while those who see their bond as more permanent could choose the option that imposes a longer waiting period. Once couples had children, they would be subject to the more restrictive requirements, regardless of their initial choice. Scott observes that such "precommitments" can be effective in other instances in helping people resist the pursuit of short-term gratification that may undermine their ability to achieve long-term goals. First, they can help improve the quality of important decisions, because research indicates that time enhances the quality of the deliberative process. Second, they make short-term alternatives more costly, thus creating a disincentive to deviate from the pursuit of long-term aspirations.

Longer waiting periods for divorce could serve these functions. Ideally, they would help ensure that decisions about divorce were made with considered reflection, making it harder to be swayed by temporary discontent or passions. Furthermore, as Scott suggests, a waiting period "defines the relationship as one that is not easily set aside, thus subtly influencing the spouses' attitudes and behavior." In this way, it signifies that marriage is a serious commitment of moral significance for society as a whole, rather than a matter of purely private concern.

A second approach to making divorce more difficult, reflected in the proposal that Jesse Dalman has sought to enact in Michigan, would place greater reliance on determinations of fault.[1] Such proposals generally provide that spouses must obtain a fault-based divorce unless they seek divorce by mutual consent. This alternative relies more explicitly on moral discourse than does an extended waiting period. It expresses the idea that marriage is a commitment that cannot be unilaterally shirked unless one of the partners has engaged in marital misconduct. With the effective elimination of unilateral divorce, this proposal would increase the number of instances in which a court considering a divorce petition would be required to make moral judgments about the behavior of spouses. In this way, divorce law would impress upon both putative divorcing spouses and society as a whole that marriage is governed by certain shared norms.

How should we evaluate these two suggestions that the gravity of marriage be communicated by making divorce somewhat more difficult? Is the requirement of a longer waiting period or of fault-based divorce in nonconsensual divorces a more desirable option? Might we even combine them in some way?

I believe that, of the two, a longer waiting period is preferable. Studies indicate that the deliberative process is improved with greater time in which to make a final decision. I am willing at least to entertain the possibility that this would be the case with respect to divorce as well. Indeed, this would seem particularly to be true with respect to such an emotionally charged decision such as divorce. In addition, research demonstrates that preferences tend to some degree to be context-dependent. That is, the constraints within which people make decisions can affect what they value in different settings.[2] There is no reason to believe that this is not true of divorce as well—no reason, that is, to believe that longer waiting periods serve only to prevent people from obtaining divorces that they "really" want. Furthermore, it seems plausible to maintain that such a reform would convey the importance of marriage more strongly than current divorce laws.

By contrast, greater reliance on fault-based divorce seems problematic. The spouse who wants to stay in a marriage will not always be the one who has acted honorably. He or she may make life quite difficult for the other partner, even though his or her conduct may not satisfy the criteria for fault. In such a case, a spouse who may have a good reason for wanting to leave a marriage may have to make significant concessions in order to win the other's consent. My concern, however, goes beyond mere reluctance to rely more on fault as a condition for divorce. For waiting periods effectively to serve their purpose, we need to reduce, rather than increase, even our current level of reliance on fault-based divorce. Not only should we reject a requirement of fault grounds for nonconsensual divorces. We also need to restrict the availability of fault-based divorce more generally. My argument is that the ability of law to send a moral message about marriage by making divorce more difficult ironically may depend on largely eschewing the overtly moral language of fault.

Why is this so? My explanation begins with Ira Ellman's criticism of Elizabeth Scott's suggestion of longer waiting periods for divorce (see chapter 12 in this volume). Ellman performs a valuable service by directing our attention to how people likely will react to the adoption of longer waiting periods. He points to data that suggest that when people have to wait longer than they want to obtain a divorce, they collude to obtain a more easily available fault-based divorce. That is, they fabricate evidence or perjure themselves to establish that one party has engaged in misconduct that warrants termination of the marriage. As a result, says Ellman, longer waiting periods are unlikely to be effective because spouses can easily evade them by conspiring to obtain a fault-based divorce that generally will be granted sooner. On this view, the effect of Scott's proposal would be simply to return us to the hypocrisy of a primarily fault-based divorce system, which undermines, rather than reinforces, respect for divorce law.

I am willing to accept that people may react to longer waiting periods in the way that Ellman suggests. I draw a different conclusion, however, than he does. If we want to give waiting periods a chance to work, we should sharply restrict the availability of fault grounds that afford an opportunity to circumvent waiting requirements. If fault-based divorce requests become more common, it is likely that, as under the prior exclusive fault system, courts faced with an increase in petitions would begin to interpret criteria such as "cruelty" or "mental distress" in a relaxed fashion. Indeed, the studies that Ellman cites suggest that this already happens when waiting periods are regarded as too long. It is hard to believe, for instance, that 86 percent of all marriages end in Wisconsin because of "cruel and inhuman treatment."

To put the point differently, many couples in what Galston calls "lower-conflict" marriages (see chapter 11) or those who simply thought that they might be happier elsewhere, probably could avoid a waiting period by obtaining a fault-based divorce. Yet these are precisely the instances in which a longer waiting period might lead spouses on reflection to conclude that their marriage is worth preserving. Given the ease with which fault-based divorce often tends to be obtained, limiting the availability of such divorces to cases of egregious misconduct seems necessary if longer waiting periods are to have any chance of working. Fault-based grounds for divorce should be available only in cases of "high-conflict" marriages, in which serious misbehavior and perhaps abuse occur. This approach, in fact, seems consistent with the views of many critics of no-fault divorce: that such divorces should not be so easy to obtain, except in cases in which a partner is in an abusive relationship. I take Galston as well to have this at least partially in mind when he talks about an "updated fault system" that takes into account spousal abuse (although he may prefer more expansive availability of fault-based divorce than I suggest).

Ironically, then, we may be most effective in sending a moral message about the gravity of marriage by reducing reliance on the overt moral language of fault in determining eligibility for divorce. Waiting periods that cannot be easily circumvented convey the idea that marriage is a serious commitment that should not be abandoned without serious reflection or egregious misconduct by one's partner. Grafting longer waiting periods onto divorce regimes that include a standard fault-based option would suppress this message by making the waiting periods easier to avoid. Furthermore, it would return us to a predominantly fault-based system that, judging from past experience, likely would diminish rather than enhance our respect for divorce law.

I have said that, although I am not completely convinced of their efficacy, I am at least willing to give waiting periods a chance to work. What would be the costs of doing so? Once again, Ira Ellman forces us to consider more precisely what we hope to accomplish with such provisions. I agree with him that a longer wait for divorce may be of limited value without efforts to force spouses to focus their attention on appreciating and, if necessary, ultimately planning for, the consequences of divorce. Indeed, involvement in the latter project may provide important information for the former. Measures such as the formulation of a parenting plan,[3] preparation of specific financial provisions, and the provision of counseling all are useful in this process. In addition, I agree that we need to consider carefully what interim financial and custody arrangements are appropriate during the waiting period.

Ellman goes on to suggest, however, that even if these steps are taken, longer waiting periods would be undesirable (see chapter 12). They would, he argues, only prevent parties from leaving a marriage to which they are no longer committed, and inhibit their ability to get on with their lives. This may be of particular concern for women with custody of children, for whom remarriage often is the most important avenue for reattaining some measure of financial security.

This delay in making a fresh start may not be altogether a bad thing, however. With respect to remarriage, for instance, some data suggest that remarriages tend to be less successful than first marriages.[4] A longer waiting period for divorce may serve to promote greater deliberation with respect to not only divorce but remarriage as well. It thus may help avert some choices about new marriages that otherwise would have been unwise. More broadly, we should not necessarily place the highest priority on allowing people to move on with their lives after divorce. The point of precommitment devices is to increase the cost of breaking a commitment—that is, to make it harder immediately to change course simply because of a desire to do so.

One reason in the divorce context for placing some impediment to moving on to a new life, of course, is the consequences of divorce for children. Too often, for instance, divorced fathers embrace their fresh start with a vengeance, failing to support or even to have any regular contact with their children. In addition, women may be particularly disadvantaged by divorce because their earning power generally is lower than that of their husbands, often because of financial sacrifices they have made for the sake of children and the household in general.

There is, however, a broader reason that we should try at least to temper the desire to begin anew. With respect to commitments in general and marriage in particular, it is not always undesirable for people to feel some tension between the claims of the past and of the future. Most marriages that end began with fond hopes and high aspirations. Even unhappy ones involve considerable vulnerability, reliance, and interdependence. Indeed, it may be precisely because of such expectations and experiences that disappointment can be so acute and acrimony so pronounced at divorce. Attempts to build something as fragile and valuable as ongoing human relationships warrant respect, and their failure should be an occasion tinged with at least some measure of regret. When considered decisions are made that they should end, we should do all we can to enable partners to get on with their lives. At the same time, however, we should try to increase the prospect that those decisions *are* considered ones.

The balance is a delicate one, because divorcing spouses are poised between two worlds. We do not want to imprison them in the past, but neither should we seek to propel them as rapidly as possible into the future. Ellman is confident that partners already do take decisions to divorce seriously and that any effort to use law to reinforce this is both unnecessary and misguided. He may be right on the first point, but even if he is, we cannot assume that this approach will continue regardless of how the larger culture treats marriage and divorce. To reiterate an earlier point, every legal provision sends *some* kind of message, which means that we can't ignore the story that divorce law may be telling.

My focus on the importance of commitment leads me to depart in a couple of ways from Scott's analysis. First, I would not distinguish dramatically between divorce prerequisites for couples with and without children. Doing so suggests that only the latter marriages are of social concern—that the former involve merely private arrangements that are of interest principally to the individuals within them. In fact, society has good reasons to be concerned about all marriages, whether or not they involve children. As I have suggested, we have an interest in promoting a society in which commitments, particularly in intimate relationships, are taken seriously. Furthermore, a large number of married couples eventually do have children. If we even indirectly convey the idea that marriage per se is a matter between the partners, it may be hard to change this orientation when couples have children. Spouses may conclude that divorce also is of interest primarily to the adults, as long as there is sufficient child support and fair custody and visitation arrangements. It is unlikely, however, that the effects of divorce can be so easily confined (see, e.g., McLanahan and Sandefur 1994). Since so many marriages do involve children, it may be best from the outset of marriage to seek to foster an other-regarding orientation among spouses. Finally, data indicate that separated or divorced persons experience "heightened levels of mortality and psychological and physical morbidity" compared to other individuals (Kitson and Morgan 1990: 913; see also Larson et al. 1996). Society has at least some interest in trying to encourage couples to take time to decide whether divorce is really in their long-term interest. For these reasons, it may be wise to have a standard waiting period for all divorces and to impose it by statute, rather than by relying on private agreement between couples who marry.

A second way in which I would depart from Scott's suggestions is that I would not support the idea of a "menu" of marriage options, with differing divorce requirements depending on different professed levels of commitment. I believe that there is value in preserving marriage as a distinctive relationship that involves the strongest expectations of commitment. I fear that diluting the significance of marriage in an effort to encourage more people to marry ultimately would only weaken the institution and deprive it of some of its moral force. Furthermore, it seems undesirable to permit couples to choose a lesser committed marriage at the outset and then require them to adhere to more stringent requirements when they have a child. Since most married couples have children, it would seem preferable to encourage spouses to be strongly committed to their marriage from the start, rather than attempt by law to transform their relationship into a stronger bond when a child arrives.

These differences aside, I believe that Scott's suggestion of longer waiting periods warrants serious consideration. It offers a way to send a moral message about marriage without the difficulties that would attend greater reliance on fault as a basis for obtaining a divorce. Indeed, as I have suggested, we likely will need to reduce the availability of fault-based divorce if longer waiting periods are to have a chance of being effective.

MORAL MESSAGES AND FINANCIAL AWARDS

A second area of divorce law that sends a message about the significance of marriage is the law governing financial claims and responsibilities when the marriage ends. Some suggest that states have been misguided in largely excluding fault from consideration in financial allocations. One way to reintroduce moral discourse into this area of the law would be to penalize or reward spouses according to their adherence to or deviation from norms of marital behavior.

The difficulty with such a suggestion is the same as with proposals for greater reliance on fault as a condition for divorce: it may be extremely hard to trace the moral course of a marriage with any degree of confidence. Stark categories of blame and praise seem blunt instruments for assessing complex and subtle patterns of spousal interaction.[5] In addition, financial awards finely calibrated to degrees of rectitude appear to require extraordinary powers of judgment. Furthermore, given the economic stakes, spouses will have strong incentives to press claims and counterclaims of betrayal and mistreatment. The prospect of an increase in such strategic behavior seems more likely to diminish than to increase our appreciation of the moral gravity of marriage. Finally, more extensive use of fault in determining financial matters at divorce might have undesirable effects on children. A spouse deemed to have engaged in misconduct nonetheless might be named custodian because it is in the overall best interest of the child. Reducing that parent's financial award, or increasing his or her financial liability, also would reduce the resources available for raising the child.[6]

The law governing divorce awards thus appears ill suited to promote a moral vision of marriage by making judgments about the relative propriety of each spouse's behavior during marriage. As with grounds for divorce, the best approach may be to take only egregious fault into consideration. An award determination under such a standard would require a degree of moral judgment in some cases, but only with respect to behavior about which there is a relative consensus.

There is, however, another way that this body of law can send a message about the moral gravity of marriage. This is to emphasize the words of the vow that spouses take one another "for richer or for poorer." This vision is of marriage as an undertaking in which partners pledge to weather the vicissitudes of fate together—to share in one another's fortunes in the broad sense of that term. On this view, strict notions of economic desert are suspended for the sake of a communal outlook. One need not directly earn a financial benefit to share in it and need not be responsible for causing a loss to bear part of it. Because of reliance on this communal economy, spouses' lives become intertwined in ways that cannot be immediately undone by divorce. This means that the spouse in the financially superior position can have an obligation to mitigate to some degree the effects of divorce on the other.

One proposal for promoting this view is to require mutual consent divorce. Proponents of this view maintain that this will give bargaining leverage to the spouse who wants to stay in the marriage. A spouse who wants to leave will have to provide enough compensation to his or her partner to make divorce acceptable. This approach in effect would reward the spouse who sought to preserve the marriage and penalize the one who desired to leave it. A partner seeking divorce would be reminded that he or she wishes to leave a relationship on which another has relied and that some measure of compensation is necessary for defeating this expectation.

This approach contains at least two difficulties, however. First, data suggest that a mutual consent requirement for divorce does not result in financial awards any higher than in states that permit unilateral divorce (see Garrison 1990). Second, as I have pointed out, it is not always the case that the spouse who wants to leave the marriage is the morally culpable one. She may, for instance, be the victim of abuse or other misconduct by a partner who himself does not want a divorce. Creating a situation in which she must make financial concessions to get out of the marriage may exacerbate her financial hardship. Attempting to create exceptions for such cases under a mutual consent rule would require inquiry into whether a spouse had a good reason for seeking divorce. This would have many of the features, and the disadvantages, of a system that required proof of fault to obtain a divorce.

A second approach is to require that ex-spouses continue to share income after divorce for some period of time related to the length of their marriage. This kind of rule is reflected in a portion of the American Law Institute's (ALI 1997) proposal for compensatory spousal payments, for which Ellman deserves substantial credit.[7] Section 5.05 of the ALI proposal provides that a person who has been married to someone "of significantly greater wealth or earning capacity" is entitled at divorce to compensation for the reduction in her standard of living that she would suffer from divorce if he or she has been married for "a sufficient duration" that equity requires that this loss be treated as the spouses' joint responsibility (ALI 1997: 280). The section does not define how long a marriage would qualify for such treatment, but an illustration in the comment that follows the section uses a marriage of five years as an example (ALI 1997: 283).

The comment to this section offers an eloquent statement of the vision of marriage as an agreement to share one another's fate: "Spouses pool their financial affairs as part of a more general expectation of a shared life in which they have emotional and personal obligations as well as financial ones" (ALI 1997: 285). As a result, says the ALI, the principle of "gradually merging responsibility" should govern financial rights and responsibilities in such instances (286). The ALI similarly recommends income sharing for an ex-spouse who has assumed primary responsibility for child care, with assistance based on the duration of the period in which she did so (section 5.06, p. 317).

These provisions are commendable. I differ with the ALI, however, in its unwillingness to treat the idea of shared fortunes as the core principle of compensatory payments. The ALI income-sharing provision is an exception to the general rule that compensatory spousal payments should be designed to compensate one spouse either for a loss in earning power suffered during marriage (ALI 1997, section 5.12, p. 380) or for a contribution to the enhancement of a partner's earning power (section 5.15, p. 383). Under this general rule, a spouse must present specific evidence of such losses or contributions in order to receive an award. That the ALI recognizes an exception for this requirement in a marriage in which one spouse has been primary caregiver is premised at least in part on the difficulty of making the necessary calculations in this type of case, rather than on the belief that such calculations are an inappropriate basis for determining financial rights and responsibilities at divorce (section 5.06, comment d, p. 322).

The ALI's (1997) proposal therefore takes as its primary rationale for compensation the rights and responsibilities that might arise between any two economic partners, married or not. General principles of economic justice require that any partner who makes financial sacrifices for the sake of partnership profits should not be the only one to bear such losses. This approach dilutes the message that marriage is a particular kind of commitment that gives rise to distinctive obligations. The point is underscored by the ALI's insistence that need is not an appropriate justification for making a divorce award (section 5.02, comment a, p. 259). Economic partners generally have no moral obligation to respond to each other's needs, but such responsiveness is a core element of marriage. Furthermore, the comment to the section on compensation in marriages of long duration says that the principle of gradually merging responsibility means that obligation "does not arise from the marriage ceremony alone, but takes longer to develop" (section 5.06, comment c, p. 286).

One might argue, however, that the significance of the marriage ceremony is precisely that it represents a commitment to care for the needs of one's spouse. The *scope* of that commitment may depend on the length of the marriage, which is why the duration of any equalization in the ex-spouses' standard of living should depend on the length of the marriage. That is, marriage represents the onset of immediate, not gradually merging, responsibility—although the extent to which it continues after divorce should depend on the degree to which lives actually have become intertwined by the passage of time. If we want to express the moral gravity of marriage, the marriage ceremony itself should be a source of obligation, because it represents an agreement by the spouses to share in one another's fortunes. Moving this vision from the periphery to the core of the ALI proposal would enhance the ability of divorce law to promote an understanding of marriage as a significant moral undertaking.[8]

My evaluation of the ALI approach to divorce awards thus illustrates that we can meaningfully talk about the possibility of moral messages through divorce law without relying on the language of fault. Indeed, an effort to send one moral message through the greater use of fault in determining divorce awards could undermine law's ability to express a different moral message about marriage as a shared commitment of care. Difficulties in determining who is at fault, and incentives to make allegations of misconduct for strategic reasons, could leave a financially disadvantaged spouse with insufficient resources after divorce—and an economically advantaged spouse with no responsibilities. For the reasons that I have described, it seems easier and more effective to reinforce the gravity of marriage by ensuring adequate financial awards than by trying to base entitlement to awards on evaluations of marital behavior.

CONCLUSION

We should not shy away from using law to express moral judgments about marriage and divorce. Indeed, as I have suggested, law cannot help but do so. Some forms of expression are preferable to others, however. The language of fault is overtly moral but requires assessments of blame and innocence that are both difficult and controversial. This language also may exacerbate hostility at divorce, leading to widespread collusion that erodes belief in the moral integrity of divorce law. We must recognize that the discourse of fault is not the only available moral dialect. Longer wait periods and income sharing are two measures that also can convey the message that marriage is a significant commitment. By avoiding in most cases direct evaluation of marital conduct, such provisions also may be well suited for an age marked by greater moral pluralism than the era of fault-based divorce. Our efforts to express the importance of law must take account of not only the potential power of law but its limitations as well.

NOTES

1. For an overview of such proposals in different states, see Laura Gatland, "Putting the Blame on No-Fault," *American Bar Association Journal* (April 1997): 50-54.

2. For an exploration of the implications of this phenomenon for law, see Cass Sunstein, "Endogenous Preferences, Environmental Law," *Journal of Legal Studies* (1993): 217; Cass Sunstein, "Legal Interference with Private Preferences," *University of Chicago Law Review* 53 (1986): 1129.

3. See, for example, American Law Institute, *Principles of the Law of Family Dissolution: Analysis and Recommendations,* section 2.06 (Tentative Draft No. 3, Part I; March 20, 1998), requiring divorcing parents to file plans setting forth postdivorce arrangements for caring for children's needs.

4. See Teresa Castro Martin and Larry Bumpass, "Recent Trends in Marital Disruption," *Demography* 26 (1989): 37. The difference in divorce rates between first and subsequent marriages tends to disappear, however, when holding age and education constant. For a discussion of the possible implications of this point, see William J. Goode, *World Changes in Divorce Patterns* (New Haven, Conn.: Yale University Press, 1993), 158. In any event, we have an interest in ensuring that individuals who embark on subsequent marriages do so upon considered reflection.

5. For an elaboration of this point with respect to another family law issue, see Ira Mark Ellman and Stephen D. Sugarman, "Spousal Emotional Abuse as a Tort?" *Maryland Law Review* 55 (1996): 1268.

6. For a more comprehensive discussion of the debate over taking fault into account in financial decisions at divorce, see Ira Mark Ellman, "The Place of Fault in a Modern Divorce Law," *Arizona State Law Journal* 28 (1996): 773.

7. Ellman is chief reporter for this project.

8. I discuss this point in more detail in Milton C. Regan Jr., "Spouses and Strangers: Divorce Obligations and Property Rhetoric," *Georgia Law Journal* 82 (1994): 2303.

REFERENCES

American Law Institute. 1997. *Principles of the Law of Family Dissolution: Analysis and Recommendations,* Part I, chap. 5, "Compensatory Spousal Payments" (Proposed Draft, February 14). Philadelphia: Author.

Friedman, Lawrence Friedman. 1990. *The Republic of Choice*. Cambridge, Mass: Harvard University Press.

Garrison, Marsha. 1990. "The Economics of Divorce: Changing Rules, Changing Results," in *Divorce Reform at the Crossroads,* ed. Stephen Sugarman and Herma Hill Kay. New Haven, Conn.: Yale University Press.

Kitson, Gay C., and Leslie A. Morgan. 1990. "The Multiple Consequences of Divorce: A Decade Review." *Journal of Marriage and Family* 52: 913.

Larson, David B., et al. 1996. "The Costly Consequences of Divorce: Assessing the Clinical, Economic, and Public Health Impact of Marital Disruption in the United States." *Journal of Marriage and Family* 58: 1044.

Lessig, Lawrence. 1995. "The Regulation of Social Meaning." *University of Chicago Law Review* 62: 943.

McLanahan, Sara, and Gary Sandefur. 1994. *Growing Up with a Single Parent: What Hurts, What Helps*. Cambridge, Mass.: Harvard University Press.

Riessman, Catherine Kohler. 1990. *Divorce Talk*. New Brunswick, N.J.: Rutgers University Press.

Schneider, Carl. 1985. "Moral Discourse and the Transformation of Family Law." *Michigan Law Review* 83: 1803.

———. 1988. "State–Interest Analysis in Fourteenth Amendment 'Privacy' Law: An Essay on the Constitutionalization of Social Issues." *Law and Contemporary Problems* 51: 79.

Scott, Elizabeth S. 1990. "Rational Decisionmaking about Marriage and Divorce." *Virginia Law Review* 76: 9.

Part Three

Reducing the Financial Harm to
Children Produced by Divorce

14

The Family as Community: Implementing the "Children-First" Principle

Katherine Shaw Spaht

The "children-first" principle, a term coined by Professor Mary Ann Glendon of Harvard University Law School,[1] describes the proposition that in cases of divorce "the fact of having children impresses a lien upon all of the parents' income and property to the extent necessary to provide for the children's decent subsistence at least until those children reach the age of majority."[2] She argues that if this principle were given the highest rank in the law of marital property distribution, then "until the welfare of the child or children was adequately secured, there would be no such thing as 'marital' property, but only *'family' property*."[3] Obviously, the underlying, compelling motivation of the principle lies in ensuring adequate provision for the support and accommodation of the children of the marriage.

This chapter implements and expands the "children-first" principle by means of model legislation entitled the "Family as Community Act." (Specific articles of this model legislation are discussed later.) By utilizing legislation to explicitly implement the principle,[4] predictability and even-handedness result, and that result in turn facilitates fair negotiations. The application of the principle is expanded under this act to include division of *family* property at death, as well as divorce, because death of a family member also results in the creation of a new family unit.

The act reflects the high social and moral interest in providing the best possible conditions for child-raising[5] by recognizing the family as a community from its inception until an event occasions the need for *family* property division. Consistently with the approach of civil law jurisdictions, the Family as Community Act (FCA) contains a mix of fixed rules and judicial discretion, traditional in "specific areas of family and succession law."[6] Within the parameters of the fixed rules contained in the act, "the judge's main job would be to design the best possible package of property, income, and in kind personal care to meet the needs of the new family unit composed of the children and their custodian."[7]

The FCA focuses on the family as a community in which each member has a stake, recognized by an inchoate right in property acquired by all of its members which matures into a legal interest at divorce or death. Such a family property system, which exists from the moment of family formation, offers a coherent legal framework within which the fulfillment of the needs of the children at divorce are paramount.

PREAMBLE TO THE FCA

The family is the first community to which a human being is introduced; thus, its existence and stability are of vital interest to society. The family is inherently connected to the institution of marriage, which is "the foundation of *the family* and of society. Its stability is basic to morality and civilization."[8]

An element of marriage and a component of the definition of family, traditionally understood, includes childbearing.[9] As an analogy to the partnership or community model of marriage prevalent today, the purpose of the family is to accumulate and diligently shepherd[10] resources for the promotion of the interests of the members of the family unit, but particularly the children, representing the next generation who it is anticipated will build on and increase the fortunes of the family.

Child rearing unavoidably involves obligations to the individual good of the child, which involves, of course, duties to one's spouse as well and to the common good of the community. Indeed, because of the necessary inculcation of values during childhood, the condition of the moral and economic resources of the family assume critical importance.[11] The dedication of such resources to the child assures his ultimate independence and autonomy. We have posited elsewhere:

> Although the family is the locus of private life, it is also critical to public identity. . . . Families teach us our first lessons in responsibility and reciprocity. In the primary setting of the family, we either learn or fail to learn what it means to give and take; to trust or to mistrust; to practice self-restraint or self-indulgence; to be unreliable or reliable. It is for that reason, if no other, that we must begin to make the vital connections between "public" policies and "private" families, and craft policies that support families.[12]

We reaffirm these principles.

The negative effects of the divorce culture, particularly on children of divorce, have been elaborately explored and established.[13] While "divorces are necessary in some situations, many are avoidable and not in the interest of the children, the community, and probably not of most adults either."[14] Although changes in the law will not immediately and necessarily alter the landscape of the culture, laws should reflect the community's commitment to children, its most vulnerable citizens. Laws can also *enable* that commitment. This is especially true where laws can have perhaps their most direct impact—at family breakdown—by adjusting the economic consequences among members of a family.

While the economic effects of death and divorce are not the central concern of civil society, they are of great importance to the well-being of children and communities. We should first devote every effort to the task of strengthening and stabilizing families.[15] The law, one of whose "most important functions is to act as teacher, . . . should try to influence people to stay in their families until their children are grown."[16]

> The right lesson is that marriage and parenthood are not suitable activities for everyone but are only for those who are willing to sacrifice personal interest to familial interests for the time necessary to raise their children.[17]

We "call on parents to recommit themselves to their work as nurturers and stewards of the next generation and to put their children first."[18]

We should also "cancel the message that divorce puts an end to responsibilities among members of a child-raising family."[19] Instead, we must "reform the economic aspects of divorce laws so that the enormous financial burden of marriage dissolution no longer falls primarily on minor children and those parents who are their principal caretakers."[20] To an extent, but less urgently, some similar, consistent communication needs to be made upon the death of a parent during the critical years of the family's task of child rearing. The decisions must, however, be made where the most harm occurs, at the point of the divorce, not in postmarital child custody and support proceedings.[21] ("That parents have a 'right to divorce' without regard to the possible detriment to their children is taken for granted; on reflection it is puzzling. . . . the law does not assert their interests until after the harmful decision is made.") While some degree of judicial discretion is perhaps unavoidable, it can and should be reduced. A regime of fixed rules or guidelines[22] based on the principles of the family as a community would contribute to ensuring that individuals in a family honor their commitments to one another.

Recommendations

Both the public ideal of the family and the public practices of families have changed remarkably over the last few decades. From a communal but highly patriarchal form, the family has evolved into a more individualistic, if also more egalitarian, shape.[23] What has not changed is the nearly universal sense of obligation to family, particularly to children, although there appears to be a confusion and disagreement as to the extent of the obligation.[24] The paramount obligation to family has not always been well expressed in either our culture or in our laws. American family law often seems to reflect more libertarian than communitarian values.[25] We should not underestimate the task of expressing the obligation to family in the law. In fairness,

> no country has achieved a satisfactory resolution of the interrelated problems of spousal and child support, property division, and child custody. Perhaps no such resolution is possible in societies where serial family formation is common among persons of modest means.[26]

The law has, however haltingly, yet progressively begun an evolution towards a model of the family that recognizes the necessity of sharing: "Community is clearly the emerging norm."[27] This chapter and the model FCA represent another incremental step in the movement toward a family covenant of equal dignity for all its members. Indeed, "[i]n a society in which law will prescribe the economic relationships of at least half of the children and their parents, we cannot afford to disregard issues of justice between family members."[28] At least not if we hope to promote a new "culture of familism."[29]

While it has often been convenient and useful to apply economic metaphors to family law, the family is, of course, no mere economic partnership. Familial or moral obligations everywhere envelop the economic.[30] These obligations arise not on account of economic contribution but by virtue of the relationship itself. Whereas equitable doctrines at divorce have expanded the meaning of economic contributions to a marriage, the FCA explicitly recognizes the *moral* dimensions as well.[31] Property, both generally and particularly in the family, constitutes an element in a complex familial relationship of stewardship and trusteeship.[32]

The child's portion of family property could, of course, be calculated economically by the costs otherwise incurred by the general community. These may be direct (welfare) or indirect (crime). But as Cynthia Starnes points out, even when economic models are applied, they are misapplied. Indeed, the

> broad use of partnership principles produces a no-fault model that both encourages the ideal in marriage and sensibly addresses the real. Under a contemporary partnership model, divorce is seen as the dissociation of a spouse from the shared enterprise. While dissociation ends the relationship, it does not usually trigger a winding-up of any shared enterprise in which the spouses have invested. If this enterprise continues, a dissociated spouse should receive a buyout of her interest. This buyout provides a theoretical basis for maintenance.[33]

Marriage is not simply a matter of contract but includes moral and social obligations;[34] to an even greater extent, parenthood does, too.

More than most model statutes,[35] the FCA advocated in this chapter represents the idealized, if not utopian, version of desirable legislation. While my preference would perhaps prefer to see the act passed as drafted, different states will require very different arrangements.[36] The specific balance struck between recognition of individual contributions and of obligations to family members must, and perhaps should be, within our own local political communities. We believe that the act assumes and encourages an ethos of personal and social responsibility that recognizes that within the family all of its members have a stake. The FCA need not be disconnected from a wider strategy of reform and indeed would be most effective as part of a broader campaign to recognize and promote the importance of the family.[37]

The specific purpose of the FCA is to mitigate the economic and moral harm done to families, particularly to children, by the divorce or death of their parents. The act should be liberally construed and applied to promote this purpose, recognizing, however, that these are different, although related problems.[38] The basic principle puts family and children first.[39] To implement the children-first principle requires that the provisions of the FCA extend beyond child support or maintenance.[40] The central principle of this chapter applies with almost equal force to family inheritance.[41]The problem of disinheritance of children has reached an acute level because of divorce and remarriage.

FAMILY AS COMMUNITY ACT

Article 1. Family community, parent defined; familial obligations
A. For the purpose of establishing legal duties, the family community includes a father and a mother, married [or unmarried] and their children, biological or adoptive until majority or, if the child is enrolled in a school or institution providing post-secondary education, the age of twenty-two.
   1. Family member is a member of the family community as defined by this Act.
   2. Parent is the mother of the child and the husband of the mother at the time of the child's conception or birth. Parent also includes the mother and the father of a child who has been adopted [or whose filiation is established as provided by law].
B. By the act of procreation or adoption, individuals assume obligations as parents, both to their children and to the community. Parental obligations include the responsibility to nurture, educate, nourish, lodge, maintain, and discipline children. These obligations continue until the child reaches majority, or, if the child is enrolled in a school or institution providing post-secondary education, the age of twenty-two.
C. Married persons owe each other fidelity, support, and assistance. Spouses mutually assume the moral and material direction of the family, exercise parental authority, and assume the moral and material obligations resulting therefrom.
D. A child's obligations include the duty to honor and respect his parents and, as long as he remains under their legal authority, obedience in all things not contrary to law and morality. Upon majority, a child has an obligation to provide support,

in accordance with need, for his parents who are in need and who cared for or provided support for the child, to the extent that the child is able.

The specific content of parental obligations can, of course, be decided state by state; in fact, the content may already be specified by either a state's statutory or common law. The obligations of parents typically include both the ancient and universally recognized moral duties to children as well as the parent's responsibility to the greater community to rear a virtuous citizen and to prevent the child's becoming a public charge on the state. The obligations are serious and profound. Even John Stuart Mill wrote that "to bring a child into existence without a fair prospect of being able, not only to provide food for its body, but instruction and training for its mind, is a moral crime."[42] The obligations of parents extend far beyond simple maintenance; and the obligations listed here are, of course, minimal and illustrative. Because of the importance of an education to a child's future opportunity, it is strongly suggested that both pre-primary and post-secondary education or training be included.[43] The disruption of a family and the damage it leaves in its wake make fulfillment of these obligations vital.[44] *If necessary and only if necessary*, these obligations may also be characterized as the legal rights of children to nurturing, education, nourishment, lodging, and maintenance.

The obligations of parenthood, even more perhaps than to a spouse, still maintain a strong hold on our society. In an age of diminished duties to one another, most people believe parents are to be held responsible for the well-being of their children. After all, the parents created the obligation, not the child.[45] The parental relationship "may well be, in our mobile and divorce-prone society, the most permanent of ties."[46] It is therefore essential that we ensure the strength of these ties.[47]

Article 2. Family Property defined
A. Unless otherwise provided, all property of family members, however and wherever acquired, and without regard to title, is Family Property.
B. Property that is not Family Property consists of:
   1. Damages or a right to damages for personal injury, mental distress or loss of guidance, care, and companionship, or the portion of a settlement that represents those damages.
   2. Proceeds or a right to proceeds of a policy of life insurance payable on the death of the insured.
   3. Property, other than the family home, acquired by gift or inheritance from a third person after the date of the marriage of the parents.
   4. Any property acquired with excluded property.

Article 3. Member's Interest in Family Property
A. Unless otherwise provided, each family member has an equal undivided interest in Family Property, which is inchoate.

B. The interest of each family member in Family Property is necessarily affected by:
  1. the death of a family member;
  2. the divorce of the parents;
  3. the birth or adoption of a child;
  4. a child's majority, or, if the child is enrolled in a school or institution providing post-secondary education, attaining the age of twenty-two.
C. Upon death of a parent or a divorce of the parents, each family member's interest in Family Property vests, and the provisions of Articles 5 and 6 apply.
D. Upon the birth or adoption of a child, each family member's interest in Family Property is reduced proportionately so that the new child has an equal interest in Family Property.
E. Upon a child's majority or, if the child is enrolled in post-secondary education, attaining the age of twenty-two, the child forfeits his inchoate interest in Family Property which is then divided equally among the remaining family members.
F. No agreement [contract, prenuptial or marital property agreement] may alter, extinguish, or waive the interest of a family member in Family Property.

Typically, in a community property system, the spouses share a legal interest in *community property*, principally composed of income and property of the two spouses. Under this act's family property system each member of the family would have an undivided equal interest in the property of family members. The family property concept bears a striking resemblance to a deferred community property regime. In a deferred community property system, the interest of a spouse is inchoate until termination of the regime; the same is true of the interest of each family member in family property.[48] The family "community" property regime is universal, including *all* property without regard to the manner or time of acquisition.[49]

The definition of *property* as used by this act would be determined by state law.[50] States obviously may want to exclude career assets, gifts, inheritances, legal recoveries for personal injury, insurance, or the like from the family property.[51] Legislators may also wish to exclude debts or the family home from the mass of family property.[52] Most important, because the FCA is designed to protect children's interests, states may desire to exclude property already reserved under state law for children.

Since family property interests are inchoate and vest only at termination of the "family community," issues of title to property and of corresponding management powers during the existence of the family community assume importance. The ability of one family member to manage family community property because title to the property is in his name may appear inconsistent with the inchoate ownership interest of other members of the family in the same property. The Uniform Marital Property Act (1983) resolves the issue of title in the following manner:

While title is virtually synonymous with ownership in the common law system, it is perhaps best understood as a *nominee* relationship under the Act. Title can be viewed as something of a permeable membrane that presents one state of affairs to third parties while encompassing an ownership relationship between the spouses within that relationship which may be different from the title-side of the membrane.[53]

During the existence of the family community, management and control[54] of family property could remain with the title holder unless the title holder is a child, in which case the parent(s) would manage the particular property subject to the restrictions of state law.[55]

The concept of a family community admittedly appears novel,[56] largely because of the direction of change in society, but, actually, it is premised on an ancient idea. Historically, no such system was considered necessary since marriage generally ensured support for children even if the couple separated, divorce was prohibited, and forced heirship or social shame assured property sufficient for the support of children. The contemporary contractual model of the family assumes self-interested, completely competent, and fully informed decision makers, and thus promotes de jure equality but de facto inequities. Individual adults committed to a more robust conventional model of family are frequently penalized for their commitment to family. Children, too, suffer when their best interests, particularly financial interests, assume relevance only at the time of divorce proceedings rather than during the existence of the marriage. The family community model of property ownership would, it is hoped, play both a practical and hortatory role in promoting strong, robust families, which serve as incubators for strong, responsible individuals such families create.

Article 4. Valuation of Family Property

A. Unless otherwise excluded, the net value of Family Property shall be the market value of all property after subtracting the obligations incurred for the acquisition, improvement, maintenance, or preservation of such property.

B. The Family Property shall be valued as of the date of filing for divorce or the date of death of a family member unless the court deems it necessary to change the termination date to assure fulfillment of parental obligations.

Article 5. Family Property at Divorce

A. Divorce alters the Family Community because of the physical separation of the parents and the legal designation of a residential and a non-residential parent. [The residential parent is the parent with whom the child resides the majority of the time.]

B. The court shall ensure that parental obligations are fulfilled before the final allocation of property between the spouses and the rendition of a divorce decree.

C. [The court may, on motion of the parties and subject to the court's review, appoint a person whom the parties have selected to mediate any matter that the court specifies.]

D. At divorce, Family Property shall be allocated in the following manner:

    1. Family Property shall be divided so that each family member receives an equal share proportional in value, although not identical in kind.

2. A family member's share may [shall] be adjusted by the court if a greater portion of Family Property is equitable or necessary
   a. to fulfill parental obligations, or
   b. if proven by clear and convincing evidence, and supported by written factual findings to be unconscionable to a family member.

Rights to possession or use of Family Property may also be granted.

3. The non-residential parent shall be awarded his share. The other shares of Family Property shall remain aggregated in the altered Family Community, composed of the residential parent and the child or children.

[4. Except for fraudulent or gross mismanagement, Family Property shall be divided without regard to the marital misconduct of either parent.]

E. Upon a child's majority or, if the child is enrolled in post-secondary education, upon attaining the age of twenty-two, the child forfeits his vested interest in Family Property which is then divided equally among the remaining family members.

Although the FCA is designed to coordinate with current legal marital property regimes, it does alter many such regimes by *requiring* that parental obligations to children be fulfilled first. The imposition of a requirement that parental obligations be fulfilled first exceeds mere insistence that the needs of children be given primary or concurrent consideration when resources are allocated between the former spouses at divorce. Most divorced spouses, it is presumed, will continue to settle property disputes as they currently do.[57] But, in the absence of a settlement agreement or if the agreement does not fulfill parental obligations as imposed by this act (article 1), the court shall make an award that assures fulfillment of the parents' obligations.[58]

The FCA merges elements of both community property and separate property (traditional common-law) systems.[59] Community property states have traditionally divided community property equally between the spouses. Equitable distribution of marital and separate property, the system of property allocation employed in most states, permits the courts to divide all property between the spouses regardless of the circumstances surrounding the property's acquisition. This act combines elements of both systems, similar to the approach of many community property states and the American Law Institute (ALI) in its *Principles of the Law of Family Dissolution*. First, the FCA establishes the principle of each family member's equal share and then permits equitable distribution of the family property if the circumstances warrant. This act merely extends to children the benefits of the same approach to property division for spouses adopted by some community property states and the ALI. The Uniform Marriage and Divorce Act already provides that

the court may protect and promote the best interests of the children by setting aside a portion of the jointly and separately held estates of the parties in a separate fund or trust for the support, maintenance, education, and general welfare of any minor, dependent, or incompetent children of the parties.[60]

The family community system, then, presumes equal division of property between all family members (as in community property and many equitable distribution systems) and extends equitable considerations to the distribution of property to children (as is currently given to spouses in separate property and some community property systems), ensuring that the primary concern at divorce is for all members of the family. Approaches different from those currently employed by the court yet similar to the FCA have been suggested by commentators,[61] followed by attempts to enact such legislation.[62] In at least one jurisdiction, legislation preferring financial provision for the children first before such provision for the spouses was enacted.[63]

This act imposes the standard of "clear and convincing" evidence to adjust a family member's share for the purpose of preventing unfair or unconscionable results. At the same time the act requires a parent and a fact finder claiming such unfairness to prepare written factual findings, an attempt to make the court's judgment more objective.[64] The FCA presumes property can be shared unless a family member shows that such an arrangement is unjust. Discretion, then, does not disappear under this system of family property but is sharply curtailed.[65] Even if judicial discretion is not eliminated entirely, this act does ensure that within its limits the child and residential (or custodial) parent will not suffer economically as a result of the divorce.

Article 6. Family Property at the Death of a Parent

A. Death of a parent alters the family community.

B. At death, Family Property shall be allocated in the following manner:
1. Property shall be divided so that each family member, including the deceased, receives a share proportional in value,[66] although not identical in kind.
2. A family member's share may [shall] be adjusted by the court if a greater portion is equitable or necessary
   a. to fulfill parental obligations, or
   b. if proven by clear and convincing evidence and supported by written factual findings, to be unconscionable to a family member.

Rights to possession or use of Family Property may also be granted.

3. The share of the deceased shall devolve according to his expressed intent in a last will [and testament] or, if he died intestate, in accordance with the laws of intestate inheritance. The other shares remain aggregated in the altered family community, composed of the surviving members of the family.

C. The court may alter the share of a child in Family Property if it is proven by clear and convincing evidence that he has attempted to take or has taken the life of either parent or if he used an act of violence or coercion to affect his share in the will.[67]

D. Upon emancipation or majority of a child, or if the child is enrolled in post-secondary education upon the child's attaining the age of twenty-two, the child becomes owner of his share of Family Property.

The FCA creates a system of "protected inheritance."[68] This system resembles both civilian *forced heirship*[69]and common-law *restricted testation*[70] systems. This system of "protected inheritance" differs from common-law systems by providing a specific proportionate share and by permitting the court to consider the reasonableness of the share without first requiring the institution of an action.[71] Ralph Brashier writes:

> When we recognize that the testator's estate will do him no good in death, his act of disinheriting his minor child seems to be the ultimate abnegation of societal and moral responsibility. If upon death he has failed to recognize voluntarily his obligations to his minor children, then it is appropriate for the law to protect both the child and the state by imposing responsibility for the burden he created and leaves behind.[72]

While skeptical of the acceptability of such a system of protected shares, Brashier notes its many advantages. Such a system is, he observes, "easy to administer," "the procedural cost . . . is minimal," and it "involves little or no judicial discretion in application."[73]

Article 7. Management of a Child's Property
A. Management of a child's share of Family Property includes the power to acquire, invest, exchange, or sell the property within the limits of preserving its value. [Nonetheless], management powers may be altered by the parents' agreement or by the court.
B. During the marriage of the child's parents they mutually assume the management of the Family Property of their children.
[C. If a child's parents are unmarried, the property of the child shall be managed by the residential parent unless otherwise altered by the parents' agreement.]
D. Upon death of a parent, or upon divorce, management of a child's share of Family Property shall be assumed by the surviving parent, or the residential parent unless otherwise altered by the agreement of the parents and approved by the court.

The parent who manages the child's share of Family Property shall owe to the child the duty of prudence and loyalty, and if he has special skills or expertise, he must use those skills in the management of the child's share.

Recognition that children may have a moral and legal claim to family property does not mean that children have a right to the use of such property. A family property regime recognizes the dignity and necessity of a child's claim to the benefits of the property but does not assume that the child is a member fully capable of exercising control over the property. The typical standard of care imposed on spouses during the marriage to prudently manage marital property may have to be raised to a more demanding fiduciary duty after a marriage terminates. With an alteration of the family community, it may be necessary to provide greater protection for the child's share or its value. That is, even though the share of the child remains in an altered yet aggregated (residential parent and children) family community, the obligations imposed on the manager in the form of a standard of care, of a duty to account periodically, and of judicial review would have to be more onerous than those existing during marriage to ensure legislative and parental acceptance.[74]

Article 8. Supplementary Methods of Ensuring Parental Obligations
A. If the share of Family Property allocated to a child is insufficient to fulfill parental obligations, the court before rendition of the judgment of divorce shall order payments in the form of:
  1. an assignment of earnings to each child proportionate to his share in Family Property unless a greater portion is equitable or, if proven by clear and convincing evidence, a child's portion is unconscionable to another family member;
  2. child support in lump sum or periodic amounts.
The court may also impose equitable remedies such as a trust or a lien to ensure the fulfillment of parental obligations. In all of these cases the management of the child's property shall be in accordance with the provisions of Article 7.
B. Payments and remedies ordered by the court under paragraph A of this Article may be modified by the court if a parent proves a substantial change of circumstances material to his parental obligations.
C. Spousal support, child custody, and child support shall not be adversely affected by the allocation of Family Property.

Courts already possess and utilize a variety of devices to ensure fulfillment of the obligations of parents[75]; however, present law does not require that the issue of parental responsibility to provide financial resources for the children be determined before a divorce judgment is rendered. The FCA differs from current regimes primarily in that the extent of parental obligation, as well as the method of practical implementation, must be determined before a divorce may be finalized.

If a child's share of family property is insufficient to accomplish the purposes of this act, one form of court-ordered payment, an assignment of earnings, may provide an alternative means to accomplish the same purpose. An award based on parental earnings (i.e., income sharing) under the provisions of this act treats postdivorce income as familial.[76] The court could order income shared among the members of the family community. The FCA presumes the shares of family members are equal but provides for their adjustment if a greater portion is equitable or necessary to meet parental obligations or if proven unconscionable to a family member by clear and convincing evidence.

The advantages of equal sharing of future income include the following:

First, it fosters the kind of sharing and caring that should typify families. Second, income sharing offers a way out of the fault conundrum. Third, income sharing empowers the financially disadvantaged who may be economically trapped in destructive relationships.[77] Fourth, it provides a path to equality that automatically adjusts to reflect the actual market situation of the parties over time.[78]

Income sharing recognizes that "[p]ostdivorce income is . . . a product not just of individual effort, but of joint determinations."[79] The difficult decision in an income sharing scheme is determining whether remarriage should free a divorced spouse from these obligations. Arguably, it should not. The possibility of postdivorce adjustment in an income-sharing award, a statutory provision flexible enough to adjust to remarriage, means that an explicit rule concerning remarriage may not be necessary.

Another device, the *equitable remedy of a trust,* divides actual ownership of property from the benefits or fruits derived from it and thus permits the diversion of the benefits to the children.[80] The trust could result from an agreement between the parents or from the imposition by the court of a constructive trust. Judith McMullen argues that the

circumstances justifying the creation of a child support trust tend to fall into four categories: (a) Where the paying parent has a variable income; (2) Where the payor is financially able to establish a trust fund to cover future educational expenses; (3) Where a trust is deemed necessary because the payor or payee have acted in an irresponsible way; and (4) Where the parties have entered an agreement whereby a trust is established in lieu of monthly child support payments.[81]

Analogous legal patterns exist for imposing management duties.[82]

An equitable or "first" lien that would give the lien a priority among debts of a parent may accomplish the same objective without the onerous fiduciary duties of a trustee. However, without fiduciary duties imposed on the parent, limits must be imposed on the sale of property subject to the lien. Otherwise, a parent could deplete his or her property subject to the lien without any breach of legal duty. Some other court-ordered restrictions would be necessary to ensure that parental obligations, both general and specific, are met.

The ability of courts to ignore title to property should also extend to spousal and child support. Support for children should be based on a uniform standard realistically assessing the cost of child rearing and the standard of living of the family enjoyed during the marriage. Support reflecting a realistic assessment of the cost of child rearing should be simple to compute using fixed tables based on a uniform standard. The relationship of the cost of child rearing reflected in the tables should be adjusted to also reflect a consideration of the standard of living of the family before the divorce. Although traditional child support payments should not be eliminated as a method to fulfill parental responsibilities, the enactment of the FCA may result in fewer child support awards. This expectation can easily be explained: the award to a child of his or her share in family property makes child support payments in many cases unnecessary.

Title to the property (right to receive income and property subject to trust or lien) remains in the name of the parent or trustee, which creates a presumption of who can manage the property unless objected to by the parents or the court.[83] The court's jurisdiction to modify an award under this article would continue until the obligations no longer exist.[84] Lawmakers should consider the enactment of a standard parental trust with uniform terms,[85] including guidelines and duties of the trustee, to ensure that the purposes of this act are furthered. Trustees could be selected by the consent of the parents or the court. If the FCA is passed, it can be anticipated that the market would respond with less expensive trusts.[86]

CONCLUSION

Ideally, a society does not rely on the force of law for solutions to social and cultural problems but rather relies on the force of habit. But the two—law and habit—are not unrelated. Law can reflect the aspirations, rather than the concessions, of a culture. It can be a means to civic renewal and relationship, particularly when it is expressive and enabling.[87]This free choice would, however, be a binding legal commitment. In this way, it blends legal theory and political practice. It can serve as a guide for its citizens, guiding them to virtue and to a thriving common good. Louisiana's covenant marriage is such an example.[88] The Family as Community Act can (1) enhance economic support for children; (2) provide greater legal predictability in fixed, definable rules that permit judicial discretion only at the margins; (3) be perceived as fair as a result of the reduction in judicial discretion, less litigation, and the fact that more property remains in the family; and (4) provide an heuristic of public obligation to the welfare of children. The act is realistically targeted to the most common form of divorce involving marriages with minor children, of relatively short duration, and involving a few but some assets. The FCA combines the best of both the community property and common-law systems. For all of these reasons, parents and the public should support the policy.[89] In arguing for a related end, June Carbone writes, "The larger issue then becomes not just the fairness of the proposals standing on their own, but their ability, to contribute to the reinvigoration of societal support for childbearing."[90]

Is there a more noble aim?

NOTES

I am indebted to Sean Donlan, my research assistant and devoted "communitarian," who spent the summer of 1998 conducting research, preparing drafts of proposed legislation, and discussing ideas incorporated in this chapter.

1. See Mary Ann Glendon, *The New Family, the New Property* (Toronto: Butterworths, 1981); *Divorce and Abortion in Western Law* (Cambridge, Mass.: Harvard University Press, 1987); "Family Law Reform in the 1980s," *Louisiana Law Review* 44 (1984): 1553; "Fixed Rules and Discretion in Contemporary Family Law and Succession Law," *Tulane Law Review* 60 (1986): 1165.

2. Glendon, "Family Law Reform," 1553, 1559.

3. Ibid.; emphasis added.

4. Glendon, "Fixed Rules and Discretion,"1165, 1175: "The first and most important reason has to do with the effect a recasting of the law would have on negotiation and settlement in the great majority of cases–those that are never litigated. From the beginning, the attention of the parties would be focused on the present and future needs of their children."

5. Glendon, "Family Law Reform," 1560.

6. Glendon, "Fixed Rules and Discretion," 1165, 1168.

7. Ibid., 1174.

8. Wisconsin Statute § 765.001. The family is "the cornerstone of the moral and social formation of children." The Communitarian Network, "A Communitarian Position Paper on the Family" (Washington, D.C.: July 1, 1999), 2.

9. See Steven L. Nock, *Marriage in Men's Lives* (Oxford: Oxford University Press, 1998), 19. "On average two-parent families are better to discharge their child-raising duties if only because there are more hands—and voices—available for the task"; Communitarian Network, "Position Paper," 3. See also William Galston, "A Liberal–Democratic Case for the Two-Parent Family," *The Responsive Community* (Winter 1990/91): 21: "A primary purpose of the family is to raise children, and for this purpose families with stably married parents are best."

10. The parents in this sense act as the equivalent of a trustee for the interest of the children. Judith Younger, in her article "Light Thoughts and Night Thoughts on the American Family," *Minnesota Law Review* 76 (1992): 906, suggests, "I would put the 500-year-old common law trust, the 'greatest and most distinctive achievement performed by Englishmen in the field of jurisprudence' to work for the American family."

11. Louisiana Civil Code, article 99: "Spouses mutually assume the moral and material direction of the family, exercise parental authority, and assume the moral and material obligations resulting therefrom."

12. Communitarian Network, "Position Paper," 14. See also Galston, "A Liberal–Democratic Case," 21: "Families have primary responsibility for instilling such traits as discipline, ambition, willingness to abide by the law, and respect for others."

13. See Barbara Dafoe Whitehead, *The Divorce Culture* (New York: Knopf, 1997); Paul Amato and Alan Booth, *A Generation at Risk: Growing Up in an Era of Family Upheaval* (Cambridge, Mass.: Harvard University Press, 1997); Maggie Gallagher, *The Abolition of Marriage: How We Destroy Lasting Love* (Washington, D.C.: Regnery, 1996);

Glendon, *Divorce and Abortion in Western Law;* Judith S. Wallerstein and Julia Lewis, "The Long-Term Impact of Divorce on Children: A First Report from a 25-Year Study," presentation at the Second World Congress of Family Law and the Rights of Children and Youth in San Francisco, June 2–7, 1997 (copy on file with author); Lenore J. Weitzman, "The Economic Consequences of Divorce: Social and Economic Consequences of Property, Alimony, and Child Support Awards," *U.C.L.A. Law Review* 28 (1981): 1181; Barbara Bennett Woodhouse, "'Children's Rights': The Destruction and Promise of Family," *B.Y.U. Law Review* (1993): 497.

14. Communitarian Network, "Position Paper," 18. See also Amato and Booth, *A Generation at Risk,* in which the authors conclude that two-thirds of the divorces involve low-conflict marriages, and in those marriages children would benefit more by the preservation of the marriage rather than a divorce; and Elizabeth S. Scott, "Rational Decisionmaking about Marriage and Divorce," *Virginia Law Review* 76 (1992): 9, 27.

15. Younger, "Light Thoughts," 894: "What American children need but do not have, it seems, are stable families, and what the nation needs, but does not have, is a national policy which encourages their formation."

16. Ibid.

17. Ibid. "Being a mother or father isn't just another 'life-style choice,' but rather an ethical vocation of the weightiest sort"; Communitarian Network, "Position Paper," 16.

18. Communitarian Network, "Position Paper," 5.

19. Ibid., 18.

20. Ibid.

21. Judith T. Younger writes, "Perhaps the most telling example of parental interests being allowed to override the child's interests is the complete absence of any best interests inquiry on the vital question of family breakup"; see "Responsible Parents and Good Children," *Law and Inequality* 14 (1996): 489. In Younger's "marriage for minor children," couples with minor children would have to establish that continuing the marriage would cause either or both spouses exceptional hardship and would harm their minor children more than the divorce. See "Marital Regimes: A Story of Compromise and Demoralization, Together with Criticism and Suggestions for Reform," *Cornell Law Review* 67 (1980): 45, 90. She also suggests that couples might "opt into" such a marriage; "Light Thoughts," 903. In this respect, her suggestion resembles Louisiana's covenant marriage legislation. See Katherine Shaw Spaht, "Louisiana's Covenant Marriage: Social Analysis and Legal Implications," *Louisiana Law Review* 59 (1998): 63; Katherine Shaw Spaht, "For the Sake of the Children: Recapturing the Meaning of Marriage," *Notre Dame Law Review* 73 (1998): 1547.

22. Glendon, "Fixed Rules and Discretion," 1165.

23. See John Witte Jr., *From Sacrament to Contract: Marriage, Religion, and Law in the Western Tradition* (Louisville, Ky.: Westminster John Knox Press, 1997).

24. See, generally, the discussion in Marsha Garrison, "Autonomy or Community? An Evaluation of Two Models of Parental Obligation to Family," *California Law Review* 86 (1998): 41, which explores alternative rationales to support alteration in child support guidelines.

25. Ibid.

26. Mary Ann Glendon, *The Transformation of Family Law* (Chicago: University of Chicago Press, 1989), 197.

27. Garrison, "Autonomy or Community?" 105.

28. Ibid., 46.

29. David Popenoe, "Fostering the New Familism: A Goal for America," *The Responsive Community* (Fall 1992): 31.

30. See Elizabeth S. Scott and Robert E. Scott, "Parents as Fiduciaries," *Virginia Law Review* 81 (1995): 2401, which emphasizes a relational model. See also their article "Marriage as a Relational Contract," *Virginia Law Review* 84 (October 1998): 1225.

31. "Economy" is itself derived from the Greek concept of household management. The family predated the market. Economic value is inherently a statement of our social values.

32. See Milton Regan Jr.'s "Spouses and Strangers: Divorce Obligations and Property Rhetoric," *Georgetown Law Journal* 82 (1994): 2303, 2308: "Property rhetoric of the market domain depicts individuals and relationships between them in distinctive ways, and thus shapes the conceptual and logical framework within which the persuasiveness of their arguments must be evaluated." See also his article, "The Boundaries of Care: Constructing Community after Divorce," *Houston Law Review* 3 (1994): 425, 430-31: "Communal relationships are governed by an ethic of care." See Younger, "Light Thoughts," 10, who advocates the use of the trust model.

33. Cynthia Starnes, "Applications of a Contemporary Partnership Model for Divorce, *B.Y.U. Journal of Public Law* 8 (1998): 107, 108. See also Starnes's "Divorce and the Displaced Homemaker: A Discourse on Playing with Dolls, Partnership Buyouts and Disassociation under No-Fault," *University of Chicago Law Review* 60 (1993): 67.

34. See Eric Rasmussen and Jeffrey Evans Stake, "Lifting the Veil of Ignorance: Personalizing the Marriage Contract," *Indiana Law Journal* 73 (1998): 453, arguing for the privatization of marital obligations. While "contracting up" to higher standards in marriage, such as a covenant marriage under the law in Louisiana and Arizona, is perhaps not unreasonable or unwise, a marital laissez-faire is a dangerous notion. See also Joel A. Nichols, "Louisiana's Covenant Marriage Law: A First Step toward a More Robust Pluralism in Marriage and Divorce Law?" *Emory Law Journal* 47 (1998): 929.

35. The American Law Institute project, "Principles of the Law of Family Dissolution," makes the same assumption about modification to conform to local law.

36. As someone trained in the civil law, that of the European continent and my own state of Louisiana, and as someone who believes that the civil law approaches to property and inheritance are inherently more communitarian, I have looked first to the civil law solution and then to its closest common-law analog.

37. In discussing their own suggestions, June R. Carbone and Margaret F. Brinig, explain that

[s]uch a strategy would emphasize: (1) increased societal support for day care, parental leave, education, nutrition, medical care, and other subsidies that directly benefit children and their primary caretakers; (2) allocation of property and post-divorce income for the children's benefit before the spouse's individual claims are considered [citing Glendon]; and (3) recognition of the parents' continuing responsibility for, and benefit from, children as a primary basis for divorce adjustments.

See "Rethinking Marriage: Feminist Ideology, Economic Change, and Divorce Reform," Tulane Law Review 65 (1991): 1007-8. See also Communitarian Network, "Position Paper."

38. See the Uniform Marriage and Divorce Act, section 102 ("Purposes: Rules of Construction"), and Garrison, "Autonomy or Community?"

39. "For divorces where children are involved we need a new set of rules based on the principle of 'children first.' Issues of property division between the parents should not even be considered until adequate provision has been made for the needs of minor children." Communitarian Network, "Position Paper," 10.

40. Nothing in this act precludes a similar modification of child support guidelines to adopt "the community" model as suggested by Garrison, "Autonomy or Community?"

41. See Frank F. Furstenberg, Saul D. Hoffman, and Laura Shrestha, "The Effect of Divorce on Intergenerational Transfers: New Evidence," *Demography* 32 (1995): 319. For example, the Canadian province of Ontario's system of deferred community applies at both divorce and death. In both cases, the right must be asserted by the parties involved. See Malcom C. Kronby, *Canadian Family Law* (Toronto: Stoddart, 1997).

Civilian jurisdictions worldwide have historically guaranteed children a share of their parents' estate at death, regardless of the age of the children, through the legal institution of forced heirship. Louisiana is the only state in the union with forced heirship, which was significantly modified by amendment to the Louisiana Constitution effective in 1996. Nonetheless, there has been increasing concern in common-law states about unjust disinheritance of children by parents, particularly minor children. See Ralph Brashier, "Disinheritance and the Modern Family," *Case Western Reserve Law Review* 45 (1994): 83; Ralph Brashier, "Protecting the Child from Disinheritance: Must Louisiana Stand Alone?" *Louisiana Law Review* 57 (1996): 1; Deborah A. Batts, " 'I Didn't Ask to Be Born': The American Law of Disinheritance and a Proposal for Change to a System of Protected Inheritance," *Hastings Law Journal* 41 (1990): 1197; Tamara York, "Protecting Minor Children from Parental Disinheritance: A Proposal for Awarding a Compulsory Share of the Parental Estate," *Detroit College of Law at Michigan State University Law Review* 3 (1997): 861.

42. John S. Mill, *On Liberty* (1859; reprint, Oxford: Blackwell, 1947), 107: "As applied to relations in the family, the harm principle is transformed from its general passive form to an affirmative obligation to care." See also Elizabeth S. Scott, "Rehabilitating Liberalism in Modern Divorce Law," *Utah Law Review* (1994): 687, 731.

43. See section 3.16 entitled "Providing for a Child's Life Opportunities," in American Law Institute, "Principles of the Law of Family Dissolution" (Tentative Draft No. 3; Part II covering child support); see also Barbara Bennett Woodhouse, "Out of Children's Needs, Children's Rights: The Child's Voice in Defining the Family," *B.Y.U. Journal of Public Law* 8 (1994): 321.

44. The formulation of the act utilizing the words *parental obligation* rather than *children's rights* was purposeful. See Mary Ann Glendon, *Rights Talk: The Impoverishment of Political Discourse* (New York: Free Press, 1991). The obligations may, of course, be reciprocal. See Article 1 of FCA, para. D. Louisiana law imposes such a mutual obligation on ascendants and descendants that lasts throughout life. See Louisiana Civil Code, article 229; Barbara Bennett Woodhouse, "Out of Children's Needs, Children's Rights: The Child's Voice in Defining the Family," *B.Y.U. Journal of Public Law* 8 (1994): 321.

45. Recognition of the family as a community initiated by the relationship between the parents, and given new form by the presence of children, would provide a more realistic picture of the efforts that accompany child rearing. Redefining family obligations in terms of such a community would also aid efforts to stem the flight of resources away from chil-

dren. June Carbone, "Income Sharing: Redefining the Family in Terms of Community," *Houston Law Review* 31 (1994): 359.

46. Garrison, "Autonomy or Community?"114.

47. This chapter, as a general principle, assumes a marriage of the biological or adoptive parents. But see bracketed language in article 1 of this act. In some states, the responsibility to children could include obligations resulting from a marriage between a stepparent and biological parent. Conditions for acceptance into the family community may be independently formulated.

48. Deferred community regimes exist in Quebec, Denmark, Sweden, Norway, Finland, West Germany, and Holland. In contrast to deferred community regimes, other community property systems, such as that of Louisiana, recognize a present rather than inchoate interest in community property. See, for example, Louisiana Civil Code article 2338.

49. The system also could function as a dual classification system, dividing individual and family property, rather than an all encompassing property system. But as the equitable distribution of property allows title to be ignored, it seems an unimportant distinction to make. See the Uniform Marital Property Act, sections 12 and 13 for potential classification of life insurance and deferred employment benefits.

50. The Uniform Marital Property Act, section 1:15, defines property as "an interest, present or future, legal or equitable, vested or contingent, in real or personal property."

51. In community property systems, this type of property is designated "separate" property.

52. Community property systems sometimes refer to the result of such exclusions as a commingled "hotchpot." The pot of "net family property" in the Family Law of Ontario, Canada (Act 1986) defines such property as

the value of all of the property, except . . . [excluded property] after deducting, (a) the spouse's debts and other liabilities, and (b) the value of property, other than a matrimonial home, that the spouse owned on the date of the marriage, after deducting the spouse's debts and other liabilities, calculated as of the date of the marriage. (Section 4.1)

The Canadian system excludes the matrimonial home, granting a potential right to possession to a spouse.

53. Section 5, comments. See section 15 for "Interspousal Remedies." Compare the Uniform Marital Property Act and Louisiana Civil Code, article 2351.

54. Management and control, according to Wisconsin statute, section 766.10 (11), means "the right to buy, sell, use, transfer, exchange, abandon, lease, consume, expend, assign, create a security interest in, mortgage, encumber, dispose of, institute or defend a civil action regarding or otherwise deal with property as if it were property of an unmarried person." Compare the Uniform Marital Property Act and Louisiana Civil Code article 2351.

55. The Family as Community Act does not contain explicit, detailed provisions on the management of family property during the existence of the "family community." Such management and control will be determined by the applicable state law.

56. German law, the ultimate source of Spanish and American community property systems, established the family as its basic legal unit (the *sib* or *sippe*) and created a community of its male members. See chapter 2 of George McKay, *A Treatise on the Law of Community Property* (Indianapolis: Bobbs-Merrill, 1926). See also Joseph Dainow, "The Early Sources of Forced Heirship: Its History in Texas and Louisiana," *Louisiana Law Review* 4 (1941): 42.

57. See Garrison, "Autonomy or Community?"

58. See Scott, "Rational Decisionmaking," at 12: "A legal regime that reflects the values of commitment could further several important social interests, ranging from the concrete [reduction of divorce litigation] to the intangible [enhancement of personal happiness]."

59. The fulfillment of parental obligations may also be characterized as an award of divorce compensation. That is, given the volume of information concerning the negative effects of divorce on children, this award could attempt to compensate for (uncompensatable) damage done to the child by the divorce. French law, for example, permits an action for damages when marital fault is involved in a divorce. Such an award can perhaps be justified using the theory of either detrimental reliance or unjust enrichment. Different states would, of course, want to approach this matter differently to ensure that the interests of children and the community are protected.

60. See section 307.

61. In proposing a "children-first" principle, Glendon writes that the court's

> main task would be to piece together, from property and income and in-kind personal care [all relating to child support], the best package to meet the needs of the children and their physical custodian. Until the welfare of the children had been adequately secured in this way, there would be no question or debate about "marital property." All property, no matter when or how acquired, would be subject to the duty to provide for the children. . . . In cases where there is significant income and property left over after the children's needs have been met, the regular system of marital property division and spousal support law could be applied as a residual system.

Divorce and Abortion, 95. See also Communitarian Network, "Position Paper," 10: "Issues of property division should not even be considered until adequate provision has been made for the needs of minor children."

62. Georgia Senate Bill #309 (February 1, 1997) [Gochenour]. The proposed bill read, "Notwithstanding any other provision of this title to the contrary, on and after the effective date of this Code section (,) each award of child custody, child support, alimony, or division of property shall be made on the basis of a 'children first' rule, meaning that the best interest of the minor children of a marriage shall be the primary consideration in any such award." The bill did not pass.

63. The Family Law Act (Scotland) 1985. "Aliment for any children will therefore be determined before the court considers financial provision for the spouses; it is only after aliment for any child has been determined that the question of financial provision for the spouses will arise."

64. The court might also appoint an attorney to represent the interests of a minor or dependent child concerning the issue of what parental obligations are owed. In such case, provision should be made for the payment of costs: "The court shall enter an order for costs, fees, and disbursements in favor of the child's attorney. The order shall be made against either or both parents, except that, if the responsible party is indigent, the costs, fees, and disbursements shall be borne by the (appropriate agency)." This is virtually identical to section 310 of the Uniform Marriage and Divorce Act.

65. See Glendon, "Family Law Reform in the 1980s," 1553, 1557. A children-first principle would make "explicit what is implicit" and "mandatory what is now optional" (1560). See also Mary Ann Glendon, *The New Family and the New Property,* 80-84.

66. This statement delineating a family member's share could be phrased by the law-maker as a presumption subject to rebuttal.

67. Prior to legislative debate, consideration should be given to including more specific acts in this list which would result in the unworthiness or disinherison of a child. See former Louisiana Civil Code, article 1621 (repealed July 1, 1999).

68. See Batts, "'I Didn't Ask to Be Born,'" 1253: "Protected Inheritance is substantially similar to the *legitime*, or forced heirship found in civil law countries and in Louisiana today."

69. Forced heirship regimes already contain, implicitly, a community of obligation and rights. See Louisiana Civil Code, article 888: "The intent of this article is that the children's rights extend to all property, both community and separate, as was the case under the Civil Code of 1870." The changes in Louisiana law to forced heirship (restricting the category of forced heirs) make the actual survival of the concept questionable. Whereas forced heirship recognized certain familial and communal values, the new regime recognizes only a need-based share given more for efficiency than community. While some in Louisiana may regret this change, it is likely a more reasonable option for those states without any concept of a protected portion. See Katherine S. Spaht et al., "The New Forced Heirship Legislation: A Regrettable 'Revolution,'" *Louisiana Law Review* 50 (1990): 409.

70. The restricted testation system is also called *testator family maintenance*. These mechanisms are employed in the United Kingdom and many Commonwealth nations to alleviate the perceived inequities of common law freedom of testation. The Canadian system allows certain dependents to apply, within a restricted period, to a court for maintenance out of the estate of the deceased for "adequate provision."

71. Parental obligations should perhaps be given preference over other debts of the deceased. This would protect both the child and the surviving parent.

72. Brashier, "Protecting the Child from Disinheritance," 21.

73. Brashier, "Disinheritance and the Modern Family," 191 (discussing forced heirship regimes). See also Glendon, "Fixed Rules," "Family Law Reform in the 1980s," and *The New Family*.

74. This set of problems is perhaps the most difficult in proposing a family community and a system of family property. The entire subject deserves careful legislative deliberation to resolve the problems in a manner consistent with applicable state law.

75. See June Carbone, "Income Sharing," and Howard W. Brill, "Equity and the Restitutionary Remedies: Constructive Trust, Equitable Lien, and Subrogation," *Arkansas Law Notes* (1992)1. See also Scott, "Rational Decisionmaking," at 73; Younger, "Light Thoughts," 907; and Judith G. McMullen, "Prodding the Payor and Policing the Payee," *New England Law Review* 32 (1998): 439. See generally "Powers of the Court" in the Family Law (Ontario, Canada), Act 1986, sections 9.(1) and 34.(1).

76. This accomplishes some of what Younger, "Light Thoughts," proposed, although this act permits divorce.

77. It may also provide a bargaining chip for the spouses: "A spouse may be willing to forego income sharing for a larger share of the property or a larger share of income." Jane Rutherford, "Duty in Divorce: Shared Income as a Path to Equality," *Fordham Law Review* 58 (1990): 586.

78. Ibid., 579.

79. Carbone, "Income Sharing," 359, 373.

80. Younger, "Light Thoughts," 906. She would permit a court to "order continuation of [a] trust relationship between ex-spouses and children, delaying termination and ultimate property distribution until the children are grown" (907). See also Batts, "'I Didn't Ask to Be Born.'"

81. McMullen, "Prodding the Payor," 439. In the article, McMullen discusses at length the difficulties and possibilities of using trust devices, including funding the trust, creating the trust, and establishing trust terms.

82. See Uniform Probate Code, section 5-101: "Persons, other than the minor or any financial institution, receiving money or property for a minor, are obligated to apply the money to the support and education of the minor, but may not pay themselves except by way of reimbursement for out-of-pocket expenses for goods and services necessary for the minor's support." See also comments: "Where a minor has only a small amount of property, it would be wasteful to require protective proceedings to deal with the property." See section 7-302.

83. See Uniform Marital Property Act.

84. See Uniform Marriage and Divorce Act, section 312.

85. See, for example, Louisiana Revised Statute 9: 963 (standard provisional custody by mandate form).

86. See McMullen, "Prodding the Payor," 471: "[M]any people will simply not have sufficient property to allow payment of a significant lump sum into a trust. . . . In these cases the main purpose . . . [would be to] provide some accountability for how the money is spent."

87. Law can nourish the common good by offering citizens the choice to opt into more constructive and demanding obligations than our dominant (individualist) cultural or legal paradigm imposes. It can allow individuals to "opportune virtue." By doing so, the law enables not only a virtuous choice by citizens directly affected but also a community-wide discussion of the virtue encouraged and its value to others.

88. See "Opportuning Virtue: Lessons of the Louisiana Covenant Marriage Act" published by the Communitarian Network.

89. See Glendon, "Family Law Reform in the 1980s," 1560, and *Divorce and Abortion,* 97; and McMullen "Providing the Payor." The second most common reason not to pay child support payments was "concern that the support money will not actually be spent on the children."

90. Carbone, "Income Sharing," 412-14.

15

Reflection on Societal Change: How Government Strives to Guarantee Children the Support of Their Parents

David Gray Ross

It is no exaggeration to say that children flourish when both parents give them ample love, attention, direction, and provision. And while most of us who are parents strive to fulfill that lofty objective, we often fall short due to circumstances that rarely lie with the child. When our children have needs, most of us try to fill those needs. When other parents' children have needs, we, as a society, still try to see that their most essential needs are met. As a result, federal, state, and local governments intervene in the lives of children and parents, particularly those children whose parents are no longer living under the same roof. How this government response has taken shape over the past sixty years is a reflection of contemporary values and commitment.

THE SOCIAL SECURITY ACT OF 1935

When President Franklin Roosevelt signed the original Social Security Act on August 14, 1935,[1] the United States was in the depths of its Great Depression, enduring a staggering unemployment rate. Government as a tool to effect social and business behavior was still in its infancy, often reflected in a generation of U.S. Supreme Court decisions that struggled to define the limitations on government's reach into areas that were once considered beyond the governmental pale. Locally run poorhouses had been around since the nineteenth century, as had been the midwestern-influenced county government–based programs to help widows and orphans,[2] but these responses were checkered, often based on the fortuity of the timing of the application for assistance and the good will of the grantor. At the turn of the century, model laws were passed by several states to make it a crime not to pay child support, as the morality rather than the economics of nonpayment was stressed.[3]

The Social Security Act, not initially intended to be the primary safety net of America it later became, offered in addition to a retirement fund a benefit, later known as Aid to Families with Dependent Children (AFDC). In 1935, the out-of-wedlock birthrate was lower than today's,[4] and the number of divorces was 218,000, a rate that was 1.7 percent of all marriages, one-third of the 1980 rate.[5]

NUMBERS

Between World War II and the 1960s, the rate of out-of-wedlock births and separating and divorcing families rose, but nothing like the rate increase in the most recent twenty-five years (1970–95).[6] The explosion of out-of-wedlock births began in the 1960s and has continued until very recently.[7] Today, about 1.2 million children, or 31 percent of births, are born out of wedlock.[8] Annually, roughly half of children who are new to nonintact homes (2.4 million) are born out of wedlock (1.2 million), and half are the result of recently separated married parents.[9] About 25 percent of AFDC children of all ages still need their paternity established.[10] Even leaving aside the children born during a marriage who are not fathered by the mother's husband, paternity establishment has taken center stage for a very significant percentage of the child support caseload. Mostly as a result of the sharp increase in the rate of single-parent households, AFDC expenditures increased dramatically over the years, from $4 billion in 1970 to almost $23 billion in 1994, as the number of recipients doubled from about seven million to about fourteen million (almost ten million of whom are children).[11]

POSTWAR AMERICA

The mobility of post–World War II America spurred universal enactment of civil remedies to collect support in interstate cases. Many Americans were no longer isolated in small communities, and urbanization and suburbanization began to take its toll on family intactness. Soldiers coming back from Europe and the Pacific theaters were a bit more "worldly." America's obsession with automobiles and interstate ease of transport made distant towns close, increasing the number of interpersonal relationships one had compared to the prewar days. While divorce was not as prevalent in postwar America as it is today, it became less of a moral taboo than it was in earlier times. Consequently, and practically, the desire was to collect support to keep families self-sufficient rather than to punish the "runaway pappy" (the moniker given to the first civil model interstate child support statute). The Uniform Reciprocal Enforcement of Support Act (URESA) was first promulgated by the National Conference of Commissioners on Uniform State Laws in 1950, and for a generation it remained the main tool for collecting the child support owed in cases in which the parents resided in separate states.[12]

Interstate cases account for about 30 percent of the total caseload.[13] URESA relied heavily on the district or state attorneys to provide needed services to establish and collect child support.[14] Criminal nonsupport prosecution was becoming secondary to civil contempt based on refusal to obey a court order.[15] Gradually, child support became an important part of economic independence for custodial mothers who often reentered the workforce, if at all, after the children had reached latch-key age, and often they were paid much less than equivalent-aged males.[16] Intact households, those with two parents, did not have two working parents as a majority of two-parent households do today[17]; however, single-parent labor force participation has been traditionally high.[18]

TITLE IV-D: GOVERNMENT INVOLVEMENT IN COLLECTING SUPPORT

While Congress had taken small steps since the 1950s and 1960s to tie nonresidential-parental responsibility to AFDC payments, the big step came in the early 1970s, when Senator Russell Long of Louisiana proposed and pushed through legislation that created a unified federal/state approach to recouping welfare from "absent" parents through a state-based, federally overseen child support program.[19] This program is known as the IV-D program, after its statutory home in Part IV-D of the Social Security Act.[20] Originally, the program's focus was on welfare-only cases, although it was long-recognized that many custodial parents, regardless of income, needed child support collection assistance. Some states, such as Michigan, have been collecting support for all families for decades. Child support keeps some families off welfare, so there is a welfare cost-avoidance argument to make as well in support of universalization of services. Another factor favoring universalization of services is the disruptive nature of case handling and support collecting for persons who go on and off welfare. Without continuity of the child support collection stream, marginally self-sufficient parents can lapse to dependency on welfare for sustenance. Changes to Title IV-D in 1984 contained congressional intent that welfare and nonwelfare cases were to be treated equally in terms of priority and resources. However, while the program is free for welfare recipients, nonwelfare applicants for paternity and child support services through the IV-D governmental entities must pay up to $25 as an application fee.[21] The IV-D services include locating a missing parent, establishing paternity of a child, establishing a child support order, and enforcing the order.

While a multimillionaire could apply for IV-D services, most nonwelfare persons apply because they need the support to help make financial ends meet. Today, half of the cases and about three-quarters of the money collected through these IV-D agencies are nonwelfare cases.[22] While no definitive statistics are available, non-IV-D cases, those cases handled outside of the IV-D system, either pro se or through private counsel, probably account for less than half of the child support cases today.[23]

ESTABLISHING CHILD SUPPORT ORDERS
WITH LESS JUDICIAL INVOLVEMENT

Even the establishment of the child support order has changed, from a judge's individual determination to a guideline-based approach intended to make awards equivalent under like circumstances within a state.[24]

Overall, about eleven million residential parents are entitled to receive child support for almost eighteen million children.[25] About 62 percent of the residential parents, who are entitled to receive support, have orders.[26] Of the 38 percent without orders, the leading reasons for not having orders are (1) the residential parent did not want an award (e.g., because he or she wanted to remain financially independent, was afraid of the nonresidential parent, or did not know how to pursue it); (2) the nonresidential parent is unable to pay; (3) the residential parent is unable to locate the nonresidential parent; (4) joint custody granted and no support was awarded; (5) a final separation or support agreement or order was pending, going through legal channels; and 6) paternity first needed to be established.[27] Many parents are afraid to rock the boat by pursuing orders, or they want to avoid the legal system's adversary process.

Of the parents with orders, about half report being paid all of their child support, one-quarter some of the ordered support, and about one-quarter report receiving none of the ordered support.[28]

How much child support is potentially owed? According to the Urban Institute, in 1990 about $21 billion was owed under a support order, of which $14 billion was paid. If awards were modified to reflect the current ability of each parent to pay, using the representative Wisconsin guideline on a national basis (about one-third of the nation has a guideline similar to Wisconsin's), another $7 billion would be owed. If all persons entitled to awards received them, another $19 billion would be owed, making the gap between what was paid and what was owed approximately $34 billion.[29]

Modification of a child support order is a labor-intensive process of information gathering and verification, and true emphasis on making orders as accurate as possible takes a lot of caseworker and decision-maker time. A national trend limits the amount of review and approval time and work needed to be conducted by courts by assigning more of the work of reassessing the child support order amount level to executive branch employees in the IV-D agency.

As the IV-D caseload grew in the 1980s and 1990s, more attention was paid to cutting down on court time in all types of routine cases. The state of the science in genetic testing, which nowadays can virtually prove a man is the father of a child, and the emphasis on voluntary acknowledgment in paternity cases have made court hearings less necessary. Administrative process is used extensively in about one-third of the states,[30] a process whereby an executive branch agency rather than a court issues and enforces a child support order.

ENFORCEMENT

Child support enforcement has shifted from relying on contempt as the main tool to income withholding through continuous garnishment and state and federal tax refund offsets. Contempt is costly, requiring a court hearing and a prosecutor's time. Contempt is also subject to continuances, persuasive defendant testimony, and episodic recurrence.

With the vast majority of Americans drawing a paycheck from an employer, it made sense to focus on the traditional collection tool of creditors, the garnishment. The problem with traditional garnishment is that it often was a one-time execution, good for only one paycheck.

Child support needed a device that allowed for collection throughout the life of the support order. The spread in the 1980s of continuous garnishment, also called *income withholding* or *wage assignment,* provided the efficient collection tool child support creditors needed. Adding Federal Income Tax Refund Offset to the collection tool mix in the 1980s also boosted collections. Withholding wages and offsetting tax refunds account for 57 percent and 8 percent of total IV-D collections, respectively.[31]

IV-D NUMBERS

The IV-D agency network is vast, affecting millions of parents and children. The numbers however, sometimes exaggerate the true number of IV-D cases. Sometimes there are several IV-D cases for families living in separate states or even separate counties. Some offices open a new case each time a person goes on or off welfare, although the services are supposed to be seamless. As a result, the number of IV-D cases is much higher than the actual number of residential parents entitled to receive support on behalf of their children. (Multicase reconciling during the conversion to statewide automated systems should help remove most duplication.)

The IV-D child support system has a national caseload of over nineteen million cases, about ten million for which orders exist.[32] There are about fifty-two thousand child support workers.[33] The program costs about $3 billion each year.[34] The IV-D agencies collect the majority of support collected overall (IV-D and non-IV-D)—about $10.8 billion, $3 billion of which is to reimburse state and federal welfare expenditures.[35]

WELFARE REFORM

Child support evolution continued as part of the welfare reform bill—the Personal Responsibility and Work Opportunity Reconciliation Act of 1996

(PRWORA).[36] After the congressionally established Commission on Interstate Child Support issued its 1992 report,[37] various bills were introduced to add more enforcement tools and to streamline the child support system.[38] The President's Work and Responsibility Act of 1994's child support provisions, which built on the Interstate Commission's recommendations, were in turn incorporated almost whole in PRWORA.

It is ironic that while Congress through the PRWORA ended welfare as a federal entitlement, the same Congress made child support requirements that are more prescriptive on the states, largely due to interstate case-processing needs and automation and electronic communication purposes. Some persons believe that PRWORA, after major child support legislation in 1984[39] and 1988[40] changed the child support system fairly dramatically, is the last chance for the system to show substantial collection rate improvement before either a block grant approach or, at the other end of the spectrum, a partial federalization of the program is undertaken.[41]

Child support has been a favorite of both Republicans and Democrats since its inception.[42] Its intent, from a federal policy angle, has been to recoup tax dollars spent on welfare and to provide a service to nonwelfare parents who need paternity and/or support established and support orders enforced and/or modified. Many near-poor custodial parents, most of whom work, are only above the welfare application line because of child support. So even within the nonwelfare population, there is a significant amount of welfare cost-avoidance as a result of successful child support collection.[43]

Congress, the Clinton administration, and most governors see the importance of providing this crucial government service. Has it changed the domestic law tradition of state-based responses to family matters to one more influenced by federal government activities? Yes, because of the federal program oversight responsibilities. Has it replaced state-led initiatives in resolving family disputes? No, because states control how to structure the marital dissolution and separation process outside of child support, and even within child support, states have much freedom regarding how they approach the provision of their services. Has it changed the role of government in domestic disputes? Yes, it has made government an active participant or partner in many proceedings. Has it replaced the traditional role of private legal representation in domestic matters? Only partly and only in child support. Private attorneys still represent child support clients; but in matrimonial law practice, the emphasis has always been on custody and property division issues.

Another question that I want to spend some time answering is, Has child support through the IV-D program changed the handling of domestic cases by the judicial system and how we look at certain domestic issues? The answer is yes, and it has to do with

- the sheer magnitude of the child support undertaking;
- the recalcitrance of a large proportion of the obligors;
- funding and automation issues;
- the balance and tension between due process and mass justice;
- the nonstatic nature of the parties' incomes and needs;
- the procedural uniformity needs inherent in large bureaucratic operations that include interstate activities; and
- a history of the government addressing only part of the problems that underlie family dissolution, nonformation, and dynamics.

With almost twenty million cases being worked by fifty-two thousand people, successful automation of most routine functions is crucial. The matching of database information with case information involves millions of names and other relevant data—a huge task with obvious privacy concerns. Huge caseloads also mean the type of tailored-enforcement remedy that the private bar is often well suited to do cannot be done as well by the public sector. The public sector needs sufficient resources to handle both routine cases in mass quantities and the special cases that require more labor-intensive efforts.

The result is that those who actively seek to avoid paying child support through work in the underground economy or transfer of assets into other persons' names are all too often successful. Why are obligors not so obliging? First, it should be stated that many are. Many pay without delay. Second, those who aren't fall into two general categories: obligors who passively resist and who will comply once enforcement begins, and obligors who will go to great ends to avoid paying. The "avoiders" seem to do so for several reasons,[44] including hostility between the obligor and the residential parent; manipulation or control by the obligor of the residential parent; the impact of remarriage by either the nonresidential or residential parent (which can work either in favor of or against greater compliance); unresolved custody, access, and visitation issues; reluctance to pay support money that could be spent on one's own needs; and general antigovernment feelings.

Society-at-large strategies are needed that include a shift in how noncustodial parents view their parenting responsibility and how teenagers view parenting responsibilities in general. Stressing compliance with the law is not enough. Society needs to stress as well the inherent "manliness" in male parenting and living up to one's associated responsibilities. The message is that strong, self-assured men provide for their families and do not forsake them. Self-compliance through an image of self-reliance is needed among men. After all, about nine-tenths of obligors are male, although there is an increase in the percentage of female obligors.[45]

Conversely, society must have an effective channel for resolution of custody and access disputes to ensure that any claims of access denial can be examined and resolved swiftly, fairly and inexpensively.

As stated earlier, working the child support caseload successfully depends on well-designed and well-implemented automation and sufficient staffing. States have been engaged in automation efforts for several years, and most have or are on the verge of having statewide systems. Automation also provides an opportunity to do more data base matching than could be imagined in a case-by-case world. Based on the pioneering work of several states, particularly Massachusetts, PRWORA requires states to use new tools for enforcement that will be based on database matches, notices, opportunities to be heard, and resolution, which, in a majority of cases, will result in little or no human intervention.

When automated systems begin to take over functions once done by individuals, not only is there still an eerie "*1984*-ish" aspect of Big Brother and the attendant concerns, but there is also an uneasiness that mistakes will be made because the computer isn't facile enough to catch a nuance or individual circumstance.

Instead of rejecting the new technology, we need to adapt it to use it so that fairness is not overrun by efficiency. Automation or no automation, due process is still the law of the land, of course, and every opportunity must still be accorded to obligors to ensure that they have the chance to be heard and present evidence before an enforcement activity becomes irrevocable, especially in cases where there is little human review of the action before it is taken by an automatic system that generates notices.

That does not necessarily mean that notice and a hearing must be accorded before the property is seized or frozen and then seized.[46] If the state makes a mistake, the obligor can be made whole again soon after the mistake is discovered. The seminal Supreme Court case, *Mathews v. Eldridge,* provides a balancing of interests to determining the constitutionality of the state's act[47] and will be our beacon as we implement the enforcement provisions of PRWORA. *Mathews* has a three-pronged test to determine fairness: (1) the private interest that will be affected by the official action; (2) the risk of erroneous deprivation of such interests through the procedures used and the probable value, if any, of additional or substitute procedural safeguards; and (3) the government's interest, including the function involved and the fiscal and administrative burdens that the additional or substitute procedural requirement would entail.[48]

Each past-due child support installment is already a judgment by operation of law, meaning that no further court action is required to find that the installment can be legally enforced like a money judgment.[49] Under PRWORA, a lien now arises by operation of law based on that judgment.[50] The state must provide a quick and fair outlet to discuss any wrongful seizure, but the state may also freeze the property to prevent alienation by its owner until the issues are resolved.[51]

Interstate cases require more uniformity than do intrastate cases because two different bureaucracies need to communicate in the same language and use similar standards, and to alleviate unfairness to the parents if one state's law is taken advantage of. The new Uniform Interstate Family Support Act (UIFSA) tries to create a little order out of chaos through some uniform procedures (including electronic transmission of certain evidence and telephonic hearing availability). UIFSA was promulgated in 1992 to replace URESA and was amended slightly in 1996. PRWORA required every state to have UIFSA in effect by January 1, 1998. The intent is to reinforce uniformity in the handling of interstate child support cases, so that local procedures peculiar to one state do not hinder case-processing because of unfamiliarity in another state. This is the first time a uniform law has been mandated by Congress for all states to pass. Additionally, Congress amended the Full Faith and Credit Act (1994) twice in the past two years to add a child support provision.[52] This ensures that child support orders of one state are recognized and enforced according to their terms in a second state. Congress and the Clinton administration understand the importance of child support, the interstate difficulties inherent in child support collection, and, perhaps most important, the temporal aspect of a child support order; that is, it needs prospective attention and protection as it changes over time to reflect the parents' financial vicissitudes during the child's minor years. Full faith and credit for prospective child support—ordered support that isn't yet due—is crucial to ensuring that past and future parts of child support orders are respected and followed in other states.

Child support lasts for at least the minority of a child, and during that time it is rare that the economic circumstances of the parents do not radically change. Next to a mortgage, a child support debt is the longest ongoing debt most obligors will have, and it can vary in amount based on the parties' financial circumstances. PRWORA has streamlined modification for IV-D cases to make it easier for either party to request a review of the appropriate amount of the order and, if appropriate, modify it. Every three years the parties will receive notice of the right to request a review, and then at state discretion, the review can be done by an automated review of the financial records of the parties to which states have access (tax and employment security data), a cost-of-living adjustment, or a case-by-case review. The first two options may result in a proposed adjustment that may not match a guideline-calculated amount, so the parties have the option of requesting a guidelines application in those cases.[53] This exemplifies the interface of automation and due process, where expediency is reined in by fairness.

My last point cannot be overstressed: the need to look at child support in the larger context of family issues. Obviously, the reasons for single-parent-headed households are numerous, and each family has its complex history. That said, it is still important for the community at large and, yes, state, local, and federal government to focus resources that best produce healthy families in a manner that least interferes with parents' primary duty to raise their children. Legal, academic, bureaucratic, and community leaders need to interweave their efforts to implement a vision that supports family formation (when possible and in the best interests of all concerned), family strengthening, and family self-sufficiency. Domestic violence and abuse and neglect situations excepted, disputes between parents should not override full emotional and financial support for their children. When parents cannot, between themselves, straighten out all the disputes that affect support, access, and major decisions affecting their children, an avenue should be open to them to help them do so. The Commission on Child and Family Welfare recently issued its report, which promotes voluntary parenting plans regarding residential arrangements and access and mandatory mediation when voluntary agreements do not work.[54] This is the direction in which the nation is headed, and it takes all of us as a community to make progress toward that destination.

The government's role in collecting child support may vary over the next several generations, but the needs of the children will not. Our most important outcome is to produce as many happy and healthy children as possible, preferably by parents' efforts, but with the government's help when necessary. We must dedicate all of our own missions as bureaucrats and academics to the flourishing of the nation's children.

NOTES

The opinions expressed herein are those of the author and may not necessarily represent the position of the U.S. Department of Health and Human Services.

1. PL 74-271 (49 Stat. 620).

2. With roots in English poor laws, the United States at its most local of governmental levels sought ways to ensure that the orphans and widows did not go hungry through a communal fund. Poorhouses were much more common around the turn of the twentieth century, as were community trusts established to take care of the indigent.

3. The Uniform Desertion and Nonsupport Act, promulgated by the National Conference of Commissioners on Uniform State Laws in 1910. Some states still have this law on their books.

4. U.S. Census Bureau's *Current Population Reports* (Series P-23).

5. National Center on Health Statistics, U.S. Department of Health and Human Services.

6. Between 1970 and 1992, the number of female-headed households with children under eighteen increased 164 percent, while the number of such two-parent families declined by 4 percent. One out of every four children lives in a single-parent household; *1994 Green Book,* U.S. House of Representatives, Committee on Ways and Means, Subcommittee on Human Resources, 456.

7. In 1960, 5.5 percent of live births were to unwed mothers. That number was 28 percent in 1990 and over 30 percent in 1994. U.S. Census Bureau, *Current Population Reports* (Series P-23).

8. National Center for Health Statistics, U.S. Department of Health and Human Services.

9. Ibid.

10. Table 37, "Nineteenth Annual Report to Congress," Office of Child Support Enforcement, U.S. Department of Health and Human Services (FY94 data); Office of Family Assistance, U.S. Department of Health and Human Services, "Overview of the AFDC Program, Fiscal Year 1994."

11. See *1994 Green Book,* U.S. House of Representatives, Committee on Ways and Means, 325, table 10-1; Office of Family Assistance, "Overview of the AFDC Program, Fiscal Year 1994."

12. See M. Haynes and D. Dodson, ed., *Interstate Child Support Remedies* (Washington, D.C.: Office of Child Support Enforcement, U.S. Department of Health and Human Services).

13. See U.S. Commission on Interstate Child Support, *Supporting Our Children: A Blueprint for Reform* (Washington, D.C.: U.S. Government Printing Office, 1992).

14. See Haynes and Dodson, *Interstate Child Support Remedies.*

15. Ibid.

16. In 1993, about 60 percent of women with preschool-aged children participated in the workforce, five times the rate in 1947. *1994 Green Book,* U.S. House of Representatives, Committee on Ways and Means, 532.

17. In 1960, 19 percent of married women with preschoolers and 39 percent of married mothers with school-aged children worked. In 1986, 54 percent of married mothers with preschoolers and 68 percent of married mothers with school-aged children worked. *1994 Green Book,* U.S. House of Representatives, Committee on Ways and Means, 534, Table 12-2.

18. Between 1970 and 1993, married women with preschoolers participation in the labor force increased by 96 percent, while divorced women with preschoolers increased their participation by 7.6 percent from 63 percent to 68 percent, and divorced women with school-aged children participation increased only by 1.5 percent from 82 percent to 84 percent. Ibid.

19. PL No. 93-647, codified in 42 U.S.C. section 651 et seq.

20. Ibid.

21. Child Support Enforcement Amendments of 1984, PL 98-378 (codified in 42 U.S.C. section 651 et seq.)

22. Data from Office of Child Support Enforcement, U.S. Department of Health and Human Services, "Twentieth Annual Report to Congress" (draft, 1995).

23. Working Group on Welfare Reform, Family Support, and Independence, "Background Papers on Welfare Reform: Child Support Enforcement" (1994).

24. 42 U.S.C., section 667.

25. *1994 Green Book,* U.S. House of Representatives, Committee on Ways and Means, 458.

26. Ibid. at 462, table 11-3.

27. See U.S. Bureau of the Census, *Current Population Reports,* Series P60-187, "Child Support for Custodial Mothers and Fathers: 1991" (Washington, D.C.: U.S. Government Printing Office, 1995), 37.

28. Ibid., 13, table 1.

29. E. Sorensen, *Noncustodial Fathers: Can They Afford to Pay More Child Support?* (Washington, D.C.: Urban Institute, 1995).

30. OCSE information from state plans.

31. Data from the Office of Child Support Enforcement, "Twentieth Annual Report to Congress."

32. Ibid.

33. Ibid.

34. Ibid.

35. Ibid.

36. PL No. 104-193 (signed into law August 22, 1996), relevant child support sections to be codified at 42 U.S.C., section 651 et seq.

37. U.S. Commission on Interstate Child Support, "Supporting Our Children."

38. See, for example, the administration's bill, the Work and Responsibility Act of 1994. From 1992 through 1994, U.S. Representatives Roukema, Kennelly, Schroeder, Downey, and Hyde, among others, and Senator Bradley, introduced child support reform legislation.

39. The Child Support Enforcement Amendments of 1984, PL 98-378 (codified at 42 U.S.C., section 651 et seq.), added provisions that included the equal treatment of welfare and nonwelfare clients, mandatory wage withholding, and use of expedited process to ensure that cases are worked quickly.

40. The Family Support Act of 1988, PL 100-485 (codified at 42 U.S.C., section 651 et seq.) mandated several state practices including that states had to offer a specified modification process to parents in IV-D cases made the use of guidelines presumptive for all child support cases, and required that income withholding begin at the time the order is entered unless the parties opt out or good cause is found.

41. Various observers have warned that Congress may look for alternative ways to increase collections if this attempt fails to dramatically improve numbers. Representative Henry Hyde has favored in the past a partial federalization of the program.

42. The Child Support Enforcement Amendments of 1984 passed unanimously. PL No. 98-378.

43. No definitive study has been done on cost avoidance, although it is clear that the closer one is to the poverty line, the more vital child support payments are to keeping the obligee off assistance.

44. See D. L. Chambers, *Making Fathers Pay: The Enforcement of Child Support* (Chicago: University of Chicago Press, 1979).

45. About 88 percent of children in nonintact families live with their mother and about 12 percent with their father. *1994 Green Book,* U.S. House of Representatives, Subcommittee on Human Resources, 459.

46. See D. Motz and A. Baida, "The Due Process Rights of Postjudgment Debtors and Child Support Obligors," *Maryland Law Review* 45 (1986): 61.

47. 424 U.S. 319 (1976).

48. 424 U.S. at 335.

49. 42 U.S.C., section 666(a)(9).

50. 42 U.S.C., section 666(a)(4).

51. See, for example, how Massachusetts's Department of Revenue, in which the child support division is housed, has practically perfected the freezing and seizing of bank accounts of delinquent obligors without jeopardizing the right to redress the claims of allegedly wronged account holders.

52. 28 U.S.C., section 1738B.

53. Section 351 of PRWORA, codified at 42 U.S.C., section 666(a)(10).

54. Commission on Child and Family Welfare, *Parenting Our Children: In the Best Interest of the Nation* (Washington, D.C.: U.S. Government Printing Office, 1996).

16

Child Support Reform in Action: New Strategies and New Frontiers in Massachusetts

Marilyn Ray Smith

On August 22, 1996, President Bill Clinton signed into law the Personal Responsibility and Work Opportunity Reconciliation Act of 1996 (PL 104-193), setting in motion the most significant reform of the nation's welfare system in sixty years. This far-reaching legislation will indeed "end welfare as we know it."

Over the last decade, we have witnessed dramatic changes in our ideas about the role of government and personal responsibility. This debate has stirred controversy throughout the nation—on the talk shows and in the nightly news; in the op-ed pages and the weekly magazines; in the barber shops and around the water coolers.

While many of these discussions in the media have focused on whether some families will be hurt by welfare reform, little attention has been paid to the fact that millions of families will be helped by child support reform. The Personal Responsibility and Work Opportunity Reconciliation Act of 1996 contains the most comprehensive provisions on child support enforcement in the history of the program. But because they have enjoyed strong bipartisan support, the important changes that are taking place in the nation's child support program have been overshadowed in the public debate by the controversy over block grants, work requirements, time-limited benefits, cash benefits for teen mothers, family caps, and child care funding.

Improved child support enforcement is an integral part of achieving real welfare reform. When just one parent provides for a family, children all too often sink into poverty, and taxpayers grow weary of paying for other people's children. A regular child support check is the lifeline that keeps afloat millions of custodial parents—usually mothers—struggling to stay off welfare and to raise their families in the dignity of self-reliance. Work requirements and time limits make child support and the health insurance that often accompanies it more critical than ever for families who are forced to temporarily resort to public assistance.

This chapter will highlight the evolution of this landmark legislation, and identify its important provisions. Next, it will describe how several of these innovations have already been implemented in Massachusetts. It will then recommend some strategies for states to pursue in implementing this complex legislation. Finally, it will explore new frontiers for the child support program in its ever-expanding mission to provide financial security for the nation's children.

EVOLUTION OF CHILD SUPPORT REFORM

The nation's child support program has come a long way since its inception twenty-five years ago. But despite all our efforts, it still hasn't moved far enough, fast enough.[1] The rapid expansion of the number of children needing child support has outstripped the ability of federal, state, and local programs to meet the needs of families relying on regular child support payments for economic survival.[2]

Historically, child support programs have suffered from a fragmentation of functions across many state and local agencies, in a complex system accountable to no single authority. In some states, the welfare department performs intake and case management functions; the district attorneys handle cases that must be taken to court to establish paternity and to establish, modify, and enforce support orders; and the clerks of court collect and disburse child support payments and keep track of the payment history, which they report to the local and/or state child support agency. Other states have various degrees of centralization between state and local agencies. In some states, there are literally hundreds of collection points throughout the state to which employers or child support obligors must send weekly, biweekly, bimonthly, or monthly checks, depending on the pay cycle or the terms of the order. There may be multiple computer systems in the state, which may or may not be able to talk to each other. Or there may be no computers at all. Until very recently (all states are now in the process of installing automated systems), throughout the country, thousands of child support workers kept handwritten pay cards, on which individual notations were made every time a check arrived in the mail or was hand-delivered by the noncustodial parent.[3]

What should be simple computerized actions, such as transferring a wage assignment when a job changes or seizing a bank account when assets accumulate, all too often require hours of manual labor or trips to the courthouse. Lack of uniformity among states dooms interstate child support enforcement to a quagmire of conflicting statutes and multiple orders. Critical employment, tax, and financial information is not readily available to child support agencies. Antiquated rules on paternity establishment turn amicable relationships into adversarial ones.

Responding to this state of affairs are the child support provisions of the Personal Responsibility and Work Opportunity Reconciliation Act of 1996. They have been years in the making, and the national child support community has been involved in their development at every step of the way. The seeds for this legislation were sown in 1988 when, in the Family Support Act, Congress called for the appointment of the U.S. Commission on Interstate Child Support. For two years, the Interstate Commission combed the country, holding public hearings, consulting legal experts, analyzing successful innovations in the states, looking for effective strategies. In 1992, the commission issued its bold and comprehensive report—*Supporting Our Children: A Blueprint for Reform*—which provided detailed recommendations for specific actions Congress could take to improve the nation's child support system.

In 1993, Clinton convened the Working Group on Welfare Reform, which conducted another extensive analysis of the nation's child support system, consulting more experts and hearing further public testimony. In June 1994, the Working Group issued its recommendations and the legislative proposal which became the basic framework for the bill ultimately enacted by Congress.

Starting in 1995, Congress examined these many recommendations, holding several committee hearings throughout 1995 and 1996, seeking detailed answers to questions about the workings of new-hire reporting, how to improve paternity establishment, the effectiveness of license revocation as an enforcement tool for the self-employed, distribution of collections between the state and families, funding priorities, and what policies would encourage families to be independent of public assistance. [4]

Throughout this period, an informal network of organizations interested in child support enforcement, including the National Child Support Enforcement Association, the American Public Welfare Association (now the American Public Services Association), the Children's Defense Fund, the National Women's Law Center, the Eastern Regional Interstate Child Support Association, and the American Bar Association Child Support Project, collaborated on various provisions to reach consensus among the key players and beneficiaries of the child support program.

Recognizing the necessity for strong interstate enforcement measures, Congress did not include child support in the block grants. Nor did it federalize the program, as some had advocated. Instead, Congress continued the federal–state partnership that has been the hallmark of the child support program for more than twenty-five years. More important, Congress sent a clear message that the force of the federal government is behind the efforts of the states to secure parental financial support for the nation's children.

HIGHLIGHTS OF CHILD SUPPORT PROVISIONS

The Personal Responsibility and Work Opportunity Reconciliation Act (PRWORA) does more than require states to pass a series of laws. It pushes states to consolidate information, streamline processes, and centralize decisionmaking authority. It calls for building a network of information and automated data matches that is virtually unprecedented in government.

The key to this dramatic reengineering of child support is to shift from "retail to wholesale," to use high-volume strategies to enforce a high-volume caseload. Since 1984, Congress has recognized that the traditional method of taking each case back to court one by one was inefficient and ineffective and has passed a series of laws requiring states to have mandatory wage withholding, to intercept federal and state tax returns, to make past-due child support a judgment by operation of law, and to effect other significant procedures to streamline processes. States have been hard at work in the last twelve years to develop automated systems that will allow operations to catch up with these changes in the law. The additional requirements of the PRWORA will further drive this transition to automation.

Four strategies unite the congressional efforts in the PRWORA to increase collections and improve the nation's child support program:

- Reengineer processes to use technology to the fullest extent for high-volume, computerized data matches and automatic issuance of notices to collect support and modify orders.
- Give child support agencies the information they need to do the job— information from licensing and tax agencies, employers, banks, credit bureaus, and law enforcement agencies.
- Reduce welfare dependency by making it easy for parents to establish paternity, by allowing states to require strict cooperation with child support enforcement efforts, and by giving former welfare families priority in collecting past-due support.
- Remove unnecessary barriers in interstate cases by requiring uniform laws and procedures and by setting up computer networks for states to exchange information through electronic transmissions.

To achieve these strategies, the act contains virtually every tough enforcement tool that states have piloted. These enforcement tools are not ivory tower concepts but are tried and true, tested by innovative states such as Massachusetts, Virginia, Washington, Iowa, Maine, California, and others. The legislation requires states to take the following actions:

- Consolidate the caseload onto central registries of child support orders at the state and federal level, to make effective use of the location tools at states' disposal.
- Set up centralized collection and disbursement units using the latest in payment processing technology, so that employers will have one location in the state to send wage assignment payments and parents will have up-to-date account records.

- Streamline the process for transferring health insurance orders, so that children don't run the risk of being without coverage when the noncustodial parent changes jobs.
- Achieve the full potential of administrative enforcement remedies, by requiring regular searches of available databases of income and assets and by providing for automatic issuance of wage assignments, liens, levies, and other administrative enforcement remedies when income or assets are located.
- Make it easy for unmarried parents to establish paternity at the time of the child's birth, right at the hospital, without the necessity for a court hearing in uncontested cases, to identify a father for every child.
- Make maximum use of automation and expedited procedures, by requiring states to shift to high-volume strategies to enforce their caseloads.
- Require employers to report new hires, so that wage assignments can keep up with job hoppers as they move from job to job and from state to state.
- Adopt procedures to revoke licenses of people who owe child support but who continue to drive, work, or play while others provide financial support for their children.
- Develop a bank match program to locate bank accounts of child support delinquents who put money in the bank instead of meeting their child support obligations.
- Break down barriers in interstate cases, by requiring all states to adopt the Uniform Interstate Family Support Act, to close the net on delinquent parents who simply skip across state lines to avoid paying child support.
- Include the federal government as a model employer, by requiring it to participate in new hire and quarterly wage reporting and to honor wage assignments without unnecessary bureaucratic barriers.
- Adopt "families-first" distribution rules, giving families who leave welfare priority in the distribution of collections when past-due support is owed to both the family and the state.

There are many other detailed provisions, with requirements ranging from better exchange of information with credit reporting agencies, to laws to set aside fraudulent transfers, procedures to obtain "seek work" orders in appropriate cases, and effective enforcement of support orders against military personnel. Throughout its various requirements, the PRWORA aims to strike a balance between creating federal mandates that set standards to push states to improve their programs and maintaining states' flexibility for continued innovation that responds to local needs and charts new directions.

But, most important, by its extensive use of automation, this legislation shifts the burden of pursuing support away from the custodial parent, so she no longer has to be the "squeaky wheel" to initiate enforcement action at every step of the process. When new-hire-reporting and central case registries are fully implemented, wage assignments will be transferred before the custodial parent even knows the noncustodial parent has changed jobs. Checks for past-due support will appear out of the blue in the custodial parent's mailbox because a successful data match resulted in the seizure of a bank account. Obligors with valuable professional licenses who are not subject to wage assignments will think twice before forgetting to mail those child support payments. States will be able to cooperate in interstate cases by electronic communication instead of being buried in an avalanche of paper and overwhelmed by tedious court proceedings for the most routine cases. Fathers and mothers who want to establish paternity in uncontested cases will no longer face the barriers of an intimidating and adversarial court process.

IMPLEMENTING CHILD SUPPORT REFORM IN MASSACHUSETTS

Massachusetts has already put into practice virtually all of the major requirements of the PRWORA. It has reengineered the child support program to make maximum use of automation and administrative enforcement remedies to handle an ever-expanding caseload. It has consolidated cases onto a central case registry. All payments are processed through a central payment processing unit. It has a highly successful paternity acknowledgment program, in which parents of more than 70 percent of children born out of wedlock sign voluntary acknowledgments in the hospital or shortly thereafter. All employers are required to report new employees within fourteen days of hire, and wage assignments are issued automatically. The state has authority to suspend, revoke, or deny professional, occupational, recreational, and driver's licenses of child support delinquents who fail to honor payment agreements. Finally, Massachusetts uses data matches with tax and bank information to locate assets and then sends out thousands of liens and levies to collect millions of dollars in past-due support. Massachusetts has increased collections by 65 percent, from $177 million in 1991 to $292.5 million in 1999. The number of families receiving child support has increased by 67 percent—from 37,200 in 1991 to almost 62,000 in 1999.

Automation is the essential tool for reengineering child support operations. Without the ability to organize and analyze vast amounts of data and produce the paperwork in a few hours, there is no possibility of dramatic breakthroughs, no expectation of quantum leaps in collections. But the effective use of automation also requires structural reorganization of child support functions so that the account histories of all cases are in a central database, ready for data matches followed by automated enforcement remedies that are issued by the thousands without individualized case reviews. Staff can then be freed to tackle the difficult cases while the machine collects on the easy ones.

Massachusetts started the reengineering process in 1986 when the state legislature began implementing the Child Support Enforcement Amendments of 1984. As in many states, the Massachusetts child support program suffered from fragmentation of essential functions among several entities, lacking a single authority possessing clear accountability or control over case management.

The first step in process redesign was transferring the child support program from the Department of Public Welfare to the Department of Revenue (DOR). DOR then consolidated payment records from eighty-four local courts and sixty local welfare offices into one central payment processing location. This lockbox facility uses bar codes and scanning equipment, ensuring that checks to custodial parents are reissued in twenty-four to forty-eight hours. The staff devoted to payment processing went from almost two hundred clerks opening envelopes in the courts and local offices to thirty employees at a central location using the latest payment-processing technology. Court jurisdiction over child support and paternity cases was changed so that on any given day, a pool of some forty-five family court judges, instead of two hundred judges, could hear child support cases in special weekly sessions devoted exclusively to child support.

Wage assignments are now required in every case and, based on new hire information from employers, can be transferred by computer to the new employer without going back to court—and without human intervention. Data matches with the unemployment agency ensure that a wage assignment is in place when the first unemployment check goes out. The new-hire reporting program has transferred 240,000 wage assignments by computer.

Taking a page from tax collection strategy, Massachusetts law provides for administrative liens that arise by operation of law in every case owing past-due support, so the agency is poised to spring into action as soon as income or assets are discovered, again without a court or administrative order—again all without human intervention. Since 1992, 200,000 liens have been issued against all child support obligors owing past-due support. As a result of the first data match with the worker's compensation agency, virtually overnight, eight thousand liens were filed on workers' compensation claims, a process that previously took twenty staff working for a month to locate each worker's comp case for an obligor owing past-due support. Now these matches take place monthly and DOR's lien is there—sent by computer, not by a caseworker—whenever a case involving a delinquent child support obligor is settled.

Legislation requiring banks and other financial institutions to provide, at first, annual—and then, in 1994, quarterly—information enabled DOR to use data matches with bank account information to seize thirty-nine thousand bank accounts and further boost collections by $24 million from 1993 to 1999. Going from an annual to a quarterly bank match more than doubled the collections from this powerful enforcement remedy.

Implementation of the in-hospital paternity program has permitted parents of more than 70 percent of children born out of wedlock to sign voluntary acknowledgments in the hospital at the time of the child's birth or shortly thereafter, establishing legal fatherhood for more than seventy-five thousand Massachusetts babies since 1994.

The caseworkers' job has changed in this process. Less of their time is spent looking for income and assets or dealing directly with custodial and noncustodial parents to gather case information. Instead, caseworkers resolve account disputes and handle customer inquiries. As a result of computerization, caseworker time is freed up to tackle the tough cases where the machine cannot find assets or income or to work through the backlog of cases needing paternity established, new orders or modifications. Contempt proceedings now focus on obligors for whom the computer has not been able to locate income or assets, making more effective use of scarce and costly attorney and judicial resources. Reductions in staff for particular programs did not mean layoffs, however. In fact, the legislature, at the governor's request, added more staff to strengthen service delivery because it was willing to invest in a successful program.

Plenty of chaos and deflated morale accompanied this new style of doing business. Caseworkers were not always enthusiastic about changes in their job descriptions or the consolidation of forty-six local offices into six regional centers and two satellite offices. The telephones burned off the hook when the lien notices first went out and bank accounts were seized. There was many a nay-saying, doubting Thomas, as well as complaints to the governor's office or the press about missing checks or inadequate customer service. But the end of this five-year process saw dramatic increases in collections and in the number of families for whom regular child support payments enabled them to leave public assistance, thus saving the taxpayer millions of dollars in welfare costs not expended. In the end, staff have grown in sophistication and have developed a thoughtful pride in the program's accomplishments.

LESSONS FROM REENGINEERING

We learned a great deal throughout this often turbulent route to reengineering—lessons that may be useful to others who contemplate changes in their child support operations as part of implementing federal welfare reform. Some innovations have already been adopted in many states; others may not be appropriate in states that are larger than Massachusetts or whose child support programs are administered through counties. Massachusetts is, after all, a small state where county government is weak, and its child support caseload consists of 200,000 cases. By contrast, many states have much larger caseloads, county government is the primary point of service delivery, and there is greater diversity of population and working conditions. Nevertheless, several strategies can be recommended.

Articulate a clear vision for five years hence. In reengineering the Massachusetts child support program, the goal was to shift from "retail to wholesale," to transform a highly individualized, case-by-case process into a standardized, computerized system that automatically makes decisions and takes action on thousands of cases at a time. The objective was to ensure that child support payments are made on time and in full and that both parents receive firm, fair, and courteous treatment. Reformers have been guided by an abiding conviction that child support is not an installment debt to be paid when convenient but the most fundamental obligation that a person has in this society.

Change in state and local agencies of the magnitude described here does not happen effortlessly. A clear vision helps all players—from the caseworkers in the local office to the legislative leaders on the ways and means committees—keep their eye on the ball.

Find a "political angel" at the highest levels of government to advocate for the necessary changes. In analyzing states that have improved their programs, one will almost always find a such as person in the wings—a governor, a key legislative leader, an innovative commissioner, or better yet, all three—who provided the resources and guidance to translate into reality the vision of an effective child support program. Without clear vision and decisive leadership at the highest levels, a child support agency is not likely to have the political clout to make the necessary changes on its own, particularly to deal with the inevitable turf battles that arise over structural change and realignment of agency functions and staff duties. The governor needs to coordinate interagency cooperation, commissioners of diverse agencies need to open doors and remove bureaucratic barriers, legislators need to provide adequate funding and laws with real teeth, and judges need to interpret the news laws for the benefit of children.

In Massachusetts, we were fortunate to have support at every critical juncture. The chairman of the senate ways and means committee started the process in 1986 by sponsoring legislation to transfer the program from the welfare department to the revenue department and to give tough administrative enforcement remedies modeled on tax collection strategies. Throughout the last decade, the senate president and the house speaker have supported tough legislation. Governor Bill Weld sponsored bold and comprehensive legislation, making child support a top priority for his administration. Mitchell Adams, commissioner of revenue during this period of innovation, inspired and fostered innovation with the specific directive to emulate best practices from other states and to become a national model. Finally, the Massachusetts family court has remained a steadfast partner throughout this transition.

Convince the legislature that providing resources for child support is a sound investment. Most legislatures would rather invest in a cost-effective program that gets results, instead of one that complains about not enough staff to do the job. To attract the legislature's attention, we reformers developed measurement criteria, such as numbers of new orders established and numbers of families leaving public assistance, in addition to collections in public assistance cases. We learned how to measure cost avoidance from welfare prevention and Medicaid savings, so that the legislature could see that the benefits from the program extended far beyond reimbursement for AFDC costs.

During this period of innovation, DOR has prepared several reports for the Massachusetts legislature, documenting past successes and laying out future plans for program innovations. The charts and graphs displaying upward trends indeed spoke "better than a thousand words." To build further good relations with the legislature, we also set up a "problem resolution office" to handle constituent referrals or cases with negative press coverage, so that we could mobilize the necessary resources for cases with particularly intractable problems. The legislature has responded by passing innovative legislation and by protecting our budget even during periods of fiscal crisis.

Get control of the caseload. Key to our reengineering efforts was getting all the cases in a single database, giving us the ability to coordinate statewide data matches of all cases meeting certain criteria. No longer do individual caseworkers review a particular case to determine whether it is appropriate for a particular enforcement remedy. Instead, the computer selects the cases and initiates the enforcement action.

This is an important difference from how we understand some states are using automated data matches. In Massachusetts, when the computer makes a "hit" for a wage assignment, a bank levy, or a worker's comp lien, we do not ask the caseworker in the local office to approve the enforcement remedy for this particular case. Instead, the computer immediately sends out a wage assignment or seizure notice. The caseworker conducts a case review only if the obligor contests the amount of arrearage claimed to be owed or appeals the seizure of income or assets on the limited grounds available. Although this "complaint-driven" process is not without drawbacks, it means that thousands more cases can be enforced, since most enforcement actions are not challenged. A preseizure review unnecessarily delays the collection.

Develop partnerships with other agencies having the information the child support agency needs. A child support enforcement program is only as good as the information available to locate the noncustodial parent and his or her income and assets. If you cannot find the noncustodial parent, you cannot make him or her support his family. State child support agencies are looking for approximately 3.6 million obligors nationwide to establish an order in the first instance and for another 2.5 million obligors to modify or enforce an existing order. The key financial information about obligors is in the hands of employers, banks, credit-reporting agencies, and other state agencies, such as unemployment and worker's compensation agencies, licensing authorities, corrections and revenue departments, and registries of motor vehicles and vital statistics. Success therefore depends on developing partnerships with those who have this critical information in their possession.

In Massachusetts, we have found that other entities, both public and private, were very willing to cooperate with child support enforcement efforts, so long as we made an effort to accommodate their business needs. For new-hire reporting, this meant requiring that employers send only the information that they were already collecting and using the new hire information to also detect fraud in unemployment and worker's compensation programs funded by employers. For licensing agencies, this meant DOR assuming the responsibility for holding the hearings on license suspension and revocation. For banks, this meant developing procedures for data exchanges and executing levies that minimized paperwork and technical computer adjustments. For the registrar of vital statistics, this meant incorporating the in-hospital program for voluntary acknowledgment of paternity into the birth registration process in a way that furthered other objectives of the vital statistics registrar for accurate birth information. Our universal experience with these other entities is that they share our mission to ensure that children are supported by their parents, so long as we listen to their program requirements.

Centralize payment processing and customer service inquires. With modern technology, it is no longer necessary for all case and payment information to be kept in a file cabinet or desk drawer readily available so a caseworker can record payments, devise an individualized enforcement strategy, and answer telephone calls from parents anxious to know when the next check is coming. Significant economies of scale can be achieved by sending all payments to one location in the state, accompanied by a statewide or regional customer service center that can answer most telephone calls. Relieved of constant telephone interruptions, caseworkers have more time to work the difficult cases and to establish paternity.

Redirecting payments and telephone calls from dozens of local offices or county courts to a central post office box includes:

- assembling, verifying, and transferring payment records to the central computer;
- notifying parents and employers to send checks to the new location;
- developing procedures for identifying money, such as billing notices or payment coupons, and printing, signing, stuffing, and mailing checks;
- identifying misdirected or unidentified checks;
- instituting protocols to maintain security and controls over money handling; and
- distributing the funds to the proper payee.

Centralizing collections was the first, and probably the most difficult, step in reengineering the Massachusetts child support program, but one that enabled us to go from 140 collection points in local offices and courts relying on approximately 200 clerks to record payments by hand, to a lockbox-processing center employing about 30 staff to perform data entry, while the machines do most of the rest of the payment processing. Checks go out quicker, and payment histories are more accurate.

Closely connected to centralizing collections has been establishing a centralized customer service center, which provides one mailing address for all inquiries nationwide and one toll-free number for all telephone calls from anywhere in the continental United States—available twenty-four hours a day, seven days a week.

Under the old system, parents deluged the local offices with telephone calls. Caseworkers had to wait in line to get onto the computer to retrieve payment information; staff sometimes did not know the answers to policy questions; callers frequently had to be referred to another unit; messages were lost; client calls were not returned.

After almost ten years of transition, redeploying staff, and consolidating local offices, more than 98 percent of the forty-five thousand calls logged in each week are now handled by the customer service center. The Voice Response System (VRS) handles 75 percent of the calls, with 30 percent of those calls coming in after business hours. The VRS can provide payment histories, as well as take messages from employers wishing to notify DOR about changes in an employee's status. During business hours, the customer can always push "0" to talk to customer service staff.

Just as important, the VRS has reduced staff burnout, errors, and wasted time, while providing better service to customers seeking basic case information. After all, the VRS does not become tired, careless, or irritable when constantly answering the same questions day after day.

Improve cooperation from custodial parents. Once we streamlined the process for collecting on accounts receivable, we turned our attention to increasing the number of accounts, using a threefold strategy.

First, because collecting money was now more efficient, staff were redeployed to improve procedures for establishing more paternities and more new orders. In 1994, we set an ambitious target to double the number of new orders in one year, created teams of caseworkers and attorneys who shared the same management goals, and expanded the "block time" sessions in courts that hear only child support cases. (In some courts, as many as 130 cases are scheduled in a single day.) The number of orders in public assistance cases has gone up by 180 percent since 1991, even while the overall number of new public assistance cases has declined.

Second, the in-hospital program for voluntary acknowledgment of paternity relies on medical records clerks during the birth registration process, aided by a statutory provision that requires both parents to sign the acknowledgment in order to put the father's name on the birth certificate—a strong inducement for most new parents. This program achieved remarkable success, with more than 70 percent of parents of children born out of wedlock signing the acknowledgment at the hospital or shortly thereafter.

Third, we strengthened the cooperation requirements for applicants or recipients of public assistance. Even in the age of information technology, the best source of information about the noncustodial parent is the custodial parent. In nonwelfare cases, parents cooperate because the child support check means money in the pocket and food on the table. In welfare cases, however, all too often the custodial parent withholds critical identifying information that would otherwise enable the child support agency to tap into the databases that are now available to find income and assets.

The system in effect before welfare reform required only nominal cooperation from the custodial parent, and the existing sanction—removing the mother from the grant—proved not to be effective. Massachusetts' experience bore this out. Before we instituted stricter criteria for cooperation, a quarter of the cases referred to the child support agency needing paternity establishment or a support order were "dead on arrival"—that is, not enough information to begin looking for more. Another 20 percent fell out before an order was established because the custodial parent failed to cooperate—either the information provided was still not enough to locate the noncustodial parent, or the custodial parent failed to appear for hearings or blood test appointments.

The Massachusetts experience is not unique, as confirmed by studies from Rutgers University, the Center for Law and Social Policy, and the General Accounting Office. Custodial parents withhold information, do not report cash payments, do not show up for appointments and hearings. They undoubtedly have many reasons, some of which may be valid, but it is time for us to start asking more questions and insisting on more answers.

To get more and better information from parents applying for or receiving public assistance, in 1995, the Massachusetts Legislature strengthened the requirements for cooperation by making explicit the specific information required and by giving the child support agency the authority to determine whether parents have cooperated. Custodial parents are required to provide sufficient verifiable information to locate the noncustodial parent, which includes the noncustodial parent's full name and Social Security number, or the name and at least two of the following items:

- the noncustodial parent's date of birth;
- the noncustodial parent's address;
- the noncustodial parent's telephone number;
- the name and address of the noncustodial parent's employer;
- the names of the parents of the noncustodial parent; or
- the manufacturer, model and license number of any motor vehicle owned by the noncustodial parent.

Information that is reasonably equivalent to these items is also acceptable. In addition, DOR was given authority to determine noncooperation. Finally, the custodial parent has the burden of showing cooperation at any hearing challenging a finding of noncooperation.

Initial results when these changes were implemented in late 1995 and early 1996 were very promising. Welfare eligibility workers knew what information to ask for, custodial parents knew what information to bring to the interview, and both workers and mothers gained a heightened awareness of the importance of cooperating with child support efforts. The quality of information improved significantly, reducing by half the number of cases with insufficient information to go forward with child support enforcement.

Changes in federal rules for cooperation give a new dimension to this debate, as states have received more flexibility to define cooperation requirements. Section 333 of the Personal Responsibility and Work Opportunity Reconciliation Act of 1996 gives the states the authority to define cooperation in good faith, subject to "good cause and other exceptions," which take into account the best interests of the child.

Strict requirements for cooperation increase the importance of a more effective procedure for identifying cases where the custodial parent has "good cause" not to cooperate with child support enforcement efforts. Until welfare reform, federal regulations have defined *good cause* as circumstances where pursuit of support is "reasonably anticipated" to result in serious physical or emotional harm to the child or custodial parent, the child was conceived as a result of incest or forcible rape, or the child is the subject of adoption proceedings. The applicant or recipient must provide corroborative evidence to support the claim, such as police reports, medical records, a birth certificate showing incest, court documents indicating an adoption proceeding, child protective service records, or sworn statements of fact.

Historically, for a variety of reasons, few custodial parents have claimed good cause. For fiscal year 1997, for example, states reported to the federal Office of Child Support Enforcement that they granted 2,296 out of 4,196 good-cause claims, with thirty-one states reporting that they had fewer than fifty good-cause claims.

In Massachusetts, we know that applicants and recipients are not claiming good cause, even when they may have grounds to do so. From 1988 to 1997, Massachusetts reported zero good-cause claims. Yet in 1995, Massachusetts courts issued more than forty-six thousand domestic violence restraining orders, with an estimated 56 percent reporting the presence of children. It is likely that at least some among those obtaining protective orders were also receiving welfare benefits and therefore eligible to claim good cause. We are left to assume that many good-cause claims are hidden in the "I don't know who the father is" caseload. As we get tough about not taking "I don't know" for an answer, we must also reexamine the standards for proving good-cause claims. We must improve our procedures for explaining the good-cause provisions to applicants and recipients of public assistance and provide referrals to domestic violence counselors so that possible victims can make informed choices about safety and the benefits of child support payments.

This is an area where much remains to be done. President Clinton directed the secretary of health and human services and the attorney general to assist states in making welfare programs responsive to the needs of battered women and to study the incidence of domestic violence and sexual assault among poor families. He also strongly encouraged states to exercise the option to implement the family violence provisions of federal welfare reform, which will allow states to use block grant funds to screen and provide services to battered women on welfare.

It is important for child support programs to be actively involved in these initiatives. A regular child support check may be the financial lifeline that allows a family to leave an abusive relationship. However, it is well documented that victims of domestic violence are at greatest risk of death or serious injury at the time of separation. The answer for child support enforcement is not in granting wholesale exemptions from cooperation requirements to victims of domestic violence. Such an approach not only deprives the custodial parent of financial support needed to leave the abusive relationship but also tacitly rewards the abuser by "letting him off the hook" for child support payments. Rather, a better strategy relies on developing sophistication in how to manage this part of our caseload. This includes training staff to screen for possible abuse and to make referrals to experts who can confer with the victim to develop a safe strategy for pursuing child support. Welfare reform with time-limited benefits means that we can no longer ignore this complex and critical issue.

IMPLEMENTING FEDERAL CHILD SUPPORT REFORM

The new federal legislation will have a significant impact on the organizational structure and functions of state child support programs. This section identifies issues that states may confront in implementing this complex legislation.

As described previously, the Personal Responsibility and Work Opportunity Reconciliation Act requires states to consolidate the caseload into one central registry, send all payments to one location for entry on a single database, amass a vast array of information about income and assets of noncustodial parents from a wide variety of public and private sources, and assemble an impressive arsenal of enforcement remedies for collecting current and past-due support—all through maximum use of automated, computerized processes. It requires wage assignments in every case and new-hire reporting to make sure wage assignments keep up with job hoppers. So that enforcement remedies can locate shifting income and assets, there are provisions for states to share information by reporting case information to a federal registry of cases and the National Directory of New Hires. Automatic liens are required in every case owing past-due support. To put teeth into those liens, states must conduct data matches with banks and other financial institutions every quarter to locate bank accounts of delinquent obligors.

This legislation is replete with technical details for reengineering processes as well as precise requirements for cooperation among federal, state, and local agencies that are virtually unprecedented in government. States must build information linkages, including automated access where available, with a wide range of other state and local agencies. This network for information will extend from welfare, Medicaid, and foster care agencies to registries of birth records, motor vehicles, and real property; from state licensing boards to corrections and revenue departments; from financial institutions to insurance companies and worker's compensation agencies; from multinational employers to "mom and pop" shops; from hospitals to public utilities and cable television companies.

Agreements to obtain this information will have to be negotiated on a statewide basis, not county by county or office by office. Banks cannot be expected to negotiate individual reporting arrangements with sixty different counties in a state, nor will unemployment compensation agencies be able to conduct data matches under different agreements with every local child support office.

Moreover, for information on location, income and assets to be useful, it must be used quickly, before it is stale and the obligor or his money moves on. States must be able to take enforcement action as soon as they locate an asset. It does little good to obtain information from an automated data match and then revert to an individualized case review to decide whether to act on the information, while the case gathers dust in a crowded in-box.

The enforcement process must be automated along with the information-sharing process. The computer must automatically spit out a wage assignment or levy notice as soon as the data match identifies an income stream or asset. For the computer to act as soon as it receives relevant information, all case information must be on one database, and one entity in the state must have authority to "push the button" to command the computer to send out notices, wage assignments, liens, and levies.

From many quarters, there will undoubtedly be pressure to maintain local autonomy, to keep local control over each case to determine whether a particular enforcement remedy is appropriate or fair, according to a caseworker's personal assessment of the individual history of the family. Automated enforcement flies in the face of time-honored notions of customer service. Unfortunately, under the individualized model, while one family may be receiving outstanding personal service, four other families do without a child support payment, as the advocates have been reminding us for years. The paradigm shift of automation turns customer service upside down. It sets up automated systems to collect money on the "easy" cases where income and assets can readily be found, so that the human resources can be freed up and then redeployed for the "tough" cases requiring intensive effort to ferret out assets, to establish paternity, or to prosecute child support delinquents to the fullest extent of the law.

In the PRWORA legislation, Congress has provided a detailed blueprint for specific remedies, actions, and time frames. It is now up to the states to decide who calls the shots on the sequence of enforcement remedies and what economies of scale can be introduced to handle the never-ending stream of cases needing enforcement. States will have to determine how to allocate new functions among the diverse players in the system—among the administrative agency, the district attorney, and the court, between the state central office and the local child support office. Decisions must be made about which parts of the program are administered directly by the state and which under cooperative agreements with county courts and other agencies. Turf battles may arise, as well as efforts to avoid some of these difficult changes by seeking waivers, in the hope that Congress and the secretary of health and human services do not really mean for states to bring about the structural reorganization that must occur for this legislation to achieve its full potential.

Such a transformation means more than adding computer technology. It also means realigning decisional power and organizational functions among the multiple state and local agencies that may be involved in child support enforcement in a particular state. This will be the most difficult part of successful implementation. Other barriers will also emerge, to be sure, but those will be operational details that resourceful child support professionals can resolve.

Achieving these objectives will require strong, sustained political leadership at the highest levels of federal and state government. Child support agencies, no matter how dedicated, cannot do it alone. Without strong leadership, the requirements to centralize case information and manage cases through the use of high-volume automated enforcement remedies may be met with resistance or founder on an incomplete vision that fails to carry out the full potential of this powerful legislation. The greatest danger will be the tendency to view this legislation as a long, and some will say onerous, laundry list of individual requirements, rather than a comprehensive, rational scheme that will move the child support program into the twenty-first century and the age of information technology.

NEW FRONTIERS FOR CHILD SUPPORT

As child support becomes the critical safety net for families leaving public assistance, the mission of the program continues to expand. At its inception in 1975, the program created a federal–state partnership designed to increase child support collections as a means of reimbursing the public fiscally for public assistance costs. Welfare is, after all, child support paid by the taxpayer. In 1984, Congress expanded the mission of the child support program to require states to provide services to families not on public assistance, in the expectation that regular payment of child support would enable these families to remain self-sufficient. The Family Support Act of 1988 and the Omnibus Budget Reconciliation Act of 1993 pulled paternity establishment into the central orbit of the duties of the child support program, requiring states to simplify procedures for establishing paternity and setting demanding performance standards for paternity establishment. The Personal Responsibility and Work Opportunity Reconciliation Act of 1996 goes even further, by pushing the performance standards for paternity establishment to 90 percent of the cases (states have a choice of formulas—either all cases in the agency's caseload, or all cases in the state). In addition, beginning in fiscal year 1999, Congress is giving states an inducement to reduce the number of children born out of wedlock by making available bonus grants to the five states with the greatest decrease in out-of-wedlock births for the previous two years, combined with no increase in abortions over fiscal year 1995.

Meanwhile, states have continued to strengthen their enforcement remedies, with an ever-expanding arsenal of tough enforcement tools, ranging from wage assignments and property seizures to "Ten Most Wanted" posters and criminal extradition procedures. Automation coupled with these "get tough" measures will reach approximately 60 percent of child support obligors. In Massachusetts, for example, if the noncustodial parent has a job, a bank account, or a driver's or professional license; collects unemployment or worker's compensation; or pays taxes, the child support agency can probably collect support. It is more difficult to get at the self-employed, the unemployed, the underemployed, and the "under the table" employed.

Not all parents fail to pay child support for the same reasons. Some do not pay because they are angry at the other parent; some do not pay because withholding money is a way of continuing control; others do not pay because the pain of separation is too intense and they have withdrawn; still others do not pay because they never had or took the opportunity to develop a relationship with the child, and some do not pay because they simply do not have the money.

This remaining 40 percent will therefore require a multipronged strategy for a multidimensional problem: high-visibility criminal prosecutions and other tough enforcement initiatives to continue to galvanize public attention and encourage voluntary compliance accompanied by more sophisticated outreach programs that support positive and responsible involvement of fathers in the lives of their children and include collaboration with seek work and job training programs for unemployed fathers. For twenty-five years, child support professionals have debated whether child support is a law enforcement or a social services program. The answer is clearly that both approaches are needed to respond to the full range of needs faced by these families in crisis.

For twenty-five years, the child support program has also danced around issues relating to access and visitation, appropriately maintaining that child support and visitation are separate, independent issues. It is time to examine this issue. However, the solution is not to link child support and visitation, as some fathers' rights groups have advocated. We should not say to a father that he cannot visit his child unless he pays child support or say that he does not have to pay child support unless he can visit his child. Children have an independent right both to child support and to a relationship with both parents. This is the law in virtually every state, with deep roots in the common law of family jurisprudence.

The issues here are complex and are not readily responsive to simple formulas. We must invest more resources in a variety of programs to help parents work cooperatively in the best interests of their children. Parenting education programs as part of the divorce and a paternity establishment process are a must. Even better would be parenting education programs before people became parents—perhaps some would think twice about undertaking this awesome, lifelong responsibility. Tough cooperation requirements ensure that mothers cannot unilaterally deny the child's right to paternity establishment and still receive public assistance. Supervised visitation may be appropriate in some cases to address a history of child abuse and domestic violence. On the other hand, changing the amount of the child support order based on the amount of visitation should be viewed with caution to prevent manipulation of visitation by either parent for financial gain.

The Personal Responsibility and Work Opportunity Reconciliation Act opens the door for child support programs to begin to address these issues. Section 391 provides for grants to states for programs to support and facilitate noncustodial parents' access to and visitation of their children, including mediation (both voluntary and mandatory), counseling, education, development of parenting plans, visitation enforcement (including monitoring, supervision and neutral drop-off and pickup), and development of guidelines for alternative visitation and custody arrangements. These grants must supplement, not supplant, expenditures for any similar programs already under way in the state, and the grants may be administered directly by the state or under contracts with courts, local public agencies, or nonprofit private entities. The secretary of health and human services will also specify monitoring, evaluation, and reporting requirements, in order to assess the effectiveness of different approaches.

As a result of the welfare reform debate, Congress in a short amount of time has raised the public's awareness of the long-term harmful consequences on children of growing up in a single-parent family. With a third of children born out of wedlock and half of marriages ending in divorce, more than half of the children of this generation will spend at least part of their childhood in a single-parent household. Of these, an estimated 73 percent will experience periods of poverty during their minority, as compared to only 20 percent of children raised with two parents in the home. Perhaps worse than periodic economic deprivation are the increased risks of other social disadvantages. As McLanahan and Sandefur have documented, children growing up with only one parent—usually the mother—are three times more likely to have a child out of wedlock, 2.5 times more likely to become teen mothers, twice as likely to drop out of school, and 1.4 times as likely to be idle—out of school and out of work.[5] They are at greater risk of substance abuse, depression, juvenile delinquency, and a host of other social dysfunctions. These risk factors cut across race, sex, parents' education, and place of residence. Although most single mothers struggle valiantly against staggering odds with insufficient resources to raise children alone—and are not to be blamed for these outcomes—a caring, involved, responsible father is clearly a powerful and necessary role model for both boys and girls in their journey to responsible adulthood.

While Congress and state legislatures should not legislate morality, they can support parent education programs that strengthen marriage and discourage out-of-wedlock births. Today the cultural norms that militate against marriage—as reflected in television, movies, and just everyday life—seem well entrenched. But not too long ago, the same might have been said about drunk driving and smoking tobacco. Well-conceived and well-executed campaigns to educate the public can work. And child support agencies, as the front-line professionals who deal with the fallout of divorce and unmarried parentage, are particularly well positioned to assist in this endeavor.

CONCLUSION

By requiring states to put in place comprehensive child support programs, Congress has demonstrated its conviction that becoming a parent and having children creates an irrevocable, nontransferable lien on the income and assets of each parent. Responsibility for financial support should not be transferred to the other parent or to the taxpayer except in extraordinary circumstances. Moreover, there will never be a good record on payment of current support unless states are also tough on collection of past-due support. Today's current support unpaid becomes tomorrow's arrears. Yesterday's arrears, if not vigorously pursued, lead obligors to believe they can ignore today's current support. When an obligor is permitted to accrue an arrearage with impunity, he or she has no incentive to comply with current support payments, and there is little to deter future noncompliance. For some, this is undoubtedly a tough stance. However, children need support on time and in full every week. And for those parents who do regularly make the necessary sacrifices to pay in full, it acknowledges their commitment by taking steps to ensure that all parents fulfill their financial responsibility to their children.

With time-limited benefits and work requirements, child support is a critical part of the safety net to keep children from sinking into poverty when their parents separate or never marry. The mission of the child support agency continues to expand as it moves into its third decade, with a growing recognition that issues of visitation, unemployment and job training, domestic violence, pregnancy prevention, parent education, and strengthening marriage all have a significant impact on the ability to collect child support on time and in full for all children.

Much remains to be done to implement these major changes in child support enforcement, and it will take several years before the nation's children are able to benefit fully from these powerful enforcement provisions. These children are our future, and our strength as a society as we start a new century depends on our ability to meet our responsibility to provide them with adequate financial support to ensure that future.

NOTES

Marilyn Ray Smith is chief legal counsel and associate deputy commissioner for the Child Support Enforcement Division of the Massachusetts Department of Revenue. Any views here are her own and not necessarily those of the department.

1. Between 1970 and 1992, the number of female-headed families with children under eighteen increased by 164 percent, while the number of two-parent families declined by 4 percent; Committee on Ways and Means, U.S. House of Representatives, "Overview of Entitlement Programs," *1994 Green Book* (Washington, D.C.: U.S. Government Printing Office, 1994), 458. In 1970, the divorce rate was 3.5 divorces per 1,000 persons; by 1990, it had climbed to 4.7 per 1,000 persons, with approximately a million children a year in the United States seeing their parents divorce; U.S. Department of Commerce, Bureau of the Census, *Statistical Abstract of the United States: 1993,* 113th ed. (Washington, D.C.: U.S. Government Printing Office, 1993), 73. In 1970, almost four hundred thousand children were born out of wedlock, making up 10 percent of all births. By 1990, the number had risen to 1.2 million, a third of all births; ibid., at 78.

2. As a condition of receiving public assistance, applicants assign their child support or medical support rights to the state. Child support services for nonwelfare families may also be obtained by making an application to the state child support program. Services provided include location of noncustodial parents; establishment of paternity; and establishment, modification, and enforcement of support orders. Except to establish a temporary order for child support, child support programs do not provide services in the aspects of a case involving divorce proceedings, property division, custody and visitation, or alimony only cases where there are no minor children in the home.

3. As states move to implement the automation requirements of the Family Support Act of 1988, these manual records are being converted to computer records.

4. Hearings were held by the House Ways and Means Committee, Subcommittee on Human Resources on February 6, 1995, June 13, 1995, May 23, 1996, and September 19, 1996; and by the Senate Finance Committee on March 28, 1995.

5. Sara McLanahan and Gary Sandefur, *Growing Up with a Single Parent* (Cambridge, Mass.: Harvard University Press, 1994), 2-3.

Part Four

Concluding Thoughts

17

When Theory Meets Practice: Communitarian Ethics and the Family

Don Browning

By profession, Amitai Etzioni is a sociologist. He is also a practical thinker and public philosopher willing to take concrete positions that spark dialogue. Because his thinking generally addresses particular issues in specific historical contexts, it is easy to miss the complexity—the thickness—of the underlying moral and political philosophy. In this chapter, I want to illustrate how this is true with regard to his thinking about the family.

Communitarianism can have a variety of meanings. To some people it can mean rule by the majority. For those such as Hans-Georg Gadamer, Alastair MacIntyre, and the Roman Catholic Church, it means a presumed priority of the power and truth of a classic tradition and the communities that carry it. For others, such as Jürgen Habermas, it might mean rule by distortion-free community consensus. Etzioni's moral and political philosophy respects and to a degree absorbs all of those meanings of communitarianism, but it organizes them into a larger model.

This broader philosophy influences both Etzioni's analysis of the situation of families today and his normative understanding of good families. It is easy to become preoccupied with details of his diagnosis of families—his concern about the divorce rate, the rise of single-parent families and out-of-wedlock births, and the declining amount of time parents spend with their children. Depending on one's personal values, one can become hostile or enthusiastic about his high valuation of the two-parent family, the need for fathers in the lives of children, and the importance of a strong cultural appreciation for parents, children, and marriage. But it is best not to rush too quickly into the details of these positions. I recommend instead pausing to examine the general philosophical stance undergirding his various specific judgments.

A DEONTOLOGICAL SOCIOLOGIST?

The mantra of Etzioni's communitarian movement is this: both rights and re-sponsibilities are basic moral values and should be balanced with one another. This is true for all times and all places. Some societies, such as Iran or mainland China, may swing too far in the direction of responsibilities, order, and control; others may move too far in the direction of rights and freedoms, as is the case with the United States today. When they become extreme in one direction, soci-eties have a moral obligation, in spite of their traditions and rationalizations, to move in the other direction. This theory has implications for families as well; the extreme cultural emphasis in the United States on individual rights, freedom, and self-fulfillment has contributed to family disruption. A cultural shift back toward marital and parental responsibility is now a moral necessity.

But how does Etzioni ultimately ground the theory that all humans universally have both rights and responsibilities and that all societies *should* balance these two moral values? Answering this question will throw light on how he grounds his appreciation for intact egalitarian families. And this discussion will also open the way to offering minor suggestions for how Etzioni can strengthen his family theory.

Two texts give us special insights into the philosophical grounds for the theory of rights and responsibilities: *The Moral Dimension: Toward a New Economics* and *The New Golden Rule: Community and Morality in a Democratic Society*.[1] In these texts one gains a clear insight into a crucial aspect of Etzioni's moral and political philosophy—his *deontological* perspective. Deontologists assert that moral ideas and actions have certain intrinsic qualities that can be recognized as ethical in and of themselves, and not because they are means to non-moral goals—goals such as an increase in the instrumentally achieved satisfactions of life. In contrast, a *teleological* grounding to ethics holds that moral ideas and be-haviors are justified if they increase, for self or community, the amount of non-moral goods—goods such as pleasure, food, housing, clean air, and beauty. Al-though they differed in major ways, the great teleologists of Western philosophy have been Aristotle, St. Thomas Aquinas, the utilitarians Jeremy Bentham and John Stuart Mill, and the American pragmatists William James and John Dewey.

Most of the social sciences are broadly *functional* in their explanatory logics: psychological, social, and economic structures meet human needs and are thus functional or purposeful—which means they are teleological. Etzioni as a sociol-ogist often refers to himself as a "neofunctionalist." But what does that mean? It means that he has incorporated a deontological element into his otherwise func-tionalist sociological system. Valid moral ideas do not have functionalist origins, he claims, but they may have certain functionalist consequences in the societies in which they work.

The significance of this move can best be seen in *The Moral Dimension*'s cri-tique of the neoclassical school of economics. Neoclassical economics is mainly associated with the University of Chicago and the names of Milton Friedman, Gary Becker, and legal theorist Judge Richard Posner. This school holds that economic behavior is motivated by rational calculation designed to maximize the satisfaction of a relatively small number of hard-wired human desires. Some members of this school have extended the theory beyond the realm of economic behavior and given accounts of human behavior in education, law, and even the family. This perspective has claimed attention throughout academia because of its relatively powerful abilities to predict human behavior.

Etzioni is functionalist enough not to reject outright the neoclassical perspective. Instead, he attempts to absorb it into a more encompassing "bi-utility" theory of moral motivation. He develops a theory of multiple selves; we have at least two selves: one coming from our basic drive to satisfy our individual desires, and another more distinctively moral self that regulates these needs in light of moral concerns. Etzioni argues that this second self—this moral self grounded deontologically by insights into the intrinsic dignity of other selves—is a more or less constant presence in human life. For the most part, it constrains and guides the rational satisfaction-seeking self that neoclassical economics supposes is the only true self that exists. Yes, human beings compete to satisfy their needs, but generally within the context of moral assumptions about the worth and dignity of others. This is how we recognize that someone in the competition has broken the rules.

This subordination of functionalism to deontology is developed and nuanced in *The New Golden Rule*. Etzioni's reformulation of the ancient and nearly universal Golden Rule goes like this: "Respect and uphold society's moral order as you would have society respect and uphold your autonomy." This is clearly not only a variation on the Golden Rule and the Christian concept of neighborly love, but also a twist on Immanuel Kant's categorical imperative. But Etzioni's contextualization of these deontological principles may be as novel as his reformulation of them. It reveals the distinctively sociological and communitarian framework of his deontology.

To understand this contextualization, we should begin with Etzioni's assertion that a "good society requires sharing core values." These core values are certainly more important in the long run than a powerful economy and efficient technology. And such core values are crucial for determining what we mean by family and the content of our family ideals. But how do we arrive at our core values? First, the will of the majority in democratic rule certainly counts for determining shared values, especially if it is achieved through broad and deep dialogue at several levels in the society. But more is needed. If democratic rule is to avoid injustice to minorities, it must be consistent with a society's moral "frames" or ideals, whether they are encoded in a constitution or diffusely embedded in the culture.

But these steps are still not enough. At a third level, Etzioni advocates "cross-societal dialogue"; the core values that emerge from critical dialogue between societies may have a deeper validity than those of individual societies, especially if the dialoguing partners bring their deepest convictions into the conversation. Finally, such cross-cultural dialogue works, for Etzioni, because all people have some access to the universal, self-evident, deontological core values of the new Golden Rule—respect for both autonomy and order. Dialogue does not create these core values; it uncovers, awakens, and enhances a culture's awareness of them. Etzioni writes that the compelling nature of the basic communitarian values "can be hidden under the influence of historical and cultural factors and economic duress. Often, only after people are exposed to these virtues through continued dialogue do they realize their compelling nature."[2]

In optimal situations, the values of autonomy and social order can be learned from our communities through a process of internalization; in turn, however, our deeper deontological moral intuitions—once we become conscious of them—can lead us to affirm that which we may have first internalized from our communities of socialization. When this happens, we say, "Yes, what I learned from my family or community is indeed true." The unjust, the immature, the fanatic, the careless, and the culturally one-sided are "people who have not yet been properly engaged in communitarian dialogues—dialogues that will help them listen to their muffled inner voices, which speak for a society in which both moral order and autonomy are well nourished and balanced."[3] Such communitarian dialogues help people discover and express their inner moral voices.

THE COMMUNITARIAN FAMILY: THE FULLER PICTURE

Etzioni's neofunctionalism, with its deontological element, is still interested in consequences and the realization in human affairs of relative goods, some of which are patently instrumental. But this is a secondary interest. We should first respect individuals and the social order and then, within these moral constraints, try to maximize wealth, health, and various other indices of well-being.

From the perspective of this moral framework, we should not be surprised to discover that "peer marriage," or what I call the equal-regard family, is his ideal conjugal arrangement. Peer marriage is based on the mutual respect for the dignity and worth of both husband and wife and their equal rights to the privileges and responsibilities of both the public and domestic worlds. (See the discussion by Pepper Schwartz in chapter 4.) This means, in principle, equal access for both wife and husband to the wage market, the responsibilities of citizenship, and the demands and joys of parenthood. In light of the time and energy it takes to raise children, society should support peer marriage with a variety of special provisions—shorter workweeks, flextime, tax credits and exemptions, and much longer job leaves so that either fathers or mothers can care for their newborn infants. On this last point, Etzioni advances very robust proposals: he advocates six months of paid leave and up to one and a half years of unpaid leave. Note that most of these measures listed here are instrumental goods—more money, more time, better health. All of them, however, are guided by the deontological values of equal respect between husband and wife and their equal responsibilities for the care of their children—who themselves should be treated in a deontological fashion, as ends and never as solely means.

Within the moral framework of peer marriage, Etzioni expresses support for the intact family defined as two parents biologically related to their children. He is fully aware that many single parents do quite well with their children. But anthropological evidence from around the world, plus recent social science research, demonstrates that *on average* two-parent families are better for children. Child rearing is a labor-intensive activity requiring at least two sets of hands that are highly invested in the caring task.

However, peer marriage and the responsibilities of child care are not easily reconciled when both parents are in the wage economy. Thus, we currently have what Etzioni calls a "parental deficit," which is seen in the decline in the numbers he cites for the time parents spend with their children: from thirty hours a week in 1965 to seventeen hours in 1985. This is mainly a cultural problem—a devaluation of children and parenting in our society. According to Etzioni, therefore, the cure must entail a cultural revolution, one that gives rise to a new appreciation of children, a higher valuation of parenting, and a renunciation of consumerism and careerism. This cultural revolution should be brought about through dialogue and persuasion that awakens and gives expression to the moral voice of the community. Social systemic rearrangements, such as better relations between paid employment and home, are important but secondary to the need to reconfigure our cultural sensibilities.

It is important to point out that Etzioni sees many social system proposals as imperfect solutions. For instance, a huge expansion of the child care industry is no simple solution for the parental deficit. In addition to the difficulties of assuring quality care, the moral formation of children—which he associates with the development of self-control and empathy—requires deep attachments during the first two years of life. Parental leaves that make it possible for at least one parent to be home with children for significant amounts of time is thus the better option.

Nor is the social system solution of returning to fault divorce a good answer to family disruption stemming from the high divorce rate. There is plenty of new social science research that demonstrates that on the whole children suffer from divorce. But returning to a fault divorce system, at this stage in history, is probably too coercive. (See the debate on this issue in part 2 of this volume.) In general, Etzioni turns to the law to shape social behaviors only after extensive dialogue has failed to create a new moral consensus that remedies the problem at hand. In addition, it often takes vigorous dialogue to create a climate for good laws. In the spirit of this reluctance to turn too quickly to legal remedies, one can understand his attraction to the state of Louisiana's recent covenant marriage law. Since this law makes it optional for couples to choose between the old no-fault marriage and a more demanding covenant marriage, Etzioni sees the Louisiana experiment as a noncoercive way for law to upgrade civil morality. He calls it "opportuning virtue"—the law offers a more ideal vision of marriage, encourages it, but does not coerce people to choose it. And it may not take a general law as such to opportune virtue. Etzioni is also a supporter of Elizabeth Scott's idea that couples should be encouraged to write prenuptial agreements that will increase the expectations placed on their marriages—agreements that, once signed, would have the force of law. He refers to such agreements as "supervows." (See Scott's essay in chapter 10.)

If, finally, couples *are* driven to consider divorce, Etzioni joins William Galston and others in emphasizing counseling, education in parent responsibilities to children after divorce, and the filing of long-term financial plans covering the needs of children until they are grown. This should be done before the legal division of property between the divorcing parents. (See the "children-first" approach to family property sketched out by Katherine Shaw Spaht in chapter 14.)

But even more important than covenant marriage or supervows is Etzioni's appreciation for marriage education. This interest goes in two directions. First, he advocates a more widespread use—by schools, churches, and the state—of the new methods in premarital preparation, couples communication, and conflict resolution. Etzioni is aware of recent research by John Gottman and others showing that married couples who stay together have as much conflict as those who separate and divorce. The difference between the two groups is that the couples who remain married have better communication and conflict resolution skills. These skills can be taught. Etzioni's promotion of marriage education is in line with his general concern to renew culture and the institutions supporting social and cultural virtues, rather than resort to law or other forms of coercion.

His second direction is toward a recontextualization of sex education in public schools. He argues that there is a place for such education, but only within a context that also prepares students for marriage and parenthood and that equips them with skills in interpersonal communication. Etzioni is critical of those forms of sex education that aspire to be value-free and only provide students with technical knowledge about contraception, venereal disease, and pregnancy. He believes that through dialogue among schools, parents, and the wider community, a more encompassing moral framework for sex education can be devised that reemphasizes marriage and conveys skills in communication for intimacy. Within this context, he advocates what some call "abstinence plus." This is an approach that first emphasizes sexual abstinence for teenagers but also educates in safe sex for those who are determined to be sexually active.

AN IMPLICIT THEORY OF SUBSIDIARITY

Etzioni's strong emphasis on peer marriage and the importance of the two-parent marriage for children should not obscure his equally vigorous promotion of supports from the extended family and wider community. As he writes in *The Spirit of Community*, communities have a moral responsibility to "enable parents to . . . dedicate themselves" to their children.[4]

> Communities are best viewed as if they were Chinese nesting boxes, in which less encompassing communities (families, neighborhoods) are nested within more encompassing ones (local villages and towns), which in turn are situated within still more encompassing communities, the national and cross-national ones (such as the budding European Community). Moreover, there is room for nongeographic communities that criss-cross the others, such as professional or work-based communities. When they are intact, they are all relevant, and all lay moral claims on us by appealing to and reinforcing our values.[5]

In the ideal world, peer marriages and the communitarian family would be influenced and supported by all of these surrounding forms of community.

In taking such a stand, Etzioni's social philosophy of families becomes similar to Roman Catholic teachings on "subsidiarity." But there is a slight difference between the two perspectives, and it is this difference that points to a way to strengthen Etzioni's theory. The concept of subsidiarity has roots in Aristotelian philosophy and the social teachings of Aquinas, and it was intentionally introduced at the level of papal teachings by Pope Leo XIII and Pope Pius XI. It teaches that both families and grassroots communities should be permitted to take responsibility for areas of life that they have superior capacities to address. In the case of families, parents should have primary rights and responsibilities for their children. Etzioni would agree; parenthood entails responsibilities and, along with these, certain rights.

Subsidiarity also holds that more encompassing communities should be prepared to give *subsidum* (supports) of the kind that help families and smaller communities fulfill their primary tasks. If needed, larger communities should give additional assistance to smaller ones when difficulties emerge that undercut their normal capacities to discharge what they generally do best. It is in light of this teaching that the Roman Catholic Church became an early advocate of government supports for a just family income, reasonable working hours, and certain kinds of family welfare. All of this is in the spirit of communitarianism as well.

But there is a slight difference between the idea of subsidiarity and Etzioni's position. All the way from Aquinas to Leo XIII, the Catholic position believes that natural parents are inclined, by virtue of their biological ties, to care for their children more intensely than others. In fact, there was in the concept of subsidiarity something like an early theory of what contemporary evolutionary psychologists call "kin altruism." Modern kin altruism theory teaches that we are inclined to give preferential treatment to our blood relatives and care for our own children because they are literally (i.e., genetically) a part of ourselves. From Aristotle to Aquinas to modern evolutionary psychology, various models of kin altruism have been invoked to explain why, on average, natural parents are more invested in their children than other people. The idea of subsidiarity respects the initiatives of families partially because it acknowledges this ancient insight into our natural inclinations to care for our own.

Etzioni has been reluctant to shore up his own advocacy of the two-parent family with appeals to evolutionary psychology's theory of kin altruism. I once heard him say, "Genes do not teach morality." Of course, he is right. The psychological internalization of community values, persuasion, dialogue, and our deontological intuitions—these are the main sources of morality in the fuller sense. But the biological identification that occurs between parents and their children, accounted for in part by the theory of kin altruism, does contribute to our knowledge of the *moral psychology* of parenthood, if not the full moral understanding of it. It helps us understand why natural parents have strong inclinations toward caring for their children—inclinations that can be built on and stabilized into more enduring parental commitments. Etzioni's own advocacy of the two-parent family could be strengthened and clarified by more use of the theory of kin altruism. Furthermore, the Catholic Church's use of kin altruism in its theory of parental motivations is a good example of how this naturalistic insight can be elaborated and enriched by additional moral and religious ideas, as is the case in the church's full theology of marriage. We need not contend that only natural parents can raise children to proffer the more balanced idea that if our cultural institutions can both celebrate and undergird such families, our society will be much the better for it.

Etzioni's thinking on the family is much more than a series of interesting cultural and political proposals. When seen within the wider context of his moral philosophy and social theory, his proposals constitute a total perspective on the family that deserves both high respect and widespread discussion.

NOTES

1. Amitai Etzioni, *The Moral Dimension: Toward a New Economics* (New York: Free Press, 1988), and *The New Golden Rule: Community and Morality in a Democratic Society* (New York: Basic Books, 1996).

2. Etzioni, *The New Golden Rule,* 250.

3. Ibid., 246-47.

4. Amitai Etzioni, *The Spirit of Community: Rights on Responsibilities and the Communitarian Agenda* (New York: Crown, 1993), 54.

5. Ibid.

INDEX

About the Contributors

Enola G. Aird is an activist mother and founder and director of the Motherhood Project of the Institute for American Values. Trained as a lawyer, she spent several years in corporate law practice before leaving to devote her energies to her children and to family activism. She has served as talk-show host for a public radio station in New Haven, Connecticut, and as a member and chair of the Connecticut Commission on Children under two governors. During the mid-1990s she worked for the Children's Defense Fund in Washington D.C., directing its violence prevention program and serving as acting director of its Black Community Crusade for Children. She has served as a Lilly Leadership Workshop Fellow at the Yale Divinity School and currently serves on the board of directors and the executive committee of the National Parenting Association, where she is also an adviser to its Task Force on Revitalizing Parenting in the 21st Century. She is a member of the Waverly Extended Family and the Council on Civil Society.

Don Browning is Alexander Campbell Professor of Religious Ethics and the Social Sciences at the Divinity School of the University of Chicago. He is the director of the Religion, Culture, and Family Project, funded by a series of grants from the Division of Religion of the Lilly Endowment, Inc. His most recent book is *From Culture Wars to Common Ground: Religion and the American Family Debate* (1997, co-authored with Bonnie Miller-McLemore, Pam Couture, Bernie Lyon, and Robert Franklin) which is a summary of the findings of that project.

Sybil Carrère is a research scientist in the Department of Psychology at the University of Washington. Her research examines the influence of the marital relationship on health and well-being.

William J. Doherty is professor and director of the Marriage and Family Therapy Program, Department of Family Social Science, University of Minnesota. He is immediate past-president of the National Council on Family Relations and author of *Soul Searching: Why Psychotherapy Must Promote Moral Responsibility* (1995). He is an active researcher in the area of responsible fatherhood. His latest work is the Families and Democracy Project, which seeks to engage families as active citizens working to improve family life.

Ira Mark Ellman is professor of law and faculty fellow of the Center for the Study of Law, Science, and Technology at Arizona State University. Before joining the ASU law faculty he clerked for Supreme Court Justice William O. Douglas, was a legislative aide to Senator Adlai Stevenson III, practiced law in San Francisco, and worked as a consultant to the California legislature. He specializes in family law and has visited at the Institute for Social and Policy Studies at Yale University and at both the Earl Warren Legal Institute and the Jurisprudence and Social Policy Program of the School of Law at the University of California at Berkeley. He is the chief reporter for the American Law Institute's Principles of the Law of Family Dissolution and is senior author for a leading text on family law.

Martha F. Erickson is director of the Children Youth and Family Consortium at the University of Minnesota, which is devoted to promoting university-community partnerships that link research to practice and policy to promote the well-being of children and families. A developmental psychologist specializing in parent–child attachment, she has written and spoken extensively about the application of attachment theory in programs that support parents and young children. Since 1994 she has worked closely with Vice President Al Gore, co-chairing his annual family policy conference, Family Re-Union, and she is co-chair of the national board of Father-to-Father, an outgrowth of her work with Gore.

William A. Galston is professor in the School of Public Affairs, University of Maryland, and director of the university's Institute for Philosophy and Public Policy. He is the author of five books and numerous articles on political theory, American politics, and public policy. He has published a number of articles on policies for children and families and on the laws governing marriage and divorce. From 1993 until 1995 he was on leave from the University of Maryland, serving as deputy assistant to President Clinton for domestic policy.

John M. Gottman is James Miffin Professor of Psychology at the University of Washington in Seattle and a specialist in clinical psychology and the scientific study of marital interactions. Prior to joining the UW faculty he served a clinical psychology internship at the University of Colorado Medical Center and was on the faculties at Indiana University and the University of Illinois. He has had a research career award from the National Institute for Mental Health since 1979.

Milton C. Regan Jr. is professor of law at Georgetown University Law Center. He is the author of *Alone Together: Law and the Meanings of Marriage* (1999) and *Family Law and the Pursuit of Intimacy* (1993) and co-editor (with Anita L. Allen) of *Debating Democracy's Discontent: Essays on American Politics, Law, and Public Philosophy* (1998). He is also the author of articles on family law, legal theory, feminist theory, and legal ethics. He served as law clerk to Judge Ruth Bader Ginsburg when she sat on the U.S. Court of Appeals for the District of Columbia Circuit, and for Justice William J. Brennan Jr. on the U.S. Supreme Court.

David Gray Ross has served as commissioner of the Federal Office of Child Support Enforcement, U.S. Department of Health and Human Services, since 1994. Prior to that he served as a Circuit Court judge in Prince George's County, Maryland for sixteen years. He also served for eight years as a member of the Maryland General Assembly.

Kimberly D. Ryan is a doctoral candidate in clinical psychology at the University of Washington. She has conducted research in the areas of couple therapy and child abuse and neglect.

Pepper Schwartz is professor of sociology at the University of Washington in Seattle. She is past-president of the Society for the Scientific Study of Sexuality and the author of twelve books, among them *American Couples: Money, Work, and Sex* (with Philip Blumstein, 1983) and *The Gender of Sexuality* (1998). She has been married eighteen years and lives on a horse ranch in Snoqualmie, Washington, with her husband, two children, and many creatures.

Elizabeth S. Scott is University Professor at the University of Virginia School of Law. She is an expert on family and juvenile law and has written extensively on marriage, divorce, child custody, and juvenile delinquency. Much of her scholarship applies social science research and theory to legal policy issues relating to children and the family. With Ira Ellman and Paul Kurtz, she is co-author of a leading casebook in family law. She is co-founder of the interdisciplinary Center for Children, Families, and the Law at the University of Virginia. She is also a member of the Research Network on Adolescent Development and Juvenile Justice, a multidisciplinary group funded by the MacArthur Foundation.

Marilyn Ray Smith is currently chief legal counsel and associate deputy-commissioner at the Child Support Enforcement Division of the Massachusetts-Department of Revenue. She served as president of the National Child Support-Enforcement Association (NCSEA) in 1994–95. She has testified on several occasions before the U.S. House Ways and Means Subcommittee on Human Resources and the Senate Finance Committee on a wide variety of child support issues. She also provided technical assistance to the drafters of the Uniform Interstate Family Support Act over its four-year development, and is currently representing NCSEA as an adviser to the drafters of the upcoming revision of the Uniform Parentage Act. She has authored numerous articles on child support enforcement, including a chapter in *Enforcing Child and Spousal Support* (forthcoming). Prior to joining the Massachusetts Department of Revenue she was in private practice focusing on family law.

Katherine Shaw Spaht is Jules F. and Frances L. Landry Professor of Law at the Louisiana State University Law Center. She teaches family law, community property and successions law. She is the co-author of a treatise on Louisiana community property law and is a member of the consultative group to the American Law Institute project, Principles of Family Dissolution and the Academic Advisory Committee of the Institute for American Values. She is a reporter for the Louisiana State Law Institute Committee on Persons (family law) and chair of the advisory committee to the Louisiana Legislative Subcommittee that revised Louisiana's community property law in 1979. She drafted the Louisiana Covenant Marriage legislation that became effective August 15, 1997.

C. Eugene Steuerle is a senior fellow at the Urban Institute and author of a weekly column, "Economic Perspective," for *Tax Notes* magazine. He is the author, co-author, or editor of eight books, more than 150 reports and articles, 500 columns, and 45 congressional testimonies or reports, including *The Government We Deserve* (co-authored with Edward M. Gramlich, Demetra Nightingale, and Hugh Heclo, 1998) and *Nonprofits and Government: Collaboration and Conflict* (co-edited with Elizabeth Boris, 1999). Previous positions include deputy assistant secretary of the Treasury for tax analysis (1987–89) and economic coordinator and original organizer of the Treasury's tax reform effort (1984–86). His research on family issues includes studies on family tax credits, marriage penalties, the treatment of family and divorce in the Social Security system, the effects of tax and welfare policies on family formation, and serving children with disabilities.

Linda J. Waite is professor of sociology at the University of Chicago where, with Barbara Schneider, she co-directs the Center on Parents, Children, and Work, an Alfred P. Sloan Working Families Center. She also directs the Center on Aging at the University of Chicago. She is co-author (with Frances Goldscheider) of *New Families, No Families?: The Transformation of the American Home* (1991), which received the Duncan Award from the American Sociological Association. She has recently completed *The Case for Marriage* (forthcoming), with Maggie Gallagher, which focuses on marriage as a social institution and the benefits it produces for individuals.

Martin King Whyte was professor of sociology and chair of the Department of Sociology at George Washington University until the fall of 2000 when he became professor of sociology at Harvard University. He is also senior research associate at the Communitarian Network. He is a specialist in the sociology of the family and in comparative sociology and the sociological study of China. His previous works in family sociology include *Dating, Mating, and Marriage* (1990) and *The Status of Women in Preindustrial Societies* (1978).